WAR ON THE BASEPATHS

THE DEFINITIVE BIOGRAPHY OF
TY COBB

TIM HORNBAKER

SPORTS
PUBLISHING

Visit our website at www.sportspubbooks.com.

10 9 8 7 6 5 4 3 2 1

Library of Congress Cataloging-in-Publication Data:

Hornbaker, Tim.
  War on the basepaths : the definitive biography of Ty Cobb / Tim Hornbaker.
    pages cm
  ISBN 978-1-61321-765-8 (hardcover : alk. paper) 1. Cobb, Ty, 1886-1961. 2. Baseball players–United States–Biography. I. Title.
  GV865.C6H67 2015
  796.357092–dc23
  [B]
                              2015004100

Cover design by Rich Rossiter
Front cover photograph by Bain News Service
Back cover and spine photograph courtesy of the National Baseball Hall of Fame Library, Cooperstown, NY

Paperback ISBN: 978-1-61321-951-5
Ebook ISBN: 978-1-61321-793-1

Printed in the United States of America

To the love of my life, Jodi.

CONTENTS

INTRODUCTION

Off in the distance, a swell of commotion attracted onlookers and the spectacle likely resembled a circus. Regulars to the Northern California course were sidetracked by the unusual display—especially for a Sunday on the links. All the attention seemed to be centered on one man, and to the uninformed observer, the individual was not unlike many others playing golf that day. He was in his mid-to-late forties, balding, and slightly overweight. In fact, nothing was particularly exceptional about him, visually speaking. But for those crowded around the man, wearing exceptionally large smiles and hoping for an autograph or handshake, they understood his significance. They realized they were around American sporting excellence, a one-of-a-kind legend that had cemented his place in the annals of Major League Baseball history. Their focus was none other than Tyrus Raymond Cobb, a twenty-four-year veteran of the national pastime.

On that day, February 2, 1936, the news broke that Cobb had received the largest amount of votes for modern inductees into the newly fashioned Baseball Hall of Fame, soon to be opened at Cooperstown, New York. He was essentially chosen number one by writers over all his contemporaries, including Babe Ruth, Honus Wagner, and literally thousands of other players. The 222 votes in his favor were just four short of unanimous, clearly indicative of his widespread esteem, and sportswriter Dick Farrington, amongst others, wondered "how it happened that four experts overlooked him."[1] Cobb, who was in the midst of a golfing round when informed of the balloting results, told a reporter: "I deeply appreciate the honor. I am overwhelmed. I am glad they feel that way about me. I want to thank them all. I've played hard, applied myself, and tried to do my best in every case."[2]

Playing hard was Cobb's keystone to success, and his intensity was visible on the field from his earliest games in small-town Georgia until his final big league appearance seven years and five months before. Understandably, the image of the ex-ballplayer on the golf course in 1936 was a distant reality from the energetic and brawny competitor lighting basepaths afire during his prime. But even all those years later, Cobb continued to live and breathe the sport. Baseball was in his blood, and the honor bestowed upon him was a fitting acknowledgment of his extraordinary dedication to the game. As amazing as it might sound, when the exalted "Georgia Peach" retired in 1928, he had established ninety baseball records over the course of his career, creating a sphere of dominance that only he could claim. Cobb topped even Babe Ruth, who reportedly retired with seventy-eight baseball records.[3]

As a member of the Detroit Tigers (1905–26) and Connie Mack's Philadelphia Athletics (1927–28), Cobb put up statistics that were simply staggering. He owned a lifetime batting average of .367, 4,191 hits, 2,244 runs, 5,863 total bases, and 892 stolen bases, according to the official statistics recorded by Major League Baseball. [Other sources, including baseball-reference.com, acknowledge revised figures to include a .366 batting average, 4,189 hits, 5,854 total bases, and 897 stolen bases.] He hit .300 or better for twenty-three consecutive years every season, but his first (1905), and played 3,033 total games. The American League batting championship was awarded to Cobb 12 times, and he won the 1909 Triple Crown and the 1911 league MVP.[4] Additionally, he captured the "Honey Boy" Evans trophy four times from 1909 to '12 for the best batting average in the majors. By 1939, over three dozen of Cobb's records were still holding strong, and some of them, incredibly enough, including his lifetime average and total number of batting titles, remain intact today—eighty-seven years after his last game.[5]

Aside from his hitting abilities, Cobb's speed, trickiness, and base-running feats were a legend all their own. He was unlike his predecessors in that regard, and revolutionized the game by forcing rival teams to completely alter their defense to combat his methods. On the basepaths, he combined quickness and psychology to confuse opposition players, performing stunts that no one in their right mind ever conceived. And, because of this, he got away with these peculiar maneuvers with great frequency. That included stretching base hits into doubles, running from first to third on bunts, and stealing his way around the diamond to eventually score a run. Pilfering home plate was also a specialty, and Cobb managed to slip underneath the tag of a catcher 54 times in his career, the most in history. (Second in modern times is Max Carey, who had 33 steals of home with the Pittsburgh Pirates and Brooklyn Dodgers.)

Cobb's reputation wasn't as pristine as his statistics, and in his ever-determined fierceness, he did many things to get under the skin of both teammates and rivals. He talked trash on the field, which was part of his psychological campaign, slid into the bases hard, often looking to kick the ball free from the gloves of defenders, and wasn't afraid to mix it up physically. The success of his unorthodox tactics, in itself, was aggravating, and sportswriters and fans in opposing towns were caught up in a kind of love-hate relationship with Cobb, worshipping his unbelievable athletic feats and then letting him have it through boos and taunts, sometimes for no other good reason than he was the great Ty Cobb. Plus, anytime there was even a hint of controversy, the floodgates were open for criticism, and Cobb was the pincushion for a never-ending slew of condemnation.

One of the most enduring allegations surrounding Cobb's style of play was the claim that he slid into the bases with the metal spikes on the bottom of his shoes maliciously aimed at defenders with a vicious intent to injure. It was an ugly claim, and Cobb denied any deliberate attempt to injure fellow players countless times during and after his career. There were a couple moments, he admitted, when specific animosity turned spiteful, but in terms of his daily game play, slashing rivals was not a premeditated action.[6] Another longstanding story that accompanied Cobb's life was his infamous jaunt into the grandstand in New York to pummel a verbally abusive fan. The partially handicapped spectator was the recipient of a swift beating and critics have used the event as evidence of Cobb's maniacal personality.

Of course, there were two sides to the story, but regardless of how many times Ty tried to explain his point of view, the scandalous version always reigned supreme. His colorful approach to baseball was bankable to sportswriters, and whenever the opportunity presented itself to feed into his intriguing image, journalists took advantage of the situation. The controversy sold newspapers and, since he consistently created excitement on and off the field, it was easy to lump a series of events together and portray him as baseball's number one rowdy. Interestingly, had Cobb performed in the television age, his amazing deeds and dynamic style would have fostered an even greater sensation. He was a must-see performer, and the marketability of Cobb as a mainstream TV celebrity would have been huge.

Twenty-three years after the 1936 announcement that he was headed for Cooperstown, Cobb, seventy-two, told a Boston reporter that he was in the "evening" of his life.[7] Although he was often in the news, mostly referenced in passing to this or that baseball record and in player comparisons by sportswriters, he was no longer center stage in the public's consciousness. Much of what had already been written about his devilish time in the national game was accepted as gospel, and was firmly ingrained in baseball lore. But Cobb was still intent on straightening out many of the persisting untruths about his career, and was adamant about setting forth his own life story to paper before it was too late.

Several times a year, he made public appearances at special events and reunion games, and made a sincere effort to return to New York's baseball shrine for the annual induction ceremonies. Cobb was exceedingly vocal about the failure of writers and the veterans committee to admit worthy stars from his generation to the Hall of Fame in a timely manner, particularly those he figured to be "shamefully omitted." If it meant temporarily amending the admittance process rules, Cobb was all for it. He explained to *The Sporting News,* "It won't cheapen the Hall of Fame to let them in while they are alive and can enjoy the honor. These old-time greats helped build up the game." Cobb referred to players like Edd Roush, Eppa Rixey, Sam Rice, and Joe Sewell, who would all eventually get into the Hall of Fame, just not while Cobb was alive to see it.[8]

Cobb was personally affected by the lackadaisical system earlier in the 1950s. At the time, he was advocating recognition for Harry Heilmann, a teammate of his in Detroit for twelve seasons. After Heilmann was diagnosed with terminal lung cancer, Cobb became even pushier for his Hall of Fame recognition, demanding that writers "Let him smell the roses while he's here, not after he's gone." But once it was apparent that there was not enough time for him to be admitted through the normal channels, Cobb visited his friend in the hospital and offered some important news.

"Congratulations, Harry, you've made it," Cobb said, informing him that he was indeed inducted into the Hall. The statement, however, was "a little white lie that was as gracious and as thoughtful a gesture as Ty ever made in his tempestuous life," according to Arthur Daley of the *New York Times.*[9] It wasn't until 1952, months after Heilmann's death, that Harry was actually enshrined in Cooperstown.

Illness began to hinder Cobb's mobility in 1959. That March, he entered a hospital in Nevada, and received nearly two weeks of treatment for a series of ailments, including back and neck pain, an infected tooth, neuralgia in his face, and high blood sugar.[10] These issues were compounded by heart problems and extreme bouts of tension, depression, and alcoholism. Cobb's condition improved temporarily, but worsened again during the summer. By November, he was in bad shape, and sought a thorough diagnosis from doctors outside San Diego at La Jolla.[11] On December 6, he was admitted to Emory University Hospital in Atlanta for further scrutiny and was given a complete top-to-bottom examination. "I've had more x-rays and tests in the past few days than I've ever had in my life," Cobb told the Associated Press. He remained upbeat, though, stating, "I'm all right. I'm feeling 100 per cent."[12]

According to press reports, Cobb's back was his severest complaint, and it was attributed to an injury from his active baseball days. Dr. Richard Hugh Wood, his chief physician at Emory, issued a statement, declaring that there was "nothing seriously wrong" with Cobb, and that "routine" tests were being conducted. Other than the back pain, the doctor announced that Cobb appeared "to be in good shape for a man of his age."[13] Wood protected the privacy of his patient and withheld information about his true condition, which was much more dire than revealed. Tests had uncovered that a previous injury wasn't the origin of his back problems, but that he was suffering from prostate cancer. The disease had already metastasized, spreading to his vertebrae and pelvic bone.[14] Cobb told Joe King that a "probable operation" was forthcoming in February 1960, and it remains unclear if this was a second surgery or the original prostate operation he necessitated. Most sources reference Cobb's prostate surgery as having taken place around December 1959. Regardless, between December 1959 and February 1960, Cobb underwent surgery, radiation treatment, and was placed on a score of medications.[15]

As could be expected, Cobb was in severe pain at times, and while he was considered immortalized for his baseball feats, his mortality on earth was in severe jeopardy. On December 18, 1959, he was allowed to leave the hospital briefly to spend his seventy-third birthday in his hometown of Royston, Georgia, with friends, and he put on a brave face for the public, telling the United Press International wire service that he felt "wonderful." He anticipated being fully discharged from Emory within a matter of days so he could return to California to spend Christmas with his children, he explained.[16] Shortly thereafter, he did venture west, and rested comfortably at his Nevada and California homes before traveling back to Georgia around mid-January 1960. A few weeks later, he mustered his strength for a journey to New York, where he was going to be honored at two separate dinners.

The arrival of Cobb in New York was a big deal to the local sporting community and reporters lined up to speak with him. Joe King received an especially enlightening interview and was quite attentive of Ty's behavior and mannerisms. King noted that Ty "never departed from his gay, enthusiastic manner," despite his obvious pain, and explained how gracious Cobb was, thanking the many people who came by for stopping in to see him. Cobb was happy to visit with "so many old friends," and answered a multitude of questions about his life and career.

A query was posed about his greatest thrill, and Cobb began to describe his involvement with the Royston Memorial Hospital, established in 1950, and the Ty Cobb Educational Foundation, set up in 1953. He perked up, saying: "My greatest thrill came late in life. Nothing gave me more comfort and satisfaction than being able to build the hospital at Royston, Georgia, in memory of my father and mother, and setting up my educational foundation. If my liver goes bad, I feel better just to get out those brochures and read 'em and try to figure out how we can do a little more for the winners of the scholarships. We can do a lot with the youngsters, sometimes even more than their parents can. I think of them all the time and that's the way I'm gonna walk out . . . and go into the shadows."[17] These projects were Cobb's pride and joy, emphasized in another interview later in 1960 when Cobb added, "It's the best medicine I have, reading letters from the students we have helped."[18]

Cobb was always willing to talk about the hospital and his foundation and expressed how proud he was of their success while in New York. In addition to chatting with King, he sat down with sportswriter Dan Daniel of the *New York World-Telegram and Sun*. Daniel, a longtime baseball pundit, was known for his astute commentary and insight into the players themselves. When it came to Cobb, he didn't mince words, and there was often a blatant sharpness to his remarks that many of his star-struck peers couldn't manage to equal. Years earlier, he wrote, "Ty Cobb was not hard to talk to—if he liked you. If he didn't, you knew it. He was caustic. Very shrewd in his observations, but the most sarcastic hombre baseball has seen—or heard."[19]

Daniel's conversation with Cobb in February 1960 was, again, very revealing for a man in the "evening" of his life.

"In the old days I rarely was received in New York with cheers and acclaim," Cobb said, reflectively. "It was here that I chased into the stands after a heckler. It was here that I got into so much trouble with the umpires and with Ban Johnson, president of the league. In New York, I fought about as desperately as I ever did to make good. The fans here must have admired me as a player. But they evidently didn't like me as a personality."[20] It was true, and the way he was perceived wasn't limited to New York. Cobb was colorful in terms of grit, hustle, and intensity, and he'd banter with fans on occasion, usually in an acrimonious way, but he wasn't seen as a personable character like Babe Ruth was. He'd sneer before he'd smile on the field and fans didn't naturally gravitate to him for his charm and charisma like they did other popular stars.

But Cobb's skills superseded any kind of popularity contest, and over-shadowed his more amiable contemporaries. Nevertheless, fans enjoyed razzing Cobb, and hoped their taunts would throw him off his game enough to give their team a chance to win. And if they jostled Cobb enough to get him angry, they'd either see him tantrum in one way or another, or deliver a special performance at the plate—all for the crowd's benefit. He was good at inspiring awe and, in the end, it didn't matter who liked him, as he had to be revered for his achievements. Cobb told Daniel that he ventured to New York with "humility and with thanks. I should get down on my hands and knees and thank the game for what it has done for me." Daniels responded in his column by stating, "Maybe it never occurred to Ty to think about the things he had done for baseball."[21]

Daniel, notably, mentioned the fact that Cobb hadn't penned his auto-biography, and wrote that it was "to be deplored" that such a volume hadn't yet been released. Ty, however, was inching toward the evitable at his own speed, and may have actually spoken to potential editors during his stay in New York. After being readmitted to Emory Hospital in Atlanta a few days later, he continued his treatment, but it became known that Cobb was negotiating with two publishing houses to finally create the authorized story of his life.[22] A deal was reached with the largest operation in the business, Doubleday and Company, and the only major component left to decide was who would work as Cobb's coauthor (ghostwriter). The obvious answer was George "Stoney" McLinn, the newspaperman Cobb had worked with covering the World Series for syndicated news outlets decades earlier. It was reported that prior to his death, McLinn was working on a book of "baseball lore" with Cobb, slated for a 1954 release. However, nothing came of it, as McLinn passed away in 1953.[23] Conversely, Shirley Cobb Beckworth, Ty's daughter, said that her father wanted Gene Fowler to work with him on his autobiography. Fowler, the author of biographies on Jimmy Durante and John Barrymore, was also ill and was unable to help Cobb at the time.[24]

The Sporting News, in June 1960, revealed Cobb's collaborator to be Clem Boddington, an eminent sports cartoonist and magazine writer from New York City. The two were going to meet at Cobb's Nevada home near Lake Tahoe and record stories on a tape recorder, then figure out what material was going into the book. Cobb envisioned the project featuring biographical information about his life, clarifications on certain controversial moments, and instructional content for youngsters on how to play ball. Cobb was motivated to get started, telling Dick O'Connor, "It's about time [I wrote my memoirs]. Everybody else has written stories about me."[25] For reasons unknown, Boddington's tour of duty alongside Cobb was brief, and after several other interim writers, another magazine writer, Alvin J. "Al" Stump, a forty-three-year-old from Santa Barbara, California, took over.[26]

Stump's interest in Ty Cobb got off on the wrong foot very early in his writing career. In 1946, as a journalist for the *Portland Oregonian*, he inaccurately claimed that Joe Percival, a small-time manager in Sheffield, Alabama, in 1904, had been "Cobb's first manager and the man who pointed his first steps along the diamond trail."[27] By 1960, Stump was a more polished writer, and had contributed innumerable articles in national periodicals. The task of transforming a wealth of memories and documentation into story form for baseball's "Georgia Peach" was all his, and the two men got to work. It wasn't long before Cobb's irrationality, brought upon by his severe health problems, became an issue. Stump held firm, and refused to relent in spite of the enormous, multilayered job.[28]

Aware of his duty as a man of the public and a baseball Hall of Famer, Cobb was respectful, dignified, and humble when in New York speaking to the press months earlier. These qualities were representative of his true self, and his professional attitude was admirable when his health condition was taken into consideration. Stump was afforded a lengthy glimpse into Cobb's private life, and there he witnessed the other side of Cobb's true self, a world in which things weren't neatly packaged and righteous. It must be said that Cobb was a difficult man to begin with, but his progressive cancer and the tremendous pain he was suffering challenged him—and those around him—from morning to night, and made the simplest of things at times almost impossible to bear.

To deal with his pain, Cobb binged on alcoholic concoctions, and his struggle with liquor had been a lingering problem for some years.[29] The demands of writing his long awaited autobiography, his natural high tension personality, and the cancer eating away at his insides undoubtedly created a combustible perfect storm that few individuals could tolerate. But Cobb wasn't the kind of man to throw in the towel, and once he set out to produce the final word on his life and career, he was thoroughly dedicated to finishing the job. Wild horses, or, in his case, a deadly disease, wasn't going to be enough to drag him away from completion, and in Stump, Ty had put his absolute trust. He believed that the sportswriter would do his diligence to tell his story accurately, setting the record straight once and for all.

Ty Cobb passed away at 1:18 p.m. on July 17, 1961, at Emory Hospital in Atlanta, and his physician, Dr. Wood, told the press that he died "peacefully and without pain."[30] A few days later, from Santa Barbara, Stump informed the Associated Press that Cobb, shortly before going into the hospital in early June, had indeed completed the principal work on his autobiography, an amazing triumph.[31] To capitalize on the publicity surrounding his passing, Stump and Doubleday worked overtime to hurry the story through the editing process. Advance reading copies were mailed out to newspaper sports editors and book reviewers across the nation by September, and a little at a time, notices about the forthcoming release were printed. The interest was astonishing. Wally Provost in the *Omaha World Herald* wrote, "Five men in our newsroom already are on the waiting list for this Doubleday publication."[32]

The book, entitled *Ty Cobb: My Life in Baseball*, was 283 pages with a foreword by General Douglas MacArthur. It featured a range of stories and descriptions, including tales from his childhood, his tumultuous early days in the majors, and covered a scattering of important events from his career. In the publicity circulating around, Cobb was quoted as saying, "My critics have had their innings. I will have mine now." And rectifying the misconceptions about his time in baseball was the crux of his autobiography; although, he asserted that it wasn't an "alibi book." George W. Clark of the *Washington Evening Star* stated, "Ty attempted to refute many of the anti-Cobb legends . . . [and] he made some good arguments in his favor."[33] L. H. Gregory of the *Portland Oregonian* called it the "finest baseball book ever written," and stated, "while it confirms some impressions of Ty Cobb, it also gives you others you wouldn't have dreamed of about him."[34]

Cobb's collaborator had to be praised too, and Gregory noted, "Stump no doubt did organize, put the book together, and perhaps suggest topics, and did it all extremely well."[35] In the *Springfield Republican*, Donald Bagg wrote, "Mr. Stump rates a cheer for conveying so much of Cobb's competitive spirit and will to win."[36] The compliments continued and Cobb's legacy, particularly the voice he wanted to communicate to the world, seemed assured going into the future. But within a matter of months, his voice was going to be completely drowned out by an unexpected source in one of sporting history's most noteworthy turnabouts. Stump, himself, had organized a separate work about Cobb on the sly, and proponents of the "Georgia Peach" were not prepared for the atom bomb that was about to explode in their collective faces.

Unquestionably, the fascinating personal life of Cobb was of interest to readers and people wanted more insight into the man who set so many baseball records. But was the public clamoring for a firsthand chronicle of Cobb's brutal last months, a detailed story about his struggle with terminal cancer, focusing on the ugliest and most embarrassing moments of his losing battle? Stump believed so, and his article, titled "Ty Cobb's Wild, 10-Month Fight to Live," was featured in the December 1961 edition of *True—The Man's Magazine.* Apparently Stump felt it was appropriate to share his experiences during an extremely private time in Cobb's life, even though his last months were not exactly necessary for public consumption. Instead of considering the personal feelings of Ty's family and respecting the recently deceased, Stump went forward with the article, and to supporters of Cobb, it was in incredibly bad taste.

Needless to say, there was plenty of material to exploit, and Stump was not holding anything back. He made cruel allegations and cited many examples of Cobb's out-of-control and contemptible behavior. These ranged from recklessly firing a pistol to his quick-tempered, hateful outbursts that were unacceptable in any civilized society. His actions were presumably spawned by his excessive alcohol and pill intake and by the effects of his aggressive cancer. Stump made startling generalizations, and found ways to connect the downcast personality of Cobb in 1960 (once again, the man near death in his early seventies) to the baseball warrior of decades before. He used much of what he garnered to sweepingly paint the rest of

Cobb's life story, utilizing a creative mix of disputed theories, assumptions, and the use of nameless informants.

Ironically, this wasn't the first time Stump had created similar controversy. Seven years before, a flurry of backlash was ignited by his article on football star Hugh McElhenny, a graduate of the University of Washington and a member of the San Francisco 49ers, also featured in *True* magazine. Eugene H. Russell, sports editor of the *Seattle Times*, responded by saying that Stump "apparently doesn't let facts interfere with his writing, as we know much of his McElhenny tale is pure fiction, derogatory of the university and of Hugh." Additionally, he cited embellishments "with incidents critical of the university and derisive of McElhenny." Russell then proceeded to pick apart a number of Stump's inaccurate statements, offering a rebuttal in each case with confirmed facts.[37]

Stump likely didn't all-out fabricate his stories about Cobb, but that makes the public release of such information all the sadder. Cobb's antics were genuine; at least the stories cannot be completely dispelled as inauthentic. The fact is that Cobb was severely troubled, mentally and physically, and in the kind of pain suffered by terminal cancer patients. Dr. Stewart Brown Jr., a close friend of Cobb's, did what Russell of the *Seattle Times* did by taking portions of the Stump article, piece by piece, and offering a rejoinder. His response was printed in full in *The Sporting News* on January 3, 1962. Brown explained that he met Stump in December 1960 and thought he "seemed like a top-notch type man." Yet after reading Stump's article on Cobb, Brown had to ask, "What is the make-up of a man who would write such an article? Principle and honor have been sacrificed." He added that "Surely [Stump] knew that Cobb's entire body was riddled with cancer and that certainly he could not be responsible for any of his acts or deeds. Surely one would not judge a person by his acts when in such a state of both physical and mental collapse."[38]

"If Stump had truly known the physical make-up of this man," Brown continued, "he would have realized that in Cobb was a heart that wouldn't give up—that refused to remain dormant. He had to be active even though his multiple diseases were making him lose his finer grades of discrimination, memory, concentration, insight, equilibrium and such." Brown was adamant that Stump didn't know the real Ty Cobb.[39] Jack McDonald, a sportswriter in San Francisco and another longtime friend of Cobb, agreed wholeheartedly. He also said he spent time with Cobb during his final year and stated that he "witnessed no wild temper tantrums and there was no eccentric, bizarre behavior such as described in the magazine piece." He addressed Stump's claim that Ty was cheap, insisting that although he wasn't "the last of the big spenders," he could "cite examples of his generous moments."[40]

Brown and McDonald were in concert with the belief that Stump overlooked the "tender and human" side of Cobb and didn't offer a balanced portrayal of their friend. This was the same complaint Cobb had for decades. Time and again, he lambasted writers with an agenda, asking one sportswriter in 1960, "Why is it that everybody has to have an angle? Just say it the way it happened. I played baseball for a long time and I gave it everything I had . . . everything."[41]

With regard to the unfair reporting, he told ex-boxer James J. Corbett in 1918, "Jesse James and Captain Kidd didn't have much on me in fierceness—if you'll take the word of some folks for it. Sometimes when I'd read articles written about me by some of the newspaper boys, I'd actually get afraid of myself—that's the kind of desperado they pictured me."[42]

How would Cobb have felt had he read the Stump article? He wanted his book to set the record straight, but now, as Francis Stann of the *Washington Evening Star* put it, Stump's article "perhaps [would] be better remembered than the biography itself."[43] That essentially meant that a ten-page article, harping on the author's days with a medicated, drunk, dying Ty Cobb was more important than a lifetime of memories offered by Cobb himself—the book he believed people wanted to read—his true memoirs. That was the story that needed to be featured in a 1994 biopic? That was truly, of all the possible narratives, the best, most interesting representation of Cobb? Sensationalism sells. And in the case of Cobb, it did in the 1910s, the 1960s, the 1990s, and everywhere in between. As a result, people are still greatly misinformed about Cobb today, and the exaggerated stories continue to perpetuate.

A major part of Cobb's contemporary image is the supposition that he was racially prejudiced. As a Southern man from Georgia, he definitely acknowledged the color line and had certain expectations and boundaries, both on the baseball field and off during his playing days. But to casually define him "racist" is far too simplistic, and like everything else about him, certain events in his life have to be thoroughly explained in context. One thing can be said for sure, no one can honestly say what beliefs were in his heart one way or another. The facts can be studied, but the absolute truth will never be known.

Whether Ty Cobb was the most talented ballplayer in history is something to be argued. He can be endlessly compared to the superstars of baseball history and his numbers will be admired for the rest of time. But his statistics don't tell the whole story. Cobb was more than the myths and the tales passed down through the years by colorful sportswriters. To really know Cobb, the man, people have to look past the fiction and the work of Hollywood and entertain the idea that he was much more complicated and complex than ever realized before. The exploitative version of his life story did sell books and newspapers, but it left the Cobb legacy with decades of regurgitated yarns. These twisted truths and innuendos have just about crippled the memory of Cobb in the modern era.

Cobb, in 1909, discussed the claims that he was deliberately spiking basemen with a St. Louis writer. He told his side of the story, denying that he was purposefully cutting down rivals, and pleaded for a sense of fairness. "I don't mind the bleachers roasting me," he said, "but put me right, will you?"[44] The St. Louis journalist likely did what he could, but over one hundred years have passed with many of the old-time allegations still intact. With this volume, readers can absorb the full account of Cobb's life and make a more informed decision on their own about Cobb's standing as of 2015. It is hoped that this definitive story will show his competitive fire and highlight his natural yearning to not only win but to be the best. He was in a war each and every time he stepped onto the field, and regardless of what any defender said, the basepaths were his and his alone.

1

"DON'T COME HOME A FAILURE"

As the American Civil War entered its second year in April 1862, thirty-year-old John Franklin Cobb was facing a life-altering set of circumstances. He was days away from being wed to his sweetheart, Sarah Ann Waldroup, and within a few weeks, would be enlisted in the Confederate Army. The call to duty was an honor, but since the future of an unskilled private in combat was anything but guaranteed, he looked forward to cementing his bonds to Sarah while he still had the chance. On May 4, the couple exchanged their vows, and by June 20 he was in uniform, fully committed to serving the war effort.[1] Although he lived in Georgia, Cobb joined Company C, 39th Infantry Regiment in his native North Carolina.[2] However, for reasons unknown, Cobb's obligations to the military lasted only fifty-six days, and he returned to Sarah, who was now pregnant with their first child.

Prior to getting married, John Cobb had resided in the Ivy Log area of Union County, Georgia, in the homestead created by his parents, William and Charlotte. But after the 1861 death of his mother, and his father's hasty second marriage in 1862, John had a hankering to plant roots near his birthplace in the far westernmost region of North Carolina.[3] The area of Notla Township in Cherokee County was about ten miles north and it offered a beautiful landscape up against the Blue Ridge Mountains.[4] That's where the newlyweds settled, and on February 23, 1863, Sarah delivered a baby boy named William Herschel. Over the next seventeen years, five other children were born to the Cobbs, including daughters Mary Jane and Nora, and sons John, Schuyler, and James.

As the sole provider, John labored long hours on the family farm and was well known in the community for his wisdom and fairness. For that reason, he often was called upon by neighbors to mediate quarrels. People respected and trusted his word as final.[5] Cobb stressed hard work to his children, but he wanted them to get an education before anything else in life. He sent William Herschel to Hayesville in adjoining Clay County to learn from Professor John O. Hicks at the renowned Hicksville Academy.[6] An astute student, William gravitated to scholarship from a young age, thriving in mathematics, history, and language. Through his studies, he gained a wealth of confidence and became an exceptional speaker and debater.

In 1880, seventeen-year-old William was engaged as a farm employee in Notla, but he had far greater aspirations.[7] According to one source, William initially traveled to Georgia to work as a book agent. [8] Within the next couple years, he sought labor and teaching opportunities, and received advice from family still living in Ivy Log. He was spirited and outgoing, and was willing to relocate for better job prospects. Around 60 miles to the southeast of Ivy Log, he met Caleb C. Chitwood, an influential landowner in the Columbia District of Banks County. Like Cobb's father, Chitwood was a veteran, but the latter was active in the conflict for a sustained period of time and highly distinguished as a captain. In fact, he was briefly held as a prisoner of war after the Battle of Vicksburg in Mississippi, in July 1863.[9] Also, similar to Cobb's father, he was a prominent member of the community and took a liking to William almost immediately.

Tall, self-assured, and sociable, William was an impressive figure and, despite the fact that he was barely out of his teens, he was admired for his all-around knowledge. It was only natural that he'd begin to teach locally in Banks County and soon developed a relationship with Amanda Chitwood, Caleb's fifteen-year-old daughter. The two were married before Baptist Pastor L. J. Duncan on February 11, 1886.[10] Not before very long, the Cobbs were expecting, and on the following December 18, a healthy baby named Tyrus Raymond, better known to the public as "Ty Cobb," was born in the family's remote cabin. Regarding his rather unusual name, Cobb explained that it came from a "Tyrian leader" from Tyre, which is today in modern-day Lebanon. He disavowed any claim that it was from Tyr, the Norse God of War.[11]

"My grandfather was a Chitwood," Cobb told a reporter in 1944. "I was born on his plantation, which is four miles from Mount Airy and about six miles from Cornelia. There's nothing there but the land today."[12] Cobb described his birthplace as taking place in the community of Narrows, an unincorporated stretch of land that included parts of Banks, Habersham, and Stephens Counties.[13] Narrows, Georgia, was the location of a locally important Civil War battle often referred to as the "Battle of Narrows." According to Mark McCoy of the Banks County Historical Society, the battle was fought in October 1864 and ended in a victory for "Home Guard" members of the Confederacy against scavenger elements of the Union Army.[14] At present, the area is more known as the Broad River region, and is actually within the city limits of Baldwin, Georgia. The exact address is 1366 Georgia Highway 105 and a marker remains there to signify his birth.

William H. Cobb was extremely motivated to further his education— maybe even more so after the arrival of his first son. He likely read the articles in local newspapers advertising the academic offerings at the North Georgia Agricultural College at Dahlonega, particularly with the prominent military department, and went forward and enrolled for the 1887–88 term. His brothers-in-law, Stephen and Carter Chitwood, also attended the college, and the trio likely traveled together back and forth between Dahlonega and Banks County. He was a model student and because of his staunch discipline and the leadership qualities demonstrated in military drill, was quickly promoted to the rank of sergeant by 1889 and sergeant major in 1890. He served as a lieutenant in his final year at the college and was part of the Class of 1892, graduating with a Bachelor of Arts and a teacher's license. The college today is known as the University of North Georgia and the "military department" of Cobb's day is acknowledged as the "Military College of Georgia."[15]

In reporting on the Dahlonega graduates, the *Atlanta Constitution* stated that Cobb was a "man of intellect, a tireless worker, and of exemplary deportment."[16] Cobb was a member of the Decora Palaestra Society, and throughout his tenure at the North Georgia Agricultural College, he continued to progress as an orator.[17] It got to the point that he was not only starring in debate competitions, but delivering presentation speeches during school exercises. He was said to be headed toward a career in law, but instead chose to remain an educator, taking up a position as principal of a school in Lavonia, later in 1892.[18] The next year, he assumed direction at Harmony Grove High School in Jackson County. On September 11, 1893, he launched the fall term at the institution, offering a "splendid address" to the students and faculty.[19]

When Cobb spoke, he tended to combine a vast knowledge of his subject matter with words of inspiration. For instance, before the pupils at Harmony Grove, he extolled the virtues of higher education, stimulating the youth to seek out advanced enlightenment. Undoubtedly, that is what he envisioned for his son Tyrus and their two other children, John Paul and Florence Leslie, born in 1889 and 1892 respectively.[20] He wanted to encourage the same kind of love for books that his father instilled in him.

During the summer of 1895, the Cobb Family moved to Carnesville, the county seat of Franklin County, and settled into their fourth home in four years. The Cobbs had lived in Banks County at the Chitwood residence in early 1892, Lavonia in 1892–93, Harmony Grove in 1893–95, and finally in Carnesville. As one might expect, the relocation was as a result of another job opportunity for William, this time as the principal at Carnesville High School. It also brought him closer to the movers and shakers of the county, including local politicians, bankers, businessmen, and other individuals who saw the potential in "Professor" Cobb. High schools in the late nineteenth century were different than they are commonly known today, and Carnesville taught students from at least first through ninth grades, meaning it was mostly comprised of children from ages seven to sixteen. Ty Cobb turned nine in December 1895, and would have likely been in third or fourth grade at the time. His studies would have included mathematics, reading, grammar, and spelling, as well as advanced classes in bookkeeping, correspondence, and business.[21]

Franklin County in northeastern Georgia was spread out across 344 square miles and, amidst the foothills of the Appalachian Mountains, was both scenic and economically viable. William Cobb was positive that it offered the kind of life he wanted for his family. There was the availability to develop a plantation of his own, prospects to expand the school system, and a possible political future (if he decided to take that route). Carnesville was just about dead center of the county and it was fairly simple to venture northeast to Lavonia or southeast to Franklin Springs and Royston. In an early 1890s promotional piece, Carnesville was described as an "ideal place," mostly because the "water [was] pure and abundant" and the "citizens [were] moral, progressive, and united."[22]

These were small communities, however, and there were just over 14,000 inhabitants in the entire county during the early-to-mid 1890s. But that gave Cobb a better chance to make his mark as a leader, helping foster a more prosperous life for not only his family, but his neighbors as well. The Cobb family moved from Carnesville to Royston sometime around 1897, and once again, William transferred from one school job to another. Royston High School would be his final endeavor as a principal, although he'd never give up his work as an educator.[23] In the late stages of the decade, he traveled back to Carnesville to mentor future teachers in what was called a "Normal" class. The local newspaper recommended that anyone "desiring to stand state examination would do well to attend."[24]

Similar to their previous moves, Ty had to adjust to his new surroundings in Royston, and it wasn't easy for the high-strung, sometimes elusive young man. Most of the kids around him had known their friends their whole lives, and he was essentially an outsider, trying to fit in with the crowd. Prone to be a bit cynical and cautious, he didn't stray too far from his father's wishes, and attended school like he was told. But he wasn't entirely fascinated by studies in the way his father had been, and his attention seemed to wander. When around others, he was always on heightened defense, protective, and any perceived insult from a peer could easily draw out his temper.

"Ty has always been impetuous and head strong," his mother Amanda explained in 1919. "Even when he was just a little tot in short clothes, he hated to lose an argument and he never did lose many. He was full of mischief in his boyhood days and he had fights in school. If a stronger boy would get the best of him, Ty would fight him every day or two until he finally won the verdict. He would never give up or admit that a lad could get the best of him."[25]

Ty had an insatiable desire to win. Regardless of the competition, he centered his entire being on that solitary goal. But the reasoning behind his drive revealed a major characteristic of his personality that he would never grow out of. In his 1961 memoir, he explained how he felt "merely adequate" as a student, simply ordinary in terms of scholastic ambition and the antithesis of his father. Despite his young age, the "Professor" wanted him preoccupied with studies and working in the direction of a professional career. Ty wasn't ready to make that kind of decision. He sought adventure, not confinement to a desk. But he wanted to measure up to his father and was frustrated by his natural inability to contend with Professor Cobb, mentally or physically. As a consequence, he became discouraged and ridden with anxieties. He also became immensely insecure, harboring a great need to prove himself a "real man."[26]

In that state of self-doubt, he manifested his energy into physical attempts to substantiate his manhood, initially through schoolyard fighting. In his autobiography, Cobb said that he walked a precarious tightrope in Royston trying to prove he "could match the bigger boys."[27] But soon he'd enter the healthier realm of organized competition and apply himself the same way. Though, it wasn't until he became utterly fascinated with baseball that he began to exhibit the type of passion that his father wanted him to give his schoolwork. Ty commented: "My first knowledge that I liked baseball was when I made my debut at school in Lavonia, Franklin County, Georgia. I was seven years old."[28] "He was always at play," said Amanda Cobb, "and it was most always baseball, providing he could find any other boys of the neighborhood to play with him." His mother admitted that her husband "scolded" Ty, hoping to dissuade him from wasting time on so useless of an activity.[29] For a young man with college options or a possible West Point Military Academy appointment ahead of him, baseball was an ill-advised pursuit.

Attorney R. L. J. Smith told the *Atlanta Journal* in 1907 that "Young Tyrus first learned to play the great American game of baseball" in Harmony Grove, and since Cobb lived in that village between the ages of seven and nine, he was probably right. Smith added that Cobb, "as a typical Georgia boy, [had] spent some of his happiest childhood days upon the local diamond." [30] According to Howell Foreman's 1912 article in *Baseball Magazine*, Cobb participated in his "first real games" while residing in Carnesville and Ty would have been ten or eleven years old at the time. He represented the West End squad and played catcher against a team from the East End.[31] These games were spirited encounters and Cobb enjoyed the rivalry. He was essentially still a novice, but loved the challenge baseball offered and wanted to do nothing else. He was thrilled whenever there was an opportunity to play in a corner lot or even a game of catch, and his enthusiasm only served to get stronger once the family moved to Royston.

Annoyed by his son's infatuation, William worked tirelessly to alter Ty's mindset. At the very least, he wanted to keep him busy enough so that he'd have no extra time to play ball. That meant chores, chores, and more chores on the fifteen-hundred acre family farm.[32] After Ty expressed an inkling of interest in becoming a physician, William encouraged him to spend time with Fountain G. Moss, a Royston doctor. After helping "Doc" perform an operation and getting a good perspective of what a physician in rural America did on a daily basis, Cobb left the option open for his future.[33] But, again, he wasn't ready to make any long-term decisions. William, incidentally, was partial to Ty becoming a lawyer. Cobb, in 1947, wrote about his father, saying: "He hoped that I would follow his footsteps into public affairs and felt that legal training would be the best preparation. Many were the times we debated the matter, but neither of us budged."[34]

The public affairs that Ty mentioned were Georgia politics, which William Cobb entered during the late 1890s. Unlike his father in North Carolina, William was a staunch Democrat and, not surprisingly, education was a key aspect of his platform. He was a proponent of fairness and respect toward African Americans and, by August 1899, had gained such a wide popularity that people were already touting a 1900 bid for Georgia State Senator.[35] The following July, he won his party's primary for the 31st District and the *Atlanta Constitution* predicted the election would probably end "in his favor."[36] On October 3, 1900, Cobb gained a majority of the vote over J. C. McCarter and became senator, a position he'd execute with the same kind of astuteness that he did everything else. Cobb was also elected Mayor of Royston, but the specific time-frame he served was not revealed.[37] According to one unidentified source, Cobb was Royston Mayor in 1903.

The baseball culture in Franklin and surrounding counties was quite robust. In 1886, the *Toccoa News* declared that "Baseball threatens to become an extensive southern industry. It is very good for amusement, but it is a poor occupation."[38] And that's the way it was treated: as a leisurely, yet spirited pursuit for young men already engaged in full-time schooling or careers. Teams represented just about every small village in the region from Harmony Grove to Elberton, and there was heavy encouragement for boys to head to the neighborhood diamond. In 1900, a journalist in Hartwell noticed a little too much "lounging listlessly around town" and told the kids to "shake your flabby muscles, shuffle off that lazy spell, and 'play ball!'"[39]

Perhaps the most important aspect of localized baseball was the competitive nature of both the players and supporters, and the honor that was on the line in games against adjacent municipalities. Rooters went out to the park to cheer on their fellow townsmen and the athletes involved in the heated contests were often on the verge of fisticuffs. The bottom line was that no one wanted to lose and give away bragging rights. While no one on the regional circuit could make a living just playing ball, the more talented players were able to venture from location to location and garner extra coinage performing away from their hometown.

It was only fitting that Royston inaugurated a team of its own to enter the scramble for area baseball laurels. With an energetic citizenry, Royston had a population of just over 1,000, and featured a number of business and agricultural firms, helping it grow in size. The cotton gins, grocery and hardware stores, plus a variety of specialty shops offered residents an expanse of employment and shopping opportunities. Reverend Frank M. Hauser, who did a lengthy profile on the relatively young Royston community for the *Augusta Chronicle*, said, "It would put to shame many towns in Georgia twice her age in push and pluck."[40] Hence, when the baseball boom hit, not only was there a championship-level squad formed, but two others comprised of aspiring players striving for a shot with the big boys.

Ty Cobb was one of those youngsters. Pretty much guaranteed a slot on a secondary team, he turned up his nose and wanted nothing less than to stand alongside the older guys and prove to his father that his so-called wasted time was worthwhile. The preeminent club was managed by twenty-six-year-old Robert "Bob" McCrary, a bank clerk by trade. A short gentleman with an easygoing disposition, McCrary didn't play favorites on his team and allowed open trials to find the very best athletes at each station. Along came thirteen-year-old Cobb, full of vim and vigor, and as animated as could be. What he lacked in experience he made up in energy, and McCrary was quite impressed. Even though Cobb only weighed somewhere between 90 and 100 pounds and appeared far too skinny, the manager acknowledged his potential and brought him into the fold.[41]

The decision wasn't universally embraced, as many observers felt he was a good fielder, but lacking at the plate. McCrary ignored those comments and worked with Cobb at length, building up his batting "eye." Cobb's improvements were soon evident. In advance of a game in Elberton, there was a problem with the team's regular center fielder, and suddenly Cobb, who usually remained home when the squad went on the road, became a much needed substitute. What is believed to be another version of this same story was told by Ty's uncle Clifford Ginn. However, he said the game was against Harmony Grove (Commerce) and the team was missing its shortstop, thus, the need for Cobb to participate. He said, "All were grown men except Cobb." But Cobb was a starring feature in the contest, making three hits and accepting eight chances in the field without an error. Professor Cobb, who was reportedly at the game, rode back to the family farm with his son, and Ty "crawled under the buggy cushion and slept all the way home."[42] Cobb knew asking for his father's permission was futile. There was no way the "Professor" would allow his teenage son to leave Royston to play foolish ball. And, actually, he had much more productive things for him to do, including work in the fields. McCrary, however, knew Ty's father personally. They were both part of the Mason Brotherhood and, through that connection, he obtained the okay for Ty to travel with the club.[43]

In Professor Cobb's mind, there were several concerns. For one, he wasn't convinced baseball was a principled field of endeavor. He was aware of the rowdiness that sporadically took place that overshadowed any wholesome rivalry. The other concern was about Ty himself. When Howell Foreman obtained stories from the residents of Carnesville about Ty, he explained that locals remembered him for being a "chronic, continual scrapper."[44] Cobb knew his son was prone to aggression and he didn't want his family embarrassed by some kind of outburst. Frankly, he wanted McCrary to supervise his son in Elberton, and the manager agreed. Young Cobb didn't underachieve on that occasion. He hit demonically, leading Royston to victory. Later, Ty explained: "Let me tell you something, once an athlete feels that peculiar thrill that goes with victory and public praise, the fascination holds him for life. He can never get away from it. On the way back home from that game I made up my mind that I would try and be a great ballplayer and I worked at it by day and dreamed of it by night."[45]

In addition to McCrary's teachings, Cobb was proactive on his own as well. He made efforts to increase his speed, read publications offering tips, and in a desperate need to supplant his ragged glove, resorted to a bit of thievery. He snuck into his father's office, pulled two ancient-looking books from the shelves, and dealt them for a new mitt.[46] It was the perfect irony, swapping academic text—which his father wanted him so much to appreciate—for a tool of the ball yard, and essentially allowing him to further his real ambition.

The Royston Reds carried a roster of about ten players, and Cobb was several years younger than his teammates.[47] But his age and lack of size were not going to hold him back, and when he was goaded by rivals or spectators, he used his anger as motivation. He nevertheless heard comments such as, "We're not running a kindergarten class. This is a man's baseball nine!"[48] Laughter and mocking accompanied the barbs, and Cobb was immensely sensitive to the ridicule. He wasn't a quitter, though, and he performed his duties at shortstop to the best of his abilities, learning from his mistakes, and fueled by the desire to show his critics how wrong they were. Ever determined, he experienced bumps in the road but, after all, as he said it years later, "I was simply a kid playing with grownups."[49]

Joseph Cunningham, a right fielder for Royston, was four years older than Cobb and one of his closest friends. Cunningham lived down the street from Cobb, and the two bonded over baseball, fashioning their own home-produced bats using Cunningham's father's carpentry tools.[50] Balls were created in an equally creative way. They would take little rubber spheres, wind string around them, and then apply leather covers. It also wasn't unusual to see small town players wearing coarse, hand-crafted uniforms, and the athletes in Franklin County were no exception.[51] From the ages of thirteen to sixteen, Cobb took great pride in wearing the red attire, and developed from an undersized boy into a robust young man while partaking in games for the honor of his hometown. In that same time, he morphed from a greenhorn into a pretty crafty ballplayer . . . but he still had much to learn.

Interestingly enough, he'd adopted a habit early in his baseball days that remained throughout his career, and that was the way he gripped a bat. He was inclined to space his hands a few inches apart on the handle, whereas most other players swung with both fists together. The technique wasn't based on an instinctive personal knowledge of how to successfully garner hits, but because, as a skinny kid, he was unable to swing the bat using the standard form. Cobb, who batted left-handed, compensated for his weakness and figured out the best way to be productive at the plate.[52] As he got older and stronger, he could have reworked his methods to be more traditional, but wasn't comfortable making the change.

In July 1903, a squad from nearby Hartwell entered a three-game series versus Anderson, South Carolina, its top rival from just over the Savannah River. A formidable lineup, Hartwell proceeded to trample the visiting club, 11–1 and 10–1 in the first two contests. Before the final game, several Anderson players deserted the team, refusing to suffer any more shame, and manager McKinney, in a terrific bind, sought local substitutes. From Royston, 15 miles away, he recruited either Bob or Jim McCrary, Emory Bagwell, Clifford Ginn, and, according to the *Hartwell Sun*, two athletes named Cobb. The newspaper indicated that one of the players was "T. Cobb," and it can be surmised that this was, indeed, Ty. The other Cobb might have been his younger brother, Paul, fourteen years old at the time. A third "Cobb" was also in the game, but this one, Joe Cobb, played for Hartwell and had no direct relation. The influx of local blood turned the competition into "the most brilliant, the most exciting, and by far the best game ever played in Hartwell." After 12 innings, the home team squeezed out a win, 2–1.[53]

For his involvement, Ty earned a little over a dollar and became a professional ballplayer. After Cobb became famous, a more dramatic narrative of his pro debut was distributed, and colorful sportswriters painted a breathtaking and heroic finish for Cobb. Chicago Cubs catcher Jimmy Archer, who played with Detroit and Cobb briefly in 1907, told the version he heard, which was Ty's "favorite story." He said that Cobb, with two outs in the bottom of the 14th inning, hit a dramatic home run to give his team the victory.[54] In reality, Ty played no part in the finish of the game. There are innumerable other inconsistencies between what really happened in 1903 and the "legend" that was created for Cobb in later years. Almost every account is different. In his autobiography, Cobb said he became pro after playing two games for Anderson and earned $2.50. He regretted it because he had wanted to retain his amateur status.[55]

Back home, Professor Cobb wasn't altogether excited by the sudden advancement of his teenaged son's career. While he certainly expected Ty to become an expert in his vocation of choice, he was steadfast in his belief that baseball was not an appropriate occupation. "Ty used to worry his father very much," Amanda Cobb explained in 1912. "Mr. Cobb insisted that he should become a professional man, as he maintained that we had the means to give him the best possible education. He was the oldest child and he took up the most of our time."[56] But the endless attempts to discourage baseball were falling on deaf ears, and Professor Cobb was starting to believe that perhaps the best way to deal with the matter was to let Ty learn from his mistakes, of which, a venture into baseball surely was.

Clued into the neighborhood buzz, Professor Cobb received numerous reports about the extraordinary success of his son on the diamond. Finally, for a contest against Harmony Grove, he decided to go out and see for himself. That was a special, yet nerve-racking afternoon for Ty, and it was hard not to be overwhelmed by his father's presence. But he was even more motivated than ever to show his value as a ballplayer and, in the eighth inning, Ty (now playing center field) made a heroic diving catch. "The catch saved the game, and I can truthfully say I never made a better one in my life," he said years later. "When I came in, the spectators were crazy with joy and they began tossing me money. I picked up eleven dollars in quarters and half dollars. My father was so carried away with my performance that he immediately became a fan."[57]

The Royston club played exceptionally well during the summer of 1903. Over two days in August, Cobb and his mates beat a combination of players (called "picked teams") from Harmony Grove, Ashland, and other local towns, and the scores, 5–0 and 16–3, were decidedly in their favor.[58] The solid pitching of Emory Bagwell and Stewart Brown were noteworthy, as was the ever-increasing offensive display from Cobb. Add the upsurge of Cobb's daring on the basepaths and he was quickly becoming the talk of northeastern Georgia. Meanwhile, the club had received a letter from an ex-teammate, Thomas Van Bagwell, Emory's older brother, who had traveled up into the Southern Association to get a tryout with the Nashville Volunteers.[59] He shared information about his experiences, from what pros were like at that level to the hotels they stayed at. "I read it and reread it," Cobb later said.[60]

"Nothing could keep me down from satisfying my ambition of showing that I could be as good as any of them," Cobb remembered.[61] His itch to prove himself was evident, and even though Bagwell would return to the Georgia circuit, not having achieved a regular berth on a minor league club, Cobb was determined to be a success.

In late 1903, news reached Royston that the city of Augusta, about 100 miles southeast, was joining the newly structured South Atlantic League, a Class C organization governed by Organized Baseball. Augusta would be known as the "Tourists" and the South Atlantic League was also called the Sally League. It was comprised of clubs representing the following cities: Augusta, Savannah, and Macon, Georgia; Jacksonville, Florida; and Columbia and Charleston, South Carolina. Inspired by the report, Cobb smartly realized that there was a hunt under way for competent players to fill the rosters of the six teams in the new league and mailed off inquiries to each of the various clubs about a possible tryout. A back channel to the Augusta team was opened when Reverend John F. Yarborough, a Methodist preacher in Franklin County, contacted W. H. Sherman, who had managed the Augusta independent club in 1903, and was well connected.[62] A few decades later, however, Cobb took offense to the claims that Yarborough was an influence on him as a young player. He wrote in his book that the Reverend had "nothing whatever to do with my development."[63] In his autobiography, Cobb said that only one manager responded to his inquiries, and that was Strouthers. But in a 1913 article, he noted that George "King" Kelly of the Jacksonville franchise also "politely answered," but told him there were no opportunities on his team.[64] In the end, it was

Augusta manager John "Con" Strothers who agreed to give Cobb a trial, but the youngster was responsible for his own expenses, including travel, room and board.

With what he understood to be the opportunity of a lifetime in front of him, Cobb was overjoyed and a little overwhelmed. The challenge of competing against older players was something he'd faced his entire life, but he'd never stepped onto a league diamond and matched up against real professionals. It was now a matter of flying the coop and either performing up to league standards or returning to Royston a failure. On the eve of his Augustan venture, he broke the news to his father and the two debated for hours. The professor knew his son was capable and he'd witnessed his excellent play firsthand, but in a last ditch effort to convince him to attend college instead, he applied a "sound and logical" argument. Cobb endured the eloquent lecture, his mind firm, and his father had no choice but to give in. His father gave him six checks at $15 apiece to pay for expenses while in Augusta.[65] Grateful to have his father's consent, Cobb later said, "I left with a great new love and respect for the man."[66]

Accompanied by his teammate Stewart Brown, who was also interested in a pro career, Cobb headed for Augusta and was amongst the first batch of players to appear at Warren Park for spring training in early April 1904. He stood out in his red hometown jersey, and his black bat was conspicuous, especially as he awed spectators with his hitting.[67] Almost from his arrival, the *Augusta Chronicle* lauded his work, and his childlike enthusiasm was on display in everything he did. Tourists catcher Dave Edmunds applied the first baseball-related nickname to the high-energy outfielder, calling him "Sleuth," and a newspaper writer explained that it was presumably because he copped all the balls hit in his direction.[68]

But his abundance of pep was creating an annoyance for manager Strothers. The latter explained: "Cobb was a player that couldn't help being noticed by any manager. He never was still a minute. He would run up to the bat, and if he happened to be thrown out at first, he would run all the way back to the bench like a racehorse. Of course, he was nothing but a kid then, and no matter how often I told him to keep cool, he would persist in skipping about on the dead run, which made my ball team look amateurish. I used to say to him, 'Now, walk up to the bat and look the situation over, see who is on the bases, where the fielders are playing for you and get your signal.'"[69] The words of wisdom didn't resonate and

Cobb continued to do things his way, dashing around the diamond with a gleeful exuberance.

Strouthers cut his excess talent, including Brown, and worked to stay under the $1,000 salary limit for each team in the league. Cobb was expected to remain, but play off the bench as a utility player receiving $90 a month, though Strouthers later said, "I signed him for $50 a month."[70] In advance of the season opener on April 26, Andy Roth, a high-profile signee, was barred from competing after a controversy sprung up involving the National Baseball Commission. As a result, Cobb went into the game, participating in his first league contest. Most Cobb books claim that it was first baseman Harry Bussey who had trouble prior to the opener, but Roth had been recalled by the Nashville club, and the National Commission stepped in. Strouthers went forward and paid a sum to clear Roth to play in the second game. Bussey was in the lineup for both the first and second games of the season. In game two, Cobb, Bussey and Roth were in the lineup.[71] Cobb was seventh in the lineup and played center, and, without question, made a big splash with the 2,000 people in attendance at the local park. He doubled in the eighth inning, stole third, and scored. In the ninth he blasted a solo home run over the left-field fence, trying to set up a last minute rally. Unfortunately Augusta faltered, and Columbia won, 8–7. The next afternoon, Cobb went 0-for-2 with a run, and shortly thereafter was abruptly released.[72] It has been reported that Cobb was let go for not going through with a sacrifice bunt when told.[73] Strothers it seemed, had no use for the Royston prodigy.

Dejected, Cobb called his father looking for guidance. He explained his predicament and told the professor that a pitcher named Fred Hays, also released from Augusta, discussed an opportunity to play with a club in Anniston, Alabama, in the Tennessee-Alabama League.[74] "You accept that offer, and don't come home a failure," his father told him, now fully pulling for him to succeed in his baseball endeavors. Cobb later explained, "Those, I think, were the most important words in my life."[75]

The weight of his father's support was immeasurable, and Cobb's determination was renewed en route to Anniston, which was 237 miles away in the eastern part of Alabama. Before him was another test of his fortitude, and the newly instituted independent organization, made up of eight clubs to include Knoxville and Chattanooga, was on less sturdier financial ground than the Sally League. But Cobb didn't hesitate to sign a $50 per month contract on April 29, and boarded with the family of Edna Darden, a widow originally from Georgia.[76] The season launched seventeen days later, but Anniston was defeated in their opener by Bessemer, Alabama, 9–4. Cobb got four hits over his next two games, kick-starting a winning streak that sent Anniston to the top of the league with an 8–1 record. However, the team nosedived in June, falling to sixth place (14–18).[77]

Fielding errors by the club were a constant problem and crowds became indifferent to the shoddy work. Cobb went through some tough growing pains of his own, and the routine hazing of young players was at the root of his troubles. Teammates got a thrill out of calling him "Kid," a name he utterly despised, and he felt the nickname was disrespectful to the point of wanting to fight whoever used it toward him. Ed Darden, son of his house-mother and roommate, remembered Cobb some years later: "He wasn't too aggressive when he first came here, but as his skills grew, you could see his spirit grow. I remember he had a couple of fights with members of his own team because of the kidding [at his expense]."[78] Homesickness and the stress brought on by the bullying tactics caused him to throw in the towel at one point. He packed his bags and began for Royston, only to be convinced to stay at the last minute.[79]

Long before the season was set to end, Anniston unceremoniously folded on July 11 and management difficulties were to blame.[80] Cobb had been a bright spot for the doomed franchise, running the bases and field-ing with skill, and batting over .300. In 1968, a comprehensive study of his time there was conducted by a handful of researchers and 27 box-scores involving Cobb were located. It was found that he had achieved a .336 batting average with 37 hits, 20 runs, 10 stolen bases, three doubles, seven triples, and four errors. This information was still incomplete because it was believed that Cobb played a total of 45 games while in Anniston.[81] Ironically, back in Augusta, Strothers was struggling and in serious need of a consistent hitter. He sought to regain custody of Cobb, but Ty declined the job, demonstrating his pride in not wanting to work for the man who fired him. Within days, the Augusta club changed owners and H. W. Wing-ard, the new manager, made the same efforts to retrieve Cobb. This time, the latter was receptive. He reported on August 9 and played out the final month. He was one of only two players in the lineup on the final day of the season who appeared in the opener in April—the other being third baseman William Spratt.[82] Not unlike Anniston, Augusta was dreadful from top to bottom, and firmly settled in the basement of the South Atlan-tic League, finishing 1904 with a 41–73 record.

Cobb batted .237 in 37 games for Augusta, and although there wasn't much to celebrate, he was one of the first five players engaged for spring camp by new team manager Andy Roth. His potential had been recognized, but it was up to him to shine on the field if he wanted a real spot on the roster.[83] Beginning in mid-March 1905, he pulled out all the stops at Warren Park and, once again, an observer for the local newspaper predicated nothing but good things for the youngster. In exhibition games against the Detroit Tigers of the American League, in what was Cobb's first look at major league pitching, he displayed versatility at bat, hitting out long triples and reaching first on bunts.[84] His quickness leaving the plate was also noteworthy and it was hard not to notice that he stood out a little more than his contemporaries.

Oddly, the *Augusta Chronicle* offered advice to Cobb in what was likely an extension of Roth's managerial guidance in the dugout. The paper cautioned the outfielder to withhold his "reckless endeavors" on the basepaths, telling him, "You are not in the amateur game now."[85] In another edition, a journalist stated, "A little improvement in his judgment on the bases," and he would "land safe and sound."[86] But that isn't what Cobb wanted to hear. He wanted to run on his own instincts, regardless of what Roth or anyone else advised. After making the team and heading into the regular season, Cobb continued his rebellious ways. During a game versus Jacksonville, he doubled, but unadvisedly decided to try to extend the hit into a triple. He was easily thrown out and the team eventually lost.

The embarrassment was personal, Cobb felt, and he certainly didn't want to be lectured about it. Roth later recalled the incident, saying, "When I censured him, [Cobb] threatened to pull his revolver on me in a local cigar store and I seized a hatchet. Bystanders interfered and Cobb and I had a serious talk over the matter to the satisfaction of both of us."[87] Based on his independent nature and the fact that it didn't take much to make him mad, Cobb's teammates applied the same type of schoolyard harassment that was seen in Anniston. One of his primary tormentors was third baseman Gus Ruhland, and the two were destined to come to blows. Cobb did eventually fight Ruhland and "proceeded to make hamburger" out of him.[88] But thirty-four-year-old George Leidy of Phillipsburg, New Jersey, a fellow outfielder, recommended that Cobb avoid trouble. To that point, in almost every situation, Cobb had simply refused to listen to advice, but somehow, Leidy was able to get through to him.

Prior to being influenced by Leidy, Cobb was a lot less focused on baseball success. He said: "My main trouble at the start was that I didn't take my job on the Augusta team seriously. I will never forget the first time I was benched. I used to like my peanut taffy, and one day I went out to centre field chewing on a big hunk of this candy. A fly ball was hit out to me, but I forgot to throw away the candy, and everything got so mixed up that I lost the ball and, incidentally, the game. For that I was benched, and I should have been."[89]

It took time for Cobb to see this, and Leidy helped, soon becoming his primary mentor. Involved in some form of the sport since the late 1880s, Leidy was a bona fide veteran of baseball and knew all the tricks to the game. His real talent lay in the way he related to and educated others, and he provided a wealth of knowledge to younger players at the drop of a hat. With Cobb, he saw outstanding potential and committed to teaching him everything from aiming bunts to specific parts of the infield to sliding properly to the famous hit-and-run. Additionally, Leidy not only enlightened Cobb to the psychology of baseball, but used a little psychology of his own to further inspire the prodigious teen. He relayed enthralling stories of life in the majors and confidently said that Cobb, if he continued to develop, was a surefire future big leaguer.[90] In response, Ty's imagination ran wild.

Between May and June, 1905, Cobb's batting average rose nearly 70 points from .243 to .312. At the end of July, he became the first player in the league to attain 100 hits and a reporter wrote, "It is interesting to note that he is ten or fifteen hits ahead" of his peers in that regard.[91] There were rumors of major league scouts roaming the circuit, and it was apparent that Cobb was being closely watched. Augusta played a doubleheader at Columbia on August 5 with Cobb in the lineup, and then journeyed to Jacksonville for a series beginning on Monday, August 7. For whatever reason, and possibly because of a thumb injury, Cobb sat out the next two games. In fact, it is unclear whether Cobb went to Jacksonville for the series at all.[92] On the evening of August 8, a tragedy was suffered back home in Royston, and yet hours would go by before Ty learned the news that his beloved father had been shot and killed.

Professor Cobb, state senator in 1900–01 and the Franklin County School Commissioner since 1902, was a gentleman of great distinction in Georgia. The forty-two-year-old dignitary had done admirable work in advancing the cause of education in his county and there were preliminary rumblings that he was on a short list to one day become state school commissioner. He was the proud father of three children, the husband of a "very beautiful woman," and seemingly enjoying an honorable existence.[93]

But in the aftermath of his murder, people were left to speculate why his wife of nineteen years pulled the trigger on that fateful night and sentenced him to death.

The stunning news was front page material across Georgia, including in both the *Atlanta Journal* and *Atlanta Constitution*, and received some national coverage. Almost immediately, Amanda Cobb was a suspect in what was believed to be a case of manslaughter. Before the Franklin County Coroner's Jury, she offered a lengthy statement, explaining that she had awoken overnight and heard a "kind of rustling" outside the window. Upon examination, she spotted a human figure, but was unable to see who it was or what the individual was doing on the veranda of the home. "The form seemed to crouch down," she said, armed with a pistol her husband had given her for home defense.[94] "I stood at the upper side of the window and pulled the shade to one side and shot twice." Her aim was unfortunately impeccable, and Professor Cobb was hit twice, once in the head and again in the stomach. Amanda claimed that Professor Cobb was a sleepwalker and may have been walking in his sleep.[95]

Despite her explanation, Amanda was encircled by suspicion. After the burial of her husband on August 10, she was arrested. She never denied pulling the trigger, but thought the house was being burglarized and said it was a horrible accident. As far as she knew, her husband had left for Atlanta earlier in the day and was not expected home until Thursday. She never thought for a minute it was him outside their home and once she realized what had occurred, became "prostrate with grief," according to the *Columbus Ledger*.[96] The story was quickly sensationalized by reports of Amanda's alleged infidelity and the assertion that Cobb had been told to "keep watch over his home." In an effort to do so without anyone knowing, he initially left home on business, only to return on foot that night with a rock and a pistol in his coat pocket. En route home, Cobb was spotted, but a witness thought he was trying not to be identified. Soon thereafter, the accidental murder transpired.

The once impeccable Cobb family was subjected to intense public scrutiny as Amanda Cobb's trial was scheduled for March 1906 and she was released on $7,000 bond.[97] Eighteen-year-old Ty was overcome with sadness and shame. His father's death was beyond comprehension and he expressed very little, if anything, publicly. The Cobb children denied the scandalous rumors of domestic discord and cited "perfect harmony" in their family.[98] Ty was the recipient of the baseball public's sympathy in Augusta and the local paper stated, "Being only a boy yet in his teens, the blow will be partic-ularly a hard one, especially on account of its tragic nature."[99] Swallowing his pain, Cobb returned to the lineup for a doubleheader on August 16, but three days later, he heard what should have been the greatest bit of infor-mation in his young life. The Detroit Tigers were in need of a good hitting outfielder, and with the help of scouts Henry Youngman, a deal for Cobb was made.[100] But, considering all that was going on, his sale to the Detroit Tigers was overshadowed by anguish. Nonetheless, he was headed for the major leagues.

All things considered, Ty Cobb was a rare phenom with the kind of innate value that could one day be the foundation of a championship team. Augusta had seen his fine play all year and in his final appearance on August 25, 1905, he was given a gold watch as a gift from the club and fans. Cobb relished the special recognition of his work, calling it his "proudest posses-sion."[101] His .326 average in 103 games spoke volumes about his ability to hit, but there was a significant jump in the quality of pitchers from Class C to the majors, and whether Cobb had what it took to be successful was something still to be determined. But in the back of his mind, echoing loudly, were his father's words: "Don't come home a failure." He didn't intend to.

2

NOT A BORN BALLPLAYER

Resting north of the Mason-Dixon Line, approximately 767 miles from Royston, Georgia, was the lively metropolis of Detroit, a city culturally and economically infused in contemporary American life. Embellished by striking and ever-growing structures in the downtown area, electric railways along the streets and a vast industrial complex, the urban sprawl, including an array of easy-to-reach suburbs, was a great attraction for people looking to settle in the Midwest.[1] Life in Detroit was going to further improve, as the economic stability created by the exportation of chemicals, cattle, and stoves, plus the heavy enterprises of railroad cars, were going to be augmented by the thriving horseless carriage industry that was better known as the all-encompassing realm of automobiles.

Motorcars and Detroit would forever be synonymous. In terms of pioneers in the field, Charles B. King, the first man to drive a gasoline powered auto in the city limits, Ransom E. Olds, and Henry Ford were innovators, setting an extraordinary trend for the world to follow. The Ford Motor Company, incorporated in 1903, grew from 31 employees in its second year to 229 in its third, and ultimately to over 55,000 by 1920. In that same amount of time, the number of cars produced went from under 2,000 a year to in excess of a million.[2] The Detroit population also skyrocketed from 285,704 to 465,766 between 1900 and 1910, and by 1920 it was the fourth biggest city in the nation.[3]

Baseball was a fixture in Detroit, commonly expected from a virile and prosperous community, and beginning in 1881, it fielded a team in the National League known as the Wolverines. In 1887, the local nine, managed by Bill Watkins and headed by the renowned "Big Four," comprised of Jack Rowe, Dan Brouthers, Deacon White, and Hardy Richardson, won both the league pennant and the world's championship.[4] Resoundingly, it was the biggest moment to date in area sports history, but the Wolverines fell from grace after the following season and faded into obscurity with only the memories of its accomplishments remaining behind. The game continued to be played on a smaller scale in the years that followed, but attendance waivered and the merit of competition was far below championship level.

By 1893, a West Coast entrepreneur named George A. Vanderbeck was actively seeking a position amongst the newly developing Western League and, frankly, he didn't seem to care what city he represented as long as he had a franchise.[5] However, soon after obtaining the rights to the Detroit club, he sought to relocate to Fort Wayne, Indiana.[6] Nevertheless, league president Ban Johnson negated the idea, and plans to initiate a squad in Detroit went forward for the 1894 season. Initially known as the "Detroit Creams," Vanderbeck adjusted the name to the "Tigers" in 1895 and, over the next five years, he wadded along but fell short of winning a pennant. Vanderbeck dropped out of the team's ownership in 1900, right around the time the Western League morphed into the American League.

Between 1900–01, as the Detroit Tigers and the rest of the eight-club American League broke from the National Agreement and became a major league in opposition to the National League, the local franchise went through some growing pains behind the scenes. The club passed from the ownership of the Vanderbecks to James D. Burns and then to a syndicate led by Samuel F. Angus. Angus, forty-six years old, was a shrewd businessman, having spent years in the life insurance racket, as well as working to establish electric railway systems in both his native Ohio and Michigan.[7] Amongst the other shareholders of the syndicate were James McNamara, E. H. Doyle, and Frank C. Cook. The team was managed by Frank Dwyer, who replaced George Stallings, in 1902. Angus ultimately bought out his partners and, along with manager Ed Barrow, improved the team standings from seventh place in 1902 to fifth in '03. Regrettably, the ongoing "war" between the leagues wore Angus thin, and he became more and more frustrated by his venture into baseball.[8]

Known for his class and personality, Angus was motivated to give dedicated fans a championship. He heeded the advice of a longtime trusted employee of his insurance business, Frank J. Navin, who was exceedingly interested in the business end of baseball. Navin stepped in and helped coordinate the reorganization of the Detroit Tigers in December 1903. The deal evenly split the $100,000 capital stock between Angus and twenty-eight-year-old business tycoon William H. Yawkey, giving each 40 percent. Navin joined in the ownership as a minority stockholder.[9] This new triumvirate was short-lived and, a few weeks later, Angus sold the remainder of his interest in the Tigers to Yawkey and retired.[10] Angus later endured a debilitating three-year illness and died on February 6, 1908. He was well liked and an important part of the Detroit community for more than fifteen years.[11]

The Yawkey-Navin combination, along with Barrow at the helm, appeared to be a formidable pairing. Previous pickups Jimmy Barrett, Sam Crawford, Bill Donovan, and George Mullin were joined by Charley O'Leary, Ed Killian, and Matty McIntyre, and followers believed they were surefire contenders. That was not the case. While respected by members of the team, Barrow was unable to fashion a winning record even though he clearly had competent talent. Sportswriters believed that Barrow made a dire error when he traded Kid Gleason for George "Heinie" Smith, and the move hindered his entire managerial stay in Detroit. *The Sporting News* called it the "biggest gold-brick deal in the history of baseball," and felt it was utterly detrimental to the team because it also led to the loss of Kid Elberfeld, who was schooled by Gleason.[12] The 1904 Tigers once again fell to seventh in the standings, with a 62–90–10 record, and were 32 games behind champion Boston. Barrow tendered his resignation before the season was over (the Tigers record before he stepped down was 32–46), and was replaced by veteran infielder Bobby Lowe.[13]

Quick, aggressive maneuvering was needed, and management stepped up to purchase third baseman Bill Coughlin, a Pennsylvanian upstart and future team captain, from Washington for a reported $7,000.[14] The next logical step was finding a battle-tested manager and Navin felt William R. "Bill" Armour, another Pennsylvania product, would fit the mold. An ex-player himself, Armour had recently walked away from his job as leader of the American League's Cleveland franchise after a three-year tenure. In that time, he supervised the signing of Napoleon Lajoie, the sensational second baseman, and transformed the team from a financial loser into one that was firmly on solid ground and in the green from a financial stand-point. In 1904, Cleveland won 86 games, but landed in fourth place, and Armour was displeased so much so that he promptly resigned. (Armour's resignation was effective at the end of the 1904 season.)[15]

Rumored animosity between Armour and Lajoie was also bandied about. But whatever the strife in Cleveland, Navin didn't care. He rushed to

Detroit in September 1904, sporting a blank check in his pocket, and immediately met with Armour to discuss terms. Armour initially sidestepped an agreement, claiming to have offers from other teams on the table.[16] He soon changed his tune and signed a contract, but the deal was kept quiet because of Armour's lingering responsibilities in Cleveland through the end of the season. Notably, Armour made a move in September, signing Arthur L. "Bugs" Raymond, a pitcher, not to Cleveland but for Detroit, which was obviously indicative of his future plans.[17] Official confirmation of his status didn't come until the second week of October.[18]

Armour was exceedingly motivated to get started and by the first part of November, he was established in Detroit and finalizing plans for spring training at Augusta in March 1905. On the other hand, Navin was busy handling the club finances and figured that the team broke about even during the course of the recent season. The news was altogether surprising considering Detroit was seventh in the league in attendance and not faring too well on the road. Additional investments for personnel and refurbishments to Bennett Park, the home stadium of the Tigers, put the franchise into the red, but there was no way getting around it—that was the cost of doing business.[19] Navin, however, had a shrewd proposal to guarantee financial capital for shareholders in 1905, but the idea worked adversely toward the players themselves.

The concept was to take advantage of the cessation of hostilities between the American and National Leagues, which came about in 1903, and the elimination of all war-time contracts. For the two years of battle, owners were compelled to lock their athletes into long-term and inflated contracts to ensure team loyalty at a time when jumping leagues was prevalent. Those multi-year agreements were coming to an end, and Navin revealed to the press that he figured to save as much as $14,000 by making widespread salary cuts.[20] Poor performances in 1904 made the dramatic decline in payroll easier to stomach, at least from the managerial perspective, and *The Sporting News* attributed a telling statement to both Armour and Navin, saying, "Not a man on the team played $3,000 ball. Why should any of them expect [a] $3,000 salary?"[21]

There was a certain amount of understanding amongst major league athletes in the post-war years that contracts would be downsized, but the knowledge of such a reduction didn't make the application of such a move any easier to cope with. The possibility of holdouts or disgruntled players didn't alarm Navin, and he sent out contracts ranging from a low of $1,800 to a high of $3,000.[22] "Wild" Bill Donovan, a standout right-hander, went 16–16 in 1904 and saw a significant decrease. With a clear right to be angry, Donovan turned the other cheek, expressed a level-headed response to the pay cut, and looked forward to a promising new year in the box.[23] Other members of the Tigers weren't as forgiving.

A slightly elevated amount of enthusiasm surrounded Detroit during spring training at Augusta, but predictions placed the club seventh in the American League by season's end.[24] Trying to disprove preseason "dope," Armour's men opened on a positive note in April and had a brief stint in first place before settling into fourth, where they'd linger most of the season. One of the foremost problems was that a handful of individuals, players Armour hoped would prove suitable in the outfield and behind the plate, failed to make the grade. The difficulties began when first baseman Charlie Hickman, known as "Cheerful Charlie," was late to spring training and, upon arrival, nursing a lame wrist. That compelled Armour to shift Sam Crawford to first, leaving the outfield to Jimmy Barrett, Matty McIntyre, and rookie Denny Sullivan. When Sullivan proved inadequate, Hickman was sent to replace him. He too lacked the instincts of an outfielder and later deserted the team.[25] This issue was compounded by the devastating injury to center fielder Jimmy Barrett, who was knocked out with a twisted left knee in the seventh game of the season against Cleveland on April 26, 1905.[26] The catching position was also a hardship because both John Sullivan and Bob Wood washed out early in the season due to their inability to perform at the major league level. Armour only had two reliable backstops, Lew Drill and Tom Doran, until Jack Warner was added in August. These issues combined severely handicapped Detroit.

Quick on his feet, a superlative outfielder with a rocket arm, and a capable .300 hitter, Barrett was, according to Detroit sportswriter B. F. Wright, the "most popular player who ever wore a Tiger uniform."[27] He was a well-liked teammate and fans grew to love his fleet heroics, whether it was in the field making a great catch or laying down a bunt to get on base. The loss of Barrett was immeasurable and changed the complexion of the team. The addition of Chris Lindsay at first allowed Crawford to return to right field, while recent signee Dick "Duff" Cooley, a grizzled major league veteran, patrolled center. With the talented Matty McIntyre in left, the outfield was somewhat stabilized, but Armour knew there was a missing cog in his machine.

During the latter stages of July and into August, the Tigers put up an abysmal record (going 9–22 from July 23 through August 28), and the team began to free fall from fourth into sixth place.[28] Sensing imminent disaster, Navin and Armour signed Jack Warner, a thirty-two-year-old catcher with ten years of major league experience, hoping he could offer some semblance of leadership to the struggling pitching staff, and maybe help groom some of the younger players.[29] Warner was a good choice to balance duties with Lew Drill and Tom Doran, but he had a history of butting heads with management. In fact, he ventured off the grid to the independents after problems with St. Louis Cardinals manager Jimmy Burke earlier in 1905. He also fought with Pittsburgh's Otis Clymer, illustrating the disposition of a roughneck.[30]

Ty Cobb was the next major acquisition, and it was the single most important move Detroit made to date—and arguably in history. The visual reports of Cobb's worthiness came that spring at Augusta and word of his impressive batting during the 1905 South Athletic League season circulated freely throughout the nation. Bill Coughlin and Bill Donovan, active Detroit players, both would later take responsibility for "discovering" Cobb, and they weren't the only ones. But regardless of who put the thought in the minds of Armour and Navin or that Detroit representatives initially thought he was a "nut" during the 1905 spring training games, the trigger was pulled, and arrangements were made to sign Cobb.[31] A total of $500 was paid to Augusta for his release, with an additional $200 sent to ensure that he joined the club as soon as humanly possible. Cobb would reportedly agree to a standard rookie salary of $1,800, which amounted to about $300 a month.[32]

The purchase of Cobb was arranged to supplement Detroit's weakened outfield. Although Cooley was batting well and popular with fans, he was not the blazing center field leadoff man that Barrett was. Cooley was also either ill or reportedly injured at the time of Cobb's importation. Cobb was uniquely speedy, a report in The Sporting News stating that veterans of the South Athletic League believed Cobb was "the fastest youngster that ever broke into professional ball," and Armour wanted to test his quality against major-league competition.[33] It was a rare opportunity for an eighteen-year-old to step into the limelight of a big-time stadium and display his wares outside the harsh regular spring audition period. For Cobb, he was joining the team in late August and facing no real job competition. Nowhere was his future position with the Tigers guaranteed, but it was a chance of a lifetime. Unfortunately, the stroke of good fortune had emerged only weeks after the death of his father.

Cobb's emotions, unquestionably, were mixed. The excitement of becoming a ballplayer on the grandest stage was balanced against the loss of the most influential person in his life. He was excited and enthusiastic, but anxious and angry at the same time. The reasoning behind his father's killing remained murky and, logically, he knew that it was something that didn't necessarily have to happen. A certain amount of confusion still remained, and there was no way to know whether the answers rested on the baseball diamond or in a courtroom. But his destiny was already decided for him, as his services were purchased by Detroit.

Announcement of Cobb's procurement was made by club officials on August 22, 1905, and, exactly seven days later, he arrived in Detroit for the first time.[34] The city, which was three times more populated than Atlanta—the largest metropolis Cobb had seen in his young life—was dark but still intimidating. The fact that the team didn't send anyone to meet him at the train depot didn't help his apprehensive nature, but he plugged on, found a hotel, and rested his head.[35] He held on to the words members of his family had given him before he left Royston, reminding him to heed the directives of his leaders and conduct himself in a responsible manner.[36]

In a way, he hoped that the same kind of mentorship and encouragement his Augusta manager George Leidy offered was prevalent on the Tigers. It seemed reasonable enough that even though his first instinct was to distrust, if he was met by a generally welcoming atmosphere, there was little doubt he'd react positively both on and off the field.

The bottom line was that Cobb wasn't a well-adjusted young man. Being asked to report to the majors so soon after his father's murder was almost asking too much of anyone, let alone a born fighter with a Rock of Gibraltar-sized monkey on his back. His body was almost moving too fast for his mind, completing physical tasks, but not altering his mindset to deal with the enormity of what had occurred back home. But he was certainly following his dreams. Cobb was acting, for the most part, on complete intuition and pushed by an inner fire to succeed at all costs. Failure was not an option.

Even before his first appearance at Bennett Field, Cobb was hyped in local newspapers. The *Detroit Free Press* stated he was a "natural born hitter," reflecting on his .326 average in the South Atlantic League, and acknowledged that he was a "tricky" batter, able to disorientate fielders by utilizing a skillful bunt and impressive speed.[37] Other reports labeled him "Cyrus Cobb," but the written content remained positive. He was a leading prospect and his midweek debut on August 30 was highly anticipated by those who'd read the exciting headlines. To Cobb himself, donning Tigers garb for the first time was a proud moment.[38] He was wearing the uniform of a big leaguer and ready to challenge his own capabilities on the field of play against the best that baseball had to offer.

The leadership of Armour, with an assist from Captain Coughlin, inspired Detroit at times to demonstrate an unusual degree of heart, and optimism renewed itself on occasion.[39] Armour was getting solid work from many of his hired guns, especially right-fielder Sam Crawford. Crawford, nicknamed "Wahoo" after his hometown of Wahoo, Nebraska, a hamlet 40-odd miles west of Omaha, was the heaviest hitter on the Tigers and one of the best sluggers in the majors.[40] At six-feet tall and upwards of 190 pounds, he was powerfully built (for that time) and, routinely through the years, sportswriters have commented that had Crawford played in the live-ball era, he surely would be amongst the all-time home run leaders. He was known for his long swing, his shockingly potent right-field drives, and was popular around the clubhouse.[41]

Coming off his worst year in 1904, having batted just .254, Crawford was determined to return to his former self. His move to first base also showed his versatility and value to the team as an all-round athlete. Over in left field, Matty McIntyre, a twenty-five-year-old in his third major-league season, was a top-notch fielder and a promising hitter. Originally from Connecticut, he grew up on Staten Island, New York, of Irish descent and was a genuinely intelligent ballplayer. He was also a practical joker, and often-times went out of his way to razz teammates. A good example of McIntyre's light-hearted nature came later in his career, when he first joined the Chicago White Sox for the 1911 spring training camp in Texas. He went to great lengths to stage a fake break-in at the clubhouse by moving all of the team's equipment and personal items out prior to the arrival of players one morning. Needless to say, after a few scary moments for the team, McIntyre had a good laugh.[42] Of Cobb's two future outfield partners, it was hard not to admire Crawford and difficult not to occasionally smirk at the shenanigans of McIntyre.

Upon his first meeting with Armour, Cobb was impressed by the leadership and methodology of his new manager.[43] There wasn't much time for a lengthy orientation process, as he was going straight into the lineup on August 30. Cobb absorbed what little information and advice he received, but was obviously travel wary and nearly overwhelmed by the sheer magnitude of the happenings around him. That afternoon, he tried to shed his nervousness and allow his instincts to kick in because, essentially, the game of baseball was the only thing he could relate to the others around him. The different style of mannerisms, conversation, and attitudes were foreign, and although he wasn't from a distant planet, being from a smallish corner of the South limited his worldly experience. Overall, Cobb stood out like a sore thumb.

Despite Cobb's efforts to maintain his coolness, observers still sensed his anxiety. H.G. Salsinger, viewing the 5'10", 155 pound Cobb, described him as "gawky-looking" in his first appearance.[44] As he stood at the plate for the initial time in the bottom of the first inning, looking across from future Hall of Fame pitcher Jack Chesbro of the New York Highlanders, one could only imagine what was coursing through his mind. With two outs and Chris Lindsay on second, Cobb swung and missed the first pitch, and then watched another go by for a strike. The tension rose, but Cobb didn't back down. He reached out for another Chesbro offering and made contact, launching the ball to center field and over the head of Ed Hahn. Lindsay scored and Cobb raced to second, where he'd remain until the end of the inning.[45] Cobb also walked and made two putouts in the field. It was an impressive start to say the least.

For a rookie feeling the weight of the world, Cobb didn't lose his composure, and while not immediately recognized as an All-Star caliber player, he was given his due in the press. The *Detroit Free Press* called his debut "satisfactory," and mentioned how he was "well-received."[46] Another report in the *Free Press* explained that if Cobb hit .275, it would be satisfactory to all and that no one expected him to lead the American League in batting like he did in the South Atlantic League.[47] Before the end of the series against New York, he had a run-in with Highlander shortstop Kid Elberfeld, which was recounted in Cobb's 1961 biography, *Ty Cobb: My Life in Baseball.* Cobb remembered sliding headfirst into second and Elberfeld dropping his knee onto his neck in what would ultimately become a significant early base-running lesson. Not only was he out on the play, but he realized that many of the tricks he made successful at Augusta were not going to work against big leaguers.

The next time the two teams met, Cobb demonstrated a smarter, more potent feet-first slide, and was actually safe against Elberfeld. The latter paid him a small compliment for his efforts and Cobb noted that nothing gave him "a greater lift than Elberfeld's spontaneous gesture of sportsmanship" in either 1905 or '06.[48] Such a statement was somewhat shocking, considering he played 139 games in that period and was around innumerable teammates, coaches, managers, and other officials. But it was indicative of the cold environment Cobb found himself in and the lack of real, personal tutelage and encouragement he had while a rookie member of the Tigers.

Barrett made several unsuccessful attempts to return from injury and Cooley, who was said to have had a poor arm from the outfield, was ultimately released in favor of Cobb.[49] With firm hold of the center-field position, the youngster expectedly performed as a raw recruit would: making outstanding plays and absurd mistakes. Sometimes his own enthusiasm got the best of him, causing him to overstep, over-slide, or overreach his recommended bounds. B. F. Wright believed that Cobb was "too fast" for the health of the Tigers, demonstrated by his willingness to run into right and left field, intruding on the regions covered by Crawford and McIntyre to snare flies.[50] Maybe it was just Cobb trying too hard. One example occurred in the second game of a doubleheader against the White Sox on September 5, 1905, when he went after a ball clearly in McIntyre's grasp, knocking it loose and causing an error credited to McIntyre. The game was close and in the ninth inning, so the blunder could have cost Detroit the game. It didn't, fortunately, and the Tigers won 3–2.[51]

Such a maneuver fed the early perception that Cobb was trying to "hot dog" and steal the limelight out from under his teammates. Even if the error was chalked up to general anxiousness that couldn't really be controlled, Cobb was still figured as a scene stealer and McIntyre was the first to develop bad feelings. Incidentally, the day before the gaffe, Cobb reacted perfectly to a drive by White Sox first baseman Jiggs Donahue in the fourth inning and made what the *Detroit Free Press* called a "sensational catch." The Detroit crowd of 7,500 gave him a standing ovation and Cobb lifted his cap several times in response to the ruckus en route to the dugout.[52]

Cobb's daring was also already on display. Versus Addie Joss of Cleveland on September 12, he reached first in the ninth inning on a slow grounder by speed and speed alone. After getting to second on a sacrifice, he waited for the right moment to advance and it came when McIntyre attained an infield hit. Cobb rushed to third and although any further running was inadvisable, he kept going and compelled Cleveland's George Stovall to make a rushed throw to the plate. It was off target and Cobb scored. Detroit took the game, 4–3.[53]

Going through the circuit and facing each team, Cobb started to pick up various tidbits of information; which runners were faster than others, and particularly the dynamics of certain pitchers. He made assists from the outfield, completed at least one double-play, and aided his pitchers when they were in a jam. On offense, he sacrificed, stole a few bases, and offered occasional timely hitting. He had much to learn, but Armour was impressed by his abilities, as were baseball fans around the league.

Over the final stretch of the 1905 season, the Tigers battled back to .500, then soon returned to the top four and captured victories in 24 of 37 games played.[54] Some people believed it was Cobb's spark that kickstarted the successful run of the Tigers.[55] Detroit would finish third when the final bell tolled with a 79–74 record, their first winning record since their inaugural season of 1901. The remarkable turnaround was the talk of baseball in many quarters and, without any delay, predictions for 1906 had the Tigers amongst the top clubs in the American League. But there was a dark undercurrent to all the hype, statistics, and fanaticism. Detroit had the worst home attendance in the league and when Boston sportswriter Fred P. O'Connell called it a "dead baseball town" in August, he was seemingly right. He intimated that, if any consolidation of teams was to occur in the majors, Detroit would be a surefire candidate for elimination.[56] Another rumor circulated that Detroit management was going to transfer the Tigers to Toledo.[57] These topics, however, were more gossip than anything else.

Cobb finished 1905 with a .240 batting average.[58] He was honest in his 1961 biography, stating that he wasn't a "born ballplayer" and that it was "highly dubious" that he'd be brought back the following season based on his ghastly performance.[59] He was, in his own head, revealing his self-doubt, but Cobb was not going to be left off the 1906 spring training roster regardless of how he felt at the conclusion of 1905. That was the opinion of manager Bill Armour, the man pulling the strings. Armour knew there would be more competition for outfield slots in the coming year, but if Cobb still yearned to prove himself, he'd have many more opportunities to do so.

Two exhibition games followed the regular season, one in Jackson, Michigan, and the other a benefit send-off at Bennett Park. The Tigers won both, garnering about $80 extra per player.[60] The funds came in handy for road expenses going home, and *Sporting Life* revealed that Cobb was headed back to Royston with a particularly grueling job ahead. He was responsible for the finalization of his late father's estate and, because of the length of time required to do so, he needed an assist from an uncle to ensure he could return to baseball on time the following year.[61] On November 30, he attended the Georgia Tech–Clemson football game at Atlanta and spoke with a local newspaper. He apparently repressed any of his concerns and boldly gave his opinion that he'd be in center field for the Tigers in 1906.[62]

The only problem with acquiring any semblance of overconfidence was that Armour and Navin had made previous arrangements to bolster the club's outfield. The August before, Davy Jones, a Wisconsin athlete with several years of pro experience (including spells with the Chicago Cubs and St. Louis Browns), was obtained from the Minneapolis Millers of the American Association.[63] Jones was an incredible speedster and claimed to have race victories over Archie Hahn prior to the latter's Olympic track conquests in the early 1900s.[64] He was touted as the fastest man in the American Association and his .346 batting average was nothing to sneeze at. A graduate of law school, Jones never originally figured on becoming a ballplayer, but his athletic skills were too advanced to ignore.

The expected arrival of Jones should have reduced Cobb's confidence in any automatic return to the outfield. It was now a matter of competition and which player wanted the position most. Nevertheless, Cobb had reason to be content. A few months earlier, he spoke with Armour about a proposed contract for '06, and the manager offered him $1,200 for the upcoming season. Seeming reasonable enough, Cobb verbally accepted the terms. When the document arrived in January 1906, he saw that the amount had been bumped up to $1,500 for the season of work. Armour, in a letter sent around the same time, informed Cobb that he had a "bright future," and management wanted to ensure he was pleased by their offering.[65] He was, and his contract was signed and promptly returned.[66]

With the contract offered, Armour did have a singular request for Cobb. The Tigers were returning to Augusta for spring training in 1906, and since Cobb was already spending time in the region, Armour wanted him to venture over to Warren Park, the central ball field in town, and get a look at the playing ground to assess its condition. Cobb did what he was asked and sent a missive back to Armour, explaining that the field was in awful shape.[67] A carnival had recently used the land and destroyed what was considered a superior field, and Armour didn't take the news lightly. In fact, word of the terrible conditions at Augusta circulated far and wide. Locals, according to the *Detroit Free Press*, took offense to Cobb's assertions about Warren Park, demonstrating the pride they had in their community.[68] This report was contradicted by later stories that Augusta was firmly behind Cobb during spring training.[69] But the truth of the matter remained the same and the field needed intensive care to be ready for the Tigers to train.

Cobb had a request for Armour too. He asked for permission to accept a fine proposal to coach a college prep baseball squad at the University

School for Boys in Stone Mountain, Georgia. The gig would eat into the first few days of spring workouts and, for that reason, Armour refused.[70] He wanted Cobb to get the most from their training sessions, and, in turn, the press claimed that Cobb had come to the same conclusion, rejecting the opportunity.[71]

But that isn't what happened. Cobb ended up going to Stone Mountain anyway and spent about two weeks as an instructor there. He met with the Tigers as they passed through Atlanta en route to Augusta on March 4,[72] but he personally didn't report until four days later.[73] It is unclear whether Cobb directly defied Armour by taking the coaching position or whether there was a mutual agreement. However, it didn't appear to affect their relationship.

From the initial training session at Warren Park, which was up to snuff by the time Detroit was ready to take the field, Davy Jones displayed an awesome presence. Paul H. Bruske of *Sporting Life* declared him the "foremost" of all recruits and it was obvious that Cobb was in the fight of his young career to maintain a spot on the everyday roster.[74] Furthermore, Armour felt Jones was the greatest outfielder ever surrendered by the American Association.[75] While no decisions were yet made, Jones looked to be the favorite for the outfield slot.

Cobb, notably, had an influential supporter in Joe S. Jackson of the *Detroit Free Press*, who, throughout the spring, praised his abilities. Almost from his arrival, Jackson noticed that Cobb was conditioned and ready to play. Others routinely waited for the spring to get into shape and often entered the regular season at a bit less than top speed. But Cobb was prepared, and because of his extra dedication to training, he was a better base runner, an improved slider, and his bunts were more along the lines of a professional at the major league level.[76] He even turned out to the grounds on a cold, wet morning after Armour announced that workouts had been cancelled, just to get in some added exercise.[77]

Another component of spring training was the general bonding of teammates. Old acquaintances were renewed, introductions were made, and usually cordiality was shared throughout. The Tigers possessed a good number of established friendships, some of which were fostered by sharing teams in the past. For instance, Davy Jones was teammates with new Detroit catcher Charley "Boss" Schmidt and pitcher Ed Siever in Minneapolis in 1905. Three years earlier, he also teamed with pitcher Red Donahue of the St. Louis Browns and infielder Herman "Germany" Schaefer of the Chicago

Orphans. Siever and Donahue were on the same St. Louis club in 1903, and Barrett was an old friend of Crawford going back to Cincinnati in 1899–1900.[78] Others like McIntyre and pitcher Ed Killian were roommates and shared the same ideals, making friendship easy.

The more outgoing and charming personalities were, expectedly, easier to get along with. Those who quickly jumped into the ongoing conversations, made jokes, and related by interests or vices, were generally welcomed, regardless of their experience. Cobb was neither outgoing nor charming. He didn't relate to his teammates through hobbies, vices, religion, background, or outlook. Cobb didn't drink or smoke, and refrained from using foul language. He was from a Baptist household, whereas baseball historian Fred Lieb suggested that "perhaps half" of Cobb's teammates were Catholics.[79] Cobb didn't tell stories, laugh at jokes, and certainly avoided sociable situations.[80] The humor of those around him didn't compute in his rigid mind and, instead of trying to understand and grow from personal interaction, he backed further away. It was a tremendous character fault, and early in 1906, it hampered his development as both a player and as an adult.

Years later Cobb explained: "I have been accused frequently of keeping off by myself and not mixing very much with my teammates. People have construed that to mean [I have felt I'm] a whole lot better than my teammates. But they have misjudged me. I have always been a poor mixer, not because I wanted to be a poor mixer, but simply because nature intended me that way."[81]

Undoubtedly, Cobb's mind was rather fractured by the approaching court action that involved his mother in the death of his father, a drama that was literally days away.[82] He did his best to keep his focus on baseball and little else. Communal happenings and finding friendly companionship was the last thing on his mind. In total, Cobb remained the odd man out, and that status didn't work against him, surprisingly, as one might think. It made him sharper, more passionate about doing his best and his work improved day after day.

His mother, Amanda Cobb, was well represented when proceedings opened at Lavonia, Georgia, on March 30, 1906.[83] Charged with murder, she was supported by five attorneys, including Judge George C. Thomas and Judge William R. Little, of Athens and Lavonia, respectively. For the prosecution, Solicitor General S. J. Tribble led a four-man team and, altogether, the trial drew impressive attention from the local populace, mostly because of the high profile of the deceased. The case unfolded shortly after a jury was selected, but finding the right twelve individuals to be impaneled was no easy task.[84] Evidence, testimony, and arguments dominated the next day and a half, and one of the most striking moments occurred when Cobb spoke in her own defense, fully denying the crime she was accused of. The jury watched as she firmly announced that she didn't know it was her husband when she fired the deadly weapon.

That evening, Ty Cobb left Augusta en route to Lavonia and witnessed the closing arguments on March 31.[85] The lawyers on both sides were passionate, and Mrs. Cobb's lead attorney, Judge Thomas, was said to have given "one of the greatest efforts" of his long, esteemed career.[86] Once the final words were spoken in open court, jury deliberations began, and the panel required an hour and forty minutes to find Amanda Cobb not guilty. She beamed at the decision, and the correspondent for the *Atlanta Journal* noted that it appeared that the acquittal was "no surprise" to her. Ty responded by sending news to the team in Augusta via telegraph wire.[87] Interestingly enough, Amanda spoke with the *Denver News* when in that city six years later and was quoted as saying that she was "unable to follow" Ty's early baseball career because her husband was "ill." She noted that "he died soon after that."[88]

Perhaps trying to break the lingering stress, Cobb went out one evening with a couple of friends and attended Kittie Baldwin's mind reading performance at an Augusta theater. The gimmick of the show was that audience members could write down a question on a piece of paper, and Kittie would call an individual's name, broadcast their question, and then divulge the answer. Cobb followed the rules, asking her how Detroit would finish in the American League standings. Baldwin called his name, and then didn't hesitate to proclaim the Tigers' fate as being fifth place in the 1906 race. So upset by the prediction, Cobb quickly called it an evening and rushed back to the hotel to clear his mind.[89]

A rash of injuries and illnesses seized Detroit as the team entered the early April exhibition schedule. Tom Doran and Bobby Lowe were joined by both Jones and Armour on the inactive list, and at Cincinnati, Crawford suffered a painful strain. Jones was initially sidelined by tonsillitis, but then suffered a head injury in an accident on the train from Indianapolis to Toledo.[90] Jones's bout with tonsillitis was healing when Cobb went down with the same problem. The agony began while at Birmingham, and Cobb tried to brush off the continuous ache, hoping it would heal on its own.

Also gripped by an intense fever, he needed swift medical attention. Guided by teammate "Germany" Schaefer, he visited the resident physician at the Boody House, the team's hotel in Toledo, and was operated on three separate times over the course of three days, without anesthetic. Cobb told the story in his autobiography, claiming that his doctor was later committed to an asylum. However, no further details can be located, and the Toledo doctor who worked on Cobb remains a mystery.[91]

Living through a bloody nightmare, Cobb survived the ordeal and on the third day, hopped on a train for Columbus, Ohio, to rejoin the club. He arrived just hours after being operated on, entered the game in the sixth inning, demonstrating his tremendous grit.[92] Despite his obvious tenacity and improved play, Cobb was headed for the dreadful role of utility-man, and his long-term status was up in the air. Other teams requested his services, but Armour declined their offers. There was something special about Ty Cobb, and, as far as he was concerned, Detroit fans were going to be the ones to watch him develop from a young, immature tiger cub into a baseball luminary.

3

WAITING FOR THE COBB TO CRACK

Ty Cobb returned to the baseball diamond with a vengeance following his mother's acquittal. The seven months between the death of his father, William Herschel Cobb, and the eventual trial was an unimaginably taxing period for Ty and his siblings. They were confronted by wild public accusations, stories portraying one or both of their parents to be adulterers, and, living in a small town, couldn't get away from the endless murmurs of gawking neighbors. Ty, now nineteen years of age, was an exceptionally proud young man. He yearned to retain the nobility of the Cobb family name and honor the outstanding legacy of his pioneering father. The desires were admirable, but the truth was that the entire situation brought immense embarrassment and shame. It was a needless tragedy and the emotional scars would never completely heal.

Later in Cobb's life, he spoke little about his father's death and rarely talked about his mother. Historians and biographers have tried to tap into Cobb's mind, sort of channeling him from the grave, and worked to put the loss of his father into a certain perspective. After all, people wanted to understand Ty Cobb the human being, and of course, the violent death of his beloved father at the hands of his mother was a life-altering incident. Upon studying the facts, the data is overwhelmingly strong in favor of the belief that the death of Professor Cobb added to the already burning fire brewing within Ty's soul. He undoubtedly turned the devastating trauma into a burning desire to be successful. At the same time, his quick temper and inner aggression sharpened, and both would linger on a hair-trigger for years.

But Cobb was still an immature boy in early 1906, everlastingly headstrong and withdrawn. His confidence on the field was growing by the day, and even the barbaric Toledo surgeries demonstrated his perseverance in the face of extreme pain. But he was more and more frequently being forced to deal with another serious challenge, one that had first reared its ugly head at Anniston in 1904. The renewal of inner-club hazing, an age-old tradition in baseball, was a terrific hardship for Cobb and would nearly siphon all of his love for the sport. The wisecracks toward Cobb while a member of the Tigers likely began in response to all the favorable crowd reactions he received from locals.[1] Soon, he'd find himself at odds with more than half his ballclub, and in a constant struggle with a pack of mischievous teammates out to run him out of baseball. Cobb explained that this period of his life was the "most miserable and humiliating experience" he'd ever gone through. Because of the seriousness of the situation, he explicitly wanted to tell this portion of his life-story in his autobiography before backtracking to talk about his childhood so people could understand the astronomical challenges he faced when he was starting as a ballplayer in 1905–06. By emphasizing the critical nature of what happened, he hoped some of the distortions about his career would be better understood.

Rookies and recruits dealing with a moderate ritualistic initiation process was nothing new. It had existed for years and included a number of different techniques, from making the newcomers carry equipment to flat-out ignoring their earthly existence. The most common was basic ribbing, which oftentimes crossed the line into mocking and ridicule, but it was all meant to test the nerves of the youngster. The disparagement usually wasn't intended to be hateful and Crawford said that "most" youngsters just laughed about it.[2] But for an uptight individual with a propensity to misinterpret words, it was definitely a hostile act. That's the way Cobb construed it to be. He didn't realize that the best way to cope with such behavior was to smile and laugh it off, quickly defusing the intensity of the nonsense.

Cobb had a natural tendency to be respectful and his first inclination was to look up to the veteran ballplayers. But his naïveté and quiet, courteous personality worked against him, and the club bullies used it to their advantage. In turn, the more Cobb resisted and protested the daily harangue, the more his tormentors picked on him. They found it all to be great entertainment. Examples of his torment were offered in his autobiography and included being locked out of the bathroom at the team hotel, having wet newspapers thrown at him on train trips, and called various names. He felt it was a "carefully schemed campaign" to wreck his spirit and send him running back to the minors.[3] Once this wound was ripped open,

Cobb stopped listening to them and rejected any advice regarding business on the field. The veterans reacted by cutting off all communications to Cobb entirely, isolating him for the most part, including on train rides and during team meals.[4]

Before the 1906 season got under way, the complicated outfield situation in Detroit was made even more difficult to understand when reporters began touting Jimmy Barrett's return. Barrett himself expressed confidence in being the opening day center fielder, although business manager Frank Navin told him that he wasn't immediately needed, as Detroit had five men vying for outfield slots.[5] The decision had already been made that Davy Jones was the top man for the position, and, at the time, Joe. S. Jackson of the *Detroit Free Press* lambasted the choice. He wrote that Jones's selection illuminated "the lack of wisdom of those who [placed] too much dependence on spring form." Jackson personally liked Cobb's work more and felt Jones was picked because he had previous major league experience. While praising Cobb, Jackson managed to criticize both Jones and Matty McIntyre in his article. Such commentary didn't go a long way in erasing any of the building jealousy and the belief that Cobb was the club's "golden boy."[7]

Warming the bench, Cobb waited patiently for his opportunity to enter the lineup and it came in the fifth game at Chicago on April 21, after Sam Crawford went down with an injury.[7] He occupied right field alongside Jones and Matty McIntyre, and worked to overcome early growing pains in a part of the outfield he was not as qualified. The lack of cohesion between the players was also apparent. On April 25 versus Cleveland, Cobb and Jones were entangled after an awkward fly by pitcher Addie Joss and the ball dropped for a double. A sportswriter for the *Detroit Free Press* thought Cobb "might have got to it if left alone."[8] Teamwork improved the longer they worked together, but as Crawford was making his way back, the injury-prone Jones went down with a charley horse.[9] That meant Cobb would now have to shift from right to center.

The ill-fate of Crawford and Jones in early 1906 gave Cobb a chance to perform, and he made the most of the opportunity. On April 30 at Chicago, he hit a timely double in the 10th inning with a man on first. The runner advanced to third and later scored on a sacrifice, giving Detroit a 2–1 victory.[10] In Washington two weeks later, Cobb pulled more 10th inning heroics when he tapped a two-out grounder to the right side and launched into a maddening dash for first base. The fielder appeared to have him dead to rights when Cobb slid headfirst, jostling a cloud of dust in the process.

Much to the agony of the audience, the umpire with his vision impaired, called him safe and Detroit scored the go-ahead run. Another run was scored when Cobb threatened a break for second and the catcher threw the ball away, allowing Jack Warner to safely cross the plate. The umpire, Tom Connor, needed police protection from an angry mob of fans after the game.[11]

Facing twenty-nine-year-old lefty Rube Waddell of Philadelphia on May 17, Cobb bunted for the only recorded hit by Detroit in the first inning. Detroit shortstop Charley O'Leary also bunted successfully in the fifth inning, but an error was ruled on the fielder, leaving Cobb to have the only successful hit of the day.[12] Waddell brushed the anomaly off and dominated the remainder of the game, winning 5–0. Further along on Detroit's eastern road trip, at Boston's Huntington Avenue Grounds May 22, Cobb snagged a nearly impossible drive in the eighth, preventing at least one runner from scoring. He went to bat the following inning and drove in two of his teammates with a sharp drive to the outfield, leading the Tigers to victory. Cobb's blend of speed, frequent hitting, and glimpses of defensive greatness fascinated spectators and writers on the road. While Jones was considered the better fielder, Cobb was leading Detroit in hitting with a .318 average by the end of May.[13] Boston's manager Jimmy Collins wanted to make a cash purchase for either Cobb or Jones, but Armour wasn't hearing it.[14]

Fans were watching the season develop with optimism, but only insiders realized the complete and utter corruption bubbling underneath the surface in Detroit. The environment was fully enveloped by a plague that was to spread like wildfire. The negative influence increased and swelled to the point that manager Bill Armour couldn't take it anymore. In the early part of May, he flatly resigned, desiring to turn his back altogether on the Tigers franchise. Navin quickly stepped in and convinced him to stay.[15] Months later, Armour revealed that had he left the team, six members of the Detroit squad, valued at $15,000, would have jumped their contracts to go with him.[16] Though he stayed, the adverse conditions continued without much of a difference.

The contaminated atmosphere was several years in the making and couldn't be blamed on any one man. Despite the common belief, Cobb wasn't directly at the center of the controversy. In fact, he was almost an innocent, wholly affected by the outgrowths of the terrible environment rather than be responsible for it in the first place. He was more of a punching bag for the clique of rabble-rousers and the abuse he suffered was beyond words for the young man living through it. Going back to at least 1904, the notable reductions in salaries by team owners caused an irreparable rift that continued to resonate two years later. Additionally, a nauseating stipulation was slipped into selected contracts withholding as much as $500, to be paid after the season, all to guarantee that the players would keep in shape.[17] The replacement of Ed Barrow with Bill Armour was also fodder for a bit of displeasure.

Speaking of Armour, catcher Jack Warner and pitchers Red Donahue, who Armour previously managed in Cleveland, and Bill Donovan were said to be unhappy with his management style and wanted the job themselves.[18] Silly jealousies were popping up in many different incarnations, from Warner's opinion of recruit backstop Charley "Boss" Schmidt to McIntyre's attitude of Cobb. A *Cleveland Plain Dealer* sportswriter wondered if the pessimism stemmed from an overall resentment for the success of both Schmidt and Cobb, two of Armour's developmental prodigies. Cobb and Schmidt were particularly lauded by *Sporting Life*. Cobb "is a fine of the first water," and Schmidt was a "treasure," the paper exclaimed.[19] Warner, who was battling consistent arm problems, watched as Schmidt seamlessly entered the picture and, perhaps, jeopardized the security of his employment. Then there was Cobb, batting after McIntyre in the lineup and producing the only .300 average on the team.

The festering bitterness was not aided by critical sportswriters, touting Cobb and putting down the other athletes. Joe S. Jackson of the *Detroit Free Press* wrote that "if a few more of the boys" could attain Cobb's secret to hitting, "the team would gain a bit."[20] Needless to say, that kind of rhetoric didn't help the Tigers clubhouse environment.

The particular cliques, as previously mentioned, built in friendships established years earlier, were highly active in causing detriment to the team. There were guys who wanted either Barrett to return to center field, or wanted Jones, Crawford, and McIntyre to hold down the outfield spots. That meant Cobb was the odd man out. If Armour and Schmidt were to join him in no man's land, so be it, according to the insolent group.

McIntyre was, historically, a unique personality and his viewpoints occasionally strayed from reasonable. He produced a .253 batting average in 1904, yet held out for more money in 1905.[21] That year he hit .263, which was well under expectations. Cobb's introduction to the team never particularly imperiled his left field station, but McIntyre seemed to take Cobb's dedication and achievements to date as a personal insult. He perceived some of the Georgian's actions such as carrying three bats into the batter's circle to lighten the swinging of a single bat at the plate to be showboating, and never felt comfortable with him as a regular outfielder partner. Cobb unquestionably made mistakes as a young outfielder and likely overstepped his bounds on occasion by running too far into the radius of McIntyre or Crawford. To have this be perceived as showing off would not be unexpected. But Cobb was still learning the trade and had a ways to go before he was considered an expert of any kind.[22] In turn, McIntyre's roommate, pitcher Ed Killian, also joined the fracas with no good reason other than to show favoritism toward his buddy.[23] If Warner who had good relations with the pitching staff and Donahue were to throw their two cents into the mix, Cobb was at odds with a formidable bunch.

Neither Crawford nor Jones was acknowledged as an overbearing force amongst those opposing Armour and Cobb. Nonetheless, Cobb believed Crawford, specifically, was an instigator like all the rest. Crawford felt Cobb entered the majors with "an antagonistic attitude," and believed "everybody was ganging up against him." Crawford added that the members of the Tigers "weren't cannibals or heathens," and that they were just athletes trying to "get along."[24] In Cobb's biography, he described confronting Crawford during a session of batting practice, but the row diminished almost as fast as it started and nothing was accomplished.[25] As far as Jones was concerned, he tried to be amiable to Cobb off the field, and claimed to be Cobb's "best friend" on the Tigers.[26] But Jones labored to comprehend the intricacies of Cobb's mind on hops between cities, and because of Cobb's inner demons, it was "damn hard to be his friend." The protective shell that protected Cobb from the outside world was too hard to crack.

Of all the Tigers players, McIntyre was Cobb's number one enemy and things took a drastic turn following a game in Chicago that Cobb didn't even participate in. The incident occurred on June 22, 1906, when Tigers pitcher Ed Siever watched in horror as a drive to the outfield dropped into an abyss between McIntyre and Jones. McIntyre was apparently in a better position to get the ball but failed to do so, causing three runs to score, and Detroit to eventually lose the game 5–0.[27] Afterwards, Siever had some harsh words for the left fielder, opening up a wider dialogue involving club management.[28] It was revealed that other complaints had been made about McIntyre, and Armour was ready to silence all the unruliness up and down his roster in one swoop.[29]

McIntyre was indefinitely suspended for "indifferent" play and Armour wanted every member of the team to realize that they too could suffer the same fate if this nonsense continued.[30] *The Sporting News* stated that McIntyre had "played his last game with Detroit." Along with Killian, McIntyre was expected to be sold or traded. Although there were rumors, Armour refused to sell or trade McIntyre.[31] The situation was uncomfortable but worked in Cobb's favor because he reentered the game as the team's new left fielder.[32] In the meantime, more about McIntyre's "indifferent" ways were uncovered by sleuthing sportswriters. *The Sporting News* explained that when Cobb was on base and McIntyre batted after him, the latter "made no apparent effort" to make contact with the ball. The paper even featured a secondhand quote from an American League catcher who heard McIntyre say about Cobb, "You don't suppose I am going to help that *** *** to the plate, do you?" Cobb, at the time, was on base waiting for support, and his teammate did the reverse by going down on strikes.[33] John B. Foster wrote that McIntyre refused to help Cobb because he "was just breaking into the game." Yet McIntyre, he added, wasn't such a superstar that he didn't need assistance once in a while himself.[34]

This was no longer the ritualistic hazing most rookie players endured, but something far more sinister. When asked by Armour, McIntyre admitted he hated Cobb and refused to take part in any game in which the Georgian participated.[35] For Cobb, he knew things had been purposefully manipulated to make him look bad and leave him hanging in either the outfield or on the bases. He realized that he'd been made a fool of on numerous occasions and the mockery was painfully combined with periods of alienation. It wasn't all in fun, but caused by hatred, and when it came to burrowing down into the recesses of anger and a true fighting spirit, Cobb was instinctively a master. He'd fight all of his teammates if need be, but on the field, he was a hard worker and knew his offensive numbers would ultimately speak for themselves.[36]

The depressing reality of Cobb's full integration into the majors was that he was unable to centrally focus on baseball. He was instead dealing with jealousy, backstabbing, hazing, and all types of tumult. But for him to still be productive in any way was a demonstration, once again, of his perseverance over and above all challenges. The chaos made him a strong person at heart and clarified his status as a fighter, for every inch and every goal. Cobb was human, though, and there were many moments of self-doubt.

He considered leaving baseball behind and the conflict with his teammates made going to park a task he reviled.[37]

The suspension of McIntyre was fitting, Armour knew that for sure, but the club had no plans to cash in on his bankability by making a deal. McIntyre fumed, threatening to take his grievance before the National Baseball Commission, and join an independent squad in Chicago. However, much of the tension disappeared when team representatives announced that McIntyre could return as soon as he agreed to play at full speed, alongside Cobb or whoever else was in the Tigers lineup.[38] Within days, McIntyre met with Armour and Navin and worked matters out, returning to the field on June 30. Cobb shifted to center and the two resumed life together as outfield cohorts. Unfortunately, the hatred that existed prior to the suspension remained, and Armour's threat to oust other dissenters did little to eradicate the overall hostilities. The troublemakers were as fiery as ever.

Cobb hit a batting slump around the same time. In the span of a week, he dropped 28 points from .352 and third in the league to eleventh place with a .324 average.[39] Sensing that Cobb needed a little breathing room, Armour worked Jones in center field and gave his prodigy a little extra rest. But when he needed a talented pinch hitter to step up in the ninth inning at Philadelphia on July 13, Armour didn't hesitate to insert Cobb into the game. Cobb followed through with a bunt to the left side, and would have been out had the first baseman maintained control of the ball. He proceeded to move around the bases as Detroit added runners to first and second, and then scored the winning run.[40]

Almost immediately after the showing, Cobb was hospitalized and two doctors were summoned to observe and treat what the press called "stomach trouble."[41] The *Detroit Times* reported the situation to be a strain of some type, suffered in the Philadelphia contest, but noted that it was not a hernia.[42] No other details were offered, leaving pundits to speculate further about Cobb's well-being.[43] He was barely able to make it to Boston for the team's next series, but Armour realized he was of no use in any playing capacity and sent him back to Detroit. Club physician Peter C. McEwen made arrangements for Cobb to be admitted to the Detroit Sanitarium and it was expected that he'd be a resident there for at least several weeks, if not longer.[44]

The anguish from months of painstaking torture had worked on his mental state, and now for his body to physically give out, Cobb was in dire

shape. He had been a robust 176-pounder earlier in the year, but his condition necessitated a painful operation, and by the end of July, he had lost
twenty pounds.[45] Out of harm's way, Cobb needed rest and plenty of it
before even thinking about returning to the diamond. He was entirely
determined to regain his footing, and made a special trip out to Bennett
Park to watch the Tigers perform one afternoon. He also joined a friend,
independent league pitcher Tom Leith, for a camping excursion near
Brighton, Michigan, where he regained his appetite and most of his weight
by eating fried bluegill fish. It was alluded, however, that Cobb's northern
diet caused his later stomach ailment and that he needed to get back to
"blue-stem collards."[46]

Interestingly, early in Cobb's hospital stay, he was visited by teammates,
although the newspaper didn't indicate who, it only stated "most of the team"
was there to wish him well in his recovery.[47] With that kind of report, one
would think that harmony had dawned on the Tigers, but there was no such
luck. Armour was still being undermined on a regular basis, and in August,
he sold catcher Jack Warner to Washington for $2,000 and suspended pitcher
Ed Killian after a drunken incident where the latter ran amok and busted up
the clubhouse. Notably, the problems of the Tigers continued to occur while
Cobb was hospitalized, which is evidence that he wasn't the only aggravating
factor for disgruntled members of the club. Sportswriters pegged Warner
and Killian as two of the principal malcontents, and with the duo flushed,
Armour was again working to find clubhouse stability. He wanted his mainstays to be happy and, with Cobb returning, he had an idea that he hoped
would solve many of the team's persistent issues.

First baseman Chris Lindsay was underperforming in 1906, batting in the
low .200 range, and Armour deduced that Cobb would make a suitable
replacement at the initial bag. He saw the youngster as having a long reach
and being an able fielder, meaning the only thing he really needed was
appropriate training.[48] Thus, with Cobb at first, he could maintain the hitting power of his Georgian firecracker, plus keep his outfield core of McIntyre, Jones, and Crawford together. It was a win-win for everyone. The
imaginative concept received about a day's worth of attention and was forgotten. Cobb was a schooled outfielder and was going to remain one going
forward.

Detroit was definitely having a year from hell, and, honestly, it was almost laughable because their problems never ceased. There were broken bones, illnesses, family difficulties, internal strife, and just about any kind of bad luck that could occur did. The latest hardship came in the form of a serious injury to Davy Jones, sending him to the infirmary.[49] His status for the rest of the year was questionable, and Armour was left without a full outfield, which was highly ironic considering the overflow of fielders at the beginning of the season. In response, the Tigers hired former Detroit Wolverines legend Sam Thompson, who, at forty-six years of age, would play eight games for Armour in right field and drum up plenty of nostalgia.[50]

In total, Cobb missed fifty-one days of active major league duty. Prior to making his return, Cobb played for several Detroit-area semi-professional squads to round out his recovery process. One of the teams was the Detroit Athletic Club (DAC), a private organization with an upper-crust membership roster, including many prosperous entrepreneurs. During this time, Cobb made friends with Albert V. McClure and John C. Kelsey, prominent members of the club.[51] He made his return on September 2, 1906, at St. Louis, and was victimized by a burst of outfield dust in deep center, causing some heartache when he couldn't get control of the ball. It was an inauspicious affair, and the game ended in six innings because of rain with Detroit on the losing end of a 1–0 score.[52] Cobb would regain his batting stride and, by the middle of the month, was back amongst the league leaders with a .323 average. Detroit as a team was no longer a contender for the pennant, and Armour was engaged in the stockpile of new recruits for the next season of play when he was blindsided by a rumor from East Coast correspondents. The gossip claimed he was being pushed out and replaced by Baltimore Orioles manager Hugh Jennings, who had been in Baltimore since 1903.[53]

Jennings was a sizable name in the baseball world. In the 1890s, he was a strong component of the three-time National League champion Baltimore Orioles franchise, a team that featured the likes of John McGraw, Wilbert Robinson, and Willie Keeler. He was a star shortstop, a skilled baserunner, and with averages of .386 and .401 in 1895 and 1896, respectively, he was a superior batsman.[54] The Orioles were notorious for their hard-hitting style of baseball and the legend of their antics was fresh in many minds in 1906. Jennings was well-liked, but he perpetuated an off-color brand of sport, one that utilized unorthodox techniques to attain a psychological advantage. His specialty was standing along the baselines on one leg with his arms raised high, shouting at the rivaling team. "Ee-yah!" was his favorite slogan.

In reaction to the rumors, Navin made a swift denial, but it didn't put a halt to the whispers. Detroit newspapermen labored in defense of Armour and the extreme conditions he faced all year. They didn't want him blamed for the catastrophic failure of the team to succeed, instead turning it back on the unruly cliques.[55] But many people thought Armour allowed the negativity to fester for far too long before taking action. He oftentimes worked to pacify the troublemakers rather than casting them out. The suspensions of McIntyre and Killian and the sale of Warner were important steps, but perhaps he waited too long to invoke a harder line of discipline.

On September 3, 1906, the news officially broke that Armour was being replaced by Jennings, and the Tigers proceeded to go out and lose both games of a doubleheader to St. Louis. Armour blamed American League President Ban Johnson for coordinating his ouster from Detroit, and felt he deserved another year as manager.[56] Baltimore owner Ned Hanlon refused to sell Jennings for $5,000, but Johnson and Navin used the rules of Organized Baseball to sidestep Hanlon completely and drafted Jennings for $1,000.[57] Detroit went through the motions of finishing the season, and the infamous "Hitless Wonders" of Chicago captured the American League pennant. Pundits accused the Tigers of "laying down" in games against the White Sox; essentially helping Chicago beat out the New York Highlanders in what was a close race. B. F. Wright denied this, claiming that Detroit won half of the 22 games played against Chicago.[58] Paul H. Bruske in *Sporting Life* indicated that the team was taking a good amount of punishment from fans and sportswriters alike, and there was immense disappointment in what was supposed to be Detroit's big year.[59] The team finished in sixth place with a 71–78 record.

Incidentally, both Cobb and Armour were involved in separate bouts of fisticuffs during the final days of the 1906 season. The first episode happened following Detroit's defeat of the Washington Senators in two-straight on September 22 at home. Armour left the clubhouse after the long afternoon and was confronted by his former catcher, Warner, now with Washington. Warner was seemingly angry about the press reports claiming him to be the "chief" provocateur of the Tigers and he let Armour have it verbally. He then struck the manager square in the face, opening up a vicious scuffle that only ended when nearby spectators pulled them apart.[60]

   The fight Cobb was engaged in took place on the evening of October 6 at the Planters Hotel in downtown St. Louis. It was actually the continuation of an earlier argument at the ballpark, stemming from a controversial play in the seventh inning. Batting champion George Stone, who'd finish the year with a .358 average, lined through the infield into left center between Cobb and McIntyre and achieved a probable double. But when neither outfielder went for the ball, Stone kept running, scoring a runner in front of him. Cobb and McIntyre were no longer playing baseball, but locked in a battle of words versus each other, and Stone eventually raced across the plate for a home run. In the dugout, thirty-one-year-old Detroit pitcher Ed Siever accused Cobb of purposefully blowing the game, and the efforts of teammates prevented a full-fledged brawl. That day, the Tigers lost two games to St. Louis in what the press considered the "worst" performances of the year.[61] A St. Louis sportswriter added that members of the Detroit squad "loafed, jested, romped and refused to actually play ball."[62]

   Siever refused to leave the matter alone and verbally accosted Cobb at the team hotel. Wishing to avoid an altercation, Cobb calmly walked away and settled near the cigar counter in the Planters' lobby. Siever joined him, according to Cobb's autobiography, but Bill Donovan's timely interference prevented any physicality.[63] However, moments later, Siever made his move and Cobb, calm and resting up against a pillar, appeared to be vulnerable. That couldn't have been any further from the truth. Cobb was guarded, expecting an attack, and nimbly maneuvered away from his aggressor. Landing a few punches, he dropped Siever and then proceeded to kick him in the face, completing an altogether one-sided contest and leaving Siever severely disfigured.[64]

   On the train later that evening, Cobb apologized to Siever for the unnecessarily violent kick, but there were no handshakes to squash the feud.[65] In fact, Cobb remained justifiably paranoid and felt a revenge assault was right around the corner. He got little rest and was armed if the worst case scenario arrived at the foot of his train berth.[66] The retaliation never came.

   The nineteen-year-old Cobb finished his first full year of major league service ahead of all his veteran teammates in batting, and was sixth in the American League with a .317 average.[67] Under the circumstances, he performed remarkably. He was facing a situation in which only a handful of individuals were showing him any respect at all, yet he was still able to be successful on his own. And in a way, the isolation he endured worked to his benefit. In the absence of company and friendship, Cobb devoted himself to self-improvement on the baseball field and made tremendous personal strides.[68]

First and foremost, Cobb wanted to improve his hitting methodology. The generally accepted style in the majors was for a player to get up to the plate and plant his feet flat on the ground, waiting for a ball to be pitched into the zone. Two of the American League greats, Nap Lajoie and Sam Crawford, adhered to this basic formula, Cobb observed, and they were premier batters. Being the greenhorn that he was, he followed suit, but was often confused by his own results. Early in the season, more often than not, he was hitting balls to right field. Suddenly, in May, he was lifting more and more to left, without any comprehension of why. "I can't account for it," he explained. "I noticed it and remarked the same to manager Armour. He said that it is liable to happen to any batsman. I guess that's right."[69]

Cobb was a perfectionist and didn't accept Armour's words as the final answer to his conundrum. So he kept working on the problem, trying to understand the basic principles of his own batting routine. He also wanted to hit to all fields by design, not just whenever he got lucky. By watching Crawford and others, he assessed their strengths and weaknesses, and realized that those who were established in a singular batting position had highly limited mobility. That didn't work for Cobb. He wanted to be flexible and adjust on a pitch-by-pitch basis, giving him a greater opportunity to make contact.

In doing so, he kept his feet closer together rather than far apart—the more traditional pose—and stood on his toes. He found that the new stance did exactly what he wanted it to do, and he was much faster and abler at bat than he was before. Another change came in the way he attacked the ball, and it was more of a natural modification as a result of his adjustable batting posture. Cobb used a chop style, quickly slicing at the ball to get on base, and through his natural power, was able to drive the ball to all parts of the field. But mostly, he could maneuver a hit directly into the available gaps or wherever he wanted on purpose.[70] Thus, he gained significant control of his own batting ability and learned much about his personal limitations.

Holding the bat, Cobb continued to do it the same old way. He had been gripping it with his hands spaced a few inches apart even before he played at Augusta, and saw no reason to change.

Cobb's studies didn't stop there. He was also a student of pitchers throughout the American League—especially those who had his number—and he searched endlessly for an explanation to their mastery. But his central deficiency was against left-handers. At times, there appeared to be no hope to his plight because he was just too far outgunned by their proficiencies. "Doc" White, a 6'1" lefty for the Chicago White Sox, made Cobb look foolish on occasion. On May 30, 1906, at Bennett Park, he fanned him three straight times and, in the eighth inning, Armour pulled Cobb for backup catcher, Fred Payne, who achieved a single.[71] Eddie Plank of the Philadelphia Athletics was another lefty with the goods on Cobb.

"Ty Cobb couldn't hit a lefthander with a paddle when he came up," said Ed Walsh, White's Chicago cohort. "But he learned. He took a south-paw pitcher out with him for morning practice day after day until he could hit the lefties as well as the right-handers."[72]

In addition to everyday practice, Cobb figured out an important tech-nique that stayed with him for the rest of his career. Against southpaws, he moved to the extreme rear of the batter's box, which allowed him to fully see the break of the pitch, and then react accordingly.[73] The relent-less attention he gave to the methods and deliveries of lefties allowed him to overcome his shortcomings at the plate. After awhile, he stopped men-tally beating himself before stepping up to face a White or a Plank, and allowed his newfound skills to give him a fighting chance. Versus White later in the year, he was one of two Tigers to have a single off the "Doc," and although the pitcher remained nearly unhittable, Cobb was figuring him out a little at a time.[74] White was magnificent in 1906, throwing for a 1.52 ERA (best in the league) and went 18–6 en route to a World Series championship for the Chicago White Sox. In 26 lifetime games against Cobb, the latter would bat .278 against him.[75]

All of the valuable baseball lessons he'd picked up didn't fall into place overnight and, of course, his midseason hospitalization didn't help his for-ward progress. Additionally, the darkness of the torment he faced was a detrimental crisis that nearly silenced his career before it really started. Of all the experiences he faced, one of the most heartbreaking came when a teammate entered the clubhouse before practice one day and sawed up two of his precious bats. These weren't the standard, run-of-the-mill sticks, but were specially crafted from ash timber, black in color, and important tools of his trade since Augusta.[76] Cobb was superstitious and sentimental, and was seriously hurt by the destruction of his vital property. The specific indi-vidual who cut up Cobb's bats was never identified. A story later told by a friend of Charley Schmidt said it was a member of Detroit's pitching staff, but Cobb thought it was Schmidt who did it.[77]

"Selfishness, bad language, backbiting, intolerance as to religion amongst the narrow and uneducated, [plus] the unfairness and crudeness of the cliques" were the bane of Cobb's existence in 1906.[78] But he had to cope with the ugliness to not only survive, but to prevail and, as time went by, his perspective tended to mature. "A young ball player has a lot to learn," Cobb admitted. "When I broke into the big leagues, I thought everybody was fighting me. It appeared as though I was the butt of all jokes and, being a southerner and considering myself sort of an outsider, I resented familiarities. It didn't take long, however, for me to learn that I was only going through the course of mild hazing that is administered to nearly all players."[79]

Soon, it would become obvious to everyone that Cobb was adopting a harder line of play, and his attitude—on and off the diamond—was becoming fiercer. E. A. Batchelor, a Detroit sportswriter, summed up Cobb's evolving nature. "He was a product of [his] environment. He came from a decent home and decent people. He joined the 1905 Tigers when they included some of the worst muckers that ever wore a uniform. They did everything possible to drive him out of baseball. He simply had to beat them at their own game to stay in the game. Once those habits were acquired, he couldn't shake them."[80]

The poisonous vipers after Cobb waited and waited for his mind, body, and spirit to crack, doing everything imaginable to fracture his enthusiasm. They worked on his inner psyche, attacked him physically, and desired with all their might to oust the Georgian prodigy. But Cobb made it. He grew as a man, persisting in spite of the nonsense, and outlived the strife of 1906 with his integrity intact. He was going into 1907 with gained strength and confidence, and soon there would be no stopping him. His adversaries had their chance to run him out of the sport and they failed. Tyrus Raymond Cobb was to remain in the major leagues and baseball would never be the same.

4

A HUMBLED BATTING CHAMPION

Following a season of misfortune from top to bottom, business manager Frank J. Navin was in a precarious position. He represented shareholders in the day-to-day operations of the club, and, in need of results, immersed himself in retooling the Detroit Tigers. Born in Adrian, Michigan, southwest of Detroit, Navin was a clerk in the insurance office of S. F. Angus before the latter bought a stake in the Tigers.[1] He took a predominant leadership role in the team and basically learned the baseball business from the ground up. In his current situation, the thirty-five-year-old was grasping for whatever positives he could muster from the misery he'd just experienced. He knew there were many capable players in the fold, and if led by the right manager, they could be a first-rate franchise.

Hugh Jennings was a known comedian in baseball circles. He wasn't the practical disciplinarian some might have felt the Tigers needed, but Jennings, a manager of the old-school, was also not a pushover. H. G. Merrill of *The Sporting News* wrote that, in comparison to the lackadaisical days of Bill Armour, the "laddybucks" of the Tigers would "find things different when Jennings" assumed control. He concluded by adding, "Jennings will have no dissention in the ranks."[2] But no one really expected all personalities to be streamlined and magically happy once Jennings arrived at the clubhouse. There were rocky days ahead, and this would have been the case regardless of who Navin brought in as manager.

At the tail end of the 1906 season, Jennings spied a couple Detroit games so he could formulate a direct impression of the team. His overall opinion agreed with Navin: the Tigers had winning stock but direly needed to repair a weakness at first base. Jennings initially wanted Michigan product John Ganzel to play first for Detroit in 1907. However, Ganzel signed with the

Cincinnati Reds.[3] There was also a feeding frenzy for first baseman Jake Stahl, the playing-manager for the Washington Senators, who was on the market. Detroit, at different points, was one of the top contenders to land him.[4] Stahl, incidentally, sat out of Organized Baseball in 1907 because he wanted to play for Boston, but Washington owners dealt him to Chicago instead. Trade considerations were made—particularly with Matty McIntyre—but in none of the proposals did Jennings find a deal giving the Tigers comparable talent.[5] Reportedly, a team from the eastern circuit wanted to give Detroit $10,000 for McIntyre, but Jennings and Navin preferred a trade for players.[6] A swap between Detroit and Cleveland was also heavily discussed by sportswriters and the names McIntyre, Fred Payne, and Ty Cobb were, in one way or another, rumored to be involved in a transaction for hard-hitting outfielder Elmer Flick.[7] Flick was at odds with his manager in Cleveland, Nap Lajoie, but was coming off one of the best seasons of his career, batting .311 with 194 hits and 98 runs.[8] It was clear that neither team wanted to trade unless they were significantly compensated.

While the Flick deal went nowhere, Navin and Jennings continued to haggle with Cleveland owners and managed to score an entirely different player during the annual American League meetings from Chicago in December 1906. The duo purchased Cleveland's first baseman, Claude Rossman, which added a key element to the club.[9] Rossman was said to be the best first baseman available, but, as noted, was not Detroit's original choice.[10] Rossman, albeit slower than many of his contemporaries, was a competent offensive weapon and, time and again, he came through at the plate with runners on the bases. The acquisition of a first baseman, combined with the signing of nearly all members of the Tigers roster for the upcoming season, gave Navin and Jennings great optimism, that is, at least temporarily.

Cobb was mobile during the offseason. He spent time at the famous Georgia-Carolina Fair in Augusta in early November and shared stories about his time in big league baseball with old friends.[11] The following month he was in Atlanta proudly playing in a special ballgame between a squad of "All-Professionals" against local firemen. His two triples were a feature of the contest, which led the pros to a 6–1 victory.[12] Intermixed with his appearances in public, he spent a fair amount of time on the hunt for wild turkeys; living off the land always seemed to be a surefire boost to his health.[13] But he was also taken aback by the bombardment of strange news reports, saying that he was about to be traded to Washington or Chicago. Although he had been guaranteed a berth with Detroit in 1907, he could not help wonder what the truth actually was. The erroneous reports, originating from New York, also claimed that Detroit was going to get rid of Crawford and McIntyre as well, leaving Jennings to start with a fresh squad of Tigers.[14]

With a $900 raise over the previous season, Cobb was content, but broke.[15] His strong keenness for financial security was years away, mostly because he hadn't yet earned enough to save a dime. The plight of young ballplayers in being able to survive a full year on a half year's worth of pay was always troublesome and Cobb was still trying to figure it out. In a letter to Navin in Detroit, he inquired about a possible loan to help him get by, but Navin tread lightly on the subject and instead offered to advance him $300 on his future salary, sans interest.[16] Cobb accepted the gesture of kindness and, certainly, walked away from the situation with further admiration of Navin as a boss.

Sportswriters were itching for newsworthy items and soon they learned that, of all members of the Detroit Tigers, Matty McIntyre was the only one not signed for 1907. According to the scuttlebutt, he was peeved about one thing and one thing only: Ty Cobb.[17] Of course, what else could it be? The mere existence of Cobb to those bemoaning unsportsmanlike grudges was enough to set off an avalanche of hate, and McIntyre apparently wasn't ready to give up his petty resentment. Cobb, on the other hand, wanted to start anew. He was ready to mend fences with McIntyre, but he had to be met, at least, halfway.[18]

That being said, Cobb remembered how the last season ended. The fight with Ed Siever was fresh in his mind, and he knew his actions didn't earn him any new friends on the team. If anything, it might have garnered him respect as a fighter, but as a cooperative colleague and bosom buddy, the scrap worked against the image he might have wanted to convey. He was acutely aware of potential blowback heading into spring training and was more hypersensitive than ever before.

The role of peacemaker fell to Jennings. Bridging the gaps between strained relations, altering the perceptions, and getting guys to dismiss their already formed judgments seemed to be a nearly impossible feat. Cobb, on the other hand, wasn't instinctively going to trust Jennings either. With the track record Armour put up, essentially failing to expunge team dissidents when not only Cobb's well-being was on the line, but for the sake of the entire club, it didn't bode well for anyone else. All things considered,

Cobb had seen only small glimpses of niceties in his brief pro experience, and he remembered each and every one of them.[19] For instance, he was humbled by the invitation tendered by forty-year-old veteran Bobby Lowe to go to dinner with him and his wife, and took to heart the words of encouragement by right-hander Bill Donovan.[20] In his autobiography, Cobb mentioned befriending twenty-two-year-old pitching newcomer Ed Willett of Norfolk, Virginia, who was soon convinced by the McIntyre clique to turn his back on Cobb.[21]

Second baseman William Herman "Germany" Schaefer was also willing to tutor Cobb on occasion. Part of a middle infield combination with shortstop and fellow Chicagoan Charley O'Leary, Schaefer was one of baseball's top personalities.[22] He was a fun-loving entertainer at his core, yet was not amused by the miserable way in which the Georgian was treated. Some years later, he revealed that he specifically taught Cobb the "old Chicago slide" during this time frame, encompassing a maneuver that saw the runner's body "twisting away" from the fielder, and reaching the base by hooking his foot. Schaefer was the closest Cobb had to a George Leidy on the Tigers.[23] Schaefer's lessons were of great value, and he would undoubtedly play a considerable role in Detroit's 1907 campaign, both as an amusing stress distraction and as a leader.[24]

Having heard enough stories about the rampant chaos in the clubhouse, Jennings knew he needed a different approach than Armour and his efforts to revamp the Tigers' den began upon arriving in Augusta for spring training. He established a distinct training regimen with an emphasis on running and long walks, scrutinized rookies, and made personal time to talk one-on-one with his personnel. After Cobb arrived, Jennings spent an hour with him, discussing past happenings and future expectations, and bestowing what the *Detroit Free Press* called "fatherly advice."[25] The meeting was constructive and Jennings must have been convinced that he successfully "reached" Cobb, touching the young man's sensibilities and setting a course for a widespread boost of team chemistry.

Cobb was valuable; Jennings was well aware of that fact and he hoped to suppress whatever negativity he was emitting. But unfortunately, within a matter of days, a horrendously unpleasant situation erupted at Warren Park in Augusta and cast serious doubt as to whether such a thing was even possible. On the afternoon of March 16, 1907, Cobb completed his mile walk from the hotel and was prepared to plunge into the normal training activities of the day. However, he was encountered by a somewhat familiar face,

Henry Cummings, a twenty-seven-year-old African American groundskeeper, known to the populace as "Bungey," and a strange altercation ensued.[26] The latter seemed to anticipate a reunion with the former Augustan player and reached out his hand in friendliness. Needless to say, Cobb didn't have the same response.[27]

Almost exactly a year before, during Tigers' spring training at Augusta, sportswriter Joe S. Jackson of the *Detroit Free Press* wrote about the local African American population and made a peculiar comment about Cobb. Several times, Jackson noted, Cobb remarked about the efficiency of "colored" people when prompted by white Southerners in comparison to their Northern counterparts. Cobb reportedly supported the theory that blacks "more readily" heeded the "requests or demands" of Southern white folk, a group which Jackson added, "maintain the old relation of master and man between the races." Jackson finished by stating that Northerners acknowledged the principles of the Fourteenth Amendment.[28]

The firsthand account by the scribe shed illuminating light on the mindset of Cobb and his perspective of African Americans. With that understanding, it probably didn't come as a surprise to those teammates who were cognizant of his racial outlook when Cobb recoiled and punched Cummings in the face in reaction to his hospitality. The unnamed reporter for the *Detroit Free Press* on the scene suggested that Cobb was infuriated by Cummings's attempt to be on "equal footing" with a Caucasian, and prompted the player's reaction. The violence didn't end there, as Cobb speedily pursued the park worker into the clubhouse, behind the stands beyond third base. There, Cummings's wife, who also worked at the park, intervened, only to be confronted by Cobb's reckless aggression. According to accounts, she was assailed and choked. The press report also claimed that Cummings was "partially" inebriated and spoke to Cobb as he went for a handshake, saying, "Hello, Ty, old boy."[29]

"I have my opinion of anybody who would strike a woman," said Charley "Boss" Schmidt, the 5'11", 200-pound catcher for the Tigers, a witness to the affair.[30]

Cobb was in no mood for the commentary of any of his teammates, friend or foe. Schmidt hadn't necessarily been involved in the McIntyre shenanigans of the previous year, but his words struck a chord in the maddening sphere of the young outfielder. His conscious mind didn't compute the gravity of butting heads with the toughest man on the team, and perhaps in all of major league baseball.[31] Physically brawny from years of pushing cars full of coal in Arkansas mines, Schmidt was a ready fighter, and demonstrated his fortitude by playing 68 games in 1906 with a broken bone in his ankle. Bizarrely, sportswriter Fred Lieb chronicled accounts of Cobb "tormenting" Schmidt in his 1946 book, *The Detroit Tigers*.[32] The purposeful provocation of the powerful catcher was unimaginable, basically akin to a death wish, but if Lieb was correct, Cobb was clearly searching for turbulence leading up to the event in question.

That afternoon in Augusta, he certainly found it when he tried to tackle Schmidt for offering his unsolicited remarks. His newfound enemy was all too prepared for fisticuffs and Schmidt successfully landed a blow before their scuffle was called to a halt by onlookers.[33] The entire situation couldn't have been any worse for Jennings and the Tigers, especially when harmony was the cornerstone of their rebuilding process. In the aftermath, Cobb denied choking the woman, telling the press, "I am in the right, and so long as I know that fact, I don't care what is done or said."[34]

Following the altercation, the focus shifted to Cobb's status with the Tigers and remarks about his fight with Schmidt, but little was said about Cummings or his wife. Cummings remained an employee of Warren Park and an Augusta newspaper declared him the top groundskeeper in the entire south, "known to every player in the Sally circuit."[35] "Bungey" found himself in a bit of trouble only a few months after his run-in with Cobb when he appeared drunk at the home of an Augusta citizen and uttered foul language in front of the homeowner's wife. The man claimed Cummings "deserved to be shot," according to the paper, and the latter was arrested.[36]

Jennings was justifiably livid and within hours of the calamity was working to rekindle talks with Cleveland to trade Cobb for Elmer Flick. He was no longer hesitant to lose a man of great promise if, and it was a big if, he was able to secure a talent of equal ability. Flick, to Jennings, fit that mark, even though he was already thirty-one years of age and of his four seasons left in the majors, only one of them would be played full-time. Ultimately, the deal was nixed by Cleveland co-owner Charley Somers, who didn't want the destabilizing influence of Cobb infecting his roster as it had in Detroit. Incidentally, both the Tigers and the Cleveland Naps were in Macon, Georgia, at the same time, seemingly opening the door for trade talks. But Somers put his foot down and there was no room to negotiate.[37] New York Highlander manager Clark Griffith also proposed a Cobb-Frank Delahanty deal, but Jennings laughed it off as a "humorous effort."[38] In regard to the possible trade to New York in 1907, Cobb talked about two benefits, stronger press and being away from owner Frank Navin.[39]

Back in the Tigers clubhouse, a state of uncertainty reigned. Cobb and Schmidt were said to be at peace, but the way Cobb eluded teammates exhibited anything but tranquility for the Detroit franchise. He walked alone, purposefully scheduled meals so he'd be segregated from the others, and was quieter than normal. Sportswriters didn't help matters by saying that Cobb was essentially friendless on the team. But Cobb relied on his personal allies in Augusta, people he trusted, and he withdrew further to be with them when not on the field.[40]

Cobb was feeling the pinch, and sincerely mulled jumping his contract.[41] Despite his impulsive anger problems and a developing propensity for violence, he was conscientious and remained with the team. He was, however, determined to get answers from Jennings about what exactly was being done to ship him elsewhere. Jennings told him that he believed Cobb's fate rested in New York, but again, a trade was not finalized because Detroit felt the offerings were uneven.[42]

Indicative of his mind-state and perhaps doing a little trade encouragement of his own, Cobb neglected orders during an exhibition versus Augusta, refusing to bunt when told, and received a "severe reprimand" from Jennings as a result. The reporter acknowledged that Cobb "played well," having a triple, a sacrifice, and a stolen base, but was rather indifferent. Cobb's "insubordination" was big news.[43] Things remained status quo as the Tigers departed camp and ventured to Meridian, Mississippi, for a game versus the local White Ribbons squad of the Cotton States League. The departure from Georgia worked in Jennings's favor, as he wanted to break Cobb free from his friends and get him back circulating with teammates. But one of Cobb's pals in Atlanta erred when he told a writer how Cobb could win a fight against any member of the Tigers, including Schmidt.[44] The brawling catcher, as expected, heard the story.

That little yarn helped instigate the second Cobb-Schmidt battle, and the clay field of Meridian was the location of the clash. Jennings explained it another way. He said Schmidt harbored bitterness toward Cobb stemming from the first fight and wanted to continue the struggle once the team left Georgia.[45] Through the decades since the fight, there have been about a dozen or more accounts of what occurred and the most common characteristic of all versions was that Schmidt won easily. The specific details of how it started and who did what varied from story to story. Cobb personally claimed he was sucker-punched, caught completely off guard, and suffered a broken nose by the opening blow.[46] Third baseman Bill Coughlin disagreed. He said that Cobb and Schmidt consented to go out to the park and fight one morning to clear the air.[47] Either way, the result was the same.

That winter, *The Sporting News* gave space for player quotes and Cobb made the paper on April 6, 1907, delivering some interesting insights. "The fact that I am a southern man has never made any difference in the way I have been treated by the public in the north. The fans all over the American League have always been kind to me. In Detroit, I feel that I have many friends among the fans, and they have treated me with the greatest consideration. I like them and I want them to like me. I always do my best when it comes to playing ball and just as long as I am in the game, intend to continue to do so. The Detroit club [pays] me to play ball, the very best I know how, and I am not going to disappoint the management."[48]

Jennings had been impressive as a manager all spring, encouraging his men to the utmost degree and earning high praise from the lowliest recruit up to the grayest veteran. But nothing he did compared to the magic he pulled the evening of the second Cobb-Schmidt battle in Meridian. It was there, at a team meeting shortly after dinner, that he established himself as the rarest of baseball reconcilers. The night of the famous Meridian meeting, Jennings asked four of his veterans, Coughlin, Donovan, Schaefer, and O'Leary to take Cobb out on the town to illustrate to the young outfielder the new team unity and kinship of the Tigers.[49] Instead of giving the men a hard time, lashing out with threats of suspensions, he motivated them with a range of captivating stories, fueling notions of teamwork and camaraderie. "From that day on, there was a change in the ranks of the Tigers," one player explained. "The fellows woke up to what harmony meant." In unison, the athletes agreed to watch out for each other in a unified fight for one goal: the American League pennant.[50]

For Cobb, he too experienced a metamorphosis. By standing tall against the mighty oak, Charley "Boss" Schmidt, he added to his growing reputation and gained a striking amount of confidence. His relations amongst teammates improved steadily, and although the Tigers would never be completely stable behind the scenes, Cobb demonstrated a willingness to conform as much as he could. "Perhaps [the second encounter versus Schmidt] was the best thing that could have happened to Ty," Coughlin explained. "He was getting a bit cocky and I have always thought the scrap with Schmidt helped to make a great ball player out of him."[51]

Bidding farewell to spring training with an exhibition record of 14–0–1, the Tigers were remarkably healthy. Cobb had developed a "severe cold" and was hampered by a back problem, but he kept playing despite being told to sit it out.[52] Matty McIntyre was back in the fold in time for opening day versus Cleveland on April 11, 1907, and Jennings wisely arranged his outfield and lineup to keep him separated from Cobb. McIntyre would lead off and play left field; Sam Crawford was in the third slot and in center; and Cobb batted fourth and manned the right side. In the position following Cobb was new first baseman Claude Rossman and his role, as it affected Cobb, was far more important than anyone else on the team. Rossman was a sure hitter and a man of excellent bunting skills. Cobb would rely greatly upon his ability to sacrifice him over and the cunning tactic was displayed in that first game against Cleveland in a 2–0 victory. Cobb scored both Detroit runs and would have had a third, but was thrown out at the plate in the sixth inning.[53]

The stories of continued infighting and disorder caused many baseball observers to write Detroit off from the start, but pundits were in for a major shock. The vibrant cohesion of the Tigers was palpable, and Jennings had successfully turned a rag-tag mess of malcontents into a competitive force of nature. Players were aggressive, hustling for every ball and digging for base hits, and showing an energetic willingness to exert themselves unlike in previous years.[54] On the sidelines, Jennings provoked increased intensity by his constant running, flailing, and commentary. He'd whistle and shout catchphrases in support of his men, while at the same time unnerving rivals. Fans were often thoroughly entertained by his riotous skit in the coach's box, and it didn't matter if he was standing on one leg or using noise makers to garner a reaction.

A marked improvement in teamwork was noticeable as well. Communication in the field was fluid and persistently helpful in snagging flies and routing throws. The cooperation was beneficial to Cobb and his adequate defense brightened sharply. Against New York on May 14, he made a diving snag of Frank LaPorte's liner in what a reporter dubbed, the "greatest catch of the season" to date.[55] Weeks later, at New York, Cobb was unable to repeat the performance against LaPorte and committed an error when he dropped the latter's fly in a 9–3 loss on June 10.[56] Sporadic errors were an expected part of baseball, and some were more costly than others. Cobb was specifically troubled by roped off sections necessitated because of overflow crowds, and every now and then, he crossed signals with Crawford.[57] During the first road trip east, Cobb put his best foot forward and appeared to be a master fielder. He robbed extra bases with regularity and made a number of bullet throws to double up runners. Cobb would end the season with 30 assists, which led all outfielders.

McIntyre was playing his usual high level of ball but, twenty games into the season, went out with a broken ankle and wouldn't return. B. F. Wright, after McIntyre went down, wrote that there wasn't a player on the Detroit roster who could "come within a mile of filling Matty's place."[58] Davy Jones went to left and overall, the adjustment didn't significantly weaken the club on offense or defense. Batting .316 by the middle of June, Crawford was at his best and Cobb complemented his work by adding the only other .300-plus average to the roster, earning a percentage of .305 with over 50 hits. As a team, the Tigers set an impressive American League record by scoring nine runs in the fifth inning against the Highlanders on June 11, and then doing the same thing in the second inning the follow day. Detroit won the first game, 10–2, and then the second, 16–4. It was an awesome expression of power and Detroit's third place standing was due to the work of the entire team, not just a couple notable stars.

Cobb's growth as a daring baserunner was more defined in 1907. He perfected the trick of dashing from first to third on sacrifice bunts and took it a step further by going from first to home on the base hits of teammates placed in front of outfielders. Human nature was human nature, he understood, and was a great believer in the mathematical probabilities of errant actions during a heated situation on the paths. So he worked to instigate them by giving the defense added pressure by teasing steals and constantly causing a distraction. Cobb was eagle-eyed about what was happening around him, and in response to the success he was having, many oppositional players were becoming incensed by his so-called unorthodox tactics.

A manifestation of frustrations emerged in the second inning against Cleveland on June 29, when Cobb refused to halt at third to accept a triple and stampeded home against catcher Harry Bemis. Bemis, who had the ball in advance of Cobb's arrival, obstructed the plate and waited for what he anticipated to be an easy out.[59] Cobb had other ideas. He never stopped running and propelled himself, headfirst, slamming his right shoulder into the backstop, forcing Bemis to drop the ball. The run scored and Bemis immediately became irate, punching the immobilized Cobb several times in his head. Cobb was never able to hit his rival back. Al Stump, in his 1994 biography *Cobb*, wrote that no members of the Detroit team went out to help Cobb when he was being pummeled by Bemis. This statement portrays Cobb as being completely exiled from his teammates, practically hated. But players from both benches rushed to the scene, and Davy Jones was the first man from the Tigers to help Cobb. The press specifically mentioned how quickly he managed to grab Bemis. Crawford and Jennings were also on the scene within seconds.[60] Aside from an exchange of words and Bemis being dismissed from the game, nothing more in the way of violence occurred.

Cobb instead let his play do the talking. In the sixth inning, he capped a 4-for-5 showing with a dramatic steal of home, the first time he'd ever accomplished the deed in the majors.[61] Nonetheless, the Bemis event was the major story. Cleveland sportswriter Ed Bang said Bemis "could scarcely be blamed" for reacting the way he did because Cobb endangered him physically and that he was "not even reprimanded," while Bemis earned a $25 fine. He called it "unnecessary roughness," and the notion that Cobb was reckless to the point of being willing to injure opponents was essentially born.[62] But however the Bemis situation was viewed, Cobb did not play illegally. He was well within his right to charge the catcher in such a manner.

July was a month of achievement and quick deterioration for Cobb. On one end, he became the first American Leaguer to score 100 hits and, as a reward for the latter accomplishment, admirers gave him a special diamond watch fob.[63] Within the next week, he slumped at bat and reporters were compelled to comment on his lack of production.[64] As Detroit ventured back east, Cobb rebounded, and was the star of the series at Boston and New York. He was so thoroughly determined against the Highlanders on July 30, that the reporter felt he was "trying to beat another team single-handed." Cobb went 4-for-5 and impressed fans as a hitter, runner, and fielder in a 6–1 victory over New York.[65] A few days later, he was confronted by a nineteen-year-old right-hander for Washington named Walter Johnson, making his major league debut.

Johnson would undoubtedly be Cobb's nemesis for years and develop arguably into baseball's greatest pitcher. In 1907, he was a fresh-faced rookie from the ball diamonds of Idaho. Little did many people know that the Tigers were given an early opportunity to sign the 6'1" pitching prodigy, but Frank Navin overlooked the hype and an inside tip, and blew it.[66]

On August 2, 1907, Johnson trotted out for the Senators and was mighty impressive against the Tigers, flashing exceptional speed. Cobb and his mates relied on bunts and speed until Crawford could stand no more, powering out a homer in the eighth. Detroit won the game, 3–2.[67] Cobb admitted that Johnson, in that game, was the "most threatening sight" he ever witnessed on the playing field.[68] Johnson would end the season 5–9 but would win 412 more before his career was through. Cobb and Johnson had a contentious rivalry, but had mutual respect. That didn't stop Cobb from trying to intimidate the passive pitcher. Early in their combat, he told Johnson that if he ever got in his way while he was trying to beat out a bunt, there would be serious trouble. Johnson smartly replied, "I feel it is only fair to warn you my control is a little off today."[69]

As the pennant race entered the final two months, all the excitement mainly surrounded the two front-runners, Detroit and Philadelphia. The heat was turned up after the Tigers slid into first place during the first week of August and continued when Jennings and his men arrived at the doorstep of Connie Mack's Athletics on August 7. The following afternoon, the two teams battled in a scrappy contest, and Cobb figured into a collision with catcher "Doc" Powers. Words were exchanged, enticing the already raucous audience. The next time at bat, Cobb doubled and was involved in more physicality with shortstop Simon Nicholls, although no violence broke out. Nicholls toppled onto him at the base and his spikes tore Cobb's garb, which needed safety pins to mend. The crowd was riled beyond belief, and Cobb was the perceived rowdy causing their fury.[70]

Philadelphia, it is important to observe, had a principal provocateur in Horace S. Fogel, sports editor of the *Evening Telegraph*. Fogel was also a columnist for *The Sporting News* and his loaded commentary was read high and low in the baseball community. His contribution to the sportsmanship of the Tigers-Athletics rivalry was to refer to the work of Jennings as "hoodlum coaching" and cited Cobb as a "dirty" player who purposefully tried to maim Powers. He further agitated things by claiming to have heard a report stating that Detroit players wanted to get their hands on him personally, as in to harm him.[71] Responding to the outrageous remarks, Detroit sportswriters tended to believe the words were being used as a way to inflame tempers amongst the public in Philadelphia against the Tigers. It was psychological warfare, and Fogel was doing his part in effort to sidetrack Detroit.

B. F. Wright hammered back, giving Cobb and his mates a prominent voice in the feud. He declared Fogel's charges to be "partisan hearsay," and clearly defended Cobb against accusations of immoral behavior on the field, specifically in the Bemis case. He explained that Cobb went in head first, not spikes first, and reiterated the right of way of a baserunner.[72] In the meantime, Cobb was relentless against Philadelphia. On August 8, he sprinted from first to third on a Rossman bunt, and then proceeded home on a wild throw.[73] In another game on August 14, he batted a hit off each of four Athletics pitchers, Rube Waddell, Jimmy Dygert, Bill Bartley, and Jack Coombs, in a 9–2 victory.[74] His high octane efforts were exceedingly distinguishable and the press corps across the American League circuit marveled at his abilities.

As could be expected, Cobb's body suffered from the frequency of his slides, which often occurred numerous times a game. Bruises were plentiful along his sides and legs, and open wounds were not an uncommon occurrence. Cobb occasionally wore sliding pads, but felt they slowed him down. He played through the pain, and his awe-inspiring quickness didn't seem to miss much of a step. On September 3, 1907, in Chicago, he blazed a path around the bases for an inside the park home run, the first ever at South Side Park, and a feat some baseball authorities deemed impossible because of the "dead" qualities of the South Side Field.[75] The agony of a sliced right hand, cut by shards of broken bottles when he accidentally fell in the overflow section of a crowd, also tested his resolve.[76] It got so bad that at one juncture he was unable to grip a bat.

Detroit and Philadelphia flipped the first and second positions in the hunt for the league championship, and Fogel unflinchingly declared the Tigers out of contention.[77] Jennings and his players did stumble, but managed to keep pace headed into the most important road trip of the year. The Tigers were revved up, and after finishing a three-game sweep of Boston, the Tigers returned to Philadelphia on September 27 and beat their foes 5–4 before 18,000 fans. A contest the next day, Saturday, was washed out, leaving both teams to stew for the remainder of the weekend since Sunday games were outlawed in the state. Anticipation was great and, prior to the 2 p.m. game time for the first of a doubleheader on Monday, September 30, more than 25,000 spectators were fixated on the Columbia Park field.[78]

Cobb and the Tigers lined up against pitcher Jimmy Dygert, and later both Rube Waddell and Eddie Plank, in what would ultimately be a singular,

17-inning battle. The lone game was an instant classic, featuring a heroic comeback by the Tigers after being down 7–1, a homer by Cobb in the ninth to tie the score, and a masterful pitching exhibition by "Wild" Bill Donovan. Additionally, there were fisticuffs as Rossman battled both Monte Cross and Waddell, and was subsequently arrested, and a called interference on a play Crawford was trying to make that could have given the Athletics the game. Connie Mack wildly protested the decision of umpires Silk O'Loughlin and Tommy Connolly, but there was little he could do other than complain. As darkness came over the stadium, the battle was called and the result was a 9–9 tie.[79]

The game was classified by Cobb as his "greatest diamond thrill" and he described the conflict in detail in *The Sporting News*.[80] Cobb named Donovan, who went the distance for the Tigers, the star of the fracas. Bill Coughlin offered comments about the battle and noted that Detroit players didn't dress at the stadium after the game, but went straight to the hotel. En route through rowdy fans, he was punched in the face by a spectator.[81] When Cobb returned to the hotel, he fell fast asleep, still wearing his uniform.

The pennant was within reach, but a few games yet remained. Eighth place Washington was next for the Tigers, and on October 3, Cobb performed dramatically in the nation's capital, but at the conclusion of the event, his status was again in question. Between the soreness of his legs and his hand injury, he was already less than a hundred percent. Moreover, his vast conditioning was being pushed to its limits. In the sixth inning at Washington, his body physically broke down following a steal of second and third, and then a rundown on the third baseline. His Herculean effort was valorous, but unsuccessful. He crumpled to the dirt feet from home plate and was tagged out. Cobb needed to be aided off the field, and in the eighth, he went to the hotel to recuperate.[82] He was in the lineup at St. Louis on October 5 and homered.

Hell-bent on winning the pennant, Detroit won five of its last seven games, including a four-game sweep at Washington, and annexed the American League championship. Around the same time, when the American League gave out its final numbers on the 1907 season, the twenty-year-old Cobb was awarded a .352 batting average. This was roundly disputed, as most pundits had him batting .350 instead, in a statistical tie for "world" title honors against National League batting champion Honus Wagner. Ernest J. Lanigan, a well-respected baseball writer, declared Cobb's record "a mite the better of Wagner."[83] The dueling honors flooded Detroit with contentment, and it was a fitting culmination to a hectic struggle. Fans at the beginning of the year weren't exactly convinced they were watching a championship-caliber squad, but they stuck it out, and the numbers increased measurably as the pennant race tightened. By season's end, people were crowding wire machines all across the city waiting for game results. The Tigers didn't disappoint, and the enthusiasts were convinced that the National League titleholders, the Chicago Cubs, didn't stand a chance.

Unfortunately, though, the Cubs had Frank Chance, the renowned first baseman and manager leading its club. Chance led Chicago to an utterly dominant 107–45 record, finishing a full 17 games ahead of second place Pittsburgh. They were imposing adversaries and Detroit was going to need its very best to pull out a winner. But the realities of the exhausting pennant chase were coming to the forefront, and it was impossible to say they were in the greatest of fighting shape. That important, but maybe overlooked, fact was going to prove paramount as the Tigers faced what Cobb called "one of the most amazing teams of all-time."[84]

The World Series of 1907 began on October 8 at the West Side ballpark in Chicago. Donovan, the winner of 25 games during the regular season, held the Cubs to three runs in twelve innings of competitive baseball, but the result was a 3–3 stalemate called because of darkness. Cobb was less remarkable, going 0-for-5, but was singled out before the game for his extraordinary performance in the batting championship race. The Chicago audience showered him with appreciation as he was given a special diamond medal, specifically fashioned by Mermod, Jaccard & King, a St. Louis jeweler, and worth about $500, for the occasion. The subsequent afternoon, the Cubs handcuffed the Tigers' offense and were well guarded against the hit and run, a bread-and-butter play for Detroit. Cobb logged his first hit of the series, but the Cubs were victorious, 3–1.[85]

The pitching of Orval Overall, Jack Pfiester, and Ed Reulbach, who went to the box for Chicago in the third game, were successful in restraining the powerful Cobb-Crawford combination, and that, to Joe S. Jackson of the *Detroit Free Press*, was a significant factor in whether the Tigers won or lost all season.[86] The duo was not complementing each other, and that was symbolic of the catastrophic failure Detroit was facing. Game Three was another lopsided confrontation and the Cubs were winners, 5–1.[87] The situation didn't improve in the fourth and Jackson explained that only three members of the Tigers were playing at their customary speed. Cobb was not one of them. He did manage to triple to center in the fourth inning and later scored, but Chicago held a 6–1 advantage to win.[88]

The lack of synergy between Cobb and Crawford was never more apparent than in the fourth inning of the fifth game on October 12 at Detroit, when the latter doubled and in dire need of assistance from the league batting kingpin. Cobb's input in what could have been a major rally was to strike out. Two innings later he hit a two-bagger himself (which was ruled a single and an error) but, in an attempt to pilfer third, was thrown out. Jackson complimented the competitive nature of the game and felt there had been a glimpse of the genuine Tigers, but it still wasn't enough. The Cubs won 2–0 behind Mordecai Brown and captured the World Series championship in a clean sweep.[89] Cobb ended up with four hits in 20 at-bats and a .200 average and no stolen bases. No one was harder on themselves in the defeat than him.

But fans saw it another way. They were overjoyed by the accomplishments of the Tigers in such a tight race, and particularly of their champion batsman. "Who's the best man in this town?" A coordinated chant asked following the game, "Tyrus Cobb! Tyrus Cobb!" Upwards of six thousand adoring enthusiasts marched through the streets of Detroit following the loss, demonstrating full and hearty support of their league titleholders.[90] A special banquet for the Tigers was held at the Cadillac Hotel on October 16 in honor of their splendid work, and a poem by Professor Edward J. Eaton of the Michigan Military Academy, entitled "Ty Cobb at Bat" was read to the audience.[91] Cobb made a few humble remarks at the event, declaring the pennant victory a united, team effort.[92] The outburst of admiration had to be meaningful to the downcast players, and upon receiving the loser's share of the purse, an amount of $1,945 and some change, attitudes all around likely brightened. A majority of the squad returned to Chicago to cash in on some additional exhibition games for a little extra money, including Cobb.

The brief barnstorming tour garnered a little positive press for Cobb because of his terrific play, but baseball fans in Chicago were already well aware of his skill.[93] His lack of production in the Series was a rare and unique anomaly, and was only going to serve to push Cobb harder. Upon returning to Georgia, he was snagged by a reporter at the State Fair and offered the following comment: "I had a good year in baseball, perhaps the best one that I will ever have."[94] No one could have known at the time, but Cobb's extraordinary season was not the limit of his abilities. There were plenty of better years ahead.

5

"UP HERE, THEY DON'T UNDERSTAND ME"

With over two years of big league experience under his belt, Ty Cobb was considerably better equipped to handle the constant strain and stress, plus the lifestyle adjustments he needed to make both at home in Detroit and on the road. He found a comfortable dwelling separate from clamorous team-mates, many of whom lived at the Brunswick Hotel, and spent endless hours in solitude studying all facets of baseball.[1] It helped that his mother, Amanda, had decided to spend the summer of 1907 in Detroit, and sister, Florence, often spent time in Detroit during baseball season, giving him a sense of family in region.[2] Additionally, his brother Paul, a young player of some ability, graduated from the Royston amateur squad and joined the Kalamazoo White Sox of the Southern Michigan League as a right fielder. Paul was expected to train with the Tigers at Augusta, but for whatever rea-son, the plan was scrapped.[3] His play was often compared to his older sib-ling, but there wasn't much in common.

Adapting to the baseball world was a unique adventure, and Cobb solved a number of his quandaries through repetition of the American League circuit. He made friends in visiting cities, found dining establishments that touched his fancy, and ensured he maintained his Southern customs. But there was one thing he was still having trouble with, and it couldn't have been more glaring than during Game Five of the 1907 World Series.

On the mound for Chicago was Mordecai Brown, a sly right-hander who'd heard enough stories about young Cobb to know he was dangerous at the plate. He also knew that he was easily ruffled. There, Brown took advantage of one of the largest known chinks in Cobb's steel-plated armor, and overtly teased Cobb with his words. The actions were clearly reminiscent of the lat-ter's early hazing episodes in Detroit and worked majestically. Cobb couldn't just see the clowning for what it was and played right into Brown's hands by becoming instantaneously furious. At one point, Brown told his catcher, "Now, don't be signaling me for any wild pitches, for they are all this guy can hit," loud enough for the Southerner to hear. Cobb's mind was clouded beyond belief, and he was simply putty in the pitcher's hands.[4]

The public probably didn't notice any of the needling, but Cobb took it all to heart. He was completely vulnerable to the words of others, and if his emotions got away from him, he was easy competitive prey. The razzing served to make Cobb immensely angry and slowly he was learning to channel all of his anger into increased drive on the field. Soon enough, it would be against the words of wisdom to prod him in any fashion. However, in his infancy as a player, rivals enjoyed badgering him. Billy Sullivan, a catcher for the White Sox, and pitcher "Doc" White had a blast at Cobb's expense. "Remember how we used to get Ty's goat?" Sullivan asked his mate by letter. "[It] makes me laugh every time I think of it."[5]

Following the exhausting 1907 campaign, Cobb yearned to return home and his Georgia neighbors were ready to receive him. The *Atlanta Journal* collected over $150 in public donations to purchase him an engraved watch and a special testimonial was held on November 12 at the Orpheum Theater.[6] It was apparent from the falderal that while Detroit appreciated Cobb's style of play, Georgia claimed ownership of the athlete and Cobb was receptive. He said that he was highly pleased by his American League batting medal, but a "different feeling" came over him when he heard about what his friends were planning. Comparing the medal and the watch, he said, "One is a trophy that might have gone to some other player. The other is something that is to be given me by my own people and it makes a fellow feel mighty proud."[7]

A speaker during the testimonial acknowledged the significance of the "Cobb" name in Georgia, and, in a prior statement, Governor Hoke Smith invoked a deeply personal element by mentioning the man who had meant the most to the young athlete. "I knew Cobb's father intimately," Smith explained, "and he was one of my staunchest friends. I am very glad to know that his son has attained such distinction on the diamond, but it is not surprising to me to find a Georgia boy at the top in any field of endeavor which he enters. While I don't have the leisure to attend ball games, or to read the 'dope,' as the news of the ball field is called, still one couldn't live in the remotest corner of Georgia without hearing of the fame of Cobb as a ball player."[8]

Unlike his father, Cobb was not a confident speaker. "I must tell you at the very start, that I am unable to make a speech," he nervously told the packed house during his testimonial. "If I could make one of the best in the world I would not then be able to say to you how I feel tonight and how much I appreciate what you have done for me. You have been very kind to me; more so than I can find language to express. You have given me credit for which I am deeply thankful. Perhaps there is a game that I know something about, but this game of speaking is one that I know nothing of, and the best that is in my heart, is, thank you one and all."[9]

The modest nature of Cobb illustrated by his statements in Detroit and Atlanta directly contradicted reports declaring him "chesty," and the "freshest youngster that ever broke into the big leagues." He further defied the circulating stories about his cockiness when he praised a number of teammates during a stint as sports editor for the *Atlanta Journal* on December 22. He wrote that Matty McIntyre had "about the best throwing arm" of any player he'd seen in left field; Sam Crawford was, simply, the "most valuable man"; and Schmidt deserved "great credit for his gameness." He complimented Hugh Jennings, George Mullin, Bill Armour, Elmer Flick, and many others in over twenty articles in the edition, and displayed a wide baseball insight of both history and current "dope." Nowhere in the articles did he hype himself. Cobb was also said to have a detailed personal scrapbook collection of articles and photos that contributed to his wide knowledge of players around the league.[10] Sam Crane of the *New York Evening Journal*, however, believed Cobb had the "perfect right" to have "an abnormal chest expansion" due to his exceptional play on the field.[11] Sidestepping vaudeville offers, Cobb retreated to Royston, where he thanked old friends for their unyielding support.

Over the winter months, Cobb took a long, hard look at the big picture, and assessed his commitment to baseball and the value of his endeavor. He spoke with family members and friends, and gleaned much advice from professionals who thought he was of a class better than athletics.[12] It was true that he was considering all prospects, from entering the business field to returning to college. Baseball was, nevertheless, still at the forefront of his mind. He decided to keep all his options open, while at the same time pursuing what he felt was a wiser contract deal with the Tigers. Frank Navin, who became President of the Detroit franchise in January 1908, mailed an offer to Cobb on the ninth of that month, and upon review, Cobb quickly rejected the terms.[13] Navin was slick in the way he presented the 1908 contract to Cobb. He gave him a number of reasons why he should sign, stating that the economy wasn't that healthy and reminded him of the poor showing during the World Series. He also stated that both Bill Donovan and Sam Crawford were "perfectly satisfied" with the terms the team offered.[14] However, the Tigers weren't exactly the most financially stable team in the league.

Everyone in baseball knew Cobb was getting a raise from the $2,400 he made in 1907. After all, he was the American League batting champion. The *Atlanta Journal* expected him to make greater pay than the Georgia State Governor and predicted his salary would be three times higher than it was previously.[15] Navin's offer was reportedly $3,500, nowhere near three times the $2,400 figure, but that wasn't the only reason Cobb turned the contract down.[16] Cobb sought to safeguard his interests, consciously realizing the kinds of risks he took on the field. He wanted a three-year agreement with a special clause, covering illnesses or injury, and guaranteeing him full salary if he went down from either. In addition, he wanted upwards of $5,000 a year for the length of the contract. Cobb was "sticking up for the rights of all ball players" by asking for the accident clause.[17] He was willing to bend from the $5,000 figure, but the three-year deal with the clause was mandatory. Asking for the stipulation was pointless, according to Detroit club representatives, because it had repeatedly demonstrated a willingness to pay full salary to players out with injury, citing both the Matty McIntyre and Jimmy Barrett situations.[18] Wary of his financial situation, Navin backed away and a stalemate began.

"It is up to Ty Cobb now," Navin told a sportswriter. "The policy of the Detroit club is to send out no special inducements and I hope Cobb will come to a realization of this fact. Of course, we all hope Cobb will be on hand when we start training, but if matters come to a showdown, an outfield composed of McIntyre, Jones, and Crawford would be the best in the American League, to my way of thinking."[19]

The hardball tact of Navin perturbed Jennings, mostly because he understood the contentious sensibilities of Cobb. A verbal confrontation, combined with threats to easily move forward without the batting champion, worked against the kind of harmony he promoted. Jennings went on record in defense of Cobb, telling Navin to "handle [Cobb] carefully," and taking blame for Cobb's holdout. The result was a halt to the decline in relations between the player and club.[20] However, the situation continued to evolve and there were reports that Cobb had received financial offers to jump to the Washington franchise of the Union Baseball League, a new organization headed by A. W. Lawson and the Logan Squares, a semi-pro team in Chicago. Reportedly, the Union Baseball League wanted Cobb so badly that owners were ready to give him the greatest salary ever paid a baseball player, a sum greater than $10,000.[21] In *The Sporting News*, H. G. Merrill had a unique reaction, declaring that Cobb was "in no sense indispensable" and if he departed the majors, "he would be forgotten" within a brief period of time.[22]

Confusion reigned as newspapermen ran wild with erroneous information and ridiculous claims. Cobb refused to listen to the propaganda. "I am not making any rash declarations," he explained, "and am not responsible for a lot of things that have been said. I am only trying to get what I feel I am worth and am not seeking any notoriety."[23] The chaos was amplified after two sportswriters, Tom Hamilton of the *Augusta Herald* and Malcolm Bingay of the *Detroit News,* entered the picture and purportedly brokered a compromise. Hamilton and Bingay, along with the latter's assistant Anderson, were ready to take credit for brokering Cobb's new $5,000-a-year contract, minus any additional clause. This was a false report, as Detroit management didn't agree to those terms. Jennings said the two men had involved themselves in search of "fame."[24] The problem was they had no permission to speak on behalf of the parties and their work was a waste of time. Cobb was rightfully fed up by the hearsay and ventured to Detroit to see Navin. Cobb arrived in Detroit on March 18, accompanied by attorney Julian McCurry of Hartwell, Georgia, and discussed terms at great length the next morning. He also spoke with former Detroit Mayor George P. Codd, who acted as a middleman in the negotiations.[25] On the evening of March 20, 1908, he approved the details laid out in a revamped one-year contract and signed on the bottom line. Neither side would confirm the amount, but it was believed to be for $4,000, plus an $800 bonus if he batted over .300.[26]

"I am glad to have the matter settled," Cobb said. "I would rather play in Detroit than any other city in the country, as I have many friends here and think that I have made good. Of course I will do my best for the club, and expect to play ball from the start. I don't care to make any predictions as to my work this year, but I think the public may count on me to do my share. The terms of my contract are perfectly satisfactory, and my relations with Mr. Navin are friendly as they have been all through our little discussion."[27]

After signing with Detroit, Cobb returned to Georgia and spent a small amount of time in Royston and Augusta before stopping in Western North

Carolina to see extended family en route to meet up with the club.[28] Having missed weeks of spring training from spending innumerable days traveling via train, Cobb was haggard, a bit fleshy, and slightly sick when he met the team in Little Rock on March 30. He didn't pause for a moment and jumped right into the action, fully confident that he'd be ready when the season started. Jennings was undoubtedly thrilled to have Cobb back in the fold and demonstrated it by ignoring him completely during workouts. Cobb understood why. That wasn't the case the year prior when he was mystified by Jennings's actions and inquired to a sportswriter why the manager spent so much time coaching others, but disregarded him. Jennings finally explained to the young athlete that of all members of the Tigers, he was the one individual who could better teach himself. He assured Cobb to trust and go with his own judgment on the field and, essentially, act as he pleased.[29]

Their system seemed to be working, Jennings believed, and Cobb was thriving at his own pace. Any overly aggressive orders or conflict was sure to derail his mindset, and Jennings, ever the diplomat, figured out the best way to handle his temperamental outfielder. To Cobb, he had the perfect amount of breathing room to study himself and zero in on his weaknesses, and there was no question that he scrutinized his own play harder than any coach ever could. Speed was a constant anxiety, and Cobb went to great lengths to increase his swiftness on the bases. He engaged a shoemaker and had lead weights imbedded in his soles. The added poundage pushed him harder and served to strengthen his lower body. Once the lead was removed, he felt as nimble as a cat. He applied the same theory to carrying three bats before heading to the plate.

Cobb was a true competitor, and there was a sustained rivalry on the Tigers about just who was the fastest runner on the team, and it boiled down to Cobb and Davy Jones. Back in 1906, Cobb was arguably at his quickest and made the home to first base jaunt in just 3.2 seconds.[30] Two years later, though, he was doing it in 3.6, while Jones was a tenth of a second faster.[31] As far as going around the bases was concerned, Cobb was number one. In fact, he might have set the world record at one point with a time of 13.2 seconds, but for whatever reason, it wasn't formally logged by pundits.[32] During games, he launched himself from the plate and ran with a fierce motion that appeared untamed and certainly unrivaled.

With the season approaching, the members of the Detroit squad expelled a host of ugly offseason talk including Detroit being ousted from

the American League, trade rumors such as McIntyre going to the Highlanders, and nonstop Cobb gossip, and managed to go undefeated in spring
exhibitions. They began on a high note at Chicago on April 14, 1908, but
couldn't find a winning groove. The White Sox overpowered them in a
15–8 victory, despite Cobb's 3-for-5 effort, including a double and home
run.[33] The Tigers opened up at home on April 17 and lost that game as well,
12–8 to Cleveland. A record attendance of 14,051 packed Bennett Park,
which underwent massive upgrades during the winter.[34] The Tigers would
lose nine of twelve games played in April and culminate the awful month in
last place. Personally, Cobb was flourishing. He was batting over .350 and
laboring to produce twice as much to cover his struggling teammates. His
mood took a downward shift when his favorite bat was stolen from Detroit's
home field.[35] Superstitious in nature, he liked to break in a bat and stay with
it, and hated to lose something so prized at a pivotal time.

Detroit rebounded on their eastern road trip, sweeping Boston and
taking three of four from Washington, and would end May one game
ahead of New York with a 20–16 record. Cobb, playing with extreme passion, momentarily was under the threat of a league suspension—the first of
his career—after he was thrown out at the plate going for an inside-the-
park home run. He loudly remarked to umpire Silk O'Loughlin and was
tossed from the field, but no punishment was handed out.[36] Throughout
his life, Cobb would long dispute being a full-fledged umpire-baiter. In
1918, he said, "During my league career, I've played in something like
1,800 games and been chased out of perhaps a dozen. That means one
expulsion in every 150 games. How many players of even the most docile
nature can show a cleaner record than that?"[37] Notably, his outfield work
was probably the best of his career to date. In back-to-back games against
Chicago, on May 30–31, he made superhuman catches, preventing a number of runs from scoring. A week later, he nabbed runners headed home
twice in two successive days.[38]

During his off hours, Cobb was enjoying life and the luxuries of the
newly constructed Pontchartrain Hotel in downtown Detroit, where he was
residing.[39] Early in the afternoon of June 6, 1908, he departed the elegant
structure, along with Rossman who was also staying there, and headed
across Woodward Avenue en route to the park for a game against Boston.
A voice then bellowed, "You can't cross here." Cobb instantly reacted, his
face red with anger and focused on the speaker, an African American
employee of the Detroit United Railway. The latter was a member of an

efficient crew striving to improve asphalt conditions for streetcars and was responsible for cautioning all traffic about the work being done.[40]

"What the **** have you got to say about it, nigger?" Cobb shouted.[41]

"I didn't [say] anything more than I tell hundreds of people every day," the worker, later identified as twenty-seven-year-old Fred Ernest Collins, said, "and, in fact, I wasn't talking to him. I warned some people in an automobile not to cross the soft asphalt, and he thought I meant him. Then he insulted me. I could see that he was a southerner, and I tried to explain to him, but he kept on insulting me."[42]

Cobb had plenty of opportunity to take a deep breath and walk away from the situation, but instead, in front of an estimated 200 people on the street, he approached Collins and initiated a physical conflict. Throwing punches with a rabid fury, Cobb displayed the same sort of reckless abandon he showed in Augusta the year before, and was unrelenting in his efforts to gain retribution for the so-called slight he perceived Collins to have made. Collins fought back the best he could, but was mainly on the defensive, and the arrival of his coworkers and pedestrians finally put a halt to the several-minute fracas. Rossman pulled his teammate from the scene and the two continued on their way to the park, but Cobb's face and head showed the obvious signs of participation in an altercation.[43]

There was another version of this story that was printed in various newspapers. It claimed that Cobb was on a bus in front of the hotel, preparing to leave for the park, when an African American yelled something derogatory at him. He then proceeded off the vehicle and brawled with the man. It was also said that spectators at Bennett Park ran onto the field in defense of Cobb, when it was thought police were going to arrest him that same day.[44]

The behavior of Cobb was unreasonable, and his frenzied actions greatly resembled those he took against the Warren Park groundskeeper. It wasn't that big of a leap to suspect the color of the man's skin had something to do with his overzealous reaction. Even a *Detroit Free Press* reporter mentioned the fact that Collins apparently didn't show Cobb the same kind of respect African Americans displayed to whites in Georgia.[45] And the particular decorum and courtesies shown by blacks toward Caucasians was very important to Cobb, as illustrated by sportswriter Joe S. Jackson in his previously mentioned 1906 article in chapter four.

The overall sum of evidence paints Cobb to be the kind of man who refused to take anything less than perfect etiquette from people of color.

However, he certainly coexisted with African Americans his entire life, and was influenced by several blacks in his hometown of Royston growing up. But in the south, there was a certain expectation by a segment of whites toward their black counterparts. For instance, the prominent Joseph B. Cumming, a Civil War veteran-turned-lawyer in Augusta, Georgia, preached the superiority of the white race and wanted teachers to impress that fact upon young African American students. He believed that blacks were at the "mercy" of whites.[46] This wasn't something he spoke about prior to the war in the 1860s, but in 1900 when Cobb was a boy. There is no telling whether Cobb ever read anything about Cumming or his ilk, but the rancid stain of racism was still prevalent across his state.

It was, in truth, rampant in Franklin County, Cobb's part of Georgia. As a youth, Cobb would have been exposed to the story of Bud Jones's murder in 1896 and the lynching of John Ware just outside Royston in 1904.[47] Local newspapers covered regional news of further acts of violence to blacks, such as the lynchings of three individuals in 1899 in Early County, featured on the front page of the *Franklin County Press*.[48] That same paper commented that Carnesville, the county seat, was a "bad town for 'bad niggers.'"[49] The Cobb household, it should be understood, was far from ignorant or intolerant and W. H. Cobb was a staunch supporter of fair education to blacks. As a state senator, he was firmly against the Bell Bill, which would have limited capital to African American schools to money brought in by black properties.[50]

Ty Cobb didn't naturally hate blacks, but he was aware of a Southern-propagated color boundary and he commanded respect from everyone on both sides of the line. As an already aggressive twenty-one-year-old in 1908, he was keenly alert to the mutterings and scowls of those around him, regardless of their color. But unfortunately, since his perceptions of rudeness were skewed by a general suspicion of nearly everyone, something exceedingly small could trigger an abrasive outburst. For a man so remarkably sensitive about every little thing, he didn't seem to acknowledge or comprehend even the slightest of sensitivity in others, and there was one route in most instances, straight to anger, and then, in some cases, violence.

Three days after the Collins incident, Cobb was found by a journalist in the Hotel Pontchartrain lobby and appeared melancholy. He was self-assured that his actions were just, but was obviously distressed about recent events. The writer reiterated the belief that Cobb was "tremendously sensitive to criticism," adding that he hated to be "misunderstood and misinterpreted." Cobb proceeded to offer the following insight into his perspective: "Up here, they don't understand me, see? Course being from Georgia, I think different about Negroes from what they do up here. I don't say my opinion is worth anything."[51] It seemed he was acutely aware of how this event was going to spawn theories about his racial outlook. In his autobiography, Cobb disavowed any notion he was a "black-hater."[52]

Collins pressed charges against Cobb and the ballplayer was arraigned on an assault and battery charge on June 8. He pled not guilty before Justice Jeffries and the case, after several continuances, was concluded on June 20 when Cobb paid a $75 fine. Cobb said, "I settled not because I thought I was the offending party, but because I thought I did not want to be inconvenienced later on. I would act again in a similar manner under the same conditions. When a man is insulted, it is worth $75 to get satisfaction."[53]

Batting clean-up, Cobb maintained his average over .300, but was exhibiting symptoms of a scatterbrain during the last half of June. On the bases, he made a number of incautious attempts to extend a single into extra bases when he clearly had no chance, didn't return to a bag to tag up on an outfield fly, and broke up a rally by trying to steal third and being thrown out. He also lost concentration on a towering shot in the wind that he normally would have caught and dashed for a liner into right center, only to dive and miss, causing runs to score. To close out the month of June, he struck out three times against his old nemesis, "Doc" White, in a 2–1 loss at Chicago.[54] Joe S. Jackson of the *Detroit Free Press* called his elongated quarrel with an umpire on June 27 "foolish," particularly because he was ejected for arguing a strike called on a teammate.[55]

Surprisingly, the teammate Cobb was standing up for was Matty McIntyre and the gesture wasn't glossed over. Later that night, outside the Michigan Central train station, the perennial rivals found common ground, shook hands, and put an end to their nearly four-year feud. A prominent rooter for the Tigers, Billy Rooks was credited with bringing about the Cobb-McIntyre peace accord. Rooks, a member of the Elks club in Detroit, was close friends with McIntyre, Rube Waddell, and many other ballplayers.[56] In his autobiography, however, Cobb claimed that McIntyre passed away in 1920 "without ever shaking my hand" to clear the air between them.[57] A sense of peacefulness in the Tigers clubhouse had been building for months and months, and the removal of friction between Cobb and McIntyre eradicated the final element of the old anti-Cobb hazing group. Pitcher Ed Siever had been sent to the minors and troublesome Ed Killian was photographed shaking the hands of a smiling Cobb, indicative of their improved relations.[58] Killian had made positive comments about Cobb in the press the September before, essentially extending an olive branch.[59] Cobb displayed a personal sentiment by saying that he was "awfully sorry" to hear that Killian was ill in January 1908.[60] Cobb later wrote about corresponding with Killian on friendly terms after the latter retired from the majors, as well.[61] B. F. Wright and Paul H. Bruske, expert sportswriters covering all-things Tigers, noticed the lightening of tensions and the greater respect teammates offered Cobb, specifically, because the latter had earned it.[62]

Cobb's rapport with Sam Crawford was utterly unique. At times, they had a mentor-pupil relationship, but as Cobb developed, he fostered a more fiery competitiveness with his fellow outfielder in his mind, similar but more intense, than that with McIntyre and Jones. He knew in his everlasting pursuit to be the best that he had to contend with the statistical numbers of Crawford, one of baseball's most potent sluggers. Cobb and Crawford shared a few qualities, but when it came to opinion, attitude, and playing style, they typically differed. For example, the sophomoric Cobb didn't believe luck played any part in baseball, and it was all up to the ability of the players themselves.[63] Crawford, a bit more worldly, disagreed. He felt the Tigers were altogether lucky to win the pennant and said it was always "a big factor."[64]

Crawford was an early riser and the first man in the clubhouse, whereas Cobb liked to sleep a little late and would frequently be the last man to arrive. As far as temperament went, Cobb was insufferable at times, while "Wahoo" was easygoing and likeable. On the field, the Georgia product ran for each base with a nearly unparalleled hustle and it didn't matter if it was a soft bunt or a smash to the fence. Crawford was known to drag a bit on shorter hits, even though he had the speed to challenge most throws to first.[65] During a batting slump, he rarely, if at all, changed his style, and waited it out, believing that he was bound to regain his stride in due course. Cobb was the opposite. He made adjustments, and went to the park in his spare time to work through it. "Practice makes perfect," he told a reporter.[66]

Dissimilarities aside, in 1908, things between the two was somewhat cordial, and Crawford, showing an affinity for the same type of bat as his co-outfielder, actually used the "Ty Cobb model" fashioned by Spalding Sporting Goods for much of the season.[67]

Usually able to ignore annoyances, Crawford fumed when Cobb ran in front of him and caught a ball during an 11–1 defeat of Cleveland on July 2. "Let that man Cobb get a couple of hits in a game and he goes crazy," the Nebraskan said after the game. "He thinks he is the only man in the team that can catch a ball."[68]

"Sam and I have always had an understanding," Cobb replied, "that either one of us could go into the other's field to catch a ball providing that neither he nor I yelled that he would take it. When the ball was hit to center, Thursday, I saw I could take it. I thought the sun was bothering Sam so went after it for I did not hear him yell that he would take it. Then he got a grouch on and has been crabbing ever since about it. I can't see anything for him to get mad about. When a team is after the pennant, every man is expected to play for anything he can get and I got it, didn't I."[69]

The outburst by Crawford made Cobb defensive and angry. It was one more thing on his mind, but he continued to battle at the plate, becoming the first American Leaguer to score 100 hits and lead the Tigers into sole ownership of first place in mid-July. On July 17, at Philadelphia, Detroit put up an astonishing 21 runs on 25 hits, establishing league records for both while holding the Athletics to only two scores. Cobb went 5-for-6 with a pair of doubles and a triple, and received a nice ovation by the Philadelphia crowd the next afternoon. The newspaper stated that the Philly crowd, after the show of respect, turned on him and jeered him every chance they got.[70] By early August, he was batting over .340, but still seemed distracted. The reasoning behind his occasional preoccupation was because in a matter of days, he was going to be wed and begin his life anew with a young lady from Augusta, Georgia by his side.

Cobb's wedding had been in the works for months, in fact, he was engaged as early as December 1907.[71] His approaching matrimony was also a likely contributing factor to his preseason holdout, as he knew he was soon responsible for his wife as well. The future Mrs. Cobb, Charlotte (Charlie) Marion Lombard, was about a month over eighteen years of age, and a graduate of St. Mary's Academy, an Augusta girls' school run by the Sisters of Mercy.[72] Her father, Roswell Lombard, was a successful entrepreneur and amassed a fortune of over $218,000 through land and business investments.[73] Living nine miles southwest of Augusta in "The Oaks," a rolling estate, Charlie's mother, Nancy, raised four children in total, including siblings Alfred, Francis, and Roswell.

The Lombards were no strangers to baseball. The Lombard Iron Works, the company founded by Charlie's grandfather, long employed an amateur team, and her brother Alfred was involved in Augusta's Indoor Baseball League as a member of the Olglethorpes squad.[74] Press reports claimed Cobb met his soon-to-be bride during his stint as a player in Augusta, and since he was at least four years older than Charlie, he was relegated to a long-distance relationship after leaving for the majors in 1905. Following each season, he spent more and more time in the Augusta area, and it was apparent that the two were inseparable.

Finally, a summer wedding was planned, but the date was up in the air due to Cobb's Detroit commitments. He spoke with Hugh Jennings and received the blessing of the team, and expected to be out anywhere from five to seven days.[75] "With Davy [Jones] there," Cobb said, "they won't miss me."[76] Because of the irregularity of train schedules, Cobb still didn't know which day he'd arrive at "The Oaks" for the ceremony, and the Lombards left final preparations open until things were definite. Their home was decorated in a simple yet beautiful manner, and only the closest friends and family were invited. Notably, Amanda, Florence, and Paul Cobb were not in attendance for Ty's wedding. The reason why is unexplained. Keeping everything basic, the wedding didn't include any groomsmen or bridesmaids.

Word came to Augusta that Cobb was to arrive on the morning of August 6, 1908, and a large delegation awaited his disembarkation at 7:15 a.m., when the train pulled into the station. However, in a very Cobb-like fashion, he wasn't where he was expected to be. More than two hours later, he turned up on a different train, along with his uncle Clifford Ginn, and dressed at the home of a local friend.[77] From there they drove to the ceremony, and arrived a minute before the formal start time at "high noon." With Reverend Thomas Walker officiating and a brass band providing the music, the wedding went off without a hitch and guests returned to Augusta to continue festivities at the Hotel Genesta.

It was originally reported that Mr. and Mrs. Cobb would depart on the 3:30 p.m. train headed to Detroit, but instead, they enjoyed the pageantry at the special reception, and didn't leave town until after 11 p.m. that night.[78] The newlyweds missed a train at Cincinnati, but returned in time for a game against Washington on August 9. In a 5–2 win, Cobb went 1-for-3 with a triple, stolen base, and two runs to his credit. He also struck out and a sportswriter on hand felt Cobb showed more anxiety than usual.[79] But despite leaving during the midst of a pennant chance, there wasn't an overflowing backlash to Cobb's six-day departure, either from his teammates or the fans. The crowd loudly cheered for him upon his first appearance on the field and high society contributed innumerable presents to the couple. His fellow players gave him a $300 gift, and Cobb was right: the team would play well in his absence.[80] They went 3–1.

Hoping to keep amongst the leaders, Detroit went east and Cobb fell into an odd slump. He was making contact, but unable to drive the ball for distance, and the deterioration of his offense affected all areas of his play. At New York on August 20, he misjudged a fly in the ninth and allowed the winning run to score. His two errors, plus two strikeouts contributed to what he called the worst day he'd ever experienced in baseball. Cobb went 0-for-5 and the Yankees won 4 to 3.[81] During the Boston series, he nearly fought Cy Morgan after the Red Sox pitcher almost hit him in the head with a ball. Cobb thought Morgan's act was purposeful and Cobb's riotous language drew calls to ban him from the local stadium for a year.[82] In all, the Tigers completed the "most disastrous eastern jump" since Jennings took over as manager, going 6–7, and Cobb's lack of hitting in conjunction with Crawford before him in the lineup and Rossman behind, was a significant reason.

Between July 14 and September 20, the Tigers held first place, but began to slide, falling to third on September 23 before snapping off a 10-game winning streak that helped them withstand the historic challenge of both the Cleveland Naps and Chicago White Sox. The American League pennant was officially snagged by Detroit on October 6 behind Bill Donovan's 7–0, two-hit masterpiece at Chicago. Detroit finished with a 90–63 record and Cleveland was only 0.5 games back at the finish. Chicago was in third, 1.5 games behind the Tigers. The enthusiasm and abilities of young shortstop Donie Bush, a recent call-up from Indianapolis, was a big element in Detroit's strong finish.[83] For Cobb, it was a grand achievement. He personally battled stomach trouble and a sore leg, but with Charlie on the road with him, her company was enough to keep his spirits up.[84]

Cobb worked through a number of rocky patches, but found his rhythm at the plate and headed for his second-straight batting championship with a .324 average. Cobb led the American League in hits (188), doubles (36), triples (20), RBIs (108), total bases (276), and slugging percentage (.475). Crawford came in second in the league with a .311 batting average. Honus Wagner, however, batted .354 in 1908 and had better all around numbers. Cobb's .324 would be the lowest average for an American League batting champion until Snuffy Stirnweiss of the New York Yankees won the title with a .309 in 1945.[85]

The year before, after losing to Chicago in four consecutive games, Detroit was ridiculed. Cobb was reduced "from a world beater to a large amateur," one pundit said, and the dominant Cubs walked right over them.[86] With Chicago effectively going over the New York Giants in a one-game playoff and capturing their league flag, a rematch was established, and it was a remarkable opportunity for the Tigers to regain credibility against their superiors of 1907.

As expected, the Cubs were the favorites, but outside hardcore enthusiasts, baseball fans didn't want the same match-up again. A Chicago-Cleveland or New York–Detroit battle would have been much more popular. Nevertheless, the Series kicked off at Detroit on October 10, 1908, and Cobb was determined to show his critics that he was a capable postseason batter.

To start the Series on October 10, less than 11,000 fans were present at Bennett Park on a rainy afternoon, but the Tigers caused much excitement by overcoming a deficit to grab a one-run lead going into the ninth. Rookie pitcher Eddie Summers, who'd gone 24–12 during the regular season, was trusted to close the game away and send the crowd home happy. He instead managed to give up five runs and Detroit lost, 10–6. Cobb went 2-for-4, and was a spirited baserunner throughout the contest, grabbing extra bases and pushing the defense to make risky throws. He tried to extend a single with two outs in the first, but Cubs right-fielder Frank Schulte saw the writing on the wall and threw him out.[87]

Game Two was another loss for the Detroit Tigers and Donovan, despite giving up one hit in the first seven innings, was unable to prevent a 6–1 rout. Cobb's base hit in the ninth scored the lone run, but other than that, there wasn't much to speak of.[88] That would change in Game Three on October 12. Chicago fans saw the Tigers in their best form to date, and Cobb was the star attraction. He went 4-for-5 with a double and two RBIs, and in the ninth, he stole second and third before attempting to sneak home as part of a double-steal with Rossman. He was caught, but it didn't matter, as Detroit sailed to its first victory over the Cubs, 8–3.[89] Turning right around, Cobb's offense was stifled against Mordecai Brown in Game Four and his error trying to catch a drive by Frank Chance in the ninth gave the Cubs its third and final run, while the Tigers were held scoreless.[90]

Down three games to one, the Series was eerily reminiscent of 1907, and any lingering enthusiasm was yanked from Detroit baseball fans. On October 14, for Game Five, Bennett Park was filled by less than half capacity in what would ultimately be the smallest crowd in World Series history (6,210). The big right-hander for Chicago, Orval Overall, proved to be far too much for the Tigers to handle, striking out 10 and allowing three hits in a 2–0 win. Cobb went 0-for-3 with a strikeout and a walk.[91] And just like that, the Cubs had repeated as world's champions and the members of the Tigers were left to pick up the pieces and make sense of their defeat. The team batting average of .209 had a lot to do with it, and a weakened pitching staff didn't help. Both Donovan and Summers lost two games apiece for Detroit, and Mullin was the only winning pitcher. Cobb batted .368, the only Detroit starter to bat better than .300, which undoubtedly went a long way to help his credibility.[92]

With the campaign over, Cobb was ready for a full and exciting winter, and wasn't about to let inactivity wear down his conditioning and strength. He had grandiose plans, and while his original idea to venture to Asia with his new bride fell through, he was going to stay busy enough.[93] And most importantly, contrasting from the situation in 1908, he'd be the first man to sign his 1909 Tigers contract.[94]

6

THE LUCKY STIFF

The playing style of Tyrus Raymond Cobb was distinctive in more ways than one. As sportswriter H. G. Salsinger put it, he was leading a "revolution" and his fresh perspective to running bases and hitting the ball was extraordinary. At the same time, he flatly ignored many of the recommendations of veterans who tried to coach him, all because he wanted to implement his own methods. Salsinger noted that conventionality was the golden rule in baseball and anyone that stepped outside the traditional customs was generally considered loony.[1] Cobb challenged that establishment. He was doing things his own way and, headed into his fifth season, he'd already proven to many American League spectators that he wasn't a temporary flash of greatness, but fit to be amongst the superstars of the game.

A number of Cobb's colleagues disagreed with that line of thought. They considered his achievements to be the work of a "lucky stiff," someone clearly in over their head and catching the breaks of an extremely fortunate man.[2] Ex-major leaguer Dick Harley said, "Cobb is a wonderful ball player, but I fear his playing days are numbered if he continues his daring base-running. It will get him sooner or later."[3] Others made similar comments, basically limiting Cobb's future in baseball to a handful of years. They predicted serious injury because of his reckless techniques and, seeing Cobb play, who could question it? But Salsinger chalked up much of the commentary to old-fashioned jealousy. It was simply amazing the way Cobb had made an impact on baseball in such a short amount of time and his opponents were envious.

Detroit's Bill Donovan, known as "Smiling Bill," was a congenial guy and always level-headed. When he remarked about Cobb following the 1907 season, people took notice. "He won't finish in the league next year,"

Donovan explained. "He plays contrary to all baseball law and he won't last. He can't. He's a wild man. Next year, they will just throw the ball to the home plate and wait for him to dash around to it. These freak players never last because they go contrary to the law."[4] Donovan couldn't have been more wrong.

Cobb was practical in his methodology, not careless. He used his intellect to figure out the best path to success, and to a lesser degree he tossed caution to the wind and played on pure intuition. As he often admitted, baseball didn't come naturally to him and he regulated himself to extreme amounts of practice to even the playing field with his contemporaries. But that is also where he began to prove superior by strengthening his weaknesses to the point they were no longer weaknesses at all. His extreme level of commitment to self-improvement was a rarity in baseball circles. Now that's not saying his peers weren't devoted athletes, but Cobb was on another plateau of dedication. He had a deep, subconscious-type determination that was ever pushing him to be the best—almost a personal compulsion—and there was no room for anything less.

Doting on his flaws, Cobb religiously studied baseball, nit-picking what he did right and wrong with his game. He observed his rivals with a keen eye and searched for ways to exploit their mistakes. Most of the time his brain was consumed by the deeper psychology of the sport, and when his mind and body were connected, he was usually able to outthink and outrun his opponents by a fair clip. Understanding his commitment to enhancing his skills, one could see why he didn't believe in luck. Based on his hard work and dedication to the sport, he felt as though he controlled his own destiny on the diamond.[5] Interestingly, though, his opinion of luck and how it applied to his career would soon change.

Engaged in his private ruminations, Cobb preferred to be alone. But a number of times in 1908, he stepped out of his protective shell and was sociable. On one occasion, he joined Herman Schaefer, Claude Rossman, and Charley Schmidt for a Detroit Wheelmen club function on Lake St. Clair. Cobb was pressured to make a speech where he thanked everyone for their support, but made a point to remind those in attendance that the other Detroit players were just as responsible as he was, if not more, for the club's achievements.[6] He also mingled with coworkers at theaters in Detroit and St. Louis prior to a major jamboree on October 8 at the Detroit Opera House.[7] That night, in a gala celebration to honor the Tigers, Ty and Charlie Cobb mixed with teammates, including Sam Crawford and Davy Jones and their wives, as well as former major leaguers like Sam Thompson and Charlie Bennett.[8]

A couple of weeks later, he was the centerpiece attraction amongst the new recruits into the Order of Freemasonry at Royston. After a baseball-related initiation where Lodge members made Cobb perform baseball slides as they hit him with an oversized bat, he bestowed an Entered Apprentice degree.[9] He visited family, rested, and went hunting as part of his post-season exercises. But on November 14, he was back in the saddle, playing ball in New Orleans for a semi-pro squad known as the Eddys, managed by G. E. P. Murray. Cobb saw his participation as a way to not only stay in shape, but to gather a little extra money and visit a town he always wanted to see. In his first game, he went 3-for-4 in an 8–0 squash, and a sportswriter noted that Cobb played to the limit of his abilities, just as if it was the World Series.[10] Things were strained, however, by Charlie's prolonged stomach ailment and her illness cast a shadow over the entire winter.

Cobb returned to the Augusta area shortly before Christmas and was surrounded by family and friends throughout the holidays. Elsewhere, baseball maneuverings were rampant and he received reports on the acquisition of third baseman George Moriarty, the departure of Bill Coughlin, and the elevation of Herman Schaefer to team captain.[11] He was excited about the reports, especially the arrival of Moriarty and wrote numerous letters to Detroit pals, extolling the virtues of the Tigers in the coming campaign.[12] When he wasn't penning missives, he managed the Royston club in regional contests and made an appearance at Elberton, Georgia, where he blasted three homers in an impressive display of power.[13] On the afternoon of March 9, 1909, he even donned a "Boston" uniform he had found at a local YMCA and took part in a friendly practice with members of the National League Boston Doves at Warren Park.[14]

All of his aforementioned activities on Georgia fields were a preamble to spring training at San Antonio, Texas, and Cobb arrived for official duties on March 16, a few days late. He was in excellent shape and predicted that he was on his way to his best season in the majors.[15] So confident in his diamond competence, Cobb was itching to pitch and boasted about his work on the mound at New Orleans. His aspiration to be a pitcher wasn't a secret. For the past two years, at least, he'd shown an interest, and often joined the hurler corps during training sessions to develop what he thought was a fine understanding of the craft.[16]

"Cut out this monkey business," Schaefer finally told him, fed up by Cobb's pipedream. "You ain't got no more stuff than a high school boy."[17] Schaefer wasn't the only one to feel this way. Hugh Jennings, Frank Navin, Addie Joss, and Willie Keeler were others who discouraged Cobb's attempt to become a pitcher. Navin, who had spoken personally to Keeler and Joss about the subject, gave Cobb his opinion in a letter dated December 15, 1908, telling Cobb to "be more careful of your arm."[18] Cobb was undoubtedly stung by the harsh words, but he refused to accept failure of any kind and continued to work on his delivery. It was obvious to those around him that he wasn't cultivating a major league arm.

San Antonio was a fine venue for spring workouts and Hugh Jennings was more than satisfied with the progress of his team entering early April. Cobb's old mentor George Leidy was the player-manager for the local San Antonio club, and on March 28, the latter played Detroit in an exhibition. Realizing what he could do on the bases, Leidy warned his team to watch out for Cobb's tricks, but after the Georgian reached second by extending what was essentially a base hit, Leidy pulled his center fielder from the game in anger. The Tigers won, 17–4.[19] The Tigers went to Dallas for a two-game exhibition series against St. Louis on April 3–4 and Cobb was fully energized to put on a good show, provoked by the recently publicized comments of the Browns new catcher, Lou Criger. The thirty-seven-year-old Criger was coming off eight seasons with the Boston Americans and the legendary Cy Young felt he was the "greatest" backstop in the business.[20] Criger had faced Cobb innumerable times, but that March, he was suddenly incited by an incident in which Cobb blocked him, he told a St. Louis reporter that he had Cobb's "goat," and with regard to stealing bases, he "never had any trouble with him."[21] Sportswriter Joe S. Jackson later questioned the validity of the Criger article, saying that there was "no proof" to its legitimacy.[22]

Cobb was incensed, but told the same St. Louis journalist that he didn't care to "knock" a fellow athlete. He recalled that Criger had also been the catcher for Cy Morgan, the Boston pitcher who Cobb believed tried to end his career by launching a fastball at his head. (Cobb actually said that had Morgan's pitch hit him in the head, he would have been killed.)[23] During the exhibition games in Dallas, Cobb and Criger matched up in only the initial game, but didn't butt heads. Their frenzied rivalry continued into the regular season, and Cobb made sure it was known by all that he planned to steal on Criger the first opportunity he had.

That chance came on April 30, 1909, at Detroit. In the fifth inning with Cobb on first, he raced to second on the first pitch, beating a wide throw and fulfilling his promise. *St. Louis Post-Dispatch* writer James Crusinberry didn't waste any time in asserting that Cobb had regained his "goat" in the ongoing conflict, but Cobb still wasn't appeased. The next day, he swaggered to second with Crawford at third and tried to coax the flustered Criger to throw the ball. Criger knew he was being challenged, and probably bit his tongue in anguish, but he held pat and guarded the plate.[24] In another game later in the summer, Cobb displayed further brashness by taking both second and third on Criger, putting a final dagger in their struggle.[25] Cobb talked about the Criger feud at length in his autobiography, and claimed to have stolen second, third, and home on the backstop.[26] It was also suggested that Cobb demoralized Criger to the point that he retired from baseball altogether. But Criger continued to play until 1912.[27]

Remarkably, Cobb didn't attribute his base-stealing success to be a personal conquest over the catcher, but deemed it a win over the pitcher instead. It was a unique philosophy, and, in fact, *The Sporting News* stated that he might have been the first player ever to make such a declaration.[28] Nevertheless, he really believed in the theory and scrutinized pitchers from top to bottom, searching for their unconscious "tell" that would give him the insight he needed to advance safely. For example, in the case of Cy Young, Cobb realized that he pulled his hands close to his chest before throwing to the plate and never deviated from the pattern. Young would often throw over to first to keep him close to the bag, but once he entered his routine, he always went home with the ball. Cobb became aware of his customary practice and began to steal immediately after Young brought his hands to his chest.

In the instance of Young, human nature sometimes revealed too much, and for that reason, Cobb was wary about his own motions on the bases. The last thing he wanted was to give up too much information about what he was going to do, especially when it came to stealing or not stealing. "I always used the same motion," Cobb once said, "whether I was bluffing or really going down. Sometimes I took a longer lead than I did at other times, but that always depended on either the pitcher or what I had in the back of my mind."[29]

Cobb too had a "tell" that was recognized by a discerning infielder. Each time he'd go to bunt, a third baseman, unnamed in the article, noticed that Cobb bit his lower lip. The fielder put two and two together and nailed him just about every time.[30]

Running the bases, Cobb didn't always guess right, and some days, he was at the mercy of his competitors. But when he was on his game, there was a certain amazement that was shared by his teammates, rivals, and the crowd. "I [knew] I had the reputation of being a crazy base-runner who took crazy chances and I always tried to encourage that notion," he explained. "Actually, though, I never took an out-and-out chance in a close game. My craziness, if you want to call it that, came in the one-sized games. It was then that I had a chance to experiment, testing out the pitcher, the catcher, or whoever took the throw at the base."[31]

On May 11, 1909, Cobb, in all his glory, attempted a base-running ploy prohibited by the rules and regulations of major league baseball. In the seventh inning against New York, he ran mesmerizingly at full speed around third base and charged across home plate in what normally would have been a triumphant score. But this time, he was instantly declared out because standing back on third was his co-outfielder, Crawford. Cobb, in a baseline pickle, went through the motions, whereas Crawford might have had a chance to score legitimately, but decided to remain still. The contest was still a 16–5 blowout in favor of Detroit, and like Cobb said, he tried to "experiment" in such games. Needless to say, not much was garnered from that little trick.[32]

The Tigers were a perennial league leader in 1909 and overcame an early slump in batting by Cobb to maintain a lead over the Philadelphia Athletics. Between opening day and early August, the club was only out of first place one day and was getting an extraordinary showing by pitcher George Mullin, who'd finish the season with a 29–8 record. Cobb's streaked to over .300 by June, and had a number of noteworthy moments. Against Washington on July 15, he achieved two inside-the-park home runs in a single game, attaining the second one after blasting through a halt sign by Jennings in what was a relatively close play.[33] A week later, he ran all over Boston, collecting four stolen bases in the process and giving Detroit a win.[34]

Of all the notable events that year, two incidents would be infamously remembered and contribute a great deal to Cobb's longstanding reputation with the public. The first happened in the opening game of a heated series between the Tigers and Athletics at Bennett Park on August 24. Sliding feet first into third base, Cobb sliced the right forearm of Philadelphia's Frank Baker in a play in which he was tagged out. The injury was painful but manageable, and Baker remained in the game. But Athletics manager Connie Mack called Cobb out afterwards, insisting the spiking was intentional and cast aspersions on the Detroit player. It was claimed that Cobb said something about taking out a Philadelphia player before the game in which Baker was hurt. Mack was also quoted as saying that Cobb "threatened to get Baker, [Jack] Barry and [Eddie] Collins," his third baseman, shortstop, and second baseman, respectively.[35] Cobb did have a run-in with Eddie Collins in the seventh inning.[36] However, in the game rundown, the Baker incident wasn't even mentioned by the *Philadelphia Inquirer*.[37]

All year, Cobb had dealt with questions about his sportsmanship and whether he was purposefully sliding into basemen with the intent of causing harm. "Never in my life have I ever intentionally spiked a player," Cobb told a Boston sportswriter earlier in the month. "I don't slide directly into a base and consequently there is little chance of my spikes striking a fielder's feet or legs. I use entirely the fall-away slide and anyone who knows base-running realizes that a man slides around a man taking the throw. At third base, I again use the fall-away slide, but not so wide."[38]

Cobb was feeling the squeeze of the accusations. Just twenty-two years of age, he was wearing a somewhat thicker skin than when he broke into the majors, but was still supersensitive to criticism and particularly any questions about his honor. He tried to set the record straight, telling a St. Louis reporter, "I have never cut down but three men since I've been in the big league, and they're good friends of mine right now. The three men I accidently injured are Billy Sullivan, one of the finest fellows in the business, and Frank Isbell of the White Sox, and [Bill] Bradley of the Cleveland Naps, and he came to me and said, 'Ty, old boy, it wasn't your fault.'"[39]

With the arrival of the Baker affair, Cobb was backed entirely into a corner. The episode trumped everything that had happened previously and redefined his status on a national and international scale. It ignited the fury of those who already harbored ill-feelings toward him and exacerbated the sentiment that he was a dangerous, reckless, and malicious player. No amount of denials by Cobb—and there were many given to the press—could stifle the avalanche of condemnation. From that moment forth, he carried the reputation of a spikes-high demon, out to maim opponents with no second thought about the welfare of any player standing in his way.

Mack perpetuated the belief and didn't budge from his stance, telling reporters he was going to the National Baseball Commission to ensure Cobb was restrained from doing any more damage. If that meant he'd be banned from the sport altogether, so be it. The story was advancing toward a political showdown of some kind, and Cobb's future was in the balance. At that point, *Detroit News* photographer Bill Kuenzel produced an impeccably timed picture of the exact moment Cobb slid into third on Baker, proving that he went for a hook slide to avoid the outstretched arm of the fielder. Baker, in fact, was in the baseline and Cobb was working to avoid contact to get to the base.[40] Cobb and his supporters were adamant that the photo cleared his name, and in many respects it did.

The Sporting News noted that the picture, "while artistic," could not be "considered as conclusive confirmation" of Cobb's innocence in the matter. Furthermore, because of the frequency of complaints by "victims" of his spikes, there was no way all instances could be chalked up to an "accident" or the "awkwardness" of the fielder. That being said, Cobb's "mere denial [was not going to] relieve him of the claim that attaches to a player guilty of this infamous practice."[41] Philadelphia sportswriter Horace Fogel loved to hammer Cobb, and reveled in the opportunity to admonish the Detroit player. As expected, he went right on the attack.

Widespread reaction to the actual event and subsequent propaganda was out of his control, and all Cobb could do was tell his side of the story. "I have never attempted to spike another player and I deny positively the charge that I have employed rowdy tactics. Of course I run the bases hard and slide hard. But the baseline, by every rule of baseball, belongs to the runner, and if the baseman chooses deliberately to get in the path to try and block the runner off, he does so at his own peril. I did not maliciously spike third baseman Baker, of the Philadelphia team. I slide into third base, and he was on the line."[42]

Several prominent voices spoke up on Cobb's behalf, including his ex-teammate Herman Schaefer, who had been recently traded to Washington for second baseman Jim Delahanty. Schaefer was one of the most popular men on the Tigers and was instrumental in Cobb's early major league development.[43] "Cobb is a game, square fellow," Schaefer explained.

"He never cut a man with his spikes intentionally in his life."[44] Chicago Cubs owner Charles Murphy added: "No one ever observed Cobb's playing closer than I did during the last two world's championship series, and if there had been anything of the 'dirty' ball player in his make-up he surely would have brought it to the front then. In all those games, I never saw Cobb make a move that would lead one to believe that he even contemplated an act that wasn't clean baseball."[45]

"It is my honest opinion that he never thinks of putting the spikes to one who seeks to block him," explained infielder Bob Unglaub of the Washington Senators. "He thinks only of getting to a bag. A number of players say that Ty has tried to spike them, but there are mighty few who can hold up their hands and say that he really hurt them."[46] American League President Ban Johnson also offered support, issuing a statement affirming his confidence in umpires to enforce the regulations of the game, essentially saying that if they didn't call Cobb out on an illegal act, there wasn't one to be concerned about.[47]

Cobb's second infamous happening of 1909 was yet another of those scandalous off-the-field occurrences, one that he more than likely wished never took place at all. On Friday, September 3, Detroit put its amazing 14-game win streak on the line against Nap Lajoie's squad at Cleveland's League Park. Darkness crept up on the competitors and the game was called at the end of nine innings with the score tied, 1–1. Feeling sociable, Cobb went out to the theater with a friend that night, steel tycoon E. S. Burke Jr., as well as a few other Tigers players. They later met up with matinee idol Vaughan Glaser and his popular cohort Fay Courteney for dinner at the Hollenden Hotel in downtown Cleveland.[48] Undoubtedly discussing a future venture that would see Cobb transition to stage performer, the group talked until around 1:30 in the morning, when, at that time, the ballplayer returned to the team hotel.[49]

Upon arriving at the Euclid Hotel, he received a note to meet up with fellow players for a late night card game on the second floor. According to Cobb, he requested assistance in finding the room from the individual working the elevator but was essentially denied help, prompting a verbal squabble. Cobb explained that the elevator worker not only refused to show him to the room on the second floor, but then wouldn't take him up to the fifth floor where he was staying.[50] The amplification of voices drew the attention of the hotel detective, also known as the night watchman, and George Stanfield quickly made his presence known. Through the years, it has often been reported that Stanfield was African American, leaving open the question of whether it was racially motivated. However, over twenty primary sources were reviewed and an exhaustive genealogical search was conducted, but no reference to Stanfield being an African American was found. In contrast, when Cobb got into a fight with Fred Collins the year before, the fact that he had tussled with an African American was prominent in nearly every press report.

At this juncture, there are two different versions of what happened, one story by Cobb, and the other offered by Stanfield.

"When I came to the elevator, where the trouble started," Stanfield explained, "I found that Cobb had struck the elevator boy. He began calling me vile names. I struck him. We sparred and then my foot slipped and I fell striking my head against the elevator grating. Cobb was on me in an instant, saying 'I'll kill you now.' I felt the sting of a knife. The blood welled up under my collar, from a deep cut on my shoulder. It dripped down over my eyes from a gash in the scalp. Through the blood I saw his hand descending to my face, and I threw up my left hand to shield my face. The knife blade passed clear through it.

"I threw him off and started backing away, flourishing a gun. I seized my club from the hotel desk and then struck a blow that brought him to his knees. I struck him again and he raised his hands over his head, begging me not to kill him."[51]

Cobb claimed that once the fight broke out against Stanfield, and the two wrestled to the floor, the watchman dug his fingers into his left eye. "I was afraid he was going to ruin my eye. I had one hand free, and finally got out my silver penknife and raked him across the back of the hand with it. Then I got loose. I didn't stab him. I did cut my own finger so that it had to be bandaged for several days while I was playing. I didn't cut him in the shoulder, as people have said I did. The knife was too dull to go through the coat he was wearing, and my own hand was cut as badly by the knife as his was."[52]

Reportedly, neither the clerk nor the night watchman knew that the man they were bickering with was Ty Cobb and they might have suspected he was not a guest at the hotel at all.[53] The *Detroit Free Press* reported that Stanfield went back to work after things were settled.[54] But in the aftermath of the incident, and once the famous Cobb was known to be part of the mix-up, a funny thing that sometimes happens to celebrities occurred. Instead of being a capable worker, Stanfield was said to be bedridden in succeeding press accounts, ailing from numerous injuries, and had a team of attorneys preparing a $5,000 civil suit.[55]

Cobb was in a precarious position, legally, but the police investigation of the fight evolved slowly on Saturday, September 4. For that reason, Cobb did what he was supposed to do, and despite being bandaged and bruised, he mustered the strength to participate in both games of a doubleheader against Cleveland. Detroit lost both games, ending their win streak. A reporter for the local *Plain Dealer* told the story of how Cobb avoided authorities by fleeing out a side door and traveling to the train station ahead of teammates to prevent a warrant from being served.[56] Annoyed by that claim, Detroit players told a hometown paper that Cobb didn't do anything of the kind and left the ballpark with teammates like always.[57] There were murmurs that the situation in Cleveland was part of a conspiracy to knock Cobb, and the Tigers, out of the pennant race.

There was no way to conceal the Cleveland matter and combined with the Baker spiking, the notion that Cobb was an out-of-control rowdy prevailed. Philadelphia sportswriters continued to gnaw at the situation as well, creating a worrisome environment in that city heading into a late season battle between the Tigers and Athletics for first place. The public was charged up and Cobb was public enemy number one. More specifically, the underground criminal network known as the "Black Hand" was adamantly going after the Georgian athlete, sending more than a dozen letters threatening his life. One letter even had a skull and crossbones for a signature.[58] That kind of irrationality turned a baseball rivalry into a nightmare scenario, and in addition to having to play one of the best teams in the majors, Cobb had to worry about a sniper's bullets or a knife-wielding madman out for blood.

The menacing letters were going to work one of two ways, it was believed. Either Cobb was going to refrain from showing up at all, or he was going to show up and be so affected by the ominous threats that he'd be completely thrown off his game. Charlie Cobb recommended the former concept, hoping her husband would play it safe.[59] But shying away from an act of intimidation was not in his character, and although he was rightfully disturbed and distracted by the alarming letters, he appeared in his right field spot on the afternoon of September 16, 1909, before over 24,000 rambunctious individuals. He still was nearly consumed by nerves and eyed his surroundings guardedly. At one point, Crawford had to calm him down after a suspicious loud noise was revealed to be a car tire blowing out and not the crack of a rifle.[60]

Cobb was booed at every turn and completely off his game. In the third inning, he was helpless against Athletics pitcher Eddie Plank and struck out with the bases loaded. He ended the day 0-for-4 in a depressing 2–1 loss. An army of police on location prevented any physical altercations between players and spectators. No soda bottles were sold for fear they'd be thrown at athletes on the field. Though, after the game, a piece of wood was tossed in Cobb's direction, and fans wildly encircled him and teammates as officers worked to keep the peace. Detroit players were escorted by motorcycle police between the stadium and the team hotel.[61] The overt animosity toward Cobb lessened after the initial game. Philadelphia fans respectfully cheered him on several occasions and offered encouragement. But more importantly, in a sincere gesture of goodwill during the second contest, Frank Baker extended his hand to Cobb after Cobb stole third, and the two shook on the field in full view of the public. Baker said that he never felt Cobb deliberately tried to harm him, and seemingly put the entire spiking situation to rest.[62]

Ironically, before the series was over, just as Cobb was trying to close the door on the harrowing Baker episode, he spiked Philadelphia shortstop Jack Barry trying to steal second in the fourth inning of the September 20 game. Barry was nipped in the leg and needed four stitches in what most publications deemed an "accident." The *Philadelphia Inquirer* noted that, after the game, Cobb was "visibly affected" by the mishap and refused to eat.[63]

"I would not have this happen for all the money I ever made in baseball," Cobb explained. "And to think that it came at a time when the Baker affair was almost forgotten. But it was an accident, and I am sure that the fans, particularly the good class who go to see a game and look for the best team to win, will bear me out that it was an unfortunate affair and absolutely unavoidable. Barry himself shouted at me, 'Don't mind, Ty. It was not your fault.' But I am afraid that it will leave the impression in the minds of some that I am a ruffian and the dirty ball player that some try to paint me."[64]

Unfortunately for Cobb, the Baker incident would never be forgotten. The story infused into the bloodlines of baseball lore, and his reputation as a ruthless aggressor would permeate throughout popular culture for decades.

After the Philadelphia series, Cobb went on an offensive tear, building up to his third-straight batting title and a .377 average. He was correct when he predicted his best year before the season started and he lead the majors in batting average, hits (216), home runs (9), runs batted in (107), and stolen bases (76). The Tigers were equally dominant and were out of first place only about 10 days the entire season. On September 30, 1909, Jennings and his crew clinched the pennant when the White Sox toppled Philadelphia in both games of a doubleheader, knocking them out of the race. It was said that the White Sox were repaying the favor the Tigers did them in 1906, when Chicago won the American League pennant. Detroit finished with a 98–54 record, 3.5 games ahead of Philadelphia.[65] Once again, the citizens of Detroit were eager to celebrate the accomplishments of their heroes, and downtown festivities commemorated their three-peat as league champions.[66]

At the Garrick Theater on October 4, Detroit's cosmopolitan crowd pleaded with Cobb to make a speech, but he politely refused, as did his teammates.[67] Two days later, the Tigers were in New York for an exhibition against the Highlanders in the benefit for sportswriter Sam Crane. Despite facing National League sensation Christy Mathewson for three innings, Detroit was victorious, 8–4, and didn't need the services of either Cobb or Crawford.[68] The club's real challenge was right around the corner, and Fred Clarke's Pittsburgh Pirates, winners of 110 games during the regular season, were all that stood between the Tigers and their first World Series title.

The focus and concentration required for such a significant athletic spectacle was unparalleled in baseball, but Cobb's mind was fragmented. He had gotten word that back in Cleveland, authorities were pushing forward with the criminal investigation of the George Stanfield case and things were bubbling to an apex. About a month earlier, Michael P. Bourke, a Detroit attorney representing Cobb, went to Cleveland and coordinated a settlement in the civil suit to cover all of Stanfield's medical costs, plus an additional amount unspecified at the time.[69] Local private detective Jacob Mintz was involved in the inquiry and, according to the *Cleveland Plain Dealer*, held an in-state warrant for Cobb's arrest. The charge was "cutting to kill."

Mintz made it known that he was going to arrest Cobb at first opportunity. He was personal friends with Napoleon Lajoie, second baseman for Cleveland, and an important member of the Cleveland sports community. For that reason, his involvement in the Cobb case could be considered suspect, along the lines of what Jennings believed: the Stanfield situation was an attempt to derail the Tigers ballclub.[70] In the meantime, Cuyahoga County directed its Grand Jury to review the details of the case that included testimony from Stanfield and Fred Avery, manager of the Hotel Euclid. The geographic locations of Detroit and Pittsburgh made a journey through Ohio customary. But Cobb had to be concerned. If he was apprehended, his Series contributions would be minimized to say the least.

Game One occurred at Pittsburgh on October 8, 1909. During batting practice before the game began, Cobb was approached by thirty-five-year-old baseball luminary John "Honus" Wagner of the Pirates, and the two met for the first time. For the past three years, they reigned as batting champions of their respective leagues and, commonly, when writers referenced the accolades of one, they mentioned the other in some sort of comparison.[71] Besides examining the cold statistics of their impressive seasons, pundits peeled back the veneer and juxtaposed their physical appearances and dispositions. Wagner was built like a modern-day tank, combining sheer power and strength with speed. In terms of personality, Wagner was like Cobb in that he was also reportedly a loner, adjourning to his room after games, and wasn't a big talker.[72] He was quiet, cool under pressure, and well liked. Incidentally, it was said that he would rather raise chickens than continue playing ball.

Cobb was the opposite. Of course, being thirteen years younger than Wagner had something to do with it, but he wasn't about to give up baseball for any alternate vocation. He was temperamental, anxious, and his attitude tended to annoy those around him. Like Wagner, he was fast, but more graceful in the way of a greyhound, whereas his counterpart was exceptionally quick but lumbering. Cobb was tall and well conditioned, possessing the frame of the ideal ballplayer, and in contrast, Wagner, physically speaking, would have been equally comfortable on a football field or in a boxing ring. The two garnered baseball honors, but did it in their own distinct ways, and their styles were generally contradictive on the field.

Understanding those dynamics, it isn't surprising that when Cobb and Wagner inspected each other's baseball bats on the field the afternoon of the first Series game, they were taken aback by the specific differences in quality. Wagner used a weighty bat with a wide handle and Cobb explained that it was far too cumbersome for his tastes. Cobb's weapon of choice, according to Wagner, was overly skinny and light.[73] The duo talked for only minutes but it was a courteous discussion, both admiring the presence and ability of their friendly adversary. With the opening game moments away, they shook hands and departed and the audience warmly clapped in recognition of such a historic meeting. This was the first time league batting champions faced off in the World Series, and it wouldn't happen again until 1931 when Al Simmons and the Philadelphia Athletics met Chick Hafey and the St. Louis Cardinals.

On the mound for Pittsburgh was twenty-seven-year-old rookie Charles "Babe" Adams, a 12-game winner and a surprising starting pick by manager Fred Clarke. Somehow Clarke knew Adams would remain unnerved by the enormity of his task, and his pitcher silenced the Tigers lineup in a convincing 4–1 victory.[74] Cobb went 0-for-3, but there was a brief uproar in the fifth inning after he attained first base on a fielder's choice. The dispute occurred when he tried to steal second and Wagner took the throw in an anticipated clash between the two stars. Cobb was called safe, but was a little worse for wear due to the fact that Wagner tagged him in his mouth, drawing a little blood.

In a bit of fiction, this incident was exploited by "journalists" who tried to color the Cobb-Wagner rivalry as being antagonistic, when it was anything but. "There was a lot of talk before that 1909 Series . . . about how Cobb and I would be murdering each other," Wagner later said. "Funny thing, we didn't have a bit of trouble. There was only one unfortunate incident, and that happened in the first game. Ty tried to steal second, and [afterwards] I discovered his face was all cut up. I guess I must have accidently tagged him in the mouth."[75]

Detroit stormed back in the second contest, winning 7–2, and Cobb drew the attention of every spectator at the recently constructed Forbes Field by stealing home in the third inning. His mindset at the time was demonstrative of his psychological awareness on the field, and it was essentially a very simple decision. Standing on third, he watched as Howie Camnitz was lifted from the game by Clarke and replaced by Vic Willis. Cobb sensed that Willis was preoccupied with the batter, and took extra steps off third. When, finally, that first pitch was made, he dashed for the plate, catching everyone off guard and slid in safely. "The way I had it doped out left little chance for failure," he confidently explained.[76] Years later, Willis said: "That's one thing I'll never forget as long as I live. I didn't think Cobb could beat the throw. I often got razzed for letting Ty get away with that theft, but I don't think anybody could have prevented it."[77]

Cobb returned to Detroit on the special train carrying the entire team, and Charlie, seven months pregnant, was by his side.[78] Games Three and

Four at Bennett Park were split, Pittsburgh taking Game Three and Detroit capturing Game Four behind the outstanding pitching of George Mullin. The series was tied 2–2 returning to Pittsburgh on October 13.[79] Made further aware of the Grand Jury developments in Cleveland, Cobb decided to avoid Ohio altogether heading into Game Five at Forbes Field. Accompanied by his old friend Herman Schaefer, Cobb used Michigan Central and Pennsylvania train lines northeast into Canada to Buffalo, and then southwest to Pittsburgh.[80] The elongated journey was a depressing reminder of the absurdity of his fight with the Cleveland night watchman and the heaviness of that issue was still burning up parts of his mind, especially when reporters referenced a potential jail sentence.

Displaying great heart, the Tigers battled back in the sixth inning of Game Five to tie the score at three, but fell apart, dropping four runs in the seventh and giving Pittsburgh the win, 8–4.[81] Once again, in the sixth contest, Detroit battled back from a losing effort to gain the lead and this time they held on to win, 5–4. The Series was tied at three games apiece, and, on October 16, before a home audience, Detroit collapsed in grand fashion, losing the finale 8–0.[82] Adams, Pittsburgh's unsuspecting rookie, was the breakout star, propelling the Tigers into a third-straight Series defeat by winning the first, fifth, and seventh games.[83]

Cobb went 0-for-4 and batted a measly .231 for the Series, while Wagner, proving superior, achieved a .333.[84] The veteran, however, was impressed by the Georgian's abilities, saying: "Cobb is what I call a perfect player. He lacks nothing. There isn't a thing that a ball player should have that Cobb hasn't got and he's got a bunch of things that no other ball player has. I can't find any weakness and I see nothing that he could improve on. But I don't think that Cobb is as good as he can be or will be."[85] It was a startling testimonial, but definitively true.

7

DETROIT'S PRIMA DONNA

On the baseball field, Ty Cobb was establishing himself as the phenomenon of the ages, and each year more and more team owners, managers, and fellow players were publicly acknowledging his remarkable talents. Charles A. Comiskey, the indomitable magnate behind the Chicago White Sox, called him the greatest of all-time, an honor made even more special by the fact that Comiskey had seen and played with the legendary generation of stars prior to Cobb's arrival to the majors.[1] He was personally acquainted with the likes of Cap Anson, Dan Brouthers, and the baseball heroes of the late nineteenth century, and still recognized Cobb, with only five years in the big leagues under his belt, as the best in history. Baseball innovator Ted Sullivan placed Cobb alongside the legends of the past, and said that he was the "grandest" player of the generation.[2] Jimmy McAleer, the 1909 manager of the St. Louis Browns, said: "Ty Cobb is the greatest piece of baseball machinery that ever stepped upon a diamond. He has never had an equal on the bases and probably never will."[3] It was generally accepted by 1910 that Cobb was a rare breed of athlete, and his unusual methods were a barrier between him and the classically trained ballplayers normally seen in the pro ranks.

But also off the field, there was another facet to Cobb not all of his contemporaries shared. He was a natural entrepreneur, and being acutely aware of the existence of life after baseball, he consciously sought investments to expand his financial base. The scant salaries of his early career did little to flush out opportunities, but he was ever mindful of prospective ventures and accepted all the advice he could garner. Family and friends back in Georgia were always offering counsel, and his in-laws, the Lombards, were amongst Augusta's business leaders. In Detroit, he smartly hung out at the Pontchartrain Hotel bar and watched and eagerly listened to the pioneers of the automobile industry as they discussed the matters of the day.[4] Cobb was inspired to find his own slice of the business world to develop and ultimately profit from.

Inquisitive in nature, Cobb asked endless questions of businessmen and bankers he rubbed shoulders with, saturating his brain with data. Following the 1907 World Series, he told *The Sporting News* how he planned to lay out some of his freshly earned capital in the timber business in Georgia, and maybe it wasn't ironic that Detroit co-owner Bill Yawkey's family fortune was made in the same field.[5] Whether Yawkey conveyed suggestions to Cobb, it isn't known but it is obvious the latter was examining all options before him. That same year, he entered the real estate industry, buying up around 100 acres in the southern Georgia town of Hazlehurst. His intent was to build houses on the property and then rent the valuable land to enterprising farmers. His property was also already valued at three times what he originally paid.[6] His project expanded in December 1909 when he purchased an additional 3,000 acres in the Hazlehurst area for a reported $20,000.[7]

A bit closer to Royston, Cobb entered into another venture with two partners, buying up land and property in Toccoa, Georgia, just northwest of his hometown. "We have named this property the 'Booker Washington Heights,'" Cobb told to a St. Louis journalist. "We call this nigger property down home, for nothing but Negros live in it. There's money in it. I mean in the niggers. You see I get $3 for this, $2.50 for that one, and $2 for this house."[8] Cobb's manner of speech, while considered shocking today, was not highlighted as offensive by the news reporter in 1909, even though the use of the word "nigger" was generally deemed pejorative. Cobb, apparently, was leaning more on an accustomed lingo rather than a textbook vernacular.

His Toccoa investment had already more than doubled and he expected greater revenue in the near future. In addition to his mounting real estate holdings, Cobb bought stock in the First National Bank of Lavonia, which became the Northeast Georgia Bank, the Bank of Martin, which he later transferred to his daughter Shirley, and other financial institutions in northeastern Georgia.[9] He became a minority owner of the *Augusta Chronicle* newspaper and eyed other opportunities with great interest.

The widespread notoriety of Cobb opened up endorsement deals that boosted his net worth as well. Beginning in late September 1907, he was

featured in advertisements for the popular soft drink Coca-Cola, joining
Nap Lajoie and Rube Waddell as proponents for the soda.[10]

Spalding Sporting Goods of Chicago was another company to court
Cobb, and a special "Ty Cobb Bat" was fashioned for sale to the public in
1907–08.[11] But that partnership didn't last long. Cobb instead inked a mer-
chandising deal with the J. F. Hillerich Company of Louisville, Kentucky,
producers of the famous "Louisville Slugger," on October 5, 1908. He
became the third major leaguer to have a signature bat behind Honus Wagner and Lajoie. Hillerich, which later became the "Hillerich and Bradsby
Company," maintained a 4,000 player files at its factory, each listing the
exact bat specifications for athletes throughout Organized Ball.[12] Lastly,
also in 1908, a "Ty Cobb Cigar" was marketed by John C. Sullivan, Detroit's
premier cigar manufacturer.[13]

The positive elements of Cobb's life were indicative of a man entering a
world of heightened celebrity, but due to his penchant for violence, he still
had to step before a judge and answer for his alleged criminalities in the
George Stanfield matter. That case advanced a great deal just before Game
Seven of the 1909 World Series, when the Grand Jury in Cleveland indicted
Cobb on a charge of "stabbing to wound." Facing up to twenty years in the
penitentiary, he was being sought by way of extradition, but Detroit team
owner Frank Navin pulled his trump card to protect his star. He hired Robert E. McKisson, the former Mayor of Cleveland and a well-connected local
defense attorney. McKisson was politically powerful, wise to the law, and
used "every technicality" to keep Cobb out of jail.[14]

Cobb had little other choice but to appear in a Cleveland courtroom on
October 20, 1909, and pleaded not guilty. After agreeing to stand trial on
November 22 and posting a $500 bond, he was released but a significant
problem was apparent. His witness list included a handful of Detroit Tiger
teammates, many of whom were in Cuba for an exhibition series led by
Matty McIntyre. McKisson asked for a continuance, but was denied. Despite
the bad news, Cobb was confident. "If there any attempt to compromise,
I don't think it will come from our side," he told a reporter.[15]

A few days later, Cobb was in New York, and his legal worries were off his
mind . . . at least temporarily. He was in town to join a fifty-car procession
from that city to Atlanta, in a "Good Roads" endurance jaunt. Behind the
wheel of "Old Reliable," a Chalmers-Detroit "30," he was accompanied by
several sportswriters, and despite the good-natured sentiment of the event,
he was as competitive as ever.[16] At one juncture in Pennsylvania, he yelled at

a driver in front of him because of his "blocking" techniques. "I figure you're trying to show me up," Cobb said to his adversary in an example of early-twentieth-century road rage, "and if you do it again, I'm going to run this car right through you." The driver in front of Cobb, who reportedly caused the uproar, said his actions were unintentional. He invited Cobb to dinner to signify peace, but Cobb declined. The other driver said, "I'm glad there are no spikes on Cobb's car, or it might go bad for me."[17] Once out from behind the slowpoke, he made a point to be the first automobile into the various stops on the route, including Roanoke, Virginia, and Greenville, South Carolina.

Charlotte, North Carolina, received Cobb on October 30, and people were mightily impressed by the athlete. "He wears a smile mostly," the local paper reported. "He's a happy citizen with a fine disposition." Kids watched him from the sidewalk in admiration, while adults moved closer to shake his hand. Cobb was accommodating. He was sociable and friendly, demonstrative of his growth as a public figure.[18] He understood that he had a certain responsibility to show his face and mingle amongst the crowd, seeing that most of the populace was there to see him. On November 2, 1909, Cobb raced into Royston, a few hours ahead of his "Good Roads" cohorts, and was celebrated like a conquering hero.[19]

Not long after arriving home, Cobb was summoned to visit with President William H. Taft who was spending time in Augusta, and the two exchanged pleasantries at the local country club on the morning of November 8. Taft was in the midst of a major Southern tour and the meeting was set up by Taft's top military aide, Captain Archibald Butt, a native Augustan and friend of Cobb.[20] President Taft, incidentally, had only days earlier expressed his support for Cobb in his pending legal strife at Cleveland, telling a Savannah, Georgia, crowd that Cobb was "being made the victim of a damnable conspiracy." He continued: "I hope that the Georgia bar will rush to his defense and by a writ of habeas corpus, if no other means is available, restore him to the people whom he loves and who love him."[21] Admitting Cobb was more popular in Georgia than he was, President Taft wished him "all the success in the world," and Cobb graciously appreciated the Commander-in-Chief's kind words.

With the President's vote of confidence bolstering his ego, Cobb returned to Cleveland for the Stanfield trial on November 22, but a protracted court drama was avoided. Prosecutors realized it had little evidence to find him guilty in a "stabbing to wound" case, and authorized the levy of a lesser charge, assault and battery. Cobb and his lawyers agreed to plead guilty and Judge Willis Vickery had the last word, saying: "Legally, Stanfield had no right to strike Cobb. Stanfield was the aggressor. The court is very willing to accept this plea." Cobb was fined $100 and released, though he would have to pay it later.[22] The ugliness of the entire situation was cleaned up rather quietly, and Cobb had Navin to thank for the latter's exhaustive efforts in providing and paying for a top-flight legal defense.[23]

"It is over now," Navin told Cobb in a letter, "and I hope it will prove a good lesson to you."[24] Whether that sentiment would bear out remained to be seen, but relations between the two were at an all-time high. In fact, shortly after the 1909 season, Cobb was given a three-year contract by Navin with the salary figure left blank and he signed it without hesitation. Navin then revealed his annual salary, and Cobb was altogether pleased. The terms of the contract were not revealed, and in March 1910, the press began to circulate that Cobb was to receive $9,000 per year. Cobb denied it, likely to keep any animosity from building up with lesser-paid teammates. The $9,000 rate was accurate, however.[25] It seemed that the previous lack of faith the two had for each other was gone, and the maneuverings of Navin in the Cleveland case literally preserved Cobb's baseball playing future by keeping him out of jail. "[Navin] has shown me he is my friend and in such ways that I realize I can't very well repay him except to always speak well of him and work my head off for him," Cobb explained.[26]

The prompt end of the Cleveland trial gave Cobb time to catch a hunting expedition headed down the Savannah River, made up of his brother Paul, his father-in-law R. O. Lombard, major leaguer Tommy McMillan, and several others.[27] Cobb also hunted with Bud Sharpe on George T. Stallings's Haddock, Georgia, plantation and, based on their growing friendship stemming from the recent World Series, coordinated an outdoors venture with Honus Wagner. Wagner, however, was not impressed by the action in Georgia and left after a few days, disappointed by Cobb's emphatic boasting about local hunting prospects. "Cobb is one of the most genial gentlemen I ever met, but there are two things we will never agree on, game and baseball."[28]

Nevertheless, Cobb's major league leading batting average gave him an edge over Wagner, and on December 28, 1909, he was awarded the prized George "Honey Boy" Evans Trophy in recognition of his achievement. Evans appeared in his black-faced costume. The Opera House musicians performed "Dixie" for Cobb, much to the delight of the audience.[29]

Briefly speaking before the audience at the Augusta Opera House, he reiterated that any personal accomplishments were secondary to his task of helping the Detroit franchise win in the pennant race.[30] A little over two weeks later, he was again called to the forefront to speak at a YMCA banquet in his honor and Cobb was similarly bashful, cutting his comments short. He told the crowd that he didn't want to appear self-centered, so he was going to refrain from talking about baseball and admitted that he garnered awards in the sport, not through pure athletic talent, but by luck. It was a significant comment because in years past, he discounted luck as a factor in his success.[31]

The biggest happening of the offseason was certainly the most personal to Cobb and his family. On January 30, 1910, Ty and Charlie welcomed their first child, Tyrus Raymond Cobb Jr., a bouncing nine-pounder, born at "The Oaks" south of Augusta.[32] Cobb was relentlessly proud, talking about his son every chance he got. He told journalists that the first thing Ty Jr. ever held was a baseball and bragged of his strength when he was just two months old. "He's so strong that he can stand up alone," Cobb announced, full of pride. "Of course, someone has to balance him, but he can hold himself upright on his legs."[33] Reporters already had young Cobb headed for the baseball diamond like his dad.[34]

Cobb was known to overload his schedule during the winter months and, in early 1910, he was solidly tied to his new auto business in Augusta. As the licensed agent for the Hupp Motor Company of Detroit, selling the Hupmobile and maintaining an active garage, he was incredibly busy.[35] He was up to his neck in sales and repairs, and didn't bat an eye as other members of the Detroit club ventured to San Antonio for spring training in March. His hunting exploits and supplemental work at Warren Park kept him in shape, Cobb believed, and the need to travel to Texas was minimized in effort to safeguard his investment. He never liked spring training anyway, but this time he had real justification to remain in Georgia. That was his point of view, at least.

Navin, Hugh Jennings, his teammates, and the press saw it differently. Navin, the capitalist, was antsy about the box office money he was losing all over the South because Cobb, the big draw, was absent.[36] Jennings, the manager, was searching for synergy in the field and in his lineup, but the hole created by his outfielder was too troublesome to ignore. Jennings was irritated by Cobb's absence and kept getting false reports about when Cobb would arrive in San Antonio. Cobb didn't blame his manager for being mad,

but did not seem to rush his arrival.[37] His teammates were taking daily practice and playing assorted exhibitions as called for by club officials. They were
putting in the work day in and day out, while the mighty King Cobb was
conveniently elsewhere, avoiding crummy hotels and backwater towns. He
was a bit too big for his britches, some of his fellow players were coming to
realize. The media was getting the same impression and the notion that
Cobb was a "prima donna" was becoming more accepted as true.[38]

Cobb was laboring to get his affairs in order, and part of his mission was
to sell off his business interests before leaving Augusta. "The auto selling
game is nothing for a ball player because it gets good just when he should
be reporting and making ready to earn his baseball salary," he explained.[39]
Once a deal was made removing his automobile burden, Cobb headed for
Evansville, Indiana, to meet up with one faction of the team on April 8. He
was not oblivious to the fact that his actions were unfair to the team, but felt
his timely hitting and rounded performance on the diamond would more
than make up for his absence.

The loss of a third-straight World Series didn't demoralize Detroit as
one might imagine, but for whatever reason, the Tigers were in poor shape
in early competition in 1910. They were beaten in exhibitions by teams in
Mobile and Memphis and lacked offensive firepower. Cobb's explosive hitting and base-running refreshed the lineup and, during the second week of
the season, the Tigers advanced into first place and remained there until
May 6. He was stealing bases regularly, hitting to all parts of the field, and
led his team on an 11-game winning streak. However, one of the most
important aspects of the season came by way of a defensive switch. Jennings,
in mid-May, decided to return Cobb to center field, where he played in
1905 and '06, placing Sam Crawford in his natural right-field slot, and alter-
nating Davy Jones and Matty McIntyre in left.[40]

In late May, the Tigers were blazing hot, playing their best ball of the
year so far, and were a couple of games out of first. But a strange thing happened in Washington, DC. Cobb told a reporter there that Detroit was
essentially out of the pennant race and that the Philadelphia Athletics were
headed for the championship. "Everything points that way," he said, "but I
still believe that we have the better ball team. Fate seems to have decreed
that no team shall win four pennants in a row."[41] Logic was on Cobb's side
to a certain extent, but on the other hand, he was causing irreparable damage to the spirit of the club. And because of his words and actions through
the rest of the season, another serious contention was made about Cobb,

not only seriously harming his reputation but once again cracking the foundation of team unity.

Notably, 1910 was a unique year for Organized Baseball, specifically because the Chalmers-Detroit Motor Company offered up a brand new Chalmers "30" to the best batter in the majors. Players and fans alike were delighted by the added touch to the already sensational annual competition and, needless to say, Cobb was caught up in the excitement. It wouldn't be a stretch to say he took the batting fight to be a personal challenge, and was ready to test his deepest determination for the sake of the goal. As a result, his team cooperation was risked for the sake of individual honors, setting a reckless course for not only himself but his teammates.

Fellow Tigers could sense Cobb's ambition, and winning the car was first and foremost. Some were still mad about his spring training avoidance and there was a general feeling that Detroit management looked the other way when issues concerned the Georgian star. He was doing a few other things to invoke an essence of loftiness, including arriving to the clubhouse after scheduled games had begun.[42] His actions continued to go unpunished, whereas if another player had committed the rule violations, there would have been the normal monetary fines imposed, at the very least. Jennings, more than anyone else, had yielded to Cobb's temperament and allowed the player to govern himself. That had been his policy since taking over the club.[43] But it was obvious Cobb was taking additional liberties and subtly throwing his weight around.

Cobb was aware of the statistical numbers for the batting championship on a day-to-day basis and, the tighter it became, the more he felt the squeeze on the field. The pressure turned his tightly woven personality into one that was nearly intolerable. Davy Jones and Donie Bush, the two men ahead of him in the lineup, received the worst of his wrath and Sam Crawford, in the clean-up position, also had to deal with his rage. Cobb's frustrations were generally spawned by the belief that Jones and Bush were not cooperating with him, working the hit-and-run, and following his lead. He wanted them helping him at all times and then for Crawford to further his advancement around the bases. When Jones and Bush didn't produce offensively or failed to watch him instead of Jennings for last-second sign changes, Cobb was known to go ballistic. Arguments ensued, but most of the time, it was better to let him vent.[44]

Things between Cobb, Bush, and Crawford were already estranged from a previous quarrel. Sometime during the 1909 season, he laid into the 5'6"

Bush with heightened ferocity and verbally lashed out at him for whatever Cobb thought deserved the attack. Crawford heard enough from Cobb with regard to Bush and stepped in to protect the shortstop. Crawford reportedly threatened to slap Cobb if he continued to harass Bush.[45] Insulted by the intrusion into his private business, Cobb stopped talking to Crawford altogether, a reoccurring method Cobb used to demonstrate hostility in his life. The silence extended to Bush as well and created an unhealthy dynamic for the Tigers franchise. To him, Crawford and Bush existed in the world around him, but he would offer zero personal acknowledgment to either one. In the outfield, Cobb and Crawford relied mostly on their own expectations of what the other would do in any given situation, and then reacted accordingly.

Cobb's wicked stubbornness wasn't anything new. Once he was crossed— or at least perceived that he was crossed—there was no getting around it. His feelings for Crawford and Bush only served to exacerbate his 1910 frustrations, especially when getting the vibe that he was again isolated from the team's majority, akin to his first couple of years in the majors. Rather than sorting the situation out and shaking hands with his coworkers to put it all behind them for the sake of the team, he perpetuated the feud and tended to make things worse.

Fed up by what he felt was Bush's ineptitude in front of him in the lineup, Cobb protested vehemently and pundits have since assumed that Jennings, who was caught in the crossfire, decided to once again bend the needs of the team to conform to Cobb's whims. It was no secret that Jennings wanted Bush batting second. The shortstop was proficient in getting on base, leading the league in walks in 1910 with 78, and was quick amassing 49 stolen bases.[46] But it wasn't enough for Cobb and Jennings finally caved, shifting Bush first to seventh, and then up to sixth in the lineup in July. The move might have pleased Cobb temporarily, but his moodiness was seemingly beyond repair. About ten days later, his irrational aggravations climaxed in a game against Boston and Jones, the club's faithful leadoff man, became his central target of criticism.[47]

On August 2, 1910, versus the Red Sox, Cobb had an unusually poor day in a 4–3 loss. Across the diamond from him was twenty-two-year-old Tris Speaker, a magnificent outfielder and a contender for batting honors, along with Cleveland's Nap Lajoie. Boston newspapers had rightfully touted Speaker and many comparisons were made to Cobb. For that reason, Cobb was itching to perform well, but after left-hander Ray Collins left him hitless, he became "meaner than the devil himself," Jones later recounted.[48] Herman Nickerson of the *Boston Journal* also indicated that Cobb may have "loafed" on a key drive by Red Sox first baseman Jake Stahl, adding to the overall miserable showing by the Georgian.[49] Mentally thwarted, Cobb raged at Jones for missing a hit-and-run sign and caused a huge uproar after the game. Jones spoke about this incident some years later and recalled that Cobb was foiled by Collins's pitching. After yelling at Jones about the missed signal, Cobb, who was at bat, refused to play any further and returned to the bench. Another player, Jones claimed, went in to bat for him. Jones added he was the "fall guy" in the situation, taking the blame for Cobb's inability to hit Collins. However, there is no evidence that Cobb returned to the bench and that another player went to bat for him.[50]

Not one to let things go, Cobb harbored resentment for Jones through an off day, and then removed himself from the lineup in protest on August 4 versus Boston, refusing to play if Davy was in the game.[51] Though initially passed off as a stomach ailment, Cobb's tantrum left him utterly alone. Jennings held his ground in this matter and didn't bow to Cobb by removing Jones.[52] A *Detroit Free Press* correspondent wrote that it was "absurd" to remove a man from the lineup who was helping the club win (Jones) "merely to satisfy the whim of another." There was clearly "room for both" on the team. Teammates, management, and sportswriters all knew Cobb was acting irrational, allowing his emotions to get the best of him.[53] In response, President Navin said he "took the only possible position in the affair in allowing Cobb to convince himself that he was wrong," he explained. "Cobb acted hastily. The same temperament that makes him a great ball player renders him liable to lose his temper quickly. If he were less impetuous, he would be less valuable to the club."[54]

Cobb missed two games, both victories for the Tigers, and he apparently did some soul searching in his free time. Pondering deeply, he concluded that he was the one off base in the matter, just like Navin hoped, and freely admitted his mistakes. The *Detroit Free Press* indicated that he was "sorry" for an angry remark he made, likely toward Jones, and was ready to put everything behind him. Navin added: "He is a youngster, hardly more than a boy, and comes from a section of the country where pride is strong. I am sorry that the affair ever came up, and glad that Cobb has been courageous enough to recede from a position that made him ridiculous. The management harbors no resentment toward him, and hopes that the fans will be equally willing to overlook a mistaken action, the result of a momentary loss of temper."[55]

A section of Detroit's left-field bleachers were anything but forgiving and criticized Cobb relentlessly in the latter's first game back on August 6. He did his best to ignore the abusive taunts, going 2-for-3 with two stolen bases against New York.[56] But the insults continued nearly unabated from the first inning until the end of the game, pushing the already distraught Cobb until he literally snapped. He rushed toward the bleachers in a haze of madness and focused his energy on an African American man, who was one of his most vocal critics. Police quickly broke up the melee, and the *Detroit Free Press* stated Cobb was "a Southerner, born and bred, and naturally [held] ideas of his own regarding the right of a colored man to abuse him in public." Cobb searched for his bullies following the game, yearning to inflict a little punishment of his own but the loudmouths had wisely departed in a hurry.[57]

Putting aside the clubhouse turmoil, there were a number of exciting moments in 1910 for Cobb. On June 18, he snagged a liner and touched off a triple play versus Boston.[58] At Washington, he homered in the 11th inning on August 25 that ultimately won the game and, toward the end of the season, garnered four hits against St. Louis on October 2. His speed and base-running feats were commonly a thrill for fans in all league parks, and he was headed for the highest batting average of his career. Plus, despite the presumptions about his solitary motivation, Cobb often got into the coaching box to encourage teammates on the bases.[59] But, nevertheless, Detroit fell more than ten games out of the pennant chase in July and were never in serious contention again.

"Even if we admit that a fourth pennant is now beyond us," a journalist for the *Detroit Free Press* wrote, "we can still live in hope that Ty Cobb will bring home the automobile."[60] And so went the focus of a majority of Detroit's supporters to the batting title and the battle between Cobb and Lajoie tightened. The physical health of Cobb was questioned when, during the first part of September, he was afflicted by an eye ailment and nearly two weeks of duties were affected. Newspapers ran wild theories and prognoses for his future in baseball, and none were even close to being accurate. It was determined that Cobb was a bit nearsighted in his right eye, though he considered it more of an inflammation problem.[61] He made his return, and by October 8, was leading by a little less than ten points with a .383 average. Only two games remained, and he was confident enough to break away from Detroit's final series with Chicago to end his season prematurely. Cobb missed the weekend games at Chicago on

October 8–9, 1910. Detroit lost the first contest, but won the second. Hugh E. Keough of the *Chicago Daily Tribune* called Cobb a "quitter" for abandoning his team and Cobb received similar condemnation from fans in Detroit. The Tigers would finish in third place with an 86–68 record, 18 games behind the Philadelphia Athletics.[62]

Cobb's gamesmanship was obvious as he sought to protect his average and the burden was on Lajoie to put forth a superhuman effort in Cleveland's final two games, a doubleheader at St. Louis on October 9. Amazingly enough, that's exactly what he did—going 4-for-4 in each of the two games and finishing with a triumphant .385 average. Initial press reports proclaimed Lajoie the American League batting champion, and because his numbers surpassed the National League titleholder, he was to be awarded the Chalmers "30" auto.[63] In the meantime, however, details of the games in St. Louis were expounded upon by sportswriters and a number of controversial allegations were made. The most colorful was the theory that members of the Browns laid down to Lajoie's batting, allowing him to get on base each time he was up.[64]

Part-time third baseman John "Red" Corriden, a twenty-three-year-old rookie for St. Louis, played along the edge of the outfield grass each time the right-handed Lajoie came to bat.[65] His defensive stance was in preparation for quick-moving liners in his direction. But Lajoie smartly took advantage of Corriden's positioning, successfully bunting seven times to the left side of the pitcher during the two games. Even though Corriden and St. Louis manager Jack O'Connor watched Lajoie bunt time after time, neither reevaluated the strategy to combat him because they were still worrying about hot shots down the line. Their inaction caused many sportswriters to cast doubt on the legitimacy of Lajoie's success. Corriden explained that he didn't want to get killed by a Lajoie drive by playing in too close. "I didn't give [Lajoie] anything," he told a reporter in response to the question of whether he laid down to the Clevelander. "I don't favor him a bit over Cobb."[66]

"I was surprised when I read of the result of the [St. Louis] games in the papers," Cobb told the media, "and am sorry that either Lajoie or myself did not win the prize for the highest average without anything occurring that could cause unfavorable comment. I am not prepared to make any charges against either Lajoie or members of the St. Louis team."[67]

The overall appearance of crookedness sparked an inquiry by American League President Ban Johnson, but he rather quickly absolved Corriden

and O'Connor of any wrongdoing.[68] However, O'Connor was released as
manager of the Browns in the aftermath of the controversy. Scout Harry
Howell, who was said to have tried to influence the official scorer in St. Louis
during the doubleheader versus Cleveland, in an effort to aid Lajoie, was let
go as well. Years later, Lajoie said: "The [St. Louis] players were in my corner. At any rate, they didn't try any too hard to get me out."[69] Contemporary
versions of this story have often included statements explaining a certain
sentiment amongst ballplayers, generally favoring Lajoie over Cobb in sort
of a popularity contest. While it is difficult to prove either way, it is not
unlikely.[70] In the main interest of lessening the embarrassment to Organized Baseball, Johnson ordered a complete review of all statistics relating
to Lajoie and Cobb, and a few days later, the official ruling of the American
League was released. Cobb, by mere points, was announced as the winner
of the championship, and, in turn, the Chalmers automobile. His average
was .384944 (rounded to .385) compared to Lajoie's .384084. Johnson also,
in his diligence to give the story a happy ending, approved the offer by the
Chalmers Motor Company to give Lajoie an auto as well, effectively wrap-
ping things up without a volcano of public resentment.

"I am quite satisfied," Lajoie was quoted as saying. "I am glad that the
controversy is over. I have the greatest respect for Cobb as a batter and am
glad of his success."[71]

"I am simply delighted, delighted, delighted!" Cobb said after being
told of Johnson's decision. "Is it really true? I can scarcely believe it. I am
glad that I won because I worked hard to be the champion batsman of the
two leagues, but it is equally pleasing to know that Larry will get a machine,
too. The rivalry between us was very keen, but it was of a most friendly character so far as I am concerned."[72] Cobb sent Lajoie a letter, saying: "Of all
the congratulatory telegrams I received over winning the championship,
yours was the most appreciated. I was very much elated when I heard I had
won the batting honor, but more so when I learned that you would also
receive an auto. You justly deserve it."[73]

Seventy years and six months after Johnson confirmed Cobb the 1910
batting champion, *The Sporting News* published a series of new research findings and altered the way the entire championship competition was viewed
historically. In essence, the publication declared Lajoie the rightful winner
of the 1910 title based on several noteworthy discrepancies, including the
elimination of an extra 2-for-3 hitting performance credited to Cobb that
was found to be false. The new data gave Lajoie a .383 average, bettering

Cobb's .382, and named him the indisputable batting king. The 13-member Baseball Records Committee reviewed the documentation and put forth the information to Commissioner Bowie Kuhn, but he, along with American League President Lee MacPhail, rejected any update to the official records.[74]

In a 1981 statement, Kuhn affirmed Ban Johnson's investigation and mentioned the "passage of seventy years" as constituting a "certain statute of limitation as to recognizing any changes in the records with confidence of the accuracy of such changes." Although the official records have not been changed, most modern publications either recognize Lajoie outright as the 1910 batting champion or include an asterisk, highlighting the differences between the sanctioned data and the independent research on the matter.[75]

Sportswriters looking for avenues to scrutinize the Tigers following the disappointing 1910 season began to harp on the play of Sam Crawford. At thirty years old, Crawford was still one of the great sluggers in baseball. He led the majors in triples (19) and ranked first in the American League in RBIs (120), in addition to being third in extra base hits. His .289 average was less than desirable, according to critics, and Crawford felt the need to respond in defense of his reputation. "I have played my level best for Detroit all season," he explained, "and I know of no reason why I should be censured. If the truth be known, Detroit's showing this year is not the direct result of poor playing, but because there is not the harmony on the team there should be.

"I have noticed repeatedly that the club caters to Cobb more than to any other player; if he reports late or misses an inning or two, little is said. I vouch that if I did the same thing I would be reprimanded right. This is the club's business, however, but I wish to show that others are to be criticized instead of me being singled out as responsible for the club's poor showing this year."[76] Crawford stated that Cobb's concentration in the fight for the batting title made him "forget team play and look only for base hits. This spoiled teamwork as a result." Simply, there was "too much Cobb."[77]

Who could disagree? But of all the gripes about Cobb's motives and temper, he took issue with one accusation more to heart than the rest. And that was the claim of him being self-centered. "The reason they thought I was swell-headed," Cobb said, "was because I didn't understand human nature and my success came too quickly. I was afraid that people would say I was swelled up and I tried to be a good fellow with the other players so as to change their opinion. Instead of that having the desired effect, the players thought I was fresh. If I had kept to myself at first and had not tried to be a mixer I would have done better. I guess I got familiar too soon. Many a time have I walked out to the outfield stoop-shouldered so as to keep the fans from thinking I was cocky or swelled up. I dread being called swell-headed worse than any other one thing. Really, it hurts me."[78]

Regardless of his statements to the press to the contrary, or the image he wanted to convey, sportswriters and fans continued to depict Cobb as a raging, conceited baseball fiend; a man who was so outlandish that he'd willingly hurt rivals with his spikes. The idea that Cobb and his colorful Cobb persona were being exploited by newspapermen to sell papers apparently never crossed anyone's mind. When he spoke in interviews or gave speeches, he was the opposite of arrogant. In fact, he was meek and bashful. No one wanted sound reason from Cobb, as they preferred a snarling crazy man. During one spring training appearance in Texas, fans were actually shocked that he was just a humble young man and not a "fire-breathing monster" that, based on the image concocted by writers, they expected to see.[79]

Unquestionably, Cobb was doing much to earn a certain level of criticism from teammates, especially by missing most spring training and arriving late to games. There was no way to explain his behavior. If Detroit was ever to come together again as a unit and challenge for a pennant, he needed to make a number of serious adjustments. Otherwise, the "Cobb Show" was going to persist, and his coworkers were going to stand by as he performed his customary magic at the plate and on the bases. In that case, it was no longer a team game, but a day-to-day demonstration of his otherworldly skill. Some games he'd be good enough to win by himself, but most of the time, as baseball is known, nine men were needed for victory. And the lack of cooperation would prevent any significant improvement in morale.

Cobb had to get back to a place where his love of the game was more evident than anything else, both in the clubhouse and on the field. His determination for the Chalmers automobile in 1910 clouded his judgment as far as team play was concerned, and fractured the confidence of fellow Tigers in his ability to fight for one solitary goal: to win for the fans of Detroit. Mending that perception was his challenge going into 1911, and rehabilitating his standing with Crawford, Bush, Jones, and the rest was not only on his mind, but on the minds of enthusiasts across Tigerland. The future prospects of the team depended on it. Cobb's stubbornness, unfortunately, would prove it a difficult road to travel.

8

THE PSYCHOLOGICAL ADVANTAGE

A player of superstitions and routines, Ty Cobb was heavily invested in the psychological aspects of baseball. His concentration extended to all facets of his game, from the way he approached the plate to his scrutiny of opposing pitchers. His belief in jinxes and omens ran parallel to many of his contemporaries, which meant it was pretty important to his day-to-day outlook. At times he sought mythic remedies for poor play, placing a horseshoe on his bats before a game or whipping the umpire's broom from one side to the other.[1] Not surprising, the maneuver didn't always work. For instance, after chucking the ump's broom from the left side of the plate to right prior to an at-bat in 1910, he was hit by a pitch.[2] During another game, he joined manager Hugh Jennings in dumping out a barrel full of drinking water from the dugout so they could refill it with bottled spring water, apparently believing in its special revitalizing effects.

Heading onto the field for a plate appearance, Cobb was highly ritualistic. He wielded three bats at first, and then dropped one as he approached the batter's box. The remaining two were his customized J. F. Hillerich Company model and a weathered black variety, a consequential weapon in his arsenal. Cobb called his black bat his "hit-getter and voodoo bat," and was considered the "pride of the great Cobb's life."[3] However, after wearing thin from overuse, the black bat was never officially used again. He instead held it as part of his mental and physical preparation. Cobb would initially swing both bats, but gently released the black a second before steadying himself in the box and awaiting the first pitch. To complete his routine, he always yanked down his ball cap a bit and tugged up his pants.[4] Additionally, journalist Frank P. Sibley wrote that Cobb whacked the base of his cleats with his bat to clear any dirt and also tapped the plate before readying himself for a pitch.[5] At that point—and only at that point—was he ready to glare outward at the pitcher.

There were many varieties of baseball superstitions. Some batters enjoying a healthy streak of hitting refused to launder their uniform, regardless of how dirty it became. Others felt if bats were accidentally crossed for whatever reason, a bad omen was created; also if a player stood at the plate with the barrel of his bat facing downward, he was sure to expect a poor result.[6] Cobb's theories and superstitions played a significant role in his baseball career, and if understood at the time, would have explained much about his perceived erratic behavior.

Getting a full night's sleep was a priority for Cobb and seeing that he was less likely to perform up to his standards without it, he was all too ready to miss any morning practice to achieve maximum rest. In fact, he avoided any pre-game workouts to preserve his strength. It wasn't that he was shunning the ordeal because he was full of himself, but that he played better if all his energy was conserved for the game itself. And since he wasn't going to practice prior to the game anyway, he didn't see the importance in showing up until his thoroughly rested frame absolutely needed to be there. Cobb's longtime friend Kenneth Stambaugh revealed that for a time, Cobb's pre-game ritual included stretching out on his hotel bed and playing records on a portable phonograph machine. The works of violinist Fritz Kreisler were amongst his favorites and helped settle his nerves.[7] In some cases, it was minutes before "play ball" was called, and other occasions it was after the contest already started. Cobb had his own way of looking at the game and it wasn't so much that he was purely arrogant, just ritualistic in his preparations.

Once locked into the mindset of competition, Cobb was a machine in the way he focused and worked to achieve his goals. Bill Coughlin, who played with him early in his Detroit tenure, said: "Cobb was smart. Instead of kidding when he came in from the field, he would sit in a corner of the dugout and watch the pitcher every minute. Then, when he got on base, he knew exactly how to proceed. That helped him immensely in stealing so many bases."[8] His quiet and concentrated nature was amongst his early secrets to success, and his ample studying garnered plenty of inside knowledge of players throughout the league. It wasn't until he got a little older that he mustered the courage to verbally joust with rivals and even members of the audience.

Baseball in the "Dead Ball Era," a period beginning around 1900, was full of colorful performers, striking athletes, and spirited play. Strategy rather than slugging was the priority of teams across the majors, and games were more often won by a mixture of smart base-running and sacrifices than by homers. Interestingly, the ball itself was literally considered "dead" because umpires refused to swap out the orb until it was in absolutely no condition to be used any further. Balls were pummeled mercilessly and were sometimes losing stitches and misshapen while still in the field of play. Needless to say, those balls lacked the velocity of newer ones, and many drives that would normally have been hit out of the park were caught by fielders.

The reason for hanging onto the battered balls was purely monetary, as it saved cash for club owners to keep them in use for as long as possible. Cobb, when he felt a ball was damaged, was known to request a new one from the umpire during a game. He was sometimes refused. On July 21, 1911, in the ninth inning of a contest against New York, he displayed a flattened ball to umpire John Egan. Egan checked it over, but thought it was suitable to continue. Cobb raged in response, kicking up dust, and was subsequently thrown out of the game. He didn't leave the field and dugout quietly. Instead, he tossed bats, and verbalized his anger for minutes before finally relenting.[9]

Balls during the "Dead Ball Era" were also affected by all sorts of legal tricks employed by cunning pitchers. Russell Ford of the New York Highlanders went 26–6 in 1910 utilizing the "emery ball," a type of pitch created by scuffing or cutting the exterior of the ball. The "shine ball" materialized by generating a smooth spot on the ball's surface and Cobb's former Augustan teammate Eddie Cicotte would gain great fame using that method. The "spitball" was yet another "freak delivery," and Chicago White Sox hurler Ed Walsh brilliantly doctored the ball with saliva or tobacco juice to create, at times, a virtually unhittable pitch.[10] In 1908, he won 40 games and was the last pitcher to do so. Cobb's challenge as a hitter was to not only decipher the array of atypical pitches, but to handle the complete repertoire of regular "stuff" thrown by future Hall of Famers including Rube Waddell, Addie Joss, Cy Young, and others.

Playing for the Cleveland Bronchos-Naps from 1902 to 1910, Joss had great respect for Cobb as a hitter and comically told a journalist in 1908 that he didn't mind if Cobb remained out of Detroit's lineup. Cobb, at the time, was going through a holdout with Tigers management. Joss said, "I can get along just as well with him off the team."[11]

Following the 1910 season, Cobb joined an All-Star team managed by Jimmy McAleer and selected to warm up Connie Mack's Philadelphia

Athletics for their World Series contest against the Chicago Cubs.[12] In addition, he received a $1,400 payday by Publisher John B. Townsend of the *Philadelphia Press* to provide expert coverage of the Series itself. With the experience of writing for the *Atlanta Journal* under his belt, Cobb took an active role in the creation of the articles and insisted that it was his voice represented, not the lone comments of a ghost writer. He would subsequently work with sportswriter George E. "Stoney" McLinn and translate his copious notes from each of the games into professional articles, syndicated to more than twenty newspapers. McLinn recalled that Cobb wasn't a "prima donna," and was "eager to cooperate." Cobb also contributed at least one article for the Metropolitan News Syndicate.[13]

On October 18 in Philadelphia, he was presented with his new Chalmers automobile for winning the batting title. He drove his car around the field at Shibe Park as the audience cheered. Lajoie, however, was unable to be present to receive his car.[14]

Before heading southward with his wife and son in his new Chalmers "30," Cobb took the opportunity to thank one of his most important mentors. Herman "Germany" Schaefer had been his teacher and friend for a number of years, and Cobb admitted, "If it were not for Schaefer's interest in me, I would not have made myself the ballplayer I am." Displaying his gratitude, he gave Schaefer his old automobile as a gift, and acknowledged the "many kindnesses" he exhibited through the years.[15]

Cobb agreed to participate in a best two-out-of-three heats auto race against his fellow Georgian, Nap Rucker, a pitcher for the Brooklyn National League franchise, at the Atlanta Speedway beginning on November 3, 1910.[16] But following the death of driver Al Livingstone at the same track, two days before, Tigers President Frank Navin wired an immediate termination of those plans. He was too concerned about Cobb's well-being to let the race occur, but Bill Nye, manager of the Speedway, lashed out at Cobb, claiming the latter had a "yellow streak" for pulling out. Nye also believed Cobb refused to drive because the money wasn't satisfactory. Cobb, of course, didn't take Nye's words sitting down and the two loudly argued.[17] The risk was unnecessary, Cobb concluded, and although he enjoyed the speed, there was no reason to jeopardize his life, especially with his wife pregnant with their second child. Incidentally, Cobb did do a few speed laps at the Indianapolis Raceway on April 4, 1911, in a National "40" roadster.[18]

A tour of Cuba's baseball fields was planned for the offseason, led by pitcher George Mullin and this time Cobb agreed to join his teammates.[19]

Sam Crawford, George Moriarty, Tom Jones, Charlie O'Leary, catcher Oscar Stanage, and even ex-Tiger Herman Schaefer took part in the 12-game series against the Habana and Almendares clubs.[20] Almost expectedly, Cobb was a late arrival to Havana, and his tardiness was blamed on business responsibilities.[21] Seven games had been recorded when he appeared for the contest against Almendares on November 27, and his assistance was badly needed. Offering a homer and two base hits, he led Detroit to a 4–0 win.[22] In fact, the Tigers prevailed in their last four of five games with Cobb in the lineup and were victorious in the overall series, 7–4–1.[23] Enormous crowds attended the games and Cobb's presence attributed to the great turnout. Cobb said that the series was "great sport" and that the Cubans played "good ball." He predicted that within two years, Cuba would be the "sporting center of the world." Cobb also came to the defense of the Tigers when a local Georgia paper gave an unfavorable critique of their performance. He said: "Detroit played rings around [the] Cubans and would have circled more but for their lack of condition. The Cubans could not beat our fourth league teams in this country in midseason when they are in practice, and we didn't have any trouble copping the series under adverse circumstances."[24]

Cobb batted a towering .370, but his average was behind three of his competitors, John Henry Lloyd (.500), Grant Johnson (.412), and Bruce Petway (.390), each an African American playing in Cuba to enhance the local squad. The color barrier in major league baseball prevented the integration of talented black players into the everyday ranks, and the Cuban series allowed Lloyd, Johnson, Petway, and Pete Hill—all members of Negro clubs in the United States—to display their skills against their white counterparts.[25] There was a measure of camaraderie during the games, even though, in Cobb's desire to perform well, he undoubtedly flashed his famous temperament. Regardless, Lloyd told the *New York Age* that Cobb and his teammates were "jolly good fellows on and off the field." It was believed that if ballots were circulated amongst white players, blacks would be admitted to the majors.[26]

Shortly after the holidays, the twenty-four-year-old Cobb was honored with his second "Honey Boy" Evans Trophy at Augusta's Grand Theater.[27] Spring training approached rapidly, and Jennings collected his players at the team's new Monroe, Louisiana, camp in early March 1911. Club management was rightfully concerned about Cobb's previous lack of interest in reporting anywhere on time and Navin sent him several letters expressing his anxieties. The gist of his correspondence was twofold, and he wanted Cobb to know that his failure to arrive and participate in training had a demoralizing effect on the team, similar to what was caused in 1910. Secondly, gate receipts for exhibitions were going to decrease measurably if he was not in the lineup. Southern fans, he felt, wanted to see their Southern baseball superstar.[28]

Navin directed Cobb to be in New Orleans for an exhibition on March 15, 1911, and Cobb respected his boss's wishes. His emergence in a Detroit uniform was a boon for ticket sales, but the Tigers were outgunned by the New Orleans club, losing 12–3.[29] The major feature of camp was the speculation and commentary of journalists as to the relations between Cobb and his teammates. The hubbub provided stirring content for excitable writers and everyone claimed to have insider awareness of Cobb's various feuds.[30] But the environment was topsy-turvy and even those really on the inside, including manager Hugh Jennings and George Moriarty, captain of the team, were perplexed by the seemingly unforgiving attitude of several players.

Things were evolving, however, and by the end of March, the tension appeared to be lifted. Doing his part, Cobb was putting forth an extraordinary effort to smooth things over and his bonds with Davy Jones were mended first.[31] Next, the walls separating him and Donie Bush were torn down, and, soon afterward, *Sporting Life* noted they were "best of friends."[32] Last but not least was Cobb's association with Sam Crawford, probably the most important player relationship on the team. The two superstars were locked into a mulish episode and neither wanted to be the first to give in. Despite their stubborn efforts to continue the rivalry, the two men began to exchange signals again on the field, and ultimately shook hands, demonstrative of the diminishing bad blood.[33]

The press also latched onto the gossip that Cobb was much slower than usual in his spring training performances, and, essentially, out of shape. Attributing comments to Detroit trainer Harry Tuthill, the *New York Daily Tribune* asserted that the outfielder had made "little progress" in three weeks of training, was feverish, and went forward to French Lick Springs in Indiana to receive medical help.[34] A revelation was made a few days later at Indianapolis and Cobb's alleged "slowness" was said to have been caused by his wearing of the "heaviest pair of shoes" he could find.[35] He was using the special footwear to build his leg muscles and improve his speed. He removed the weighted spikes and immediately began to display the old

Cobb rapidity. In Cincinnati, witnesses responded to the statements that he was slowing down as being the "stuff . . . dreams are made of."[36] He hadn't lost a step.

Opening the campaign with his preferred lineup, Jennings had Jones leading off followed by Bush, Cobb, and Crawford, and a fraternal spirit prevailed for the most part. Detroit took first place on the second day of the season and rampaged over its rivals, building up a nine-game advantage by mid-May.[37] The entire squad was collaborating and the Tigers often capitalized on opponents' mistakes to eke out wins. A prime example of the club's renewed energy came on April 30 against Cleveland when, down three runs in the ninth, Detroit stormed back and won the game. E. A. Batchelor of the *Detroit Free Press* summed it up by writing, "There never has been a more exciting game at Bennett Park." The 14,000 people in attendance agreed and it was Cobb's grounder at the finish that contributed to the result.[38]

Unburdened by the widespread presumption that he was only out for himself, Cobb was in tremendous form and his numbers skyrocketed. His actions on occasion were borderline unbelievable and a Detroit sportswriter, in the aftermath of Cobb's showing on May 12, said it was "the greatest individual exhibition ever given by a ball player." He scored three runs and drove in two during a 6–5 win over the New York Highlanders. The game was a streaming highlight reel for Cobb, as he made play after play in remarkable fashion. In the first inning, he astonished both teams and the crowd by running from first to home on a simple base hit by Crawford. Then in the seventh, he pulled off another stunner by stealing home on catcher Jeff Sweeney.[39] Batting better than .400, Cobb was headed toward the best season of his career and became, to this day, the youngest player to achieve 1,000 hits.[40]

But a year in the life of Ty Cobb was not fulfilled without a notable off-the-field happening and a bit of baseball controversy. On the evening of May 22, 1911, he was relaxing just outside the Hotel Pontchartrain in Detroit when he observed a man, later identified as nineteen-year-old John Miles, exhibiting a little too much interest in his Chalmers automobile. Seconds later, Miles was in the driver's seat and riding along Cadillac Square, making a hasty escape. Cobb, wearing his civilian attire, nimbly burst into a full stride, chasing down his car with fire in his eyes. Like something out of a modern-day action movie, he managed to hurdle himself into the auto while it was moving, turn off the engine, and proceeded to yank Miles out from behind the wheel. Police arrived within moments and arrested the thief. Cobb declined to press charges, but Miles was prosecuted anyway.[41]

A few weeks later, in Philadelphia, a particularly impassioned game rekindled the feud between Cobb and Frank Baker of the Athletics. The infamous incident of 1909 was thought to have been put well to rest, but in the sixth inning, after Cobb tried to steal third, members of the crowd cried foul. They vocalized their opinion that the Detroit player, once again, was out for blood in attempting to purposefully spike Baker. The *Philadelphia Inquirer* reported that Cobb's spikes touched Baker's hand in the slide, and the third baseman gave a "nice ladylike twist" to Cobb's foot in response.[42] The crowd was volcanic and a further eruption was possible. In the eighth, the exuberance of the Philadelphia audience elevated to its highest point with Cobb standing on third and looking to score. Real fireworks were about to begin.

Eddie Plank was on the mound at the time and he wanted to keep the demon of the paths hugged to the bag, so he tossed over to first. Cobb, in going back to the base, slid at Baker a second time and the two apparently made unavoidable contact. Baker was enraged by the maneuver, and tried to kick his adversary in the leg.[43] That aggression propelled Cobb into a state of fury, and the quarrel was seconds away from becoming a full-fledged duel when others stepped in to pull them apart. A segment of the crowd was incensed by the scuffle and threatened mob violence targeting Cobb. The danger was all too real, and once the game ended, Cobb was approached by a horde of angry individuals looking for some semblance of vengeance.

Appearing unruffled by the looming storm, he actually took steps toward his would-be assailants before being surrounded by teammates and police. Thousands of people were active in the chaotic display and, en route to waiting taxis, Detroit players carried bats as protection.[44] In depictions of the 1909 Baker spiking, for which Baker was blamed, writers have often alluded to a riot scene in its aftermath, which didn't occur in any shape or form.[45] It wouldn't be a stretch to believe that the 1909 incident and the ramifications of the 1911 event were somehow conjoined instead of remaining two, separate happenings. Cobb was indeed threatened by an unruly element of the Philadelphia baseball public, but it was still obvious he had many admirers in that city. It was apparent by the routine ovation he received each time he successfully made a hit.

July 4, 1911, saw the Tigers play Chicago in a doubleheader and by the end of the day, Cobb was emotionally drained. In the morning contest, he was silenced by Ed Walsh and his 40-game hit streak—the sixth longest in major league history—had ended. Cobb's achievement did establish a new American League record.[46] Detroit lost the match as well, 7–3. The second game was a lengthy battle, going 11 innings before the Tigers won, 11–10. But since Philadelphia swept their holiday games, they knocked the Tigers out of first place for the first time since April. Cobb dealt with an exceptionally abusive crowd at Bennett Park, and throughout the late innings of the second game he was battered by loud critics who seemed to delight in running him down. Tigers' players had a generally negative impression of Detroit fans. In this instance, fans were angry Cobb had not tried to snag a difficult drive by Chicago's Rollie Zeider in the eighth inning that ended up being a home run.[47] His limit of punishment was exceeded and he withdrew himself from the game in the 10th inning, simply unable to deal with the hateful taunts any longer.

The Tigers quickly regained first place, but Cobb was feeling the physical effects of his continuous superhuman effort. Suffering from a throbbing headache and a terrible cough, he was losing both sleep and weight.[48] He remained in the lineup to help his teammates in the pennant fight, and writers repeatedly made note of his outstanding play in spite of playing at less than a hundred percent. In fact, journalists joked about Cobb's so-called illness while he amazingly maintained an over .400 average and performed epic feats on the bases and in the field.[49] On top of that, he made three of what reporters called the "greatest catches" of his career during this time frame, two at Philadelphia on July 28, and the other against Chicago on August 12.[50] But in the midst of his gutsy endeavors, Detroit dropped into second place, and would remain there for the rest of the season. Conversely, the Athletics locked up the division lead and never gave it back. Philadelphia would win the American League pennant in 1911 with a 101–50 record.

"I have already stolen nearly as many bases and scored as many runs this season as I did all year in 1910," Cobb said in August. "I feel that the exertion has been too much for me. In only a few of the games in the east did I feel right."[51] Things were aggravated much worse at Boston after his prized bat was stolen in a mass rush of the field by spectators. He idiosyncratically believed the loss of his faithful weapon, a tool that had contributed greatly to his success all season, was going to propel him into a prolonged slump. Cobb offered a "liberal reward" for its return, and in the meantime, not only had to use an alternate bat but had to mentally cope with the superstitious notions such an adjustment caused, however irrational they were.[52]

The batting championship was on Cobb's mind, mostly because of his competitive sensibility, and he yearned to again finish first. His strongest challenger came in the form of twenty-four-year-old Joseph Jackson, nick-named "Shoeless Joe," a product of Pickens County, South Carolina. Three years earlier, the *Detroit Free Press* made references to Jackson following his major league debut for Philadelphia, going 1-for-4. It was mentioned that some Southern writers thought Jackson was "as good as Ty Cobb," which was a startling opinion.[53] Jackson's first full season was 1911, and he was living up to the hype. Now playing for Cleveland, he was learning much as an understudy of Nap Lajoie, but he wanted to bond with his fellow South-erner, Cobb. The two talked and Jackson inquired about Cobb's polished sliding abilities. The Georgian, without hesitation, agreed to teach Jackson what he knew and conveyed the optimal tricks of the hook slide.[54]

Cobb could plainly see that Jackson was somewhat star struck by him. Essentially a rookie, the Clevelander was a mighty ballplayer, but easily intimidated. A lack of education cut down dramatically on his reading and writing skills, and Cobb knew he could be manipulated without too much effort. As the competition for the batting title tightened, Cobb invoked a little mental warfare against Jackson, intending to get inside the head of his rival. He became condescending, sarcastic, and eventually started talking straight trash, all in the hopes that Jackson would collapse under the pres-sure.[55] Cobb's psychological advantage worked in the long run, and he ended up winning the title with a .420 average compared to Jackson's .408.

By posting additional major league leading numbers in hits (248), runs (147), RBIs (127), and stolen bases (83), he was the natural selection to win a second Chalmers auto. Unlike 1910, the award was not based strictly on batting figures, but all-round play on behalf of his team, making it essen-tially the first ever Most Valuable Player (MVP) designation for the major leagues. The newspaper writers making up the Chalmers Trophy Commis-sion were united in naming Cobb the victor.[56] American League President Ban Johnson questioned the unanimous decision, reminding the public that Cobb was fined and scolded by the National Baseball Commission for playing an unsanctioned game in New York in September. "Ty Cobb is a grand player," Johnson told the press, but then proceeded to mention how he "caused dissension" in the Tigers' ranks. His potent comments were accompanied by the partial headline "Ty is Overrated."[57]

The president of the league was entitled to his opinion, and Cobb undoubtedly withheld a vitriolic response. Short on time, the Georgian returned to his post as an expert pundit for the *Philadelphia Press* and a variety of syndicated newspapers covering the World Series. He watched as the Philadelphia Athletics won their second-straight championship, beating the New York Giants, four games to two. From there, he was off to rehearsals for his theatrical debut in the stage hit *The College Widow*, a comedy written years earlier by George Ade. Ever since 1907, producers had tried to coax Cobb to spend his winter on vaudeville, convinced his name and popularity would garner impressive money at the box office. He turned the prospects down, but relented to Cleveland's Vaughan Glaser after his longtime friend offered a nice guarantee.[58]

Surrounding Cobb with the attractive nineteen-year-old lead actress Sue MacManamy, who was relatively new to the stage, and a horde of unique characters, Glaser, as manager and producer, launched the play on October 30, 1911, at the Taylor Opera House in Trenton, New Jersey. "Shoeless" Joe Jackson was initially supposed to join Cobb, but backed out at the last minute.[59] Sports editor Marvin A. Riley of the *Trenton Evening Times* was in attendance, and said Cobb made a "credible performance" as an actor. He commented on the loud and positive reactions of the audience to his actions, and it was evident that Cobb overcame the normal jitters to remember his lines.[60] Many people were surprised by his composure throughout his performance as Billy Bolton, the star football halfback at the fictitious Atwater College. As the story went, "Bolton" was planning to transfer to rival Bingham but the "College Widow" intervened to keep his allegiance firm.[61]

The play featured a bit of intimacy between Cobb and his leading lady, and climaxed in a major football scene. Theaters as spelled below were lined up down the East Coast and across the South before heading to Detroit, Chicago, and Cleveland. "I don't know much about it yet," he told the press early in the run, "but I'm learning fast. So far I am about as enthusiastic as anybody could be. Things have gone pretty good for us. The people seem to like our show and they don't seem to dislike me as an actor."[62] Cobb did have his critics along the way and the highbrow sect of the theater probably looked down their nose at his amateur thespian abilities. But others simply appreciated his efforts. "Ty is a good actor, because he acts naturally," a writer for the *Cleveland Press* stated, and in many towns, the crowd demanded a curtain speech.[63]

Detroit spectators bided their time before celebrating the arrival of Cobb and his troupe in mid-December. He was excited about it as well,

sending out invitations to local buddies for his December 23 performance at the Lyceum Theater. After the second act, he was beckoned to
say a few words, but was interrupted from the crowd by teammate Bill
Donovan. Donovan met Cobb on stage, and the two embraced in a handshake, then "Wild Bill" proceeded to give Cobb a special gift on behalf of
his friends. It was a traveling bag, "full of base hits," Donovan explained,
and the contributors to the present included Frank Navin, Bill Yawkey,
Harry Tuthill, Eddie Cicotte, H. G. Salsinger. E. A. Batchelor, and teammates Davy Jones and Sam Crawford.[64]

"The reception given me by my Detroit friends [was] one of the most
satisfying things of my whole career," Cobb told a reporter. "This actor's life
isn't exactly the round of pleasure that some people's fancy may paint it.
The hardest thing about it, to my mind, is the fact that a man can't get his
regular sleep. When I go home after the evening performance, it is impossible to go right to sleep like I would do in the summer months, for I am all
keyed up and under a nervous strain. The stage is very well in its way, but
there is nothing about it so pleasant to me as the satisfaction of slamming
out a nice, clean hit."[65]

His eyes strained by theater lights, Cobb cut short the breadth of the
tour in January 1912, and admitted, "I am more fatigued right now than I
ever was at the end of the baseball season."[66] The tour was expected to continue until March 1912. Cobb told one reporter, "I think that a man needs
a vacation."[67] The curtain closed on *The College Widow* in Cleveland and
Cobb pined for a speedy return to his family in Detroit, where they were
spending the winter. The June before, Charlie had given birth to their second child, Shirley Marion Cobb, and Ty enjoyed a much needed rest in the
comfort of his loved ones.[68] He was a perpetual mover by heart, though,
and his time recuperating from his arduous schedule was brief. Soon, he
was seeking out new hobbies like bowling and iceboating, and in January
1912, he joined the Michigan Sovereign Consistory, a branch of Freemasonry, in Detroit. Having already joined the Order at Royston several years
before, he was welcomed as a thirty-second degree mason in a ceremony at
the Moslem Temple.[69]

The offseason gave Cobb time to contemplate the comings and goings of
the American League, particularly roster changes around the circuit. He

read varied baseball publications to get the scoop on promising recruits and immersed himself in the statistics of rivaling teams, essentially giving him the intelligence he needed as to which players were heating up or slowing down in their careers. It wasn't that he was just randomly inquisitive, but plotting a legitimate psychological blueprint for the upcoming season. In fact, ever since becoming a major leaguer, he'd kept a mental database of opposing players and became highly adept at knowing their weaknesses and routines. He found that such information played perfectly into his line of attack, consisting of skill, a set of theories, and working the percentages.

The combination was lethal. Cobb's intrinsic understanding of "enemy" limitations was astoundingly beneficial. He knew which players were poor throwers, which were high-strung and easily flustered, and those who were caught in a wicked slump. Beyond that, he went out of his way to garner certain inside information about rivals who were battling illnesses or mentally exhausted by engaging in small talk with players on other teams, intending to use a mixture of all the "dope" to gain an advantage.[70] He'd often pass off incorrect data about one of his teammates to fool the opposition, as well. Meaning, he'd customize his offensive approach specifically because of the players in the field before him. If a rookie was at third base, for example, Cobb was more likely to bunt in that direction because he felt the percentages were better for him to get to first safely. The recruit was more apt to boot, bobble, or toss the ball wildly than a hardened veteran.

Cobb analyzed baseball religiously in his free time and studied the habits of his peers. He took real notice of the way they responded to his movements, working to improve his chances for success. As one might expect, Cobb's rivals regularly established a reactionary plan to his off-beat style, planning out layered resistance to combat his techniques. But when the defense felt they had Cobb solved, he switched up his attack plan and did something a little different. His desire was to always keep opponents guessing to what his next move was going to be, and the concept worked solidly for years.

Depending on the circumstances, Cobb wasn't above using tricks to triumph in a ball game. He was occasionally known to fake an injury to his leg, limping to sell the handicap, only to erupt into a full stride and score a pivotal run in the same contest. He'd kick up clouds of dust to obscure the vision of umpires, run in the line of thrown balls, and if given the chance, he'd punt the ball out of infielders' glove. Cobb pulled one of his infamous stunts during a game against Chicago on April 30 when he slid into a ball laying on the base path, kicking it off the diamond, and then ran home to score a winning run in the 10th inning. White Sox players claimed it was a deliberate interference, while Tigers supporters said it was an accident. The umpire agreed with the latter and the score counted.[71] The legendary hidden ball trick wasn't out of the realm of possibility either. Later in the decade, while playing first base against the Chicago White Sox, he performed the deception following a meeting at the mound with his pitcher. Cobb casually returned to his position with the ball under his arm, and then tagged out runner Joe Benz when he eased off the bag.[72] These stunts were textbook Cobb and took many shapes and forms throughout his tenure in baseball.

The psychological game was a huge asset to Cobb and he went to great lengths to get into the heads of opposing players. Rivals were frequently demoralized by his clever base-running and left to wonder how in the world they were going to stop him. Notably, one of his principal concepts was based on the notion that certain aggressive maneuvers not only worked to serve a purpose in the current game he was playing, but that it would have a lasting mental effect on opponents in subsequent games as well. It applied greatly to running the bases, he felt, and the threat of stealing was remembered by adversaries regardless if he intended to follow up with a second attempt or not. Thus, it caused a disturbance and played right into his hands. The propaganda surrounding his so-called sharpened spikes created another level of intimidation entirely, and infielders psyched out by the allegations were left rattled.

Going into the 1912 season, there were rumors of a nearly complete team aversion to Hugh Jennings continuing as manager of the Tigers. Cobb publicly denied this, claiming the internal dissension was limited to a few individuals.[73] He was unenthusiastic about attending spring training camp in Monroe, Louisiana, and agreed to meet the team a few weeks later in New Orleans. In the meantime, he visited relatives in Georgia and participated in a game Royston had against nearby Elberton. With Cobb in the box, Royston was victorious, 7–0.[74] Before the end of March, he was alongside his Detroit teammates battling through an exhibition schedule, but the team appeared sluggish. Cobb was on his way to regaining his batting eye when he developed a cold in Toledo, Ohio. Suffering from a fever, sore throat and relentless cough, he was severely weakened, but still determined to start the season in the lineup.

At Cleveland on Opening Day, he was held hitless in four at-bats in the opener, and the Tigers lost a heartbreaker in eleven innings, 3–2.[75] From there, he had a few painful mishaps in the first couple of games, including a foul tip off his leg, a hit-by-pitch, and a rib injury. These added to his persistent illness and only served to frustrate him all the more. By the time Detroit reached Chicago early on April 15, he needed a thorough rest before that afternoon's game. All he wanted was peace and quiet, but unfortunately, his room at the Chicago Beach Hotel gave him a constant barrage of excruciating train sounds from the nearby tracks of the Illinois Central Railroad. Cobb protested to hotel management for another room, but after feeling dismissed by a hotel clerk, he began to flash signs of his famous temper and the Chicago Beach Hotel banned Cobb after the incident.[76]

The clerk worked to pacify Cobb, telling him that he could give him another room later in the day, but only if he kept it secret from his teammates as new rooms couldn't be offered to everyone. Additionally, the Tigers agreed to send him to another hotel, but Cobb stubbornly declined to move unless the entire team left. He didn't want to appear a prima donna, but after Cobb departed Chicago that night to return to Detroit for medical attention from his private physician, press reports spun the story to do just that. Sensationalistic headlines claimed he "quit" the Tigers because he didn't like his room and any mention of his prolonged illness was minimized.[77]

The grand opening of the brand new Navin Field, a modern steel and concrete structure, captivated Detroit baseball fans and Cobb did his best to recuperate in time to participate in the April 20 game. Seeing how important it was to the franchise, he not only appeared but pulled his superstar magic against Cleveland. In the first inning, he combined with Sam Crawford to pull the double steal twice and the second time he safely went home in a mad dash for the plate. He went 2-for-4 and had a pair of terrific defensive plays, giving the energetic audience of 26,000 a thrill in a 6–5 victory.[78] The next day, pitcher George Kahler nearly came to blows with Cobb after a mix-up around first base. As the *Detroit Free Press* noted, Cobb was perfectly willing to oblige the twenty-two-year-old, but the umpire prevented any fisticuffs.[79]

Already with signs of controversy and his inglorious fighting spirit in full view, Cobb was in rare form. Detroit was clearly not a championship caliber squad in 1912, but they had the ability to impact the pennant race by knocking around those at the top of the first division. Headed into its first eastern swing, the Tigers were much more unified than sportswriters believed, and the alleged internal dissension was not going to prove a hindrance to the team's success. In fact, going into New York, club unity was going to be tested more than any team in baseball history and the players were going to come together for the sake of one man, backing him to the fullest. That man was Ty Cobb, and he'd once again be at the center of a hailstorm of contention.

9

BRAWLS AND STRIKES

The rapport between audiences and baseball players was unique during the early twentieth century and much more personal than it is today. It wasn't uncommon for members of the bleacher section or grandstand to engage in a running dialogue with athletes on the field and the mood of the discussion ranged from comedic to vicious. Players bantered back and forth with crowds throughout a game and everyone had a hearty laugh. But there were instances when the conversation turned highly sarcastic and then crossed the line to vulgarity, leaving innocent patrons of stadiums—many with families—shocked and bewildered. Big league ballplayers were without question supposed to maintain a professional stance and ignore the profane spectators, but occasionally, things spiraled out of control.

Ty Cobb was long a target of crowd focus. Since becoming one of the most heralded athletes in the game, he was keenly watched by spectators regardless if he was standing idly in the outfield, at the plate, or even walking down the street. Many die-hard fans were fascinated by the aura of Cobb and treated him like royalty. Sportswriters were equally enthralled, often calling him the "greatest ball player" of the age, and lauding his great feats on the diamond through their written word. There was a special mystique about Cobb that separated him from other players in baseball, and the years of success and controversies only served to feed into the legend that surrounded him.

By 1912, the majority of the public had accepted Cobb as the sport's premier athlete, but with that there were certain expectations. For one, he was counted on to pull his superman act during every game he played, which was, realistically, impossible. When fans in circuit towns bought tickets to see their home team play Detroit, they figured Cobb was a lock for some type of dramatic display. He was always good for a bit of offensive splendor combined with a shade of base-running that was majestically achieved despite all odds. He was undoubtedly a boon to ticket sales all around the American League and fans, in recognizing his standout performances, routinely applauded his efforts. But when Cobb was having an average day or worse yet, in a funk, fans rapidly turned against him. There were boos, jeers, and hissing from all corners of the audience, and Cobb was forced to withstand a bombardment of negativity.

The Frank Baker incident in Philadelphia years earlier spurred on waves of backlash and Cobb was at the center of a massive rise in public abhorrence. But the venom dissipated in short time and the respect paid Cobb by grandstand spectators eventually overruled any disorder emitting from the bleachers. Other episodes were similarly handled by baseball fans, meaning that there was usually an initial uproar to an action by Cobb and a certain amount of criticism but it would generally fade fast and he was again given the respect his superlative play deserved. In essence, Cobb was loved and hated by the masses for different reasons at different times. Fans enjoyed their freedom in goading him, realizing that he was temperamental, but for the price of admission, it was well worth it to give him a little ribbing. After all, it was interaction with a true baseball superstar.

"The kidding did an awful lot to spur me on to greater efforts," Cobb explained. "Those fellows in the stands were telling me that I was a false alarm and a joke and that I wasn't even a good bush leaguer, really were friends in disguise because their joshing always made me try to show them the errors of their opinion. Ordinary spoofing by the fans was all right. It acted as an incentive for me."[1]

Cobb took much of the teasing in stride. His spring training appearances after his early 1908 holdout caused some fervor, for instance, and one of his admirers in Memphis sarcastically referred to his exorbitant salary request by yelling, "The $5,000 beauty, eh? Strike him out!"[2] Fans in Cleveland pestered him unmercifully during the 1910 Chalmers automobile competition, convinced that their own, Nap "Larry" Lajoie, was going to prevail. One rambunctious spectator told Cobb, following a strikeout, "You can be Larry's chauffeur!"[3] Cobb's thin skin thickened as years passed and a genial smile in response to the taunts quickly defused the weight of whatever was being said. From time to time, he'd give a little bow or doff his cap in acknowledgment of the clamoring and devotees were simultaneously enraged and overjoyed by his reply. But there were also times that Cobb wasn't able to gesture jokingly and laugh it off.

The early going of the 1912 campaign was decidedly irritating to Cobb and, during a heated series against the Highlanders in New York, his temper flared. He bickered with third baseman Cozy Dolan in the opener and was the recipient of howls from jokers behind the Detroit dugout for three-straight days.[4] The fourth and final game was played on Wednesday, May 15, and the loud antagonists were again in attendance. From the moment Cobb stepped onto the field, they made their presence known and it was nearly impossible for anyone around the third base line to ignore their colorful language.[5] In the second inning, to make matters worse, Cobb bobbled a base hit by Dolan and opened the floodgates for his tormentors to ridicule him. The mistake flushed Cobb with anger, but he didn't respond outwardly.

In the midst of the unruly crew was one man in particular, Claude Lucker (Claudian Northrup Lucker), a thirty-one-year-old law clerk originally from South Carolina.[6] Cobb recognized him as someone who'd picked on him in previous trips to New York and felt he was the main agitator. In fact, he told Lucker the summer before to go elsewhere with his wicked commentary because he (Cobb) was "only human" and saw "no justice" in the way he was treating him.[7] Nonetheless, Lucker and his associates were amused by the spectacle and kept up their shenanigans. Cobb was slowly losing his cool, but instead of immediately flying off the handle, he did two proactive things to avoid trouble. For one, he remained in the outfield when his team was at bat one inning because he knew he wasn't due up. Thus, he didn't have to walk by the hooligans and hear further abuse.

Additionally, after the third inning, he walked toward the New York dugout looking for a representative of Highlanders' management, hoping to get Lucker tossed out. No one was found, and Cobb returned to the Tigers' bench. As he made his way over to prepare for the top of the fourth, he received yet another barrage of comments, including one statement calling him a "half-nigger."[8] In reaction, Cobb later said, "Something seemed to snap within me. A blind, unreasoning fury engulfed me. Just what happened in the next two or three minutes I know only from hearsay, because from the moment that I lost absolute control of my temper, I remember nothing until I was climbing back into the field. But spectators saw me hurdle into the bleachers, seek out the tormentor and pummel him."[9]

Of course, the tormentor on the receiving end of the ballplayer's wrath was Lucker. Cobb sprung into the crowd and rushing toward the man in the alpaca coat sitting in the third row.[10] He didn't waste any time and there were no words, apologies, or threats of suspension that could have shaken him from his path. In tow were members of the Detroit ballclub, all of whom were carrying bats, and on a specific mission to protect Cobb from any outside interference. They wanted him to get revenge on his verbose enemy and Cobb, completely overcome with rage, unleashed a blistering assault.

"He let out with his fist and caught me on the forehead, over the left eye," Lucker explained after the incident. "You can see the big lump over there now. I was knocked over and then he jumped me. He spiked me in the left leg and kicked me in the side. Then he booted me behind the left ear. While I was down and Cobb was kicking me someone in the crowd shouted, 'Don't kick him. He is a cripple and has no hands!' Then I heard Cobb say: 'I don't care if the ***** has no feet!' I was pretty well bruised up and covered with blood when Cobb was through with me."[11]

Prior to the attack, Cobb had no idea that Lucker had suffered the loss of one hand and three fingers from his other in a newspaper press accident. It wasn't until he got up close that he noticed Lucker's right hand in his pocket, and Cobb worried that the man was going to withdraw a gun.[12] So he struck hard and fast, quickly gaining the advantage in what was a one-sided fight. Patrons yelled and strained to get a better view of the amazing sight, as police and umpires worked to regain order. Cobb was tossed from the game but remained in the dugout until the seventh inning, when he emerged to walk across the diamond to the clubhouse. The *Detroit Free Press* reported that "fully 80 percent" of the audience "cheered and clapped" for him, an unusual display in light of what happened.[13]

"I am exceedingly sorry that this happened," Cobb said afterward. "I know that the publicity I will receive will be extremely distasteful to my wife and family and it is of them I am thinking. I think the provocation was sufficient to justify my action, no matter how much I may regret the encounter."[14]

The awareness of the fact that Cobb was goaded into action prevented an all-out blitz by the New York audience and probably stopped what normally would have been a full-scale riot. Cobb wasn't ripped to shreds by the press in subsequent days, and instead, a dialogue was opened about a culture of rowdyism toward players by obscene spectators.[15] The lack of security at the Highlanders' Hilltop Park was not only blasted for the relentless verbal attack on Cobb, but for a violent barrage of bottles thrown at umpire

"Silk" O'Loughlin a few days earlier.[16] Cleveland pundit Henry P. Edwards put the onus on President Ban Johnson to "take the lead in having these abusive spectators squelched in some manner, by removal from the parks, if necessary," all in effort to ensure the purity of baseball.[17]

Johnson's priority at the time, needless to say, wasn't a universal league edict protecting players from overbearing fans, but essentially figuring out a way to deal with Cobb. He couldn't abide players jumping into the crowd to fight enthusiasts no matter the reasoning and issued an indefinite suspension the next day.[18] For those who were pro-Cobb, the punishment was harsher than anticipated. They felt a fine was better served, primarily because of the extenuating circumstances, and considered Johnson's summary banishment, without an investigation and hearing, unjust. Cobb agreed wholeheartedly. He wanted his version of the story officially on the record and opposed any form of reprimand prior to a thorough inquiry.[19] Nineteen members of the Detroit Tigers, including many guys who were rumored to be at odds with Cobb at one time or another, stood by his side, and threatened to strike if he wasn't reinstated immediately.[20]

Although Johnson disciplined Cobb precipitously, he went forward with an investigation and planned to announce a further decision with regard to his playing status. In the interim, the Tigers went to Philadelphia for a game on May 17 and Cobb watched from the stands as his mates beat the Athletics, 6–3.[21] But once it was determined that his suspension wasn't going to be lifted, the entire Tigers roster followed through with their threat and went on strike in unprecedented fashion. They adjourned to the upper pavilion and watched a make-shift squad of nine amateurs, two former professionals, and Hugh Jennings face the Athletics on May 18. Jennings had little other choice but to quickly form the replacement team to avoid massive fines because of forfeiture, and his unit was battered by Philadelphia, 24–2.[22]

The baseball world was in a state of turmoil and newspaper writers could barely keep up with all the various points of view. Cobb was vigorously defended by his friends in both Detroit and Georgia, and former Washington Senators manager Joe Cantillon said he would have done the same thing in response to a raucous fan.[23] White Sox owner Charles Comiskey was more subdued in his reaction, telling a reporter that players had always been subjected to the kind of abuse Cobb suffered, going back to when he was active, decades earlier. "It seems to be a part of the game," Comiskey added.[24] *The Sporting News*, in an editorial, opposed the players' strike, calling it Cobb's "Rebellion," and likened the star athlete to Caesar, asserting that he be "dealt with" for the sake of Organized Baseball.[25]

Cobb was humbled by the support he received from his Tigers teammates, but the situation as a whole, he felt, wasn't one of vanity or to protect his reputation.[26] He saw it as an opportunity to force change in the way that all players across the majors were treated by fans. On May 20, he convinced his fellow players to return to the field, illustrating his concern for their future in baseball plus the interests of owner Frank Navin, and successfully put an end to their hiatus. The next day, the real Detroit team played at Washington and won, 2–0. Cobb, however, remained suspended through May 25 as Johnson's punishment ultimately lasted ten days. He was handed a $50 fine and the controversy was seemingly put to bed as players and writers returned their focus to the 1912 pennant race.[27]

There was a serious residual complexity stemming from the onslaught of Lucker, one that put Cobb's well-being in jeopardy. The *New York Sun* reported in July, ahead of Detroit's first series in the city since the incident, that associates of the Sirocco Gang were seeking revenge for the damage inflicted on their friend.[28] Additionally, Cobb was privately warned by a reliable informant of potential danger, and the combination of sources only fueled his concern. Heeding the words of caution, he took "certain means" to safeguard himself, presumably by carrying a firearm.[29] Extra police were on hand when the Tigers played the Highlanders at the Hilltop on July 9, and a Detroit report, instead of commenting on a rain of disapproval, stated, "No player ever received [a] greater ovation" than Cobb.[30] Apparently the fans forgave Cobb's indiscretions.

A few months later, an incident in Detroit caused some to wonder whether New York goons were going to great lengths to extract vengeance. This happened on an August evening, and Cobb was initially en route to the train station to meet up with teammates for a late night excursion to Syracuse, New York, to play an exhibition match up. Driving along Trumbull Street with Charlie by his side, he was beckoned to stop by three half-drunken and disorderly men. "Thinking that I might have hit somebody, I did so and got out of the machine," Cobb explained. He quickly ascertained from the disposition of the trio that trouble was ahead, and yearned to get back into his vehicle and leave. But the men instigated a physical conflict and Cobb had no choice but to defend himself and his wife.

Cobb added: "I sailed in and as I did so, two of the men recognized me and made no effort to fight. In fact, they tried to stop the row, but I wasn't going to let the fellow who had hit me get away without something in return, so I gave him a whipping, and I reckon beat him up pretty badly. At any rate, after I had knocked him down, he reached over my shoulder and inflicted a slight wound in my back with a knife, hardly more than a scratch. This was the only hurt I received. All of the men apologized to me and the one that I had whipped got down on his knees trying to square things. I got back into my machine, reassured Mrs. Cobb, who was badly frightened, and went on down to the depot, where I took the train with the rest of the boys."[31]

Receiving a wound a quarter of an inch deep in his upper back, near his shoulder, Cobb was not seriously injured. Upon arriving in Syracuse, he was treated by a physician at the Yates Hotel, and given two stitches. But since he departed Detroit shortly after the attack, no official police report was filed, nor did anyone know who his attackers were. Venturing to guess, Cobb said, "There is no connection between this fracas and the trouble that I had in New York in May, so far as I know."[32] It was later revealed that Cobb quarreled with a newsboy named "Scabby" over a craps game in the clubhouse of the Tigers sometime prior to the attack. Cobb concluded that his assailants were associates of the newsboy and, outside the Ste. Claire Hotel in Detroit, he found "Scabby" and "gave him a beating."

On the field, Cobb was having another banner year. He garnered 14 hits in 19 plate appearances during two doubleheaders at Philadelphia in July, but sportswriter Jim Nasium complained that Ty was stepping forward out of the batter's box while swinging at the ball against Philadelphia pitchers, thus, gaining an advantage.[33] Things didn't change much through the remainder of the season and Cobb finished with a .409 average, leading the majors once again. With 226 hits, he tied "Shoeless" Joe Jackson, but his 61 stolen bases were distinctively less than the leader, Clyde Milan of the Senators, who set a new American League record with 88. Notably, Cobb topped the majors in being caught stealing 34 times. As a team, the Tigers won only 69 games and it marked the lowest win-total since Cobb had been with the club. Detroit finished in sixth place and was more than 36 games out of first when the season concluded.[34]

Even before the end of the 1912 campaign, rumors widely circulated that Cobb was seeking a new three-year contract from Navin at $15,000 per annum. While Cobb acknowledged that he was looking for a raise from his previous salary, he denied the new amount reported by the press. Nevertheless, his request of $12,000 made Navin wince and recoil.[35] Citing a bad financial year as a result of the poor performance of his team, the Tigers' owner was not only going to reject the salary demands of Cobb, but Sam Crawford as well. "The Detroit baseball club is not the Standard Oil Company," he exclaimed. "I know what we can pay Ty without bankrupting the club and I do not intend to go any higher."[36]

Cobb believed his high-level of success warranted a raise and decided to play a psychological card in his negotiations by mentioning a series of financial opportunities that would take him away from the game of baseball. "If the club will not meet my terms," he said, "I will stay out of the game for I have several propositions that look attractive and believe that I can make a lot of money outside of the diamond." One of the most lucrative job offerings called for him to purchase cotton in southern states for a New York corporation at $10,000 a year.[37] His love of baseball was well-established, but the salary question was fast becoming a matter of principle, and since Navin appeared unmovable on the subject, a lengthy holdout was guaranteed. Cobb put the debate out of his mind and took his family to Augusta for the winter. In early 1913, he joined the always colorful Rube Waddell for a hunting trip in Kentucky.

To strengthen his conditioning, Cobb formed an All-Georgia barnstorming squad, teaming with, at times, Nap Rucker, Tommy McMillan, Ducky Holmes, and a majority of amateurs. On March 24, his team was trounced by Brooklyn, 7–1, in Augusta, and a few days later, they were also defeated by Atlanta.[38] The series of embarrassing losses were made even worse when Cobb's nine was topped by a rural outfit of collegians and locals at Anderson, South Carolina. The losses, combined with being a full-fledged holdout at odds with his club, undoubtedly made Cobb much edgier than usual. A baggage handler in Athens, Georgia, felt his wrath over a petty amount of money due to stow his dog on a train headed for Royston. Cobb went too far by threatening the worker, but the latter, unconcerned, was said to have reached for a "lump" in his pocket, apparently a weapon, and got Cobb to back down.[39]

All things considered, it wasn't surprising that Cobb's temper flared again during the barnstorming tour, but his row with a collegiate player in South Carolina was risky and could've ended in bloodshed of the worst kind. On April 5, 1913, his team appeared in Spartanburg to face Wofford College on their home grounds. The exhibition was exceptionally heated, despite its inconsequentiality, and Cobb was determined more than ever to win. At one juncture, he slammed into a rival player standing in the baseline and sent him to the dirt in a heap. Garnering two hits and two stolen bases, he led his team to victory, 9–8. But during the ninth inning, he had a few cross words for Rutledge Osborne, an eighteen-year-old second baseman for Wofford.[40]

Osborne was not necessarily large for his age, but was an athlete of local repute. He'd soon captain his school's football team and star at quarterback. He was also a member of the South Carolina National Guard and not the kind of guy to be easily intimidated. That was confirmed when he let Cobb know that he disapproved of his roughhouse tactics, shouting from the coaches' box while the major leaguer was on the mound. Cobb was offended, of course, by the audacity of the youngster and told him to quiet down. He then offered to settle matters after the game. But as the final out was recorded, Osborne's friends and police swarmed the field and prevented any impromptu boxing.[41]

It was a coincidence that Cobb's aggregation and the Wofford squad were headed to Greenville, South Carolina, the following Monday, for both teams were booked to play Furman University. Osborne, according to his statement, heard through the grapevine that Cobb was still looking to resolve their differences and packed a loaded .32 caliber revolver in his luggage for the Greenville trip. As expected, Cobb confronted him, coaxed him into a second floor room at the hotel and proceeded to strike the first blow. Osborne withdrew his weapon, only to have it yanked away by one of Cobb's teammates and suffered a severe beating.[42] Another side of the story claimed Osborne was mouthing off at the hotel, looking for a fight, and that Cobb didn't resort to physicality until the pistol was revealed. Either way, Cobb brawling with a teenager, regardless of the reason, didn't exactly fit the expected character of the nation's top ballplayer.

Spring training for the Tigers went on at Gulfport, Mississippi, without Cobb and Navin held firm in denying any boost in salary for the 1913 season. The ramifications of his absence were felt at the box office and sportswriters continued to wonder who would crack first, the stubborn player or owner. Navin was empowered by the theory that he was acting in the interests of all major league owners by refusing such a huge monetary demand, figuring it would set a precedent that would corrupt baseball.[43] "Mr. Cobb did not make baseball," Navin said venomously, "baseball made him. He has grown to believe that his greatness precludes his being a subject to discipline. In the past I have patiently put up with a great deal from Cobb. It has now reached a point where there must be a showdown."[44]

Bound to the Tigers via the reserve clause (which tied him to the team regardless if he signed a contract or not; effectively, it meant Detroit "owned" his services), Cobb was more anxious than Navin in the argument and when Detroit kicked off the season on April 10, their star center fielder was not on the bench with his teammates. The National Commission suspended Cobb for his failure to appear and a tense situation greatly escalated. Cobb's plight received nationwide publicity and it wasn't long before he was bolstered by congressional support from Senator Hoke Smith and Representative Thomas Hardwick of Georgia. Looking to ascertain whether Organized Baseball restricted free trade and violated the laws of the Sherman Antitrust Act, Smith asked to read Cobb's contract and the latter mailed the document to Washington, DC for review.[45] *The Sporting News* reported that baseball leaders welcomed an inquiry, seemingly blasé about the threat.[46] But behind closed doors, owners seethed because it was the last thing they wanted.

A funny thing was happening between Navin and Cobb . . . a game of sorts. Navin mulishly refused to reach out to Cobb and Cobb wouldn't go to Detroit to meet with the owner until he was specifically asked. Vaughan Glaser, producer of Cobb's stage debut in *The College Widow* and a friend of both men, realized this was the nonsensical obstacle standing in the way of resolution. He quickly prompted Navin to message Cobb, asking him to Detroit, and after the magnate did, Cobb dropped everything and immediately ventured northward from Georgia.[47] Within two days, Cobb was in the budding "Motor City," and only an hour of negotiation was needed before a new contract was to be signed. The terms were not disclosed, other than it was a one-year deal, and there was contentment all around. Navin happily declared, "The war is over!"[48]

Cobb returned to the field on special permission of baseball authorities and was officially given a clean slate by the National Commission with a full reinstatement on May 1. His fine amounted to $50.[49] By that time, the Tigers were already being put through the ringer. They'd lost nine-straight between April 22 and May 3, and dropped to seventh in the league. Many roster changes had altered the look of the team, including the arrival of left fielder Bobby Veach, infield sensation Oscar Vitt, and pitcher Jean Dubuc the year before. Amongst the other stalwarts were Hugh High, Del Gainer, and George "Hooks" Dauss, and the base of veterans George Moriarty, Oscar Stanage, Sam Crawford, and Donie Bush, who were still the heart of the club. However, it was obvious that Cobb was needed to give the Tigers any kind of real competitive edge.

Unfortunately, Cobb was unable to carry the team into the first division in 1913 and he struggled along with his own set of problems, beginning with eye trouble only days into the season. In July, he was spiked on his right knee trying to steal second by Buck Weaver of the White Sox, leaving a deep wound. The injury became slightly infected and he was sent to the sidelines to recuperate.[50] Adding a further complication, his back was in poor shape and causing him plenty of pain. On July 12, Hugh Jennings placed the weakened Cobb on second base and the Georgian's performance was anything but spectacular. E. A. Batchelor of the *Detroit Free Press* was usually kind to Cobb, but he had to call things as he saw them, and simply wrote that Cobb "proved beyond question that he [was] the worst second baseman living or dead." He committed three errors in five chances and Detroit fans energetically hooted and hollered at his expense.[51]

Trade gossip involving Cobb circulated heavily during the summer and, after the negative expression of his home audience, he was agreeable to a transfer, perhaps to either New York or Boston. Paul Hale Bruske wrote that he felt Detroit enthusiasts would be accepting of a trade and confirmed the diminishing of his local popularity.[52] Fervent newspapermen prophesized that Cobb was either headed to Chicago in a deal for Hal Chase, sold to Washington for $100,000, or headed to Boston. Cobb responded to an August rumor that he was sold to New York for $40,000, saying, "It is the first I've heard of it, but I surely hope it is true."[53]

The batting race between Cobb and "Shoeless" Joe Jackson was exciting all season. At one point in June, both men were hitting over .430 in an astronomical display of offensive firepower. The *Cleveland Leader*, in an effort to write off Cobb, mentioned that he was not particularly impressive during a recent series and had "lost some of his old-time pepper."[54] But despite missing 31 games, he rallied at just the right times to ultimately lead the majors in batting average, finishing with a .390, 17 points ahead of Jackson. His other statistics suffered because of his inactivity. In fact, Cobb's 167 hits, 70 runs, and 67 RBIs were the lowest he'd achieved since 1906, his first full season in the big leagues. As for the Tigers, they ended the year in sixth place with a 66–87 record, a depressing 30 games behind the Philadelphia Athletics.

Twenty-three-year-old Oscar Vitt, at season's end, made a few pointed comments in the press about Cobb. He asserted that Cobb was, as he had been suspected in earlier years, working the solo game instead of playing for the team.[55] Cobb responded to the comments, saying: "Such a charge is ridiculous. I should think Vitt might help the team if he would accumulate a little better individual average and not attack his fellow players."[56] Vitt batted .240 in 1913. This wasn't the first time a report attributed to Vitt made mention of Cobb. In February 1913, Vitt allegedly claimed Navin was tinkering with the salaries of Detroit players, working to cut where he could because he wanted to ensure Cobb got the $15,000 he demanded. Such an accusation made Cobb look bad in the eyes of his teammates, and wasn't factually accurate. Vitt and Cobb were at odds and not speaking, stemming from several previous arguments. Cobb, as usual, had wanted to fight Vitt, but the much smaller infielder backed off and Oscar Stanage stepped in to shield him from any of Cobb's aggression.[57]

Frank Navin listened to the nonstop hullabaloo regarding Cobb's status with the Tigers and probably chuckled to himself. He certainly entertained hypothetical trade possibilities, but he had no real intention of making a deal unless he received two or three top stars in return. He wasn't going to waste time dickering with owners over his superstar and during the 1913 World Series in New York, he met privately with Cobb to discuss business. The meeting was fruitful. They verbally agreed to a two-year contract calling for a base salary of $11,250, plus another $3,750 in bonuses ($15,000 total).[58] The arrangement put to rest the notion that Cobb was going to play for any team other than the Tigers. Cobb, in response to his public declarations of wanting to be traded, clearly emphasized that he didn't want to leave Detroit and was completely happy with both management and the fans. It was a necessary public relations move.

The emergence of the Federal League in 1913 significantly jolted major league owners, and not since the American League challenged the authority of the established National League in 1901 had an independent entity caused so much concern. Reinforced by wealthy financiers, the Federals were planning an elaborate eight-team circuit stretching from Kansas City in the west to Brooklyn in the east, and including stops in Chicago, St. Louis, and Pittsburgh. Inducements were made by agents of the organization to players throughout the majors, and the likes of Joe Tinker, Russell Ford, Hal Chase, Cy Falkenberg, Steve Evans, and George Mullin were enticed to jump to the outlaw league. As early as August 1913, gossip in newspapers touted considerable monetary offerings made to Cobb in efforts to get him to defect from Detroit.[59]

The Federals direly wanted Cobb, and league executives knew that attaining him would result in a financial and psychological victory unparalleled in baseball. Fans would flock to Federal stadiums based on Cobb's name recognition alone and the maneuver would provide the kind of legitimacy the organization desired, while leaving the American League badly demoralized. News wire reports in January 1914, months before the Federal League was to officially get off the ground, disclosed annual salary amounts ranging from $15,000 to $25,000 tendered to Cobb to jump sides. In response to the chatter, Cobb sent a telegram to E. A. Batchelor of the *Detroit Free Press*, confirming his loyalty to Detroit, stating, "I would gain nothing by change."[60]

Over the winter months, Cobb immersed himself in the game of golf and it wasn't surprising to see him at the Augusta Country Club, playing 18 rounds in the morning and again that afternoon. In fact, he was more enthusiastic about attending spring training than he had been in years so he could spend time at the Mississippi Coast Country Club in Gulfport, Mississippi, a short distance from Tigers' camp. Scoring about 100 on an 18-hole course, he was ever determined to improve, and considered it a good way to enhance his hand-eye coordination, as well as his leg and arm muscles prior to the season. In a very Cobb-like fashion, he tried to be an innovator, having his caddy "pitch" balls close to the ground for him to hit but the unorthodox tactics didn't gain much traction.[61] Nevertheless, he carried his wooden clubs everywhere he went.

Joining the team at New Orleans in mid-March, Cobb was heavier than he was known to be in the past, a sign that his work on the links didn't get him in the kind of shape that hunting or winter ball had previously. The people of Gulfport were overjoyed by his presence, closing up town banks, shops, and governmental offices to attend a game between the Tigers and New Orleans Pelicans on March 19, and Cobb "performed as advertised" by hitting a two-run triple in the ninth.[62] Detroit won the game 11–10 in 12 innings. As far as the team was concerned, manager Hugh Jennings was thrilled about a few of his new recruits and optimistic about the team's chances in the pennant race. Nineteen-year-old Harry Heilmann from the Pacific Coast joined Marty Kavanagh, a second baseman, and George Burns at first. Also, Harry Coveleski, a former National Leaguer, filled a needed left-handed pitching role.

Jennings came to the realization that his idea to bat Sam Crawford in the third slot and Cobb clean-up in 1913 hadn't had the intended results, and shifted Crawford back to fourth in the lineup. The move gave Cobb better chances to score with a more consistent hitter behind him.[63] The season opened in Detroit on April 14, 1914, and went thirteen innings before St. Louis garnered a 2–0 advantage, putting the pressure on the home team to rally. In the bottom of the inning, the Tigers got two men on and Cobb exhilarated the 20,000 rooters in attendance by tripling to the fence, clearing the bases ahead of him. With the score tied, Crawford advanced on a soft hit that kept Cobb tied to the bag, but Bobby Veach proceeded to sacrifice and Cobb trotted home for the victory, 3–2.[64] It was an electrifying way to start the season.

Right from the start, the team struck a nice balance of pitching and hitting, and enjoyed a full month in first place between April and May. Cobb's batting eye seemed to tune up a little slower than anticipated, and it was hard not to suspect his preseason golfing exploits as a possible cause. Many baseball players swore off golf in the midst of training because of the differences between the two sports and a general feeling that one hindered the other. During Detroit's first road trip to New York, Cobb stepped before the prominent dignitaries of the American Booksellers' Association and gave a short, yet entertaining speech. His showing was coordinated with the launch of his first book, *Busting 'em: And Other Big League Stories*, released by publisher Edward J. Clode.[65]

The Federal League rumors were rekindled after Cobb was spotted consorting with members of the rival league in Chicago and, no matter how many times he denied jumping to the outlaws, writers loved to speculate. Jennings didn't give the gossip a second thought. He was working to maintain the stability of his club and felt that if his players could continue at their present gait, there was considerable hope of making a sincere challenge for the top position in the American League. The two things that could derail their efforts were injuries or major incidents, but, considering the odds, what were the chances they'd experience both? For the 1914 Tigers, those odds were good.

10

BUTCHERING PENNANT CHANCES

The Detroit Tigers were more than two weeks into a grueling road trip on May 18, 1914, and were capably withstanding each of their challengers to retain first place in the American League. That afternoon, however, they were confronted by twenty-six-year-old George "Rube" Foster, a skilled right-hander from Oklahoma. On the mound for Boston, Foster would later gain fame as a two-game winner in the 1915 World Series, helping the Red Sox overcome the Philadelphia Phillies. But that day in 1914 at Fenway Park, he hurled a scorching fastball into the right side of Ty Cobb, causing a "green-tree fracture" of his sixth rib, meaning that the bone had split.[1] Despite difficulties breathing, Cobb resisted the pain enough to engage in a game the next day, going 1-for-2 with an RBI before yielding to his injury. Once a diagnosis was made, it was revealed that he'd be out of the game for at least a week, but really, his recovery required about fifteen days.

In Cobb's absence, Hugh Jennings utilized Harry Heilmann and Hugh High in center, but the Tigers were cast from their leadership position and endured a five-game losing streak before the Georgian superstar was able to return on June 5. Still not fully healed, Cobb missed added time closer to the middle of the month, and then went 8-for-16 over a four-game period, reasserting himself in the club's championship drive. During the afternoon of Saturday, June 20, Cobb readied himself in his customary outfield spot and reacted to a sharp liner into right-center off the bat of Washington Senators third baseman Eddie Foster. He lost his footing en route, and the ball managed to eke past him. He then momentarily fumbled it, allowing Foster to round second and head to third on the error.[2]

Unnerved by his mistakes, Cobb was boiling with intensity and in a poor mood. Things deteriorated even further when a pair of jokesters in the right-field bleachers started riding him, calling him off-color names. Quickly pushed to his limits, he shouted back at his tormentors and let it be known that he was willing to step away from the game to settle their differences. The challenge to his manhood was too much to forgive, and between innings, he ran off the field, caught the two young men under the stands and dished out a quick pounding.[3] While he might have satisfied his immediate craving to square things up with his antagonists, he was still bent far out of shape and highly volatile. It wasn't going to take much for him to explode again.

The Cobbs were having a small dinner party at their Longfellow Avenue rental home that evening with Washington manager Clark Griffith as one of their guests.[4] Following the game, Cobb arrived home to find Charlie upset about a phone conversation she'd had with a local meat market regarding a batch of spoiled fish. Unhesitatingly, Cobb rushed out the door, his mind clouded by anger, and there was absolutely nothing that could stop his quest for vengeance toward the man who, he felt, had insulted his wife. At least, that was *his* point of view. William L. Carpenter, proprietor of the Progressive Meat Market, saw the situation differently. He didn't think he had insulted Mrs. Cobb, but clearly insisted that the fish were fresh when they left his business. He was upset enough to cancel the Cobb account and refuse any future dealings.[5]

Carpenter, however, never expected Cobb, the famous baseball player he admired, to burst through the doors of his establishment, brandishing a loaded Belgian-made .32 caliber revolver.

"Where's the man who insulted my wife?" Cobb yelled. According to Carpenter's version of events, Cobb freely pointed the weapon at him, "glaring like one insane." Later, Cobb admitted to withdrawing his revolver only after Carpenter grabbed a meat cleaver. No bullets were fired and no blood was shed in the ensuing minutes, as Cobb demanded the butcher call his wife to apologize. In possession of the superior weapon, Cobb's menacing persuaded Carpenter to make the call, and the ballplayer was sufficiently pleased, ready to pay his bill and leave.[6] But Carpenter's brother-in-law, Howard G. Harding, a tall twenty-year-old assistant in the shop, was not agreeable with anything that was taking place. He openly interfered in the conversation, sharply criticizing Cobb and the latter responded likewise.[7]

"I believe you're a coward," Harding told Cobb. "Put down your revolver and come out into the street." Cobb shifted gears again, focusing completely on his new foe and proceeded to yank Harding out onto the sidewalk. He handed his weapon to a nearby citizen, and then used his size and strength to manhandle his rival.[8] Knocking Harding down at least twice and blackening his eye, Cobb was unmatched, and there were likely few people in the area capable of dealing with his ferocity. In contrast, when police arrived and placed Cobb into a wagon headed to the station. There he was docile, seemingly awakening to the seriousness of what had occurred.

Each time Cobb experienced a moment of dubiousness, he had been forced to cope with the ramifications, going back to the beginning of his career. In the aftermath of the Fred Collins incident in 1908, the Frank Baker spiking, and, of course, the Lucker situation in New York, he was branded all sorts of ways. He was rowdy, a lunatic, a violent thug out to purposefully maim fellow players, and so on. Cobb immediately knew that his latest scrap was going to hurt him publicly, and told three newspapermen waiting for him at the Bethune Avenue police station, "I'm not going to give you a thing. This isn't going to appear in the papers. If it does, I'm ruined—ruined—my reputation's gone. They'll hoot me off the diamond. I'll have to forget the American League and go over to the Federals."[9]

When advised that he would be better served to tell his side of the story, he thought for a moment, and the *Detroit Tribune* noted that "with almost childlike simplicity, Cobb's complete attitude changed." He consented and gave a full statement.[10] But incriminating statements were provided by Carpenter and other witnesses, and there was no way to sugarcoat his behavior. "Cobb acted like a maniac," Carpenter explained. "He certainly should be restrained until he learns to control himself." Police commissioner John Gillespie said, "I am surprised, with his temperament, that he has not gotten himself into more trouble."[11]

Much like the George Stanfield affair of 1909, the Detroit Tigers and other key friends in high places protected Cobb as the news unfolded. Even though Commissioner Gillespie marveled at Cobb's rage, he was responsible for clearing the air in terms of his status. The player wasn't arrested but detained, and it was surmised that any sort of punishment "would be bad for the city of Detroit." Gillespie took it a step further by saying that Cobb should never have been brought in to the station at all.[12] Tigers' club secretary Charles Navin dropped everything to race to Cobb's side and his lawyer James O. Murfin toiled to turn a potential assault case into a simple disturbing the peace charge. Cobb pled guilty and was fined $50.[13]

"I am sorry that this incident happened," Cobb told a reporter. "Sorry for myself and anyone of my friends whom it affected. But if the same insult was offered again, I think I should take the same course."[14]

Even though Cobb was making every possible effort to move on from the embarrassment, it wasn't going to be that easy. He suffered a broken thumb in the fight with Harding and the initial assessment was that he was to miss ten days of playing time. The injury proved to be more serious and Cobb was out for more than three weeks. He returned to the field at Washington on July 14, but it was obvious he wasn't yet ready and his hand went back into a plaster cast. The Tigers fought to remain in second, but the continued absence of Cobb was believed to be the central factor why Detroit was not putting up a better fight for first against the Athletics. The club experienced a painful seven-game losing streak between July 20 and July 27, and fell to fourth in the standings. By that point, they were 11 games out of first.

Finally, Cobb reemerged on the playing roster on August 7, and hit a triple in a 3–1 victory against Boston at Navin Field. A writer for the *Detroit Free Press* heard no "unkind remarks" toward Cobb in light of his ordeal and said that he was "roundly cheered" by fans.[15] Nevertheless, the butcher incident figured heavily into the team's lack of pennant hopes and the season was technically over before it really had concluded. But Cobb was always good for some excitement. On August 24 at Washington, he engaged in a "friendly" wrestling match in the clubhouse with Joe Engel of the Senators. The jovial session took a negative turn when Engel suffered a deep cut after being thrusted into a locker, and required five stitches.[16] Cobb also accidentally wounded the thumb of Jack Bentley during a play at the plate, and was essentially connected to the injuries of two Washington pitchers in a single afternoon.[17]

At Detroit on September 7, the Tigers participated in a contest against their heated rivals, the White Sox, a game that went 12 innings before being decided in Chicago's favor. The game was far more remembered for Cobb's entanglement with Sox third baseman Jimmy Breton in the 10th inning at a point in which Ty was looking to score the winning run. Breton smartly got in Ty's way and prevented him from reaching home. The next day, fans anticipated a reprisal and, during the first inning, Cobb rushed to third in a play in which he was easily out. He slid hard to the bag anyway, spiking Breton below his knee. A Chicago reporter claimed that "Cobb bounded up and stood over him as if gloating," but Breton didn't complain and asserted that the spiking was wholly unintentional.[18]

Although he played in only 98 games, Cobb was designated the batting champion with a .368 average, while outlaw Benny Kauff of the Indianapolis Hoosiers in the Federal League topped him by two points, and is today generally considered the major league titleholder for 1914. Cobb produced 127 hits, 69 runs, 57 RBIs, and 35 stolen bases in his abbreviated season. The Tigers missed third place by a half game, finishing with an 80–73 record, and landing behind Philadelphia, Boston, and Washington. Based on the ongoing war, sportswriters predicted a tumultuous baseball economy and a number of teams faced dire financial losses. Detroit, surprisingly, drew over 400,000 people at home, the third most in the league, and took in about $30,000 in profits.[19]

Frank Navin was pleased, not only with the performance of his club, but especially with the devotion Cobb was displaying week in and week out. "Cobb showed me another side of himself when the Federal League backers were after him. They offered him every inducement under the sun and he turned his back on them. He stood by me and said he wanted to show the people of Detroit that he was loyal to the Tigers and eager to help win a pennant. Manager Jennings will tell you that in all the years he has been here, he has never seen Ty so eager to win games for Detroit nor so anxious to get along with everybody on the team. He has been the most cheerful and happiest of ball players. All this junk about the Federal League grabbing him is piffle. Cobb will not desert the Tigers."[20]

As a result of the heightened camaraderie between Navin and Cobb, and to further bind them in the midst of war, a new three-year contract agreement was established in August 1914. In fact, it not only encompassed the three seasons of 1916, 1917, and 1918, but also included renegotiated terms for 1915 that had been part of the two-year deal he signed in March 1914. The new agreement called for Cobb to receive $20,000 annually for the next four years and the contentious ten-day clause was stricken from the document.[21] Soon, he would be, without question, the highest paid man in baseball history.

Following the 1914 season, Cobb adjourned to his old haunts in Georgia and was able to help commemorate the World Series title of his friend George Stallings at a special dinner in Macon, Georgia. Stallings, as manager of the Boston Braves, won four-straight from Philadelphia in the championship series, and Cobb called him "the greatest instiller of the fighting spirit in ball players I have ever known." Master of ceremonies John T. Boifeuillet told a story about Cobb, saying he overheard a conversation at a recent game with a girl asking her friend, "Why are so many policemen standing around here?" A short time later, realizing the Detroit Tigers' star was standing on first, she answered her own question, "Oh, I know what they are for. They are trying to keep Ty Cobb from stealing bases!"[22]

Cobb, as usual, was always on the move, and spent a good amount of time golfing and hunting during the offseason.[23] His wife Charlie was enormously understanding of his "on-the-go" frame of mind and was a lot less adventurous than he was. She ducked press attention and was comfortable in her role as homemaker. A baseball fan at heart, she took great pleasure in seeing games when she was afforded the opportunity and was a staunch supporter of the Tigers. Of all her husband's tricks on the diamond, she particularly enjoyed watching him pilfer home plate, but the awesome display he put on almost daily was tremendously satisfying for the entire Cobb family.[24] Charlie, early on in their marriage, adjusted to his celebrity status and the fact that he was gone for multiple weeks throughout a given year.

Her adjustment to the demands of being a ballplayer's wife didn't necessarily mean it wasn't difficult, and she was undoubtedly distressed by stories of death threats, riotous masses, and fisticuffs involving her husband. Arguably no player in sports history had been involved in as many controversial moments as Cobb over the course of his career. Each day, perhaps hundreds of newspapers across the globe ran stories about his deft-defying heroics on the ball field, in addition to tales of his off-the-field scandals, contract negotiations, and copious gossip. His name sold newspapers and sportswriters loved to bank off his marketability. Spiking incidents and chaotic brawls were music to the ears of sports editors—and the wilder, the better.

As one might imagine, this was not glorious subject matter to the loving family of Ty Cobb, and the over-hyped stories published in papers were downright frightening. Charlie was well aware of his temperamental behavior and viciousness. He could be just as angry in private as he was in public, but she was patient with him. She allowed him to rule according to his own sensibilities and, understandably, took charge of the household once he was gone. For the sake of the children, she did her best to control the environment in a structured manner, and with the responsibilities of running the domestic side of things in both Detroit and Augusta, there was rarely a dull moment.

The Cobbs had established a permanent home at 2425 Williams Street in Augusta, in what was known as the "The Hill," and F. C. Lane of *Baseball Magazine* called it a "typical southern mansion."[25] The two-story residence featured eight rooms, two baths, and included a "hospitable" atmosphere, which Charlie cultivated and guests always enjoyed. Ty's office sanctuary rested on the first floor, and was a room Lane described as being under lock and key. Inside, Cobb kept his assortment of hunting rifles, weapons he wanted safeguarded from his young children, especially when he was out of town. Amongst the other notable items in Cobb's personal stash were a collection of historical books, his favorite cigars, and a bottle of moonshine whiskey. Other miscellaneous items picked up in his travels lined the shelves and countertops.

Winters often went by in a blur, and before anyone really had a chance to realize it, Cobb was headed back northward. On March 20, 1915, he reported to the Tigers at Mobile, Alabama, in good physical condition but, once again, appeared a tad heavy.[26] His golf game was still an essential part of his preseason focus and whenever he could sneak away from the diamond to play, he would. At Gulfport, Mississippi, spring training was a revelation and Hugh Jennings found himself surrounded by a cast of enthusiastic athletes. Outside Cobb, Sam Crawford and George Moriarty—guys with more than ten years major league experience—the roster mainly consisted of talented youngsters with a number of them being pitching hopefuls. Ralph "Pep" Young gave added life to the infield and, from the onset of the season, the team seemed infused with high energy.

To start their 1915 campaign, the Tigers snapped off an eight-game winning streak in April and rested safely in first place. Cobb was at his best, batting in the neighborhood of .400, and tackling every aspect of the game with an intense grit. Twice within a week in early May, he raised the dead with earth-shaking responses to called strikeouts by umpires Dick Nallin and George Hildebrand, and his fiery disposition was not lessened in any way by his advancing age.[27] One of the most interesting happenings of the early season didn't involve a divisional game, but an exhibition at Syracuse against the Pittsburgh Pirates of the National League. The largely forgotten contest, occurring on June 3, 1915, saw Cobb and Honus Wagner adjourn to the same ball field for the first time since the 1909 World Series.[28]

An audience of 10,000 recognized the significance of having the two legends appear before them and cheered both with great fervor. Wagner, at forty-one years of age, was in his nineteenth season as a big leaguer and had no intentions of being overshadowed. In the fourth inning, with two men on, he blasted the ball over the left-field fence for an apparent home run, but the umpire called it foul, much to the chagrin of those who clearly saw it veer to the right of the pole. It wasn't until the ninth that Wagner got what he wanted and homered without any controversy. But by then, the Tigers were well ahead and won the exhibition, 8–2. Cobb, incidentally, appeared in the third with the bases loaded and grounded to Wagner, triggering a double-play. As part of the field day exercises, Cobb participated in a relay race along with teammate Donie Bush and Max Carey and Bob Schang of the Pirates, and won over a local team.[29]

Running the bases harder than he had in years, Cobb was back to logging multiple stolen bases a game and, because of that fact, the chances for spiking accidents increased tenfold. At Boston on June 9, Red Sox shortstop Everett Scott was wounded when Cobb slid into second base during the first inning. His condition worsened when, as he favored his injury, he twisted his other ankle and missed a month of playing time.[30] The situation served to amplify the tensions between Detroit and Boston, and their feud would continue to develop as the season progressed. Cobb also gashed the hand of Senators catcher John Henry when stealing home on June 18,[31] but no one held any grudges. In fact, Cobb amusingly caught for Henry during Washington's fielding practice the next day.[32]

The never-say-die attitude of the Tigers in 1915 reminded Cobb of their 1907 campaign and, if things adhered on that path, Detroit was in line for another chance at a World Series title.[33] It wasn't guaranteed but after the club slipped from the top spot, they remained within reach for most of the summer. A major key to the team's success was the ability of Cobb and Bush to get on base, followed by the proficient hitting of Sam Crawford and Bobby Veach in batting them home.[34] The speed and surefire offensive power of team regulars was unusually robust, and pundits referred to Cobb, Crawford, and Veach as the "Wrecking Crew." In the AL pennant race, the competition was boiling down to Chicago, Boston, and Detroit, and there was no love lost between the three teams.

Cobb was also quick to incite things too. On August 24 at Detroit, he grounded out in the eighth inning and, rather than returning to the Tigers bench as one would expect, he trotted over to the Boston dugout and relaxed. Naturally, Red Sox players were incensed and umpire "Silk" O'Loughlin yelled for Cobb to remove himself at once.[35] Additionally, Cobb engaged in a loud argument with Boston manager Bill Carrigan, and his actions were the opposite of endearing to the latter's men. Red Sox fans were equally aroused, and *Boston Journal* columnist Francis Eaton took notice of a certain negative encouragement by a local group of "discredited baseball writers" hoping for pandemonium when Detroit arrived in "Bean Town" in what was the biggest series of the pennant race.[36] Troublemakers were spitefully prepared well in advance.

Over 21,000 people at Fenway Park loudly reacted to Cobb's first appearance at the plate on September 16, 1915. Cobb was somewhat good-natured about the booing and hissing, murmuring, "It sounds like the stockyards," and telling the crowd, "Come on, yell, we like it!"

Eaton believed he was having "a little fun" on the field, doffing his cap to the fans and offering "derisive glances."[37] He explained that Cobb was "so much more clever, brainy, and resourceful than the men who are trying to nibble on his heels," and instead of the crowd and sportswriters working to get under his skin, he was turning things around to use it to his advantage. But the combative atmosphere morphed from one of simple hooting to one bordering on violence. Fans threw glass bottles at Cobb and it was apparent that both teams were fuming and out for blood.

Hostilities openly erupted in the eighth inning when twenty-three-year-old Carl Mays, a pitcher with a "submarine" style of throwing, threw two balls high and inside on Cobb. Blisteringly angry at what he thought were purposeful attempts to hit him, Cobb didn't offer a full swing at the next pitch, and released the grip of his bat just as he brought it forward, sending it in the direction of the rookie right-hander. Although the bat missed its target, Cobb approached Mays and they quarreled verbally as spectators went wild. Moments later, with Cobb back in the batter's box, Mays fired yet another pitch at him and successfully nailed the Georgian on the wrist.[38] Cobb was pumping with adrenaline and, once on base, quickly stole second. Irate rooters perceived his maneuver to be an attempt to spike Everett Scott and, two batters later, he bowled into catcher "Pinch" Thomas to score, sending the audience into a deafening uproar.

The game was called with Detroit leading, 6–1, but hooligans bombarded the field and Cobb was their main object of fury. He was "jostled about and roughed up quite a bit," according to the *Boston Herald*, but he made his way to the clubhouse "leisurely" as police and teammates protected him from injury. Cobb surprisingly smiled at the near-riot scene, which was probably the opposite of what those looking to cause him harm anticipated.[39] The next day, he was received by applause and hisses, and the two-run homer he hit in the ninth was met with a nice ovation. However, the Tigers were defeated, 7–2. Losses also came in the next two meetings, pushing Boston ahead in the standings by four games. The pennant was soon out of reach for Detroit and the Red Sox not only clinched, but won the World Series over Philadelphia.[40]

Cobb led the majors in batting average (.369), hits (208), runs scored (144), and stolen bases (96, that stood as a major league record until 1962), and despite a single stretch of 23-straight plate appearances without a hit in August, he played his usual remarkable game.[41] He returned to Augusta for the winter and settled into a familiar routine of hunting birds, squirrels, and rabbits in Richmond and Screven Counties. Along with several partners, including John Phillip Sousa Jr. and Edward S. Rogers, Cobb purchased a sizable property of about 6,000 acres along the Savannah River to use as a hunting ground.[42]

In many ways, Ty Cobb was a much different man than he was a few years earlier. He was more mature, composed, and sociable, although when he was in a certain frame of mind, it didn't take much to set him off. As a veteran member of the Tigers, he had accepted a leadership role, calling for certain plays with Crawford and his teammates rather than ignoring them. For instance, he commonly worked a bunt play when Donie Bush was on second base, drawing the fielders in with a bluff and allowing Donie to steal third. During a September 1915 game at New York, Cobb ran in from center field to give pitcher George Dauss mid-inning advice and helped the latter stave off a Yankees rally, maintaining a 4–3 lead for the win.[43] He was talkative to fresh recruits and gave Jennings his opinion on the future potential of certain rookies.

Jennings enjoyed Cobb's increased mentorship of the younger players and expected him to offer guidance to teammates in the field during games. Spring training for the Tigers returned to Texas in 1916, and the people of Waxahachie were keyed up by the opportunity to see the multi-time batting champion. But as Cobb was making last minute preparations to join the team, a devastating fire consumed downtown Augusta, spreading across thirty-two blocks and destroying over seven hundred buildings. Millions of dollars in property damages were suffered and Cobb, a big proponent of real estate, was amongst those to endure losses.[44] Fortunately, his home was outside of the burn radius, but scores of his friends were directly impacted by the overwhelming ruin. Cobb was delayed by the tragedy and caught up with the club at Houston on March 31.

Houston, incidentally, was going to be the site of a highly awaited confrontation. For months and months, sportswriters had hyped Benny Kauff as the "Ty Cobb of the Federal League," and crowed about his outstanding hitting and speed. Kauff, undoubtedly, was the sensation of the outlaw organization, batting .370 as a twenty-four-year-old rookie in 1914 for the league champion Indianapolis Hoosiers and .342 in his sophomore effort for the Brooklyn Tip-Tops. His batting average, combined with a stolen base tally of 130 over those two seasons, put him in an exceptional class of ballplayers, and writers loved to compare him to Cobb.

.   The Federal League folded in December 1915, after a settlement was reached with Organized Baseball and the ongoing war concluded.[45] As a result, Kauff transitioned over to the New York Giants, presenting an opportunity for him and Cobb to meet on the field for the first time. Giants manager John McGraw and Hugh Jennings arranged a five-game series for spring training, but four of the games were already played by the time Cobb reported. That made the Houston contest on April 2 all the more intriguing. In spite of the so-called rivalry touted by the press, Cobb and Kauff didn't enter the exhibition as enemies, and the game went off without any fireworks. Both went 1-for-4 with a double, but Cobb was said to have gotten the better of the ex-Federal Leaguer by stealing a base and scoring two runs. The Tigers also prevailed, 9–2.[46]

It was customary for preseason journalists to call Cobb overweight by 1916, but as he aged, like most people, he put on extra pounds that were harder to take off and what was considered "heavy" for the Georgian athlete was now becoming his standard "healthy" weight. Being without winter or spring practice left him a little behind in finding his batting groove, but he hovered around .300 after the first eight games of the season. He'd miss the ninth contest at Navin Field against Chicago on April 21 because of illness, and remain on the sidelines until returning to center field at St. Louis on April 28. Notably, Sam Crawford was another player on the sick-list in April and, for the first two months of the 1916 campaign, Detroit mostly hovered between the third and seventh positions in the American League standings.

Detroit was struggling at the plate, and it wasn't just one or two players, but nearly all the team's regulars were batting far below expectations, Cobb included. By mid-May, Cobb had a .273 average with Crawford, Donie Bush, Oscar Vitt, and Oscar Stanage each hitting for a lower percentage. Tris Speaker, who had been traded from Boston to Cleveland in April, was batting a hundred points better than Cobb, setting a tremendous pace for American League honors.[47] Baseball critics were quick to publicly speculate whether Cobb's best days were behind him, but Cobb worked to quiet his doubters with a strong surge, pushing his average over .300 by the end of the month. Nonetheless, his detractors were coming on hard, both in the press and from the stands, and his frustrations were occasionally exposed on the diamond.

On May 15, at Washington, DC, he was caught in a third-inning run-down by Joe Boehling and fans were appalled when Cobb proceeded to toss a handful of dust into the pitcher's face. To witnesses from the crowd, it was completely unwarranted, and they let him have it with a thorough onslaught of booing. The *Detroit Free Press*, perhaps in defense of their local hero, explained that Boehling directed a "vile" epithet at Cobb when making the tag, instigating him to respond the way he did. However, the language used was inaudible to spectators, and, since Cobb's animalistic behavior was on full display, he obviously was the bad guy in the situation. E. A. Batchelor wrote that it was the "first time" that Cobb had been treated in such a manner at Washington, where he was typically very popular. The "verbal abuse" continued for the remainder of the game.[48]

Additional frustrations were apparent in Chicago on July 2, in what was the climax of a four-game sweep by the White Sox. In the seventh inning, umpire Dick Nallin called Cobb out on strikes and the latter exploded in a fit of rage. He threw his bat wildly into a section of empty seats at Comiskey Park and his "eccentric and dangerous antics" caused his ejection from the game.[49] American League President Ban Johnson suspended Cobb for three days for the tantrum and Detroit was playing its worst ball of the season. Hugh Jennings admitted Cobb was going through some hard times, but defended him from naysayers: "Every time he falls down in a pinch now or fails in an attempt to make a brilliant play, he is hooted and abused just as though he had committed some frightful crime. Cobb is as much of a gentleman as anybody in the game [and is] the last man that anybody ought to pick on. He is trying his best."[50]

Another boost of support came from Cobb's roommate, Jean Dubuc. "Let me go down as saying that a fairer, cleaner, or better ballplayer never lived than Ty. Its Cobb did this, Cobb did that, Cobb did something else all day and everywhere you go. I would be frayed out if it were me. Ty's human, remember that, and that's why he is so well liked. When he has a great day with the stick he's happy, and when a slump spreads its fist over his hitting, he bucks and riles, and that's why he does not stay in a slump. This thing of licking all the rest of the league in the batting averages every year is no pipe job. It's the hardest thing in the world. Pitchers work their ears off against Ty, fielders are on their toes the minute he comes up to the bat and the fans all want to see him fooled, too. Cobb loves baseball, that's why he is so good. If he played for the home team in every town we visit he would have more friends."[51]

The chase for the batting championship was considered, at times, to be a three-man race between Tris Speaker, Ty Cobb, and Joe Jackson, but it was evident from the beginning of the season that Speaker was having a career year. Cobb came on hard near the finish line, but his efforts resulted in a .371 average, 15 points behind Speaker, and placed him second. For the first time in nine seasons, Cobb was a runner-up in the American League batting competition and his dethronement as king wasn't met with a series of alibis.[52] He acknowledged and accepted the victory of Speaker without fuss. In the pennant race, the Tigers put up a gallant fight well into September, running neck and neck until losing several crucial games at home and dropping back to third. Detroit concluded the season with an 87–67 record, behind Boston and Chicago.

Cobb went east to offer his expert opinion about the Boston-Brooklyn World Series as a journalist and moonlighted as a barnstormer with the New Haven Colonials, an independent club managed by twenty-one-year-old George M. Weiss.[53] The Red Sox, following their 4–1 championship victory in the Series, played an exhibition against Cobb and the Colonials at New Haven on October 15. Cobb, holding down first base, collected eight assists and scored two hits off Babe Ruth, Boston's shining pitching star, in a 3–3 tie. In response to the unsanctioned game, the National Commission fined Cobb, Ruth, and other major leaguers for violating the rules of Organized Baseball by participating in the exhibition.[54]

Before rejoining his family in Augusta, Cobb had yet another endeavor to undertake. This time around, he was stepping before a camera to film a silent movie entitled *Somewhere in Georgia*. The proposition, although unusual, came together through the hard work of two friends, Vaughan Glaser, part owner in a new Cleveland-based movie picture company, and Grantland Rice, the author of the script. Glaser had been the man who successfully coaxed him to step onto the vaudeville stage and it was only fitting that he had a hand in Cobb's transition to film.[55] Work began in October 1916 in the area of Tottenville, Staten Island, New York, and director George Ridgwell said, "As a movie actor, Ty is lots more than a .380 hitter."[56]

A "story of baseball and romance," the movie centered on Cobb as a bank employee in his native Georgia, and, of course, he was the star ball-player for his local, small-town squad. He fell in love with the beautiful banker's daughter, played by veteran actress Elsie MacLeod, but, as luck would have it, he was scouted by the Detroit Tigers at the same time and called up to the majors. But as soon as trouble arose back home, Cobb returned to save the day, fighting with a crew of outlaws before emerging at the ball field to hit the winning homer. He also scored the girl of his dreams and the movie concluded "in a manner appealing to ball fans and picture fans alike."[57] With the film complete, Cobb (who was soon to turn thirty) was ready to embrace the calming environment of the South, and mentally and physically prepare to regain his lost batting title in 1917.

11

ALWAYS EXPECT THE UNEXPECTED

New York baseball statistician Al Munro Elias published an incredibly revealing look at Ty Cobb's twelve years in the major leagues in December 1916. The report, syndicated to papers throughout the country, proclaimed him to be the sport's "most remarkable batsman of all-time." Elias based his extraordinary statement on the whopping .369 career batting average of Cobb, which topped legends Ed Delahanty, Pete Browning, Nap Lajoie, and everyone else who stepped onto a big league field. Going a step further, Elias broke down Cobb's work against nearly 200 pitchers, and found that he'd achieved a better than .350 average against Cy Young, Chief Bender, Eddie Cicotte, Rube Waddell, Dutch Leonard, and a slew of other premier hurlers. His .326 against Walter Johnson was nothing to scoff at either.[1]

The impressive stats illuminated the pure mastery of Cobb behind the bat and proved that his stylized techniques were working splendidly well. Each and every day, he went out to the diamond and played *his* game of ball, unaffected by the more traditional methods of those around him. Neither his manager nor his fellow players influenced his approach to hitting, fielding, or running. It was all Cobb, implementing his own personal science of baseball. And for those observers of his unique style and mannerisms during a game, they were treated to a distinctive performance only Cobb could execute. He was a bit idiosyncratic and a lot eccentric in his routine, and no journalist captured the subtleties of his behavior better than Frank P. Sibley of the *Boston Daily Globe*.

Sibley fancied the idea of giving readers an inside sense of the Georgian's trademark habits during all phases of the game, and dissected his style and body language for a telling article aptly entitled "How Ty Cobb

Plays Ball."[2] He took notice of Cobb's habitual impulse to swing at the first pitch thrown, how he took "two or three steps forward to meet the ball" in the batter's box, and the power of his swing. Cobb garnered a base hit, Sibley noted, and once safely planted at the bag, he held the attention of the pitcher while inching off first, threatening to steal.

Cobb's jumpiness kept everyone guessing and he settled to watch the pitcher's motion with his knees bowed inward toward each other, prepared to either dash to second or slide back to first. It was the standard fare for Cobb, and his rivals across the league were in a constant struggle to overcome his unpredictable nature.

In terms of personality, Cobb was, at times, a loud rooter for teammates and a heavy instigator of opposing players. At other moments, he was withdrawn and lost in his own train of thought. But he was always observant, keenly aware of the game's circumstances. Naturally, Cobb was in a much better mood when the Tigers were winning, brazenly smirking at pitchers, smiling after close plays, and ribbing infielders with an arrogant flair.[3] A round of chuckles by Cobb easily goaded players into a rabid fury, and Sibley commented that he wasn't "ever-popular" with contemporaries but clearly, the kind of smugness he displayed had something to do with it. Interestingly, Cobb hadn't always been a shameless trash talker, but grew into the role, likely out of a necessity to both fight fire with fire and to gain a mental advantage.

However, when Detroit was on the losing end of things, Cobb was far from jovial. He was furiously doing everything in his power to score runs. After hitting into an out, he walked with his head down and was the kind of guy who'd browbeat himself for failing to produce. He'd also lash out at teammates for the same, and again, his vitriolic exhibition usually tended to turn attitudes against him. But altogether, Cobb's techniques, superstitions, and temperament were resulting in astronomical individual records. And in many ways, there was truth in the statement of a fan, who explained, "He's got 'em licked before he starts," within earshot of Sibley.[4] The reality of the matter was that Cobb *did* have great gains on his opponents because of the legend he created and the innuendos surrounding his gamesmanship.

He was a mystifying athlete, and by creating endless opportunities for the Tigers to win, die-hard enthusiasts knew to always expect the unexpected when he entered the game. Sibley wrote that Cobb added "more strength to a club than any other one man, and no man [had] so great a following of fans." It was simple: people appreciated his hard work and exciting style of play regardless of their team loyalty. For older fans, he was amongst the last of a dying breed, a reflection of Kid Gleason, Kid Elberfeld, and hard-nosed battlers of yesteryear; men who put great stock in doing everything humanly possible to win, and that meant fighting for each and every run. He wasn't out there to make friends but to achieve victory.

During the winter of 1916–17, Cobb was no less enthusiastic about golf than he had been in previous years, even though he felt that playing midseason diminished his batting "eye."[5] Tris Speaker disagreed, believing that his devotion to golf throughout 1916 was a major factor in his winning the batting title.[6] Nevertheless, Cobb was steadfast in his conviction, and planned to wind up his golf game once the season got under way. But that still left plenty of time to enjoy the sport throughout the spring, especially during training in Texas. He also centered his energy on hunting. On one of his jaunts into Louisiana to hunt duck, he was joined by two friends, Rick Woodward of Birmingham and Robert W. Woodruff of Atlanta, both prosperous businessmen.[7] Cobb's connection with the latter would be especially beneficial in the future, as the Woodruff Family became involved in leadership positions for the Coca-Cola Company.

After arriving at Tigers' camp in Waxahachie, Texas, on the evening of March 26, 1917, Cobb got in a few days of practice before the team traveled to Fort Worth to begin a rematch series against the New York Giants. The two clubs faced off the year before and Detroit won three games to two. Despite camaraderie between managers Hugh Jennings and John McGraw, and the fact that the games were supposed to be lighthearted exhibitions, there was a serious spirit of competition amongst the players of both squads. In the opening contest on March 30, Cobb doubled in the eighth to score two runs and led the Tigers to a 4–1 win. While Cobb had a good reason to be contented with his performance, Giants team captain and second baseman Charles "Buck" Herzog was not thrilled by his play, going 0-for-3 and committing three errors.[8]

McGraw was an outstanding motivator of his men and knew he had three firecracker infielders: Herzog, shortstop Art Fletcher, and third baseman Heinie Zimmerman. He long supported a rowdier side of baseball, particularly the side that embraced verbal antagonizing of opposition players. Like Cobb, he knew a little provocation went a long way to disrupt the mindset of rivals, and he encouraged the barbs thrown at Tigers players. But things intensified once Herzog and Fletcher directed their attention to

Cobb and began ribbing him unmercifully.[9] That set the stage for the second game of the series at Dallas on March 31.

"Cobb was late arriving at the park," Fletcher later explained. "He had been out at the country club playing golf. That in itself would have been enough to get us on him, for most of us shared McGraw's scorn for 'cow pasture pool,' but when he insisted he must hit a couple of practice pitches before the game got under way [because he'd missed batting practice], he left himself wide open. We called him everything in the world and since he was hot-tempered and prideful, he naturally came back at us."[10]

"When we started the second game with them at Dallas," Cobb told a reporter, "they commenced attacking me at once. Herzog was awfully raw, and I warned him that I would attend to his case if he did not stop using such vile language. He kept it up and I warned him again, but he persisted.[11] He taunted me to the limit. Finally I retorted: 'When I get on first, Herzog, I'm going down to second. You can depend on that.' I got to first in the third inning and the whole Giant team, tipped off by Herzog, knew that I planned to steal on the first ball pitched. As [Ferdie] Schupp swung his arm, I started for second. The throw was a pitch out. Herzog, instead of waiting on the bag to tag me as I was going in, deliberately took two steps up the line to meet me. And in doing so, Herzog trespassed on territory that belongs to the base-runner."[12]

Convinced that the thirty-one-year-old Herzog was trying to show him up, Cobb slid hard into the bag with "both feet high in the air," according to the *Dallas Morning News*. His spikes caught the infielder on the left leg, above the knee, cutting him open.[13] In a split second, Herzog furiously lunged at Cobb and the two scuffled in the dirt before standing, only to resume their hostilities. But Fletcher crept behind Cobb, grabbing his arms and allowed his teammate unhindered freedom to strike the Georgian. But Cobb wiggled his body, evading a punch, and slithered away from Fletcher to land a blow of his own right in the mouth of Herzog. That was just before a combination of managers, players, and police broke up the commotion.[14] Umpire Bill Brennan ruled Cobb out of the game, but strangely allowed Herzog and Fletcher to remain, even though they fully participated in the fracas.

The blame went to Cobb, and Dallas fans—about 4,000 at Gardner Park—showered him with boos while cheering Herzog.[15] Angry, frustrated, and undoubtedly wanting revenge, Cobb watched the rest of the game from the sidelines, pondering his next move. In that time, he focused his true antagonist, and it wasn't Herzog or Fletcher. The chief instigator, he felt, was sitting on the Giants' bench. "Believe me, John McGraw is a great deal worse than Charles Herzog," Cobb declared.[16] "He is a mucker of the lowest type. His language to me and other Detroit players during the games was unprintable. If I ever get him alone in a nice, quiet place, I shall be tempted to clean him up, but I understand he seldom moves without a bodyguard. The Detroit team will never play another series with his club. His work is too raw."[17]

Cobb's mind was just about made up. He had no interest in continuing to battle the unruly Giants and listening to McGraw's hot air. He especially didn't want to help McGraw fatten his wallet by adding to the box office draw. The best way to deal with the situation was to skip out on the rest of the series and train only with his teammates during practice sessions. No matter what anybody else said, he wasn't going to let the matter slide, as his mind was made up. That evening, Cobb dined in the Oriental Hotel in Dallas, the headquarters for both the Tigers and Giants during their stay in the city. A special banquet had been arranged to celebrate the occasion, and Cobb was enjoying the chow when he was approached by Herzog. It seemed he also wasn't about to let things slide.

Sportswriter Hugh S. Fullerton once called Herzog "one of the brainiest, cleverest men in baseball," and said that he was a "hard fighting . . . bundle of nerve and determination."[18] His courage was on display when he stepped to Cobb, upwards of twenty-five pounds heavier, and requested a resumption of their earlier fisticuffs. Naively, Cobb at first thought Herzog wanted to solidify harmony between them, but was quick to consent to another fight, telling the Giant infielder that he'd be in his room in a half-hour. In the meantime, he finished his supper, adjourned to his room and began shifting the furniture to create enough space for the expected brawl. He also used water to douse the carpet in effort to gain an advantage by keeping Herzog's footing off balance.[19] It might not have been necessary, but exhibited Cobb's forethought.

With Zimmerman by his side, Herzog arrived at the scheduled time and the groundwork for their clash was laid. Instead of a straight boxing bout, which might have benefitted "Buck," they agreed to a "rough and tumble" contest, allowing a mix of pugilism and wrestling. In his corner, Cobb had trusted allies Oscar Stanage and team trainer Harry Tuthill, and with everyone on the same page the battle commenced. The way Cobb explained it, the two began wilding throwing punches. "Each of us swung about six blows without a hit," he said. "Then I luckily landed a wild one on Charlie's jaw.

He went down. I helped to pick him up but when he got to his feet he started to swing at me. So I squared off again and before Herzog could get home a punch, I landed another on his chin and he went down again. That ended the fight."[20] Cobb and Herzog shook hands before the latter left the room, nursing a battered face.

McGraw naturally found out about the confrontation, as well as its result, and was livid. After locating Cobb in the lobby of the Oriental Hotel, he lashed out with a bombardment of criticism.

Cobb later explained his version of what happened: "I was talking to a Texas friend at the time and my friend turned to McGraw and said, 'If you don't shut up I'll put a bullet hole through your stomach big enough to drive a team of horses through.' McGraw must have thought my friend meant it. He shut up."[21] Other accounts of this story claimed that it was Cobb who threatened McGraw, but either way, the feud between them escalated.

The next day, an estimated 10,000 spectators were on hand to see the wild and wooly antics of the two teams, but were saddened when the primary battlers sat out. Cobb was in uniform, but took in the festivities from a stationary position in the outfield.[22] He also warmed the bench for an exhibition at Wichita Falls, and then decided to depart the tour completely because he wasn't getting anything out of the brief, pregame workouts. Jennings agreed, saying: "I would not let Cobb play against the Giants again, even if every New York player assured me on his honor that there would be no more strife. He is too valuable a piece of property to be brawling around with men that have less to risk and I am glad that he is going to be removed from this atmosphere."[23]

Notably, Cobb had no hard feelings for Herzog, telling one journalist that they "parted the best of friends."[24] In subsequent years, they bumped into each other several times, usually during spring training, but never again did they quarrel. Many years later, after it was revealed that Herzog was destitute and battling a dire case of tuberculosis at a Baltimore hospital, Cobb was one of many baseball figures to offer financial assistance.[25] But, regardless of his willingness to tender aid to his old rival, most pundits wanted to remember their scandalous duel. After all, as sportswriter Dan Daniel put it, their clash was "perhaps the most famous fight in modern baseball."[26]

Having bolted from the Tigers-Giants tour at Wichita Falls, Cobb arrived in Cincinnati on April 4 in the midst of heavy rains and registered at the

Hotel Havlin. His intentions were to join Christy Mathewson's Reds and complete his training with the National Leaguers at Redland Field. But the weather didn't cooperate and Cobb was relegated to a light workout with local players underneath the stands.[27] Manager Roger Bresnahan and his Toledo Iron Men were in town as well, but the washout cancelled a scheduled game against Cincinnati. The ex-major league catcher was leading his club back to Toledo and asked Cobb if he'd accompany them. Since his plan was to meet up with the Tigers at that city anyway, Cobb consented.[28] The move afforded him a chance to play the world champion Boston Red Sox in exhibitions that weekend.

With special permission from Detroit owner Frank Navin, Cobb lined up as a member of Bresnahan's franchise, and Dick Meade of the *News-Bee* wrote, "Cobb in a Toledo uniform will be a novel and unusual attraction and will undoubtedly draw many people."[29] Thousands poured into Swayne Field over the next two days to see Toledo beat the Red Sox twice, 6–0 and 6–1, including a pounding of Boston pitcher Babe Ruth. Although Cobb only had two hits, Meade wrote that he "hustled and gave everything he had at the plate, on the bases and afield." He added, "It isn't hard to understand why he stands at the head of his profession."[30] The Tigers arrived on April 9 and, with Cobb in the right uniform, Detroit beat Toledo, 8–5.

Jennings made a preseason adjustment to the Tigers roster, sending Cobb back to right field, placing Heilmann in center, and utilizing venerable "Wahoo" Sam Crawford as a pinch hitter. The shift didn't seem to bother Cobb, as he told the *Detroit Free Press*, "I don't care where I play. I'll hold down any position they assign to me."[31] Team defense was strengthened by the maneuver, mostly because Crawford, playing his nineteenth year in the big leagues, had slowed considerably. The thirty-seven-year-old was less than 60 hits away from 3,000 in his career, and, since most observers felt it was his final season, achieving the honor all depended on how much playing time he received.

The campaign opened on April 11, 1917, versus Cleveland, and over 25,000 fans set a new attendance record for Navin Field. But the enthusiasm of Detroit fans didn't match the team ability at the start of the season, and the Tigers not only lost the initial contest but went 3–7 over the course of their first ten games. The team's offense was horrendous, and by May 25, Cobb was the only regular hitting over .275, with several players barely batting their weight. That same day, Cobb, averaging .319, was switched back to center field prior to a home game against Philadelphia with Heilmann heading to right. The Georgian was particularly motivated to do well on that occasion, as he was roasted by an obnoxious spectator near the visitor's bench, and went 2-for-3 with two walks and two stolen bases. The team, however, lost in 11 innings, 10–6.[32]

From the New York area circulated an unsubstantiated report that Cobb, in his blind desire to regain the batting title, was once again demonstrating the qualities of a lone wolf. The claim was that he was experiencing tunnel vision and ignoring teammates all to center on that single, individual goal.[33] There was no doubt that Cobb was working extremely hard and boosting his personal numbers but, in a way, he was being forced to step it up because of the lack of production elsewhere in the lineup. The report was also slightly similar to Cobb's anti-Giants statement in April. In essence, the attack on Cobb was likely part of a propaganda-type rebuttal to dredge up controversy in the Detroit camp. But the publicity didn't hurt the team, as the Tigers began playing its best ball so far that year in June.

Detroit went 11–6 during a trip to Eastern cities, including a sweep of Boston. In that same period, Cobb batted .463 and had a 5-for-5 day in New York on June 5.[34] Additionally, he built a consecutive game hit streak that was headed toward 30 by the end of the month. At St. Louis, he was cheered riotously by local enthusiasts following an eighth inning hit to continue his streak on July 1. The run continued for a few more days, ending at 35 games on July 6.[35] In the Chicago series, an entertaining episode between Cobb and third baseman Buck Weaver occurred after the Detroiter had slid to the bag safely. Weaver, in trying to tempt Cobb to make a break for the plate, rolled the ball away from him, telling the latter to go for it. Cobb teasingly danced off the base and Weaver, with amazing agility, seized the ball and nearly made the out.[36] Whether Cobb was still in a joking mood afterwards can only be guessed upon.

On July 30, 1917, at Washington, DC, an impressive "world record" was established, according to the *Detroit Free Press*, after Cobb, Bobby Veach, and Oscar Vitt each attained five hits against Senators pitching.[37] The team improved significantly and won a number of close games with a pronounced confidence, fighting back from late inning deficits to briefly seize third place. Cobb's passion was infectious in many ways, but at times he was overbearing and caustic. For instance, on a ball hit into left field, easily playable by Veach, Cobb's gusto carried him a little too closely to his teammate, causing Veach to lose sight of the ball and commit an avoidable error.[38] On another occasion, as he coached third base, he gave a forceful shove to Detroit's George Burns, who was hesitating to advance home after a triple and a defensive error, breaking a rule prohibiting coaches from making any physical contact with players.[39]

The Tigers had little chance to catch the league-leading White Sox down the stretch, and locked up fourth place behind Chicago, Boston, and Cleveland. On August 25, Detroit took time out to honor the storied career of one of the town's iconic baseball heroes with a special "Sam Crawford Day." Crawford participated in only 61 games in 1917, his final coming on September 16, and racked up only 18 hits, leaving him 39 shy of 3,000. His displacement from the active roster was not sudden. Jennings didn't hide the fact that he wanted a younger and quicker outfield, and two years earlier dropped Crawford to fifth in the lineup to get better results from the Cobb-Veach combination. Crawford's batting remained an asset and had the designated hitter spot been available to the Tigers in 1917, it is certain he would've been a prime candidate for the job. But as things stood, he was expendable and his big league career came to an end.

Baseball history has seen plenty of rivalries between teammates, but the Cobb-Crawford relationship stands out as one of the most turbulent. They were cohabitants of the same outfield, dugout, and clubhouse for thirteen years and enjoyed three league titles together. But they were different in so many ways and prone to clash. At the base of their association, there was mutual respect, and while some people might have thought Cobb was too conceited to acknowledge the superstar qualities of his fellow Tiger, that was an erroneous assumption. In 1910, Cobb bluntly declared Crawford "one of the greatest hitters in the game," even admitting that "Wahoo" was "better" than he was.[40] The following year, Cobb named his teammate one of the twenty all-time best and also referred to him as the "Mighty Sam Crawford" in an article he authored.[41]

But Cobb was paranoid about Crawford, and that feeling went back to his earliest days with the team when he thought Sam was heading up a clique against him. Crawford had never been one of his toughest critics, but nevertheless, Cobb was ever suspicious about his motives. Bob Dunbar of the *Boston Journal* conveyed a story that shed light on just how far Cobb's distrust of Crawford went. Apparently there were times when Cobb would swing through the ball and miss, then immediately turn and glance at the Detroit dugout to see if Sam was laughing behind his back and taking joy from his failure.[42] Clark Griffith, in addition, commented on Cobb's disjointed perspective, saying: "He accused Walter [Johnson] of bearing down on him and letting up on Sam Crawford, who followed Ty in the Detroit batting order. Cobb was jealous of his own teammate."[43]

A lack of communication, punctuated by literally months and months of not talking to one another, combined with an overt passive aggressiveness, made the rapport between Cobb and Crawford difficult to mend. They definitely went through periods where they endured flawless teamwork on the field, but the smallest misinterpreted event often triggered quiet fury—particularly on Cobb's part—and turned things ugly fast. But near the end of Crawford's tenure on the team, he was the one developing hard feelings and a sense that he was being pushed out by Cobb and Jennings.[44] Long of the theory that Cobb influenced roster moves, Crawford never believed he'd ever suffer the same fate as some of his contemporaries, who'd allegedly been pushed out because of Cobb's disfavor. His attitude changed in 1917 with his own dismissal and he felt Cobb, not Jennings, was the actual manager of the Tigers.[45]

"I never tried to run the Detroit team," Cobb said in response to the charges, "and Hughie Jennings will tell you that. Often I went to Hughie with suggestions that I felt might help the team. That was my right. Every player who has the interest of his club at heart should make suggestions for betterment. But never did I try to usurp Hughie's authority." And with regard to his butting heads with his fellow players, he admitted to such wrangles, saying: "There is nothing unusual in that. I dare say that there isn't a player who was in the big leagues for a long period of years who didn't at some time or other, have a jam with a few of his teammates. This is especially true of a club that is in the thick of a pennant fight and where everybody is keyed up to the highest tension possible. But every quarrel that I ever had was patched up." In fact, friendships were formed, according to Cobb.[46]

Crawford, as far as he was concerned, later agreed with that fact, telling a reporter: "We always got along well, despite what people said. There were some differences, but none that wouldn't exist on any teams. We were friends."[47]

The 1917 batting race ended with Cobb leading both leagues with a .383 average, exactly 30 points ahead of his closest rival, twenty-four-year-old George Sisler of the St. Louis Browns.[48] Cobb was also baseball's top scorer in hits (225), doubles (44), triples (24), stolen bases (55), on-base percentage (.444), and slugging percentage (.570). He placed second in RBIs (102) and runs scored (107) behind teammates Bobby Veach (103) and Donie Bush (112), respectively. His play was consistent throughout the season and although he faced a few leg problems, mostly from excessive sliding, he participated in 152 games. In that time, he went hitless in only twenty-five contests and regained the honor of the batting championship.[49]

The importance of baseball was far overshadowed by the devastating extensiveness of World War I, which was drawing immense concern. On April 6, 1917, the United States entered the conflict, declaring war on Germany, and initiated a draft calling for men from ages twenty-one to thirty-one. Cobb, thirty, met the age criteria, but as a married man with three children, he was initially thought to be exempt from military service.[50] However, since his secure financial standing was pretty well known, the legitimate dependency of his family was drawn into question. As required, he filled out his registration card and, after being named to Class I status, accepted his eligibility for duty.[51] In the interim, he was more than willing to offer his assistance to the soldiers at Camp Hancock outside Augusta, and began helping out where he could in November 1917.

A short time later, Cobb's status was adjusted by Augustan officials and he was placed in Class II, meaning that he was temporarily deferred but still eligible for future military service. Cobb made it clear that he was willing to serve, and if not drafted, was very likely to enlist sometime late in the summer. Sportswriters, in the absence of any concrete news, connected him to trade rumors, insisting that Cobb was soon going to be a member of the New York Yankees but Navin adamantly denied the gossip.[52] For Cobb, though, he proceeded to follow his usual offseason schedule and kept his legs active by hunting regularly. On March 25, 1918, he reported to Waxahachie, Texas, joining the Tigers to begin his training, and on the first of April, Detroit began a thirteen-game exhibition series against the Cincinnati Reds.

Excelling as a team, Detroit beat the Reds ten times, and Cobb was firing on all cylinders, batting .424 during the series.[53] En route to Cleveland, where the season was to open on April 16, Cobb developed a 101-degree fever and was suffering from a bad case of the grippe, better known as influenza. The contagious disease had also sidelined pitchers "Deacon" Jones and Bill James, and yet a third hurler, Willie Mitchell, was battling pneumonia.[54] With Howard Ehmke, a 10-game winner in 1917, in the service, the Tigers were stretched thin. To make matters worse, Harry Heilmann left the club because of the death of his mother, adding to the complexities. Bad weather delayed the opener for two days, and on April 18, the Tigers took Dunn Field with Frank Walker, Lee Dressen, and Babe Ellison in spots usually occupied by Cobb, Heilmann, and Crawford.[55]

The Tigers quickly established that they were not a .500 ballclub, dropping from a third place position shortly after the season began to last, and would maintain a spot in the lower second division (sixth through eighth) for a majority of the year. Cobb's season was tumultuous.

At Washington on May 26, he received right arm and shoulder injuries after diving for a difficult ball and missed four games.[56] As he mended, he worked as a pinch hitter before stepping into the first baseman's role on June 6. He remained at the initial bag for the next eight games, doing relatively well, but with a noticeable hiccup here and there. Fans at Navin Field were evidently so riled up after he mistakenly dropped a ball thrown in the ninth inning of a game on June 8 that they booed him without relent.[57]

Aside from the team's dismal standing in the pennant race, there was another possible reason for the backlash against Cobb and that was his poor showing at the plate. His batting was far below average, around .277 when he first went out with his injury. By the middle of June, he had fought his way back to .300, but fans in Detroit were still antsy. Earlier in the month, as the Tigers were facing a no-hit bid by Boston's Dutch Leonard, patrons at Navin Field came alive to actively root for Leonard to achieve the distinction and opposed Cobb as he entered the fracas as a pinch hitter in the bottom of the ninth. Cobb popped out in foul territory and Leonard made history, much to the delight of the audience.[58]

Personally challenged by the turmoil, Cobb went on the "most remarkable batting spree he ever has taken," according to the *Detroit Free Press*, and hit .512 over a 19-game period into July, elevating his overall average to .380.[59] But despite the impressive run toward yet another batting championship, he was not completely engulfed by his baseball responsibilities. In fact, his concentration was divided between his day job and what he expected to soon be his number one responsibility, and that was serving his country in a military uniform.

"I believe every man in the United States who is able to render some service to his country should get on the job," Cobb told a reporter. "I am shaping my business affairs to that by the time the season ends, I will be able to do my part. I don't believe the people care to see a lot of big, healthy young men out on the field playing ball while their sons and brothers are abroad risking their lives to conquer the Huns. I will quit the game until the war is ended and do what I can to aid in speedily winning it."[60]

Following a "work or fight" decree from Provost Marshal General Crowder in May and the declaration that the sport was not essential employment, players throughout Organized Baseball were impelled to either enlist or join vital labor organizations. Two of Cobb's longtime on-field rivals, Eddie Collins and "Shoeless" Joe Jackson, were such examples, with Collins headed to the Marines and Jackson taking up with a shipbuilding corporation in Delaware. Cobb settled on a position in the Army Chemical Warfare Service and passed a thorough physical exam in Washington, DC, on August 16. Eight days later, before a patriotic crowd in New York, he announced his intention of being in Europe by the first of October to help the war effort.[61] The 15,000 in attendance were overwhelming in their respectful admiration.

A doubleheader at Detroit against the White Sox on September 2 ended the abbreviated campaign, which was purposefully cut short to allow players to adhere to the new laws. Cobb went 6-for-10 between the games—both victories for the Tigers—and pitched two innings in the finale.[62] It was a praiseworthy way to end the season and exemplified Cobb's status as the major league batting leader, as he finished with a .382 average, well ahead of his nearest competitor. The Detroit club didn't have much to crow about otherwise, finishing with a 55–71 record and in seventh place, 20 games behind the Boston Red Sox. The statistics didn't mean much in the big picture, and Cobb immediately embraced his new occupation as a commissioned officer in the United States Army.[63]

The newly designated Captain Tyrus R. Cobb tied up loose ends in Detroit and Augusta, said goodbye to his family, and departed for Washington on September 30. Sportswriters assumed he would head into training at the engineers school at Camp Humphreys, Virginia, and the report that he was at the latter venue engaged in studies circulated in newspapers. But Cobb didn't want to be tied up for months stateside. He wanted to sail for France as soon as possible, reaffirming that he was "not trying to avoid military duty." The perception that ballplayers were "slackers" and working to evade combat was grinding on Cobb's nerves. He told reporter Robert W. Maxwell that he was in the military to fight and that he planned to toil harder for the service of the country than he ever did on the diamond.[64]

"Nobody ever felt more proud of a uniform than I do at the present moment," Cobb explained, wearing his Army duds. Discounting the rumors that he was going to have a rear-echelon job as a physical trainer, he said, "I am in the field offensive service and my work has to do with the practical application of gas on the enemy."[65] Noisy cynics criticized the athletes who entered the chemical service as officers, believing that it was a sort of safe haven to protect the pampered stars. Cobb reiterated his motivations a half dozen times, but regardless, doubters were still going to have something negative to say.

Ex-heavyweight boxing champion James J. Corbett wrote a series of articles based on a "heart-to-heart talk" he enjoyed with Cobb in September. Cobb offered a realistic perspective of his career, saying: "I have played perhaps the last game of baseball that I ever shall play. It is my hope that I will be on the battlefields of France before winter. And I may never come back. Even if I do, there is no assurance that I'll get back in diamond harness again."[66] If there was any truth to his statement, his Army garb was perhaps the final uniform he'd ever wear.

Ty Cobb posted a lifetime batting average of .367 and was a 12-time American League batting title champion, which is still the most in Major League Baseball history.

Baseball card of Ty Cobb from the American Tobacco Company, produced between 1909 and 1911.

Cobb, standing at bat, is depicted on an American Tobacco Company baseball card from the famous T206 card series.

The likeness of Ty Cobb as a member of the Detroit Tigers is captured on an American Tobacco Company trading card from the T205 series in 1911.

Reproductions courtesy of the Library of Congress

Cobb is in the middle row, third from the left, in this 1907 Detroit Tigers team photo. The Tigers won their first American League pennant that year, but lost the World Series to the Chicago Cubs in four straight games.

The youthful exuberance of Ty Cobb is apparent as he readies himself at the plate in one of his earliest known baseball photographs, taken circa 1905.

Often relying on his awesome speed, Cobb slides into third for a successful triple during a game on August 16, 1924. His 295 triples are second all-time, only 14 behind the leader, teammate Sam Crawford (309).

Photo courtesy of AP Images

Cobb's sliding style was a relentless source of controversy, with some players and managers contending that he purposely slid with his spikes "high," intending to injure the baseman. Cobb denied the charges.

Photo courtesy of the National Baseball Hall of Fame Library, Cooperstown, NY

Playing the game with a fierce aggressiveness, Cobb took physicality on the diamond to a new level, and when he slid into bases, he did so at full velocity. As a result, collisions with basemen were commonplace.

Cobb always watched each game intensely, looking for ways to capitalize on the weaknesses of rivals. He also liked to prepare for a plate appearance by holding three heavy bats, and believed it measurably increased his bat speed.

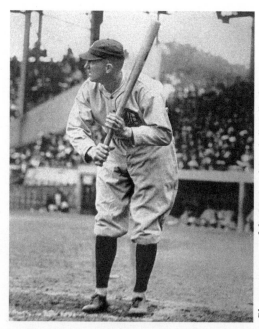

Photo courtesy of the National Baseball Hall of Fame Library, Cooperstown, NY

One of the more obvious and unique trademarks of Cobb's batting style was the way he gripped the bat, with his hands a few inches apart.

Photo courtesy of the National Baseball Hall of Fame Library, Cooperstown, NY

Although his methods at the plate were unconventional, Cobb hammered out 4,191 hits and held the Major League Baseball record for fifty-seven years. Pete Rose broke his record, making his 4,192 hit in 1985.

Automobiles were another passion for Cobb, and he enjoyed taking a ride prior to games to soothe his natural nervousness.

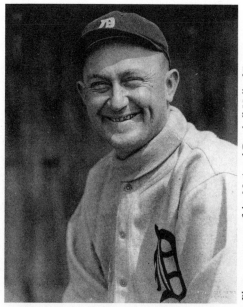

As hard as it might be for some to believe, Cobb did have a lighter side and, at times, displayed a full smile for photographers.

An amused Cobb stands ready to enter the field of play for one of his 3,034 games. He is fifth all-time for games played in Major League Baseball history.

Freely admitting that he wasn't a natural hitter, Cobb had to work extremely hard to attain the success he achieved, especially in overcoming his limitations against left-handed pitchers.

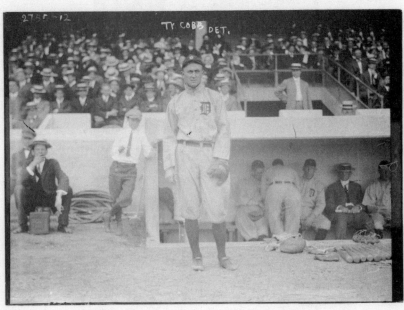

During a game, few individuals were more focused than "The Georgia Peach," but there were times when rowdy spectators shattered his concentration by verbal taunts. Once his breaking point was reached, he was unpredictable and, in 1912, rushed into a New York crowd to fight with a particularly unruly antagonist.

Photo by Louis Van Oeyen

Joe Jackson (right) was another southern product, hailing from South Carolina, and looked up to Cobb in many ways. Interestingly, many people considered Jackson to be a more natural hitter than Cobb, and Ty himself later acknowledged "Shoeless" as the greatest batsman in baseball history.

Photo courtesy of the National Baseball Hall of Fame Library, Cooperstown, NY

Three baseball legends, Cobb (left), Joe Jackson (center), and Sam Crawford (right), engage in a little pregame conversation.

For a number of years, Cobb and Judge Kenesaw Mountain Landis, the Commissioner of Baseball (right), had a solid friendship. That friendship dissolved as a result of the latter's actions during a high-profile gambling investigation in 1926–27, which threatened Cobb's position in Organized Baseball. Cobb was cleared of any wrongdoing.

Photo courtesy of the National Baseball Hall of Fame Library, Cooperstown, NY

Cobb and Tris Speaker, longtime American League rivals, became teammates in 1928 as members of the Philadelphia Athletics. Over twenty-two years, Speaker achieved a .345 career batting average and joined Cobb in the inaugural class of the National Baseball Hall of Fame in 1939.

After twenty-two years with the Detroit Tigers, Cobb joined Connie Mack's Philadelphia Athletics in 1927 and played for the A's for two years, retiring following the 1928 season.

Cobb and Babe Ruth (left) had one of the most interesting relationships in baseball history. At times they would go for each other's throats, ready to fight, while others they were jovial and joking. Through it all, though, they shared a mutual respect.

Photo courtesy of the Library of Congress

During the 1924 World Series, future Hall of Famers George Sisler (left), Babe Ruth (center), and Cobb (right) paused to shake hands for the camera.

Photo courtesy of AP Images

Displaying their famously joking manner, Babe Ruth (left) remarked about the thinning condition of Cobb's hair during a charity golf game in 1941. Cobb, who never sidestepped trash talking, undoubtedly prodded the "Bambino" in return, and the two had a good many laughs.

Later in Cobb's life, he had the opportunity to watch the eradication of baseball's color barrier and praised many African American superstars, including Willie Mays. When given a moment to bend the ear of a ball-player, Cobb didn't hesitate to offer words of advice or encouragement.

In May 1957, Cobb visited the clubhouse of the Milwaukee Braves and took a moment to display his hands-apart hitting method to (from left to right) Frank Torre, Warren Spahn, and Bobby Thomson.

Photo courtesy of AP Images

Cobb loved returning to the National Baseball Hall of Fame at Cooperstown, New York, and tried to make it an annual trip. On July 27, 1953, he placed particular importance on attending the ceremonies because one of his protégés, Al Simmons, was being enshrined. Fans always enjoyed hearing what Cobb had to say.

Photo courtesy of AP Images

Mourners in Royston, Georgia, pay their respects to Cobb during his funeral services on July 19, 1961, two days after his passing. Cobb was interred in his family's mausoleum, next to his parents and sister.

12

PATHWAY TO RICHES

Growing up the grandson of two war veterans, Ty Cobb was acutely deferential toward service in the armed forces and was fascinated by military traditions. Stories about the conquests and leadership of French Emperor Napoleon Bonaparte were amongst his favorite literary subjects and it's hard not to wonder whether the historical implications of going to Europe were on his mind in the days preceding his arrival to the combat theatre.[1] The American Civil War was another topic of great interest and he took particular pride in the actions of Southern soldiers. During a trip to Lookout Mountain at Chattanooga, Tennessee, in 1914, he lectured friends about local battles, telling them how the Confederates were often outnumbered. "If we had been able to muster as many soldiers as the north, just think what might have happened," he explained.[2]

Army officials acquiesced to Cobb's wishes in him joining the American Expeditionary Force (AEF) at once, and promptly routed him onto the troopship *HMS Baltic*, which sailed from New York around October 13, 1918. A fellow officer and passenger on the boat, Edward S. Luce, later recounted what he believed to be the "biggest scare or thrill" Cobb ever got in his life. "We were in mid-ocean, had just had supper, and were leaning over the side of the ship. It was a half-moonlit night; we could see the other ships in the convoy silhouetted against the sky, when, all of a sudden, we saw a white streak heading toward the *Baltic*. We were both frozen in our tracks. We couldn't move, and neither of us spoke a word.

"Just when that white streak we supposed was a torpedo was due to hit the side of the ship, we jumped back—and nothing happened. It was the white wave from another ship in the convoy and not a torpedo. Even now, when Ty and I meet, we always remark on 'the biggest scare we ever got in our lives.'"³ Because of the secrecy surrounding the deployment of troops, a number of newspaper writers mistakenly declared that Cobb was in either New York City or Washington, DC, even though he was well on his way to Europe. The *Baltic* arrived first at Liverpool, England, and then Le Havre, France, where Cobb and his comrades disembarked. On October 28, Detroit Tigers President Frank Navin received a notification by mail affirming that Cobb was safely overseas.⁴

Cobb received orders to Chaumont, a couple hours southeast of Paris, and the site of Allied Headquarters. His first duty station was actually located at the AEF Chemical Warfare Service training school, housed not far from the city at Hanlon Field, and there, he rendezvoused with a number of familiar faces. Included were Major Branch Rickey, formerly a manager of the St. Louis Browns, and Captain Christy Mathewson of the Cincinnati Reds. Over the previous two years, Cobb and Mathewson had become good friends, bonding in Cincinnati in the spring of 1917 and then during the Tigers-Reds exhibition series earlier in 1918. They played competitive checkers, a game Mathewson mastered, and together used their celebrity status to sell liberty war bonds.⁵

At Hanlon Field, the hazards of German warfare, specifically the poisonous gases being used in the trenches, were studied by thousands of recruits in advance of their expected transfer to the front lines. The proper uses of protective masks and defensive equipment were essential, and Cobb, Mathewson, Rickey, and their brethren passed through a specialized gas chamber as part of their training. According to Cobb's 1961 autobiography, he and others missed a signal and were exposed to a harmful dose of gas during their instruction session. He claimed that eight men died as a result and Mathewson suffered irreparable damage to his lungs.⁶ Fortunately for Cobb, he experienced only a slight illness and remained fit for combat. However, on November 11, 1918, the armistice was signed, putting an end to the combat in Europe, and he never saw Germany. Not before very long, he was back on the Atlantic Ocean sailing for home.

The USS *Leviathan* was one of the first troopships parading westward in December 1918, and Cobb was amongst the nearly 9,000 soldiers, sailors, and marines aboard. The Saturday before landing at Hoboken, New Jersey, an entertainment show was staged and the baseball fans of the crowd called Captain Cobb front and center to make a speech. He abided on the extraordinary occasion and, in what were probably the most important oratory comments he'd ever given in his life—to triumphant members of the military returning to their families—made an incredible pledge to his comrades.

A young Brooklyn war hero, who'd been seriously injured in combat, told a reporter what the baseball luminary said. "He [Cobb] told us a lot of josh stuff and when he told us some more about baseball, he says, 'If I get back in the game and I'm playing at the Polo Grounds, I want you fellas all to remember I made this trip on the Lee-vy,' that's what we call this ship, with you. 'If I'm stealing third,' says Ty, 'and it flashes on anyone of you who I am just as I'm sliding to the base, I want you to stand right up in the bleachers and yell out, *Hey, Ty, I'm a guy that was on the Lee-vy!* And I'll run right off the baseline and over to wherever you are in the bleachers and shake hands and sit down and have a talk about this trip. To hell with whether we win or lose.'" The young man then proudly said, "I'm gonna take Ty Cobb up" on that promise.[7]

Upon his arrival on American soil on December 16, 1918, Cobb was besieged by journalists looking for a headline.[8] They wanted to know what his intentions were, and if he really planned to walk away from the game of baseball. His responses were half-hearted, but it was clear that quitting the game was a possibility. Before the end of the year, there were rumors he planned to exercise his newfound freedom since receiving his uncondi-tional release from Detroit prior to his deployment and sign with the New York Yankees for the 1919 season. It was a stunning turnaround, but base-ball officials were not buying the trick for a minute. Cobb, and any other players who left for military service, were still tied to their original ballclubs, and were, in no way, free agents. That meant Cobb was going nowhere but Detroit, if he planned to resume his baseball career.

There was certainly a lot to consider and Cobb needed time to digest his future plans. Off the diamond, he'd been exceptionally shrewd with his money and demonstrated his ambitious business sensibility innumerable times over the past decade. His investments were originally based on a need to secure an income outside of what he made in baseball, due to the wobbly nature of the sport. Any number of times, a fractious break from Detroit management over contract terms could've put an end to his regular pay-checks, but since he was always enterprising, his family would never do with-out. And that was a purposeful arrangement on his part, consciously made to protect his wife and children going into the future.

Cobb, in 1916, expressed a partiality toward bank stock and real estate, but his portfolio through the years was remarkably diverse.[9] Back in 1907, he placed money in an unguaranteed Arizona gold mine, only to see his money jump from $3 a share to upwards of $100 three years later. The deal, recommended by a friend, paid off in spades, and the novice investor gained confidence in listening to the advice of others. He followed up by putting $1,000 into cotton and watching his money leap to $7,500.[10] As a citizen of Detroit, he entered a local retail sporting goods operation run by William B. Jarvis in June 1912 and a line of "Ty Cobb" branded merchandise was produced, everything from baseball equipment to tennis rackets. He saw the long-term viability of such a venture and told a reporter, "This new business is something I intend to make a life work of and it certainly looks good to me."[11]

In the baseball realm, sportswriters linked him to ownership positions with Indianapolis of the American Association and Lincoln of the Western League, but neither panned out. Then in 1911, he joined Frank Navin, William Yawkey, and Hugh Jennings to buy the Providence Grays of the International League, which became somewhat of a minor league proving ground for the Tigers.[12] Cobb again broadened his interests in September 1917, when he formed an Augusta agency to distribute Anheuser-Busch's nonalcoholic soft drink, Bevo. The beverage was sold as an alternative to beer and sponsors targeted the military in marketing strategies.[13] E. A. Batchelor predicted that the investment would bring Cobb $10,000 annually.[14] Also at Augusta, he formed the Ty Cobb–Bill Sanford Tire Company, and his firm was the exclusive vendor for the popular Diamond Tires in the district.[15]

Buying property was long a passion of Cobb, and he put money into real estate in both Detroit and Augusta. Sidney I. Busbia was his agent and partner for a number of homes and lots in the latter location and, at different points, Cobb owned hundreds of acres of land across Richmond County, Georgia.[16] Of all his properties, one in particular received a personal touch. In 1916, he incorporated the United Apartment Company with four associates and constructed a $75,000 modern apartment building at the northwest corner of Greene and Cumming Streets. The beautiful structure was named the "Shirley Apartments" for his daughter, Shirley Marion Cobb, and is still standing in the heart of Augusta, today known as the "Cobb House Apartments."[17]

Stock in the United Motors Corporation was a smart buy for Cobb, especially after the company was bought by General Motors in 1918. By the end of 1920, he would own nearly 300 shares in "GM," worth around $4,000.[18]

Another important stock purchase came in the form of the soft drink Coca Cola, and, in fact, it would ultimately be the most significant and enduring investment he'd ever make. His attention was initially drawn to the soda by Atlanta businessman Robert W. "Bob" Woodruff, whose father Ernest was an instrumental cog in the 1919 purchase of the company from the Candler family. Cobb explained in his autobiography that Woodruff convinced him to take out a loan for $10,800 so he could obtain 300 shares in 1918.[19] It was a wise decision and served as the golden goose on his pathway to riches in subsequent years.

Ironically, during Cobb's post-military period of rest and relaxation, he was confronted by the sudden serious illness of his boss, business partner, and mentor, William Yawkey. Yawkey, part owner of the Tigers since 1903, was passing through Augusta when he was overcome by influenza and hospitalized. Rushing to his bedside, Cobb offered his support, but the baseball magnate succumbed on March 5, 1919.[20] Notably, Yawkey's adopted son Tom would later enter the major leagues as an owner as well, purchasing the Boston Red Sox in 1933 and holding his position for more than forty years. He was once asked about Cobb and replied, "I've always had the greatest respect for him as a player and as a man. I've always considered him the greatest player that ever lived."[21]

Detroit players reported to spring camp at Macon, Georgia, in March and Cobb was not only absent, but his status remained unclear. He hadn't signed a new contract, and communications between the outfielder and Frank Navin were silent. In terms of conditioning, Cobb was in good shape, having spent considerable time hunting and working out with the Washington Senators at Warren Park in Augusta. Yearning to get back into the swing of things and disregarding any previous thoughts of retirement, he agreed to a two-year, $20,000 annual salary, and met the team in South Carolina on April 8.[22] The next day, he entered the lineup at Rock Hill, and in his first at bat in months, homered much to the delight of the crowd.[23] At Greensboro, North Carolina, a few days later, he was mobbed by fans of all ages, many of whom just wanted to catch a glimpse.

Although the war was over, major league owners felt the overall environment for baseball was uncertain and they agreed to shorten the 1919 season to 140 games. In contrast, Cobb expected prosperity and he couldn't have been more right. Attendance in Detroit alone was going to triple over the year prior as America's pastime was embraced by a patriotic public.[24] Cobb was set to play ball on Wednesday, April 23, for opening day at Navin Field, but rain and cold weather postponed the highly anticipated affair for two days. On Friday afternoon, 10,000 patrons braved the chill to see their hometown favorites beat Cleveland, 4–2. Cobb, having gone 2-for-4 with a double and two RBIs, looked to be in top shape.[25]

Sometime that same day—probably following the game—he encountered a maid at the Pontchartrain Hotel in what might have been, according to press reports, the most disturbing off-the-field incident Cobb ever experienced. However, at the time, few people knew the episode occurred at all. Newspaper editors were reached by influential powers prior to breaking the story locally and it was decided not to harm the reputation of the recently returned war veteran and baseball hero on the dawn of a new season. It wasn't until eight days later that the *Chicago Defender*, an African American paper, revealed what otherwise should have been front page news in all the major dailies. The *Defender* rightfully called out its counterparts for the lack of coverage and declared, "Every effort has been made by authorities connected with the Detroit club to keep the story of Cobb's brutality suppressed."[26]

Chronicling the gathered evidence, the *Defender* explained that Cobb came upon Mrs. Ada Morris, an African American woman, changing the bed linen in his room. He asked her where she was from and Morris replied, "Pennsylvania." Cobb then responded by saying, "There never was a nigger like you from Pennsylvania." Refusing to be spoken to in such a manner, Morris let Cobb know and, according to the *Defender*, the volley of words quickly turned into a physical altercation. The scrap was essentially one-sided and ended when Cobb kicked her down some stairs.[27] Morris, bruised and battered and under the care of a doctor, contacted attorney Reuben C. Nicholson and immediately initiated a $10,000 civil action.[28]

Once word of the case went public in late May, papers across the country picked up on the story and it was of great interest that Cobb completely dismissed his first court appearance.

In response, Wayne County Circuit Court Judge Clyde Webster issued a victory to Morris by default.[29] Former judge James O. Murfin, who represented Cobb in the infamous 1914 butcher assault case, contested the decision and a grueling legal battle ensued. The *Chicago Defender* mentioned that representatives of the ballplayer were endeavoring to settle out of court by offering a miniscule sum of money. That tactic had worked in yet another of Cobb's controversial affairs when an under-the-table payment of $115 was paid to night watchman George Stanfield ten years earlier.[30] But this time around, Morris and her lawyer were steadfast and denied Cobb an easy way out.[31]

The lack of rounded coverage, detailed statements from both sides, and other witness reports left the entire situation with an overtone of ambiguity. But based on Cobb's track record and the way political muscle assembled to support his defense as in times past, there was enough to bolster the credibility of the alleged evidence—at least somewhat. The fact that neither Morris nor Cobb stepped forward with a detailed description of what occurred—and there were absolutely zero independent accounts from eyewitnesses—contributed to the uncertainty of the case. Adding to the mysteriousness, the result of the $10,000 civil action was never publicly revealed by the mainstream press. The story went away in a cloud of silence, just like Cobb and his backers had hoped, and it is possible that a settlement was eventually reached.[32]

Cobb's season, in spite of the legal chaos, didn't miss much of a beat. His solo numbers were first-rate, as were customary, but the Tigers loomed as a pretty solid second division club for most of May. There was still optimism, as his production combined with Bobby Veach, Harry Heilmann, and Ira Flagstead, created many concerns for opposing pitchers.[33] Frank Navin, in trying to give Detroit better chances down the stretch, sent $12,000 to the Yankees for left-hander Dutch Leonard in May 1919, and on the surface, the move seemed like a positive step. Leonard joined "Hooks" Dauss, Bernie Boland, and Howard Ehmke to complete the club's quartet of starters, and helped push the Tigers into second place during an important road trip east in late July and early August. The excursion wrapped up with sweeps of both Washington and Philadelphia.

On September 4, 1919, a loudmouth from the stands at Navin Field was desperate for Cobb's attention and called him a number of "vile epithets." The tension slowly developed and Cobb, at first, was able to ignore the ear-splitting comments. His point of no return was inching closer and closer, and he walked over to the side of the field where the boisterous spectator was sitting and warned him on two occasions, even challenging the man to a fight after the game. The rowdy was not backing down for a moment, apparently unafraid of the consequences, and once the final out was made, he rushed onto the field to confront the Georgian. Needless to say, Cobb was in no mood for extra innings with a foolhardy hood, and he didn't waste any time kneeing the man in the groin and walking to the clubhouse, his day's work at an end.[34]

"I don't like brawls," Cobb explained, "and avoid them whenever possible. All players could avoid such unpleasantness and abuse if men like that one this afternoon were not permitted in the stands. They should be ejected from the ball park when they become as nasty and abusive as that fellow became to me this afternoon. He deliberately put himself out to ride and insult me. Some of these bullies apparently think that as soon as a man puts on a baseball uniform, he becomes fair game. I disagree with that theory. These insulting fellows wouldn't dare go into a man's office and call him the names they call ball players. They wouldn't go into a theater and abuse actors as they abuse us. This ball park is our office and we are entitled to a certain amount of respect. So far as I am concerned, I mean to insist upon that little measure of success."[35]

The Tigers lost their hold on second place in a competitive race for the American League pennant, and landed in fourth place behind Chicago, Cleveland, and New York, eight games out of first.[36] The White Sox, led by "Shoeless" Joe Jackson, Eddie Collins, and Cobb's old Augusta teammate, Eddie Cicotte, were destined for the World Series against the Cincinnati Reds, and, considering the level of talent on the club, were a reasonably safe bet to win the championship. Cobb thought so, and placed wagers on the first two games. But when the results came back, 9–1 and 4–2 in favor of Cincinnati, he was out $50 and $100 respectively.[37] The Reds captured three additional contests—surprising many observers—and won the series. Outside factors, it was later revealed, had influenced a certain element of the Chicago ballclub and the "Black Sox" were doomed for defeat in a shameful display of corruption.

Ending his year with a .384 average, Cobb won his third-straight major league batting title and eleventh overall (twelfth in the AL).[38] His accomplishment was impressive, but strikingly overshadowed by the play of twenty-four-year-old George Herman "Babe" Ruth of the Boston Red Sox. Ruth was a colorful six-year veteran and known mostly as a pitcher. But his transition to the outfield placed him in the everyday lineup and gave him the chance to demonstrate an extraordinary slugging power that was unparalleled in baseball history. In 1919, he blasted 29 home runs and set a new single-season record, electrifying crowds across the league circuit. He topped the majors in on-base percentage (.456), slugging percentage (.657), RBIs (113), runs scored (103), and total bases (284), and was fast becoming the most popular man in the game.

Cobb acknowledged Ruth as a "natural slugger" first in 1915, and was complimentary of the young up-and-comer in a couple of his syndicated articles.[39] During the subsequent Detroit-Boston rivalry, the two were undoubtedly fired up by the friction on the field, but there were no specific hints of a personal feud. That began to change in 1919, and writers fueled the mounting antagonism by almost incessant head-to-head comparisons of Cobb and Ruth. Pundits partial to Babe predicted he'd once and for all end the batting championship streak of the Georgian, and minimized Cobb's abilities to ballyhoo their hero. Detroit manager Hugh Jennings came to his player's defense, declaring, "For years Cobb has been the hitting marvel of baseball. I'd rather have one Cobb than five Ruths!"[40]

In recognizing his own increased value, Ruth created a sensation by issuing an ultimatum to Boston management, demanding $20,000 for 1920 despite the fact that he already had signed a three-year deal for half that amount. If he didn't receive the money, Ruth declared he wanted to be traded at once.[41] Cobb heard the story and spoke out against such a move, saying: "Ruth, having signed to play for $9,000 is not playing fair if he tries to hold up his employers for more while the contract is in force. I'm for a ball player getting all he's worth, but I am opposed to his breaking a contract to do it. And that's what Ruth says he intends to do."[42] The inference that he was a contract jumper made Ruth furious, and he told the press, "I'll settle the question when I meet Cobb [next spring]." Journalists took that to mean he planned to instigate a fight with his growing rival. Ruth added, "Cobb must be jealous of me because the newspapers have played me up this year as the biggest attraction in baseball."[43]

Any concerns Cobb might have about Ruth and the brewing contentiousness were shelved to attend to his ailing wife in Augusta. On September 19, she gave birth to their fourth child, an eight-pound girl they named Beverly, and was in poor health. Cobb immediately journeyed home following the season closer at Chicago and tended to his family. Business was a secondary priority, and as his wife improved, he was able to devote time to preparations for the grand opening of his tire business on October 20.[44] Through the winter, he spent time hunting, working with his dogs, and was involved in a prominent real estate transaction for the Schneider Building in downtown Augusta.[45]

Rumors at the end of Detroit's 1919 season talked of team dissension and insiders once again claimed that the majority of managerial decisions were being made by Cobb, not Jennings. Some sportswriters awaited an official announcement by Navin declaring Ty the new boss, but it never came. Spring training picked up in March 1920 at Macon, and while Cobb remained a stone's throw from his teammates, he never chose to make the trip from Augusta. When questioned about his failure to appear, Cobb said he was "already in perfect condition," and didn't believe any additional preparations were necessary. Furthermore, he mentioned the likelihood of soon retiring, a theme that bobbed up in late 1918. "This will probably be my last season on the ball field," he declared.[46]

As the Tigers went up the East Coast in an exhibition series against the Boston Braves, Cobb was scheduled to catch up with the club at Greensboro, North Carolina, on March 31, but illness put a damper on those plans.[47] He instead entered the lineup at Indianapolis on April 10, and, four days later, inaugurated the championship campaign with the Tigers squad versus Chicago in a 3–2 loss. The next twelve games ended similarly, and by May 2, the team was in last place with an embarrassing 0–13 record. There was plenty of time for recovery, but Detroit was lackluster in nearly every category and even Cobb was faltering. It was startling how inaccurate the preseason "dope" had been, as many sportswriters pegged the Tigers as challengers for, at least, second place. The club was not up amongst the league's best, but rather at the bottom of the barrel.

Struggling pitchers, low morale, and poor overall leadership was a recipe for disaster for Detroit. No remedy came from Cobb and his old-time superhero act was unavailable, primarily because he was having troubles of his own. His batting average was in the .250 range by mid-May and physical impairments were almost consistent. A shoulder injury slowed him up a bit, and his left elbow was bruised after being hit by a fastball from Allan Sothoron of the St. Louis Browns on May 30. In the 10th inning of a game at Chicago on June 6, he collided with right-fielder Ira Flagstead chasing a ball and was carried to the dugout in bad shape. The *Detroit Free Press* indicated that he was "grievously hurt" in the accident, and initial reports had him on the sidelines for up to ten days.[48]

Cobb, with torn ligaments in his left leg, was much worse off than journalists supposed and would be out of action for a month. Oddly, the speculation then went in the opposite direction, asserting that his career was finished. He scoffed at the guesswork of baseball experts and stated that he'd be back in the lineup by July 15.[49] In the meantime, he hobbled around the Augusta area recuperating, and took in a couple of local ballgames. He also signed a deal, believed to be valued at upwards of $10,000, to participate in a series of exhibitions in California after the season in what would be his first West Coast jaunt.[50] The trip was something to look forward to, but in the interim, he needed to regain his strength and rejoin his teammates.

On July 8, Cobb reemerged in a Detroit uniform and added an important RBI in a 4–3 victory at the Polo Grounds in New York.[51] Before the series in New York concluded, Cobb and Ruth gave the fans a thrill by homering in the same game on July 11. It was Babe's 27th of the year, and only the second for Cobb. A couple days later, Cobb reinjured his leg sliding into second at Fenway Park. His injury appeared devastating to one Detroit journalist, who promptly declared that he "might not play again" in 1920.[52] Cobb, however, loved to prove the naysayers wrong and fought through the pain to go 3-for-4 for Detroit two games later, on July 16. He was determined to remain on the field.

The baseball community as a whole was horrified by the news from New York on August 16, 1920, that popular shortstop Ray Chapman of the Cleveland Indians had been hit in the head by a pitch and critically wounded. Suffering a fractured skull and bleeding on the brain, he succumbed to his injuries overnight following an unsuccessful surgery at a Manhattan hospital. At the time, historian Frederick G. Lieb wrote, "The biggest tragedy that major league baseball ever has known in nearly fifty years of operation befell the great American sport this morning" when Chapman passed away.[53] His death marked the first fatality at the big league level, and, of course, there was an immediate response from the public, officials, and players to reprimand the pitcher at fault for the high and inside ball that caused his mortal wounds—accident or not. The attention was now on Carl Mays, the controversial hurler for the New York Yankees.

The Tigers were in Boston and Cobb was sound asleep when he received a late night telephone call, informing him of Chapman's death. A journalist wanted an instant reaction, and Cobb offered a few words. But the next morning's paper included statements attributed to the Detroit outfielder that Ty insisted he didn't make, specifically comments that he wanted Mays banned from baseball. In fact, Detroit and Boston players were said to be organizing an effort to sit out any game Mays was scheduled to pitch against them. New York pressmen recited the remarks reportedly said by Cobb and fans were eager for the latter's arrival at the Polo Grounds on August 21. The huge throng of more than 30,000 people bombarded Cobb with jeers, boos, and taunts, letting the Detroiter know just how they felt.[54]

"This hissing of Cobb is the most unjust thing of his career," Hugh Jennings said after the game. "He certainly does not deserve it, as he absolutely is guiltless of doing or saying anything to hurt Mays."[55] The rough treatment motivated Cobb at the plate on August 22 and he went 5-for-6 with four singles, a double, two runs, and two RBIs in an 11–9 victory. Years later, Jack Stevens, host of *The Inside of Sports* for the Mutual Radio Network, remembered the incident and recalled how Cobb responded to the booing. "Ty kept grinning and pounding out hits," Stevens said. "He hit five in a row and then the boos gave way to cheers. After Ty had slapped his fifth hit, the stands fairly rocked with applause, the gathering of 40,000 giving him the greatest ovation he ever received" at the local stadium.[56]

Cleveland, with the spirit of Chapman in their corner and the sympathy of fans nationwide, won the 1920 American League pennant and then captured the World Series title from Brooklyn, five games to two. The Tigers were 37 games behind the Indians in the race, finishing in seventh with a record of 61–93. Unstable pitching was a central problem, as the team's top five hurlers, Hooks Dauss, Howard Ehmke, Red Oldham, Dutch Leonard, and Doc Ayers each had a losing record. Cobb's .334 batting average in 112 games placed him tenth in the league behind George Sisler, Tris Speaker, Joe Jackson, Babe Ruth, Eddie Collins, and others. He didn't rate amongst the leaders in hits, runs, RBIs, or stolen bases, and actually, his 15 pilfered bags were his lowest total since 1905, his first year in the majors. Months earlier, Jennings said he noticed Cobb was slowing up, and Ty's susceptibleness to injury especially when it came to his legs, seemed to confirm that he was no longer the natural speed demon he once was.[57]

The Chicago White Sox were 96 game winners in 1920, and landed in second place just two games behind Cleveland. But the team was fractured beyond repair after a couple players who'd participated in a systematic effort to throw games during the 1919 World Series revealed their stories.

Two of Cobb's acquaintances, Eddie Cicotte and Joe Jackson, were at the heart of the swindle, and the damaging controversy threatened the sanctity of major league baseball. Regardless of the allegations and the result of the series, it was impossible to definitively say which players played crooked. Yet, it wasn't impossible to say which players took tainted money from gamblers, and both Cicotte and Jackson were guilty. They were lumped into a bunch and altogether banned from Organized Baseball forever by newly established Baseball Commissioner Judge Kenesaw M. Landis.

Cobb held "Shoeless" Joe in the highest regard. That was evidenced by his comments to a reporter in Jackson's hometown of Greenville, South Carolina in 1942. "I don't care how we feel or what some folks may say about some of the tragic incidents in that man's baseball life. You can't take away from him the fact that he was the greatest hitter the game has known. He was greater than I, although I managed to top him in the records each year we fought it out for the batting titles. Jackson could hit any kind of a pitch, from his shoe-tops to his head. There may have been some things I could do better, such as dragging bunts, and they say I had a faster getaway from the plate on the swing. But Jackson never was fooled up there, and I think he had the best eyes, and the keenest reflexes, of any hitter I ever saw."[58]

Not surprisingly, based on the listless performance of his club, Jennings tendered his resignation as manager of the Tigers on October 15, 1920.[59] In his fourteen years as skipper, the team had captured three pennants and finished in the top four of the standings—ten times. Jennings's passive style of management was unique and allowed Cobb the freedom to independently prosper without overbearing supervision. When volatile situations arose, instead of arguing with his temperamental outfielder, Hugh often looked the other way. These incidents were sometimes interpreted as Jennings playing favorites with Cobb but, all things considered, the two complemented each other in many ways. Certainly, Cobb's progression as a superstar athlete would have advanced differently under a manager other than Jennings.

Of course, Cobb was considered as a possible replacement, but he long maintained that he never wanted to manage while still an active player.[60] The June before, he'd spoken about such a duel responsibility, saying: "I am a ball player and not a manager. I have troubles enough playing the game without the additional burden of management. As I look at it now, when the last man is out, my work is over for the day. The manager stews all night figuring why the team lost or why the pitchers failed to come thru and a lot of other worries. No management for me. Perhaps when my playing days are over I may take up the task of management, but not so long as I am cavorting on the ball field."[61] Cobb's perspective was reasonable and respectable, and he appeared a man who recognized his own limitations.

On October 16, 1920, Cobb and his wife Charlie, plus their four children, arrived in San Francisco on a trip of business and pleasure.[62] He was treated like royalty by local baseball officials, government representatives, and scores of fans who'd never seen him in person before. He made a personal appearance at the Jackson Playground, putting on a baseball demonstration and answering questions for a mob of awestruck kids. His recommendation was to stay away from cigarettes if they hoped to become ballplayers and then handed out a bunch of signed balls.[63] Huge crowds turned out for exhibitions in San Francisco, Fresno, San Jose, and elsewhere; when he wasn't on the field, local mayors were beckoning him for social visits.

A highlight for Cobb in San Francisco was meeting an old-time ballplayer named Mike Finn, who was in the game before he was even born. After the meeting, Finn told a reporter: "Ty Cobb is so different from the man I expected to see that I couldn't get my breath for awhile. He is a champion hitter and somehow I had pictured him as a big roughneck with bulging muscles. Instead of that I was greeted by a boyish-looking fellow who looked as if he had to shave only once a week and would not have to use much of a razor then. He has class sticking out all over him, and I am mighty proud to have made his acquaintance."[64]

The Cobb family headed back east in December 1920 after a successful journey and the beauty of Northern California was etched in their collective minds. Ty's thoughts were preoccupied by the managerial challenge and the possibility of having to play ball for someone a little less understanding than Jennings. There were other concerns as well, but in his heart, he knew more than anything else that he had to put to rest the rumors that he was in decline. And he didn't ever want to finish a season with his batting average tenth in the league again.

13

MICROMANAGER

Prior to the 1920 baseball season, a joint committee made up of representatives of the American and National Leagues agreed to place a ban on "freak deliveries." The tactic effectively abolished the spitball, emery ball, shine ball, and other trick pitches thrown from the mound, and would greatly alter the way the game was played.[1] Hitters, for years, were at a disadvantage, and deceptive hurlers twisted them in knots on a routine basis. But once these techniques of modifying the ball were stripped from pitchers, batters were empowered at the plate. Offensive production increased and scoring was no longer contingent on clever base-running and small ball. The home run was fast becoming the primary feature of baseball and Babe Ruth's powerful clouting had turned him into an international celebrity.

Ruth, who was purchased by the New York Yankees from the Red Sox in late 1919, led the league in more than a dozen categories in 1920, and his 54 homers established a towering record that captivated the imagination of the young and old.[2] His rise to prominence in the wake of the "Black Sox" scandal couldn't have come at a better time for baseball, and the public willingly overlooked any damage to the sport's integrity to embrace Ruth as its central hero. In general, home runs were plentiful in 1920, as 630 were hit across the majors (183 more than the year before), and crowd enthusiasm was at an all-time high. Journalists and insiders spoke about the liveliness of the ball and theorized that a combination of weakened pitching, better quality yarn used in the manufacture of balls, and a pure motivation by hitters to emulate Ruth by swinging for the fences contributed to the dawn of what was dubbed the "Lively Ball Era."[3]

Following the response of Ty Cobb and Ruth's threat to jump his Boston contract if he didn't receive a raise, the latter expressed a desire to fight his

Detroit rival. But not only did he think better of a possible scrap in 1920, the two were photographed together at the Polo Grounds in New York in May. Interestingly, Cobb navigated into the tour he made of the West Coast with the aid of Ruth's business manager, Johnny Igoe of Boston. In June of 1920, the latter compared the two, and favored Cobb. "Fans go to see Ruth do one thing—that is, hit home runs. They expect him to hit one and when he does they go home thrilled. Cobb stars every day. His hits are clean and he is always thinking of some way to outsmart the opposing team. Babe doesn't hit them over the fence every day. Ty shows his assortment of wonder stuff daily."[4]

With Cobb said to be the best of the old guard and Ruth the champion of the new, people loved to pit the two against each other, and everything from their box score numbers to their salaries were judged in side-by-side comparisons. Even their personalities were fodder for discussion. New York columnist Dan Daniel wrote: "Ruth had no enemies, only friends. Every fan was his pal and every person who saw him was sold immediately on George Herman Ruth. Ty Cobb somehow had few fans friends. He had a rasping manner, an overbearing way on the field."[5] Yankees locker room manager Fred Logan added: "The greatest clubhouse character was Babe Ruth. Easy with his dough, never sulked, always in fine humor, always in hoss-play, joking, rough-housing." Regarding Cobb, he noted that Ty was "erratic in the clubhouse," but considered him the better of the two.[6]

Grantland Rice, formerly of the *Atlanta Journal* and now a syndicated columnist in New York, was honest in his perspective despite his longstanding friendship with Cobb. He stated that the Detroit outfielder was "held in admiration rather than in affection," and those "who are not inclined to cheer his personality must yield him his due as a star." Ruth, on the other hand, had "the name, the wallop, and the personality that make up a popular mixture."[7]

The game was unquestionably evolving away from the style of Cobb, and fans were no longer centering their attention on his rousing performances on the basepaths, but holding their collective breath anticipating monstrous home runs. Cobb, however, wasn't yet ready to give up his place in baseball's pecking order. He was more competitive than ever, and in battling Ruth on the field, he was prepared to fight tooth and nail to help his team win. And whenever he got the chance, he planned to antagonize the living daylights out of his foe and utilize his famous psychological methods to get inside Ruth's head. He knew it had worked on Joe Jackson and scores of others, so why not Ruth?

Rumors were rampant in late 1920. Joe LeBlanc of *Collyer's Eye*, a publication out of Chicago, announced that Cobb was sold to the White Sox for $50,000, which was, incidentally, half of Ruth's purchase price.[8] Frank Navin told a reporter that the story was, "Too ridiculous to even think of."[9] Other gossip related to the Tigers managerial job vacancy, and ex-White Sox boss Clarence "Pants" Rowland was believed to be a top candidate. George Stallings and Jimmy Burke were also apparently being considered, according to hot stove chatter. But Navin wanted Cobb first and foremost, and sent six telegrams to his star on the coast trying to induce him.[10] En route back east in December, Cobb stopped in New Orleans and discussed the opportunity at length with a trusted friend, Detroit sportswriter E. A. Batchelor. Batchelor was fond of the idea, and by the end of their meeting, Cobb was almost convinced.[11]

Yet, still, a little part of him was conflicted and he explained his anxieties to the press. On one hand, he liked the idea of imparting his philosophies and molding a championship squad. He wanted the glory that accompanied such a feat and sought to add a World Series title to his career record. On the other hand, he felt his playing skills would be hampered by managerial responsibilities. Additionally, he knew that it would take a couple years to build the Tigers into a contender and didn't want fans to become frustrated by his inability to magically construct a winner after one or two seasons.[12] He seemed confident to a certain degree, but held back by the many questions that remained. From the viewpoint of experts, though, it was more about whether or not Cobb could inhibit his own caustic disposition enough to be a successful leader.

After a brief stay in Augusta, Cobb ventured to New York for a meeting with Navin at the Vanderbilt Hotel on December 18, 1920. Contract terms, various obstacles, and other concerns were debated for several hours and, with a handshake and a signature, Cobb agreed to become the playing manager of the Detroit Tigers for 1921. In the subsequent announcement, it was made abundantly clear that his one-year, $25,000 deal made him, once again, the highest paid man in baseball, topping Ruth, and no doubt Cobb took a lot of satisfaction from that fact.[13] As manager, Cobb was given full authority to modify the team roster, and it is notable that he scouted a handful of potential recruits while in California. Southpaw pitcher Bert Cole, a twenty-four-year-old from San Francisco, was particularly impressive, and upon getting the scouting info from Cobb, Navin quickly worked out an arrangement to land the hopeful.[14]

Fighting off a winter cold, Cobb went to Detroit for an elegant day-long gala to celebrate his new position on February 1, 1921. In addition to a special breakfast and luncheon, there was an exclusive evening banquet at the Hotel Statler, and amongst the 900 dignitaries in attendance were Ban Johnson, Hugh Jennings, Sam Thompson, Jimmy Barrett, and Davy Jones. Politicians, businessmen from the auto industry, and other well-known socialites were present, and when Cobb stood to express his gratitude, he "spoke feelingly," at times holding back his emotions. He later told a journalist that the testimonial was the "greatest honor ever paid him," according to the *Detroit Free Press*.[15]

Cobb's approach to being a manager was the opposite of what was expected of him. Instead of ruling with unyielding aggressiveness, he planned to offer "encouragement and advice" to his men.[16] Beginning in spring training at San Antonio, he worked to foster the image of a brother, not as a domineering chief standing off to the side barking orders. He was right there with his players, doing everything they were doing, running laps and making sure they received appropriate accommodations. Going against his personal nature, he became more outgoing, getting to know the guys on the team and listening to their stories.[17] He disallowed the growth of destructive cliques and put a lot of thought into being the kind of ideal manager he would want for himself.

In terms of doctrine, Cobb made a number of significant changes. He called his men to report at around 1 p.m. every afternoon, having canceled morning practice. Theorizing that productivity was vastly reduced after just waking up and having breakfast, he believed he could get better results from his players later in the day. He eliminated clubhouse strategy meetings, calling them a waste of time.[18] Cobb encouraged instant reaction to the happenings on the diamond and didn't want his players trying to force a specific set play they'd figured out beforehand, especially if it didn't correspond with what was breaking down in front of them. Another change came to the club's on-field signals, which were tossed out and replaced with a completely new system. He advocated heads-up play, teamwork, and wanted a fierce fighting spirit. He also expressed the necessity of having a versatile attack to keep opponents guessing.

Weighing over 195 pounds, Cobb arrived in San Antonio the heaviest he'd ever been, but was his same old self, striving to shed his extra poundage and sharpen his batting eye. Most of his time was spent observing the thirty or so other players in camp, including the rookie upstarts, and the cumbersome job of weaning the roster down to around twenty-four was his alone. Five prospects, Lu Blue, Johnny Bassler, Carl Holling, Harvey "Suds" Sutherland, and the aforementioned Bert Cole, were imports from the Pacific Coast League, and impressed Cobb enough to earn regular berths with the team. Blue stood out as a first baseman and allowed Harry Heilmann to shift back to right field, strengthening the entire defense. Catcher Bassler was highly touted as well, and was acquired in a trade that sent veteran Tigers backstop Oscar Stanage to Los Angeles.[19]

The general consensus was that Cobb was doing well as a rookie manager in his first couple of months on the job, but he was pretty much guaranteed to face growing pains along the way. His famous temperament wasn't going to disappear no matter how much he tried to repress it, and differences between himself and his players were going to crop up from time to time. But morale was good in March and April 1921.[20] Dutch Leonard, the well-known pitcher, returned to the Tigers soon after Cobb was appointed manager, despite quitting the club the September before because of problems with Jennings.[21] Leonard apparently believed the fresh leadership of Cobb offered new potential for Detroit in the American League pennant hunt and rejoined his teammates.

Although the overall mood of the team was positive, it likely would've been undermined to a large extent had pitcher Howard Ehmke and Cobb not made peace months earlier. The two men had frequently butted heads in recent years and the feud was amongst the most harmful clubhouse dilemmas facing the Tigers. However, *The Sporting News* indicated that they "parted excellent friends" just prior to the end of the 1920 season.[22] With Leonard and Ehmke, his top two hurlers in good spirits, Cobb was enthusiastic, yet levelheaded about Detroit's chances of playing competitive ball against the likes of the Yankees and Indians. He predicted sixth place for his club and said he'd resign if they didn't fare better than seventh. "If we do better, the boys can rejoice with the fans," Cobb told a reporter.[23]

San Antonio, ironically, was the spring training locale for the New York Giants and no one had forgotten the bad blood between Cobb and John McGraw, stemming from the dust-up between the two in 1917. Nevertheless, locals welcomed a series and hoped bygones were bygones for the sake of old-fashioned, civilized baseball. The Tigers trained on a makeshift diamond at Brackenridge Park just north of downtown and stayed at the Travelers Hotel, while the Giants had the favored ball grounds at League Park, and were quartered at the Menger Hotel near the Alamo.[24]

Impatient officials scheduled two games for the proposed series without a working agreement between Cobb and McGraw, and the exhibitions slated for March 12–13 didn't come to fruition. According to Cobb, he refused to "eat humble pie" by personally asking McGraw to participate, and announced, "From now on, the Giants don't exist."[25] The pro-McGraw account claimed Cobb did turn up at the hotel to work a deal, and McGraw angrily told him, "I wouldn't play you a series if there were ten grand in it for us in every game."[26] Years later, New York Yankees manager Casey Stengel remembered the story and said McGraw ran Cobb out of the hotel lobby after the latter inquired about a series.[27] Once again, like most of baseball lore, the truth was somewhere in the middle of these versions.

The condition of the Tigers heading into the season opener on April 13 was the best in four years, Cobb believed, and excitement was not only running high in Detroit, but across the league. He invoked a little nostalgia in trying to pump up his players, harkening back to a retro style of uniform with an Old English "D" on the front, worn by the championship squads of the late 1900s. Amusingly, Cobb's superstitiousness was also prevalent, and Joey "Six-Toes" Joslin, about eleven years of age, hung around the dugout as a mascot. His job was simple: to inspire good luck and ward off any jinxes.[28] The first game versus Chicago was rained out and played on April 14 before 25,000 spectators in Detroit. Wet weather lingered in the area, but didn't damper the enthusiasm of fans. In the seventh inning, the Tigers charged back from a 5–1 deficit to tie things up, and then, in the bottom of the ninth, Harry Heilmann scored Ralph Young on a base hit in an amazing climax to Cobb's debut as manager. Detroit won, 6–5.[29]

The thrilling finish was an exceptional way to launch the 1921 campaign, but it didn't take long for Cobb's unique disposition to become apparent. At Chicago on April 21, he became aggravated to his limits by the instability of Ehmke to throw with any semblance of accuracy. He ran from center field to the pitcher's mound a number of times, halting the game in the process, and laid into Ehmke, which undoubtedly destabilized their recently mended relationship. Harry Bullion remarked that Cobb was going to be "prematurely old" if he expressed the same kind of nervousness every time the Tigers were defeated.[30] He appeared overly anxious and akin to a micromanager, trying to control each and every moving part of the game. Maybe it came with experience, but he had to learn that the fate of the season usually didn't rest in the result of a single contest. He couldn't take a loss personally, and, at the same time, hold a defeat against whichever players who were not up to par on that given day.

Rapidly sinking to the depths of the American League standings, the Tigers were failing to capitalize on opportunities and pitching was weaker than expected. Hitting and defense were above standard and even a little consistency from the mound would have gone a long way to win the games they were losing. In May, Detroit braced itself in third place and home fans continued to pour into Navin Field to see what kind of team Cobb was churning out. But things fell apart in the east, and Detroit lost nine in a row between June 11 and June 19, including sweeps by New York and Boston. The heated series against the Yankees saw Cobb resume his quarrel with Babe Ruth.

The hostilities began on June 12, when a photographer sought an updated photo of Cobb and Ruth together, and asked the latter to pose with his Detroit adversary. Babe responded in the negative, curtly dismissing the idea. The photographer instigated matters by telling Cobb about Ruth's rejection, and the Tigers' manager was prompted to do a little instigating of his own. He opened up a full barrage of criticism, sarcastic remarks, and vile epithets directed at Ruth, mocking him as a "gorilla," amongst other things. The situation developed further after both men rushed onto the field to pull Lu Blue from New York catcher Wally Schang, who'd erupted into near fisticuffs moments earlier. With the tensions heightened, they directed frantic comments at each other and came close to exchanging punches. The verbal jousting went on throughout the game, and likely the rest of the series.[31]

Ruth was very much superman-like the next day, blasting out two homers and pitching five innings in a 13–8 victory over Detroit. The *Brooklyn Standard Union* stated that he was out for "revenge" for the recent ridicule and Cobb, incidentally, was the only Tiger to go down on strikes.[32] On the whole, the June eastern tour symbolized everything that was wrong with the Tigers, from poor pitching to collapsing in the pinch. A slump by second baseman Ralph Young on defense hurt the infield significantly, and Cobb experimented with Joe Sargent at second and Ira Flagstead at shortstop, replacing veteran Donie Bush. On June 30, Cobb went out with a left knee injury, and placed Chick Shorten in center field.[33] The club temporarily rebounded, and even though his condition improved in the days following,

Cobb refused to disrupt the winning environment that was in place without him, remaining on the sidelines.[34]

The momentum trailed off, and by the end of July, he was back in the game. But the Tigers were determined to hold down sixth place in the standings and made no serious threat to improve their position for the balance of the season. Cobb, as usual, had a few colorful moments. During a midweek contest at Navin Field on July 13, he watched as his third baseman Bobby Jones was ejected for protesting a called third strike by umpire Billy Evans. Joe Sargent was slated to replace Jones, but when he didn't listen to Evans's directions, he too was tossed. Cobb was livid. He yelled his displeasure and later told a reporter that the umpire had exceeded his authority by ejecting Sargent before he even had a chance to get into the action. He said Evans smugly announced, "Get out your check books; this is going to cost you some money!"[35]

Not ordinarily intimidated on the diamond, thirty-seven-year-old Evans was a capable fighter, and had defended himself from unruly players and patrons innumerable times since becoming an American League umpire in 1906. Mixing with Cobb, whom he respected as a ballplayer, was just another day at the office, and he wasn't going to shy away from the harsh communication being passed back and forth on that occasion or any other. A little more than two months later, on September 24, 1921, at Washington, DC, Cobb and Evans picked up where they left off, and had a running dialogue that would've made a sailor cringe. Cobb was particularly expressive after being thrown out stealing a base and the final score, 5–1, in favor of the local squad, was anything but pleasing. Jawing on the way to their respective clubhouses, Cobb and Evans agreed to meet under the grandstand to settle things up, but this time using only their fists.[36]

It was easy to assume that Cobb was the aggressor, but he later refuted any such claim. "I did not challenge him," he explained in a letter to Joe Williams of the *New York World-Telegram*. "I have never challenged an umpire to fight."[37] In sync with other controversial moments from Cobb's career, his scrap with Evans became legendary, but was marred by poetic sportswriters looking for more melodrama than accuracy. He was often portrayed as a sadistic gladiator, provoking fights because he got a kick out of it. But in this case, Evans was the instigator and acknowledged it himself: "I challenged Cobb and there was nothing else he could do but accept."[38]

Agreeing beforehand to what was essentially a no-rules brawl, the player and umpire matched up and as many as fifty people watched the "savage"

encounter unfold. The fight consisted of wild punches, a modicum of wrestling, and a furious effort put forth by both individuals to gain the upper
hand. According to the *Washington Evening Star*, a total of eight wallops
successfully landed, and at the point in which the fight was halted, Cobb
was in charge.[39] Blood spilled from a cut to Evans's lip, and after cleaning
up, Evans went directly to the Tigers clubhouse and apologized. "I liked
him so much for that that I wished our quarrel had never happened," Cobb
explained. "In fact, it should never have happened, because my respect for
him was so great."[40]

Cobb silenced his critics by regaining his batting form in 1921, and his
only competition in the race for league honors came from fellow Tiger
Harry Heilmann. Heilmann, a product of San Francisco, had been with
Detroit since 1914 and was one of the most talented athletes in the game.
Standing 6'1" and weighing more than 190 pounds, he was a natural slugger with an exceptional eye at the plate. Baseball biographers have long
scrutinized the relationship of Cobb and Heilmann, and emphasized a
break in their relations after the latter was designated the 1921 batting
champion with a .394 average to Cobb's .389.[41] They offered the theory that
Cobb was bitter about losing the title and employed his old trick of not
speaking to his right fielder in a display of childish anger.

As was well known, Cobb's will to be number one in everything was a key
personality trait, and he was undoubtedly disappointed in placing second
for the batting championship. But with regard to Heilmann, he didn't
appear hostile, at least publicly. He lauded his outfielder, telling a reporter
that Heilmann stood next to Nap Lajoie as the best right-handed batter he
ever saw perform. "From the start of the recent season, he took the lead,
and, excepting one day, he never lost it," Cobb explained. "He consistently
kept his average above the .400 mark all the way, and his work didn't show
a flash in the pan at any time."[42] Heilmann also had good things to say
about his manager, declaring, "Whatever success I attain as a ball player, in
the game and financially, I owe it to Ty Cobb." He specifically attributed his
upswing in hitting, beginning in 1921, to the mentorship offered by the
Georgian.[43]

On a personal note, Cobb missed three games in June because he hur-
ried to the bedside of his sick grandmother, Sarah Ann, in Cherokee
County, North Carolina. The eighty-three year old was the matriarch of the
Cobb clan and was hugely influential in Ty's life. Throughout his childhood, he spent many summers with his father's parents in the western

mountains of North Carolina, and the wonderful visits were indelibly etched in his mind. He always held his grandmother in the highest esteem. She was wise, perceptive, and, as a "header," able to brew homemade concoctions to cure just about any kind of ailment. Cobb said that she possessed "one of the most remarkable minds, if not the most remarkable," he ever came into contact with, and that he "never knew another woman like her."[44] Sarah succumbed to her illness on October 4, 1921.[45]

Another significant family-related event occurred midseason for Ty, as he and his wife welcomed a new baby son, James Howell, on July 24. In the wake of a difficult delivery, Charlie's health was of serious concern and Ty rushed home to Augusta to tend to his wife. Many years later, his oldest daughter, Shirley, revealed to biographer Don Rhodes that Charlie suffered "eight miscarriages" in her lifetime and "wasn't supposed to have any children" after her birth in 1911.[46] Fortunately, her condition improved following the arrival of James, their fifth offspring, and he would be their final child.

The Tigers ended 1921 in sixth place with a 71–82 record, 27 games behind the pennant-winning Yankees. New York, led by Babe Ruth's amazing 59 home runs, ultimately lost the World Series to their cross-town rivals—the New York Giants. Shortly following the season finale in early October, Cobb went to San Francisco to manage a local club for the California Winter League, seemingly building upon his experiences from the prior year. Heading up the three other squads were baseball luminaries Harry Heilmann (Mission district of San Francisco), George Sisler (Vernon), and National League batting champion Rogers Hornsby (Los Angeles). While the four headliners were likely guaranteed sums at or around $10,000 apiece, the league itself was a financial bomb, and moneymen lost upwards of $40,000.[47]

Poor attendance and bad weather were a detriment, but Cobb made his presence felt on and off the field. Community leaders asked him to attend social events such as the Knights of Columbus gala at the Palace Hotel in San Francisco. He was called to make a speech, and Cobb preached clean living and regaled the audience with stories about his big league experiences.[48] On the diamond, his San Francisco team was less than successful, and finished last with a 21–29 record. Individually, he batted around .400 and his tenure on the coast included a spiking of catcher Sam Agnew and a ferocious verbal exchange with umpire Bill Phyle, leading to a forfeit, and a $150 fine, the largest penalty of that kind in his career.[49] During a game in Los Angeles, he chided a few obnoxious bleacher bums and welcomed any one of them to come down and speak with him personally about their criticisms. None responded favorably to the challenge.[50]

Already engaged in making preparations for spring training, Cobb moved camp from San Antonio to his hometown, Augusta, Georgia, and began searching for a private home to house his players. He wanted better accommodations than a hotel, improved meals, and quieter surroundings. Two colonial mansions across the Savannah River in North Augusta, South Carolina, filled the bill and Cobb arranged to rent the structures in January 1922.[51] Warren Park in Augusta, additionally, was a much better training ground than what was available in San Antonio, and Cobb believed his team was going to be better prepared for the upcoming campaign based on that fact.

Trade talks were commonplace in the winter months and Cobb sought a replacement for shortstop Donie Bush, who was placed on waivers in August and picked up by the Washington Senators. Cobb inquired about infielders Joe Dugan and Everett Scott, and Bobby Veach's name came up as a pawn in a possible swap. But because of Veach's value, Cobb wanted equal talent in any kind of trade. When nothing panned out, the Tigers embraced the combo of second baseman George Cutshaw, a ten-year veteran of the National League, recently picked off waivers from Pittsburgh, and rookie shortstop Topper Rigney of the Texas League. Cobb also convinced Detroit President Frank Navin to invest heavily in two pitching prospects from the Pacific Coast League, Herman Pillette and Sylvester Johnson.[52]

California infielder Fred Haney was another addition, joining Detroit by way of Omaha of the Western League. However, the loss of pitcher Dutch Leonard over a salary squabble offset any major gains, and left the rotation weak. Howard Ehmke, the team's other top hurler, was again at odds with Cobb and requested a trade, only to be rejected.[53] The few problems in camp were manageable, and Cobb's "merciful" training regimen was arranged to properly eradicate winter sluggishness. He told his players to work into form slowly, warning of injuries if pushed too hard and too soon.[54] At a Rotary Club barbeque on March 14, with Baseball Commissioner Judge K. M. Landis in attendance, Cobb was praised by his Augusta neighbors, and was touched when the body, in unison, sang their song, "My Hero."[55]

A series against George Stallings's Rochester franchise of the International League was launched in March, and, like Detroit's tours with Boston in 1919–20, was booked by Walter Hapgood. Hapgood was known for scheduling games in small towns on shoddy fields and he lived up to his reputation. The diamonds were dangerously substandard and accommodations were repugnant. On the first day of the torturous journey, Cobb became sick and bowed out. But his men were forced to continue on and team morale was hurt considerably. On April 4 at Americus, Georgia, Cobb was back in the lineup, and, in trying to help his team, suffered serious injuries sliding into second base. He badly twisted his right knee and ankle, and the demoralizing news highlighted the overall insignificance of the Hapgood tour.[56] No exhibition money was worth the loss of a player like Cobb.

Hobbled and in need of a cane to walk, Cobb was nixed from the opening day game at Cleveland on April 12, 1922. He did try to lend his bat for the cause in a brief pinch-hitting role, but was unsuccessful. Not counting the home opener on April 20, which he struggled to participate in for the benefit of fans and a handful of pinch-hitter appearances, Cobb missed nine games in April and was batting under his weight by the end of the month. On April 30, he was shut down, like the rest of his teammates, by twenty-six-year-old Charlie Robertson of the White Sox on a historic afternoon at Navin Field. In an epic display of mastery, Robertson threw baseball's fifth perfect game, turning Cobb and his Tigers away one at a time until twenty-seven batters had dejectedly returned to the bench. Sportswriter Harry Bullion said that Detroit was, simply, "helpless."[57]

Cobb was "crazy" during the contest, according to Sox captain Eddie Collins. He rampaged back and forth, calling for inspections of the ball by the umpire crew, and assumed Robertson was doctoring the ball in some way. Not only were innumerable balls checked and rechecked, but efforts were made to examine the pitcher's uniform as well, all in the hopes of locating evidence of trickery. Collins explained that Cobb also slid hard into first base, trying to knock the ball from Earl Sheely's grip. The tactics didn't work and Robertson's invincibility was sustained at the end of the 2–0 game. "[Detroit] tore our clubhouse to pieces that night trying to find what he had done to the ball, but they never found anything," Collins said.[58]

Despite losing the first six games of the season and seven-straight to close 1921, plus the perfect game pitched against them, Cobb was still optimistic. He felt his players were maturing quickly into a well-oiled machine— and he was right. The Tigers swept Boston and took three of four from the

Yankees on the road in May, and went from last place to third. Cobb's dramatic arguments with umpires, his precise management style, and willingness to do whatever it took to win was spreading like wildfire throughout the roster, and players who were normally passive were battling for every inch. George Chadwick, a syndicated baseball writer, called the Tigers the "sensation of both leagues," and said that Cobb's fighters were proving everyone wrong by doing exactly what pundits said couldn't be done in Detroit. They were getting timely pitching, strong fielding, and, of course, top-notch hitting up and down the lineup.[59]

Cobb's batting average shot from .176 on May 1 to .389 on May 7, helped by a 5-for–5 showing on the latter date. St. Louis fans on May 29 were treated to a rare exhibition of Cobb's offbeat shenanigans as he yelled passionately at the umpires for repeated transgressions. He crossed the line by stepping on umpire Frank Wilson's foot; he was ejected and suspended for five games by American League President Ban Johnson. The punishment was excessive, Harry Bullion believed, especially when compared to Babe Ruth's one-day suspension for throwing dirt at an umpire and running into the stands in chase of a fan at the Polo Grounds on May 25.[60] A *New Orleans States* editorial equated Ruth's actions to "hoodlumism" and the *Tampa Tribune* added that the Babe was temperamental, "like all great stars."[61]

But questions had to be asked: Was there a double-standard in baseball? Were Johnson and Judge Landis applying one set of laws for their top star, Ruth, and another for everyone else? What kind of punishment would have been levied on Cobb had he thrown dirt into the face of an umpire and again stampeded into the crowd? These were all logical queries, and Bullion was right to compare the two suspensions. However, there was another fact that had to be taken into consideration. Ruth had just come off a thirty-nine-day suspension for barnstorming during off the offseason, easily demonstrating that officials were not pampering the home run king. In fact, Johnson fined Ruth $200 for his rowdy actions at the Polo Grounds and stripped him of his Yankees team captaincy.[62]

The suspensions of Cobb and Heilmann, who was also punished for his actions in the disorderly St. Louis game, and the illness of Lu Blue temporarily halted the team's momentum. Bouncing between third and fifth place in July and August, the Tigers were in desperate need of a reliable pitcher to push them over the hump. At the plate, Cobb had a superb July, achieving five hits in each of three different contests, and his average was comfortably over .400.[63] He enjoyed a 16-game hit streak into early August and briefly overtook George Sisler at the top of the league rankings. Sisler, though, was having a career year and didn't fade far from the lead. The press followed every point gained and lost by the two competitors in the clash and displayed amazement at Cobb's perseverance in his eighteenth big league season.

Tempers flared in New York on August 16, 1922, when Yankees hurler Carl Mays was blamed for throwing a little too close to Bobby Jones, high and inside, with two outs in the ninth. Cobb protested to the umpire, and then went out to jaw at Mays near the mound. The tension was too much for Mays and he gave up a three-run homer to Jones soon thereafter and lost the game, 7–3.[64] The next afternoon, Cobb had words for Babe Ruth, in what the *Detroit Free Press* called "strong repartee."[65] Notably, Ruth's 1922 figures were down compared to the year prior, but no one could really complain that a .315 average and 35 home runs were overly disappointing.

On September 17, Sisler attained a hit in his 41-straight game, breaking a mark set by Cobb in 1911, and, in keeping with the spirit of good sportsmanship, Cobb sent his friendly rival a telegram of congratulations.[66] Sisler went on to win the batting championship, his .420 average beating out Cobb's .401, and it marked the third and final time Ty would bat over .400 in his career. With the Tigers finishing in third place, unable to touch the Yankees or St. Louis, Cobb started looking toward 1923.[67] He was making no promises, but planned for better results in the upcoming year, hoping for team unity and success. Time and again, he proved that individualism was out the window. After one particular hitless afternoon earlier in the season, he told a reporter, "What do I care? We won the game!"[68]

14

THE FIGHTING SPIRIT

Approaching his nineteenth major league season in 1923, Ty Cobb was still in a fighting frame of mind. He was fully engaged in managing the Tigers, accepting the positives and pitfalls of the complicated vocation, and was ever determined to winning a pennant that had long eluded him. On a personal level, he was facing the reality of advancing age and his body wasn't bouncing back from the wear and tear as easily as it had in the past. That was a basic truth in the life of a professional athlete, and even the most talented players were confronted by the factor of deterioration. For Cobb, he had expressed his desire to leave the game on top, and the thought of being forced off the diamond because of diminished skill was terrifying. He wouldn't stand for it. To fight the inevitable, he continued his extraordinary commitment to conditioning to keep his decline at bay.

But regardless of his mental strength and dedication to training, he was suffering the loss of a step here and there, particularly when it came to his speed. His nine stolen bases in 1922 were the lowest of his career, not counting his abbreviated first season, and he was thrown out on the basepaths thirteen times. In fact, of the 897 stolen bases he'd achieve, 815 were already pilfered by the end of 1922. Cobb's high velocity running and clever sliding had always been the cornerstone of his repertoire, and his steady progression away from the speedster he once embodied was clearly visible to the public. Sportswriters and fans who'd witnessed the madcap methods of his prime were quick to recite stories of amazing exploits that simply didn't appear possible in the realm of baseball. Somehow Cobb legitimized the off-the-wall concepts and turned the sport on its head.

Between 1907 and 1915, Cobb set several modern-day, single-season stolen base records. His 96 thefts in 1915 was a lofty standard, and with "small ball" disappearing in the Lively Era, no one was sure if it would ever be challenged.[1] In terms of competitive fire, Cobb was arguably peerless in history. A Boston advocate testified to that fact in one of Grantland Rice's columns. He told a story of how Cobb was on the receiving end of a "verbal barrage of unusual venom" from fans during a local game. In response, a vengeful Cobb hit a single to right, but instead of slowing up at first, he continued for second. The befuddled fielder threw the ball away, followed by a second throwing error trying to get Cobb at third base. "Cobb never once hesitated," the observer noted, "but rounded third for home at top speed." He slid hard, knocking the ball free, then stood up and bowed to the crowd.[2] He wanted to show up the local club in return for the abuse, and did so, mixing a colorful array of talent, daring, and showmanship.

"Cobb was reckless, a wild man on the bases," George Sisler later said. "He irritated the opposition, and that made them tense and more prone to make mistakes when he was running. He would do things you'd think were crazy, and, more often than not, he'd get away with them. Cobb was in a class by himself as a slider. He was a big man—at least 195 pounds—but could adjust his body and change direction at the last split second to avoid a tag. Many times I saw him slide past the bag and tag it from behind."[3]

Umpire Billy Evans was an exceptional baseball scholar and remarked that Cobb had "nine different slides and a thousand variations of each slide."[4] The maneuvers were perfectly timed, curtailed to the individual play, and Cobb's great knowledge of rival infielders helped give him an added advantage. This skill wasn't inborn. Cobb worked endlessly to sharpen his sliding abilities, exerting his body to the point in which his thighs were bloody from open wounds suffered in the gravely dirt.[5] There were times he'd ignore the appearance of blood on his pants in the middle of a game, disregarding cuts he'd gotten going into a base, all because he was concentrating on the contest itself. Nothing else mattered, not even his health.

Harry Tuthill, the Tigers club trainer, explained that Cobb suffered "sliders," missing layers of skin large enough for a hand palm to fit inside. Relying on liniment, tape, and ice bags, Tuthill did his best to treat Cobb and said others with similar injuries would've quit the game to rest, but not Ty. He "needed only to hear the sound of the starting bell the next day to forget all about himself and repeat his daily performances without a murmur of complaint."[6] Dr. Robert F. Hyland also cared for the injured Cobb, and said that the player's body was "fairly covered with bruises and abrasions, from his skull down to his toes."[7]

These contusions were a badge of honor, in a way, demonstrating his true grit in the pursuit of baseball glory. While he never held the men on his team to the same standard, he wanted to impress on them the need for intelligence in running the bases. The game, he told them, was not only about long swings for the fence line. The diminished speed of Cobb, who turned thirty-six years old in December 1922, was acknowledged but where he couldn't be faulted was at the plate. He was still as sharp as a tack, batting .401 in 1922, tied for second in the majors with Rogers Hornsby.[8] In September, he passed Nap Lajoie for second all-time in hits, and Honus Wagner, standing atop of the pack, was less than a full season from being surpassed if Cobb kept up his customary gait.[9] Cobb's stats and longevity threatened other longstanding baseball records as well.

A sizable controversy arose following the 1922 season regarding Cobb's batting average, and there was some dispute whether he truly batted over .400. The situation stemmed from a May 15 game on a rainy afternoon in New York, and a hit by Cobb that official scorer John Kieran recorded as an error on Yankees shortstop Everett Scott. Associated Press scorer Frederick Lieb differed from Kieran and awarded Cobb a hit. The American League utilized the AP account rather than Kieran's, thus, boosting Cobb's average over .400. However, there was protest from the Baseball Writers' Association that the AP account was unofficial and should have been superseded by the official scorer's tabulations. American League President Ban Johnson announced that the official sheet from the game was not signed and rendered "valueless" by errors. Because of those issues, the league deferred to the AP score instead, which he endorsed.

Finishing the year in third place was a big boon for baseball in Detroit and for Cobb's reputation. "Ty Cobb has shown that he is a real manager, a real leader," Chicago writer Hugh Fullerton declared. "He has ideas which a lot of managers lack. [The Tigers] are antagonistic in temperament and style." During the season, Cobb was completely lost in the moment of the daily grind, reacting positively and negatively to the happenings on the field. His emotions were overly sensitive to the smallest details of the game and fits of anger could be touched off by trivial matters that only he recognized as important. Other times, he wasn't able to control his elation. Harry Heilmann's game-winning single in the 1921 season opener was a perfect example. Cobb rushed onto the diamond in a fury of happiness and celebrated with the hero on the way back to the dugout.[10] In May 1922, Bobby Veach made a nearly impossible catch—perhaps the greatest of his career—and Cobb was so overjoyed by his feat that he jogged over and hugged him.[11]

However, with Cobb, it always seemed as if an outburst was only a breath away. He was easily aggravated, and it didn't matter if it was the opposition or his own team's poor play that provoked him, the result was the same. Even if he consciously recognized that his verbal onslaughts were hurting the morale of his players, he often couldn't stop himself from losing his cool. His loud voice and aggressiveness wasn't interpreted as sound leadership, and certainly worked against the team. As could be imagined, the stronger personalities were most offended by his raucous demeanor, but patient players—those understanding of Cobb's high-strung nature—allowed him to do his thing without any grudges and benefitted from the wealth of his baseball wisdom.

One aspect that bothered Cobb a great deal was any semblance of indifference from his men in the dugout. He wanted to look down the bench and see players rooting, yelling, and pulling for each other in a unified effort. The display of passion also helped to disrupt the mindset of opponents, which in the psychological game was essential. Versatile infielder Fred Haney, standing but 5'6", was more animated than two or three of his contemporaries put together, and Cobb loved his intensity. First baseman Lu Blue was scrappy, clashing with rivals on the field on occasion, and Harry Heilmann did the same. He wanted his players to be as edgy as he was, running at full speed from base to base, sliding hard, and doing whatever was necessary to advance the cause of the club.[12] He realized that a lineup of clones was impossible, but guys at least trying to fit the Cobb mold pleased the manager to no end.

"I would rather have a team of ball players who possessed 50 per cent ability and 50 per cent fight than a whole flock who had 90 per cent ability and only 10 per cent fighting instincts," Cobb explained in 1922.[13] Additionally, he wanted his men more angry and aggressive than happy and passive. In the case of Bobby Veach, his easygoing attitude annoyed Cobb immensely and Ty worked to dismantle his usually sunny disposition in an effort to get better production from him. He ordered Heilmann to ride Veach from the batter's box when the latter was at the plate, calling him "yellow" and other names all to get him mad.[14] The scheme was unscrupulous, but indicative of Cobb's yearning to have a team of warriors. The last thing he wanted to see was Veach at bat, smiling to the enemy, and being his naturally friendly self.

Frustrations, as can be imagined, came easy to Cobb. During a game at Boston, he stepped up to the plate and gave a hit-and-run sign to Ira Flagstead at first. Flagstead didn't acknowledge the signal and Cobb gave it two more times, hoping to convey the instruction. Finally, with no choice, he walked down the baseline and asked his player if he knew what to do. Flagstead said he didn't, leaving Cobb confounded by their lack of congruity.[15] "Some differences" between Cobb and third baseman Bobby Jones after a play were attributed to Jones being benched in the first game of a doubleheader with Cleveland on July 4, 1922, according to the *Detroit Free Press*, and one could only wonder what was said behind the scenes.[16] Nine days later, Howard Ehmke was pitching far below his standard at Philadelphia, and Cobb decided not to yank him for a reliever. He wanted Ehmke to take his medicine, purposely leaving him in to get pounded for eight earned runs and 13 hits in a 9–4 defeat.[17]

Veteran pitcher George "Hooks" Dauss got the same treatment. But sometimes Cobb couldn't stand to leave his hurler in for a second longer. At Boston on July 18, 1922, Dauss gave up three runs and four hits in just over an inning's work, and after being pulled, Cobb fined him $25 for his awful performance.[18] Monetary punishments were promised by Cobb prior to the 1922 season, and he seemed to believe it was a just form of discipline. Yet it did nothing to endear him to his athletes.

Moving players down from their regular spots in the daily lineup was considered a demotion in some regards, and Cobb used the move regularly to incite reaction and break slumps. And if that didn't work, he'd bench the troubled player for a few days to give him time to clear his head. Cobb was a big believer in one-on-one training with players struggling at the plate, trying to meticulously dissect the batter's flaws. He felt there was typically a mechanical explanation, and since he knew their techniques front and back, he could step in and correct whatever was wrong.[19] This kind of specialized coaching and outside perspective were personally helpful to Cobb when he experienced slumps throughout his career, and for that reason, he was in favor of the system as manager.

As much as egotist people might have thought Cobb was, he wasn't above removing himself from a game for a pinch hitter when a better opportunity arose to help the team. On May 5, 1922, he went 0-for-3 against lefty Bill Bayne of the St. Louis Browns and, essentially ineffective with a batting average of only .250, called for Bob Fothergill to replace him. Unfortunately, the best Fothergill could muster was a long fly out.[20] Interestingly, the tactic was reflective of one of Cobb's most noteworthy strategies. He was fanatical about using right-handed batters against left-handed pitchers, which was generally considered a more effective approach, and Fothergill, as a righty, had improved chances considering the odds. Cobb was absorbed by the odds, and the same methodology applied to his pitching staff. He wanted right-handed pitchers against right-handed batters and lefties versus lefties, utilizing the basic blueprint for baseball generalship.

That was the central reason why he withheld naming his starting pitcher until the last possible minute.[21] He didn't want to give his rivals advance knowledge of whether he was sending in a righty or lefty, and allow them time to rearrange their batting order to gain an upper hand. Cobb was tricky; at times warming up a pitcher in front of the dugout, indicative of his starter, and then another underneath the grandstand, away from prying eyes who'd ultimately head to the mound. On other occasions, he'd have a slew of pitchers warming up on the field, creating confusion for his opposition and sportswriters. He favored the heavy use of pinch hitters too, and it wasn't uncommon for more than a dozen players to head into a Tigers game on any given day. Cobb's Cleveland adversary Tris Speaker managed in a similar way and games between the two teams were always strategically executed.

The condition of his pitchers was a considerable anxiety for Cobb. He put a lot of time into supervising their actions or inactions, and Howard Ehmke's failure to meet expectations remained a thorn in his side. On October 30, 1922, Cobb decided to rid himself of the hassle once and for all. He organized a trade with the Boston Red Sox and sent Ehmke and three others (Carl Holling, Danny Clark, and Babe Herman), plus $25,000, for pitcher Rip Collins and infielder Del Pratt.[22] Collins, a twenty-six-year-old right-hander from Texas, went 14–11 in 1922 and was considered a star in the making. His counterpart in the deal, Pratt, offered the kind of experience Cobb wanted at second base. In the majors since 1912, he had played for three American League clubs and was a dependable fielder with surprising consistency at the plate. Detroit was paying a sizable toll in the deal, but to strengthen the pitching rotation and infield appeared to be well worth the cost.

Cobb's desire for high-spirited personalities on his club was never more apparent than when he picked up Ray Francis from the Washington Senators in a trade for Chick Gagnon on November 24, 1922.[23] Francis, an erratic left-hander, had demonstrated his inner fight to Cobb a few months earlier when they clashed on the field after Ty had nearly been hit by a pitch. Sent to the dirt, Cobb jumped to his feet and approached the mound, but Francis didn't flinch. They were separated before anything else transpired, and additional words were exchanged after the game. Cobb was impressed by the twenty-nine-year-old's fortitude, and told a journalist, "That's the spirit that makes winning pitchers. I could use that fellow on my club."[24]

The Tigers returned to Augusta for spring training in 1923, and Cobb again arranged for housing in private mansions instead of a downtown hotel. From the start, he was taxed by big responsibilities: surveying the recruits and assessing the health of his veterans. To deal with volume of athletes in camp, he split up the youngsters and old-timers, asking the rookies to report at 10:30 a.m. for batting practice and his mainstays an hour later.[25] Filling the instrumental role of coach was former Pittsburgh and Cleveland catcher Fred Carisch, having replaced Dan Howley, and trainer Jimmy Duggan did the best he could mending sore limbs.[26] On Cobb's laundry list of areas to improve, base-running was pivotal, and many hours were consumed by drills. Working with young pitchers was critical as well, while also trying to solve the troublesome quandaries of underperformers like Bert Cole.

On paper, Detroit looked like a pennant contender, and Cobb liked his chances a whole lot better with his rotation strengthened and Pratt sealing up the infield. He told a reporter in early March, "At this time I can see no reason why the Tigers shouldn't finish right up near the top and if Rip Collins and Ray Francis live up to expectations a part of the World's Series may be played at Navin Field next fall."[27] Further confidence was gained by the exciting play of twenty-one-year-old rookie outfielder Henry "Heinie" Manush. In 1922, Manush batted .376 for Omaha of the Western League and, along with Bob Fothergill, provided Detroit with excellent backup for Cobb, Harry Heilmann, and Bobby Veach. His arrival did away with the need for Ira Flagstead, and he was dealt away shortly after the season opened in April.

Past ordeals were seemingly forgotten and another infamous Walter Hapgood tour was scheduled because of Cobb's friendship with manager George Stallings of the Rochester Tribe. This time was no better, and the *Detroit News* described the conditions of the jaunt through Georgia and Alabama as "horrible."[28] On the lighter side of things, Cobb was given a huge reception from admirers—including hundreds of people from his hometown of Royston—during the exhibition opener at Athens, Georgia, on March 26. Royston's mayor Linton Johnson declared a half-holiday for his town to allow citizens to make the 30-odd mile jump to Athens to see their hero play. The Tigers were still shaking off their winter rust and lost 5–3 in 10 innings, and Cobb went 1-for-5.[29] In conjunction with an appearance in Griffin, Georgia, Cobb lectured intrigued students at a local high school, advocating clean living and sportsmanship in baseball.[30]

While Cobb was working his team into championship condition, negativity surrounded them in the form of bad weather, injuries, and illnesses. Of the cast of pitchers, only three or four were deemed to be in form, and the others were questionable to say the least. Cobb was almost hospitalized after being struck by the follow-through of Sylvester Johnson's bat while hitting flies to the outfield in Augusta on April 4. Nailed above his right knee, he went down in a heap and turned pale with pain. Those on the field ran to his aid and immediately figured the worst. But Ty regained his composure and necessitated nothing more than a few bags of ice in the clubhouse.[31]

Augustans highly anticipated a match-up between Detroit and the St. Louis Cardinals on April 7, 1923, pitting Cobb against superstar Rogers Hornsby, and an estimated 5,000 packed Warren Park to see the thrilling battle. Hugh Kinchley of the *Augusta Chronicle* called the first six innings of the contest the "biggest kind of big league baseball," and fans were enjoying a first-class effort. With two outs in the bottom of the sixth and no score, Cobb attempted to steal second and was called out by umpire Cy Pfirman. According to Kinchley, Cobb reacted by throwing dirt into the air, and a St. Louis player told the official what the manager had done. Pfirman then ejected Cobb from the game.[32] Harry "Steamboat" Johnson, the home plate umpire, disagreed with that version. He wrote in his 1935 book, *Standing the Gaff,* that Cobb tossed the dirt into Pfirman's face, not into the air.[33] If true, Cobb's actions certainly didn't reflect the kind of good sportsmanship he preached in Griffin days earlier.

Upon being ordered from the field, Cobb went out to center field, completely ignoring the ruling, and was ready to play the seventh inning. But Pfirman and Johnson stuck to their guns, gave him five minutes to retreat, and when he didn't move a muscle in the direction of the clubhouse, they forfeited the game to St. Louis, 9–0. The result was unsatisfactory to the large throng, and patrons ran onto the field in disgust. In his summation of events, Kinchley, of course, favored Cobb but had to acknowledge the manager's stubbornness, which ultimately robbed the thousands in attendance of an entertaining finish to the game.[34]

The underwhelming condition of the Tigers was less than pleasing to Cobb, and he put his men through a couple lengthy practice sessions with the hope of shaking off any listlessness prior to the season opener at the St. Louis Browns on April 18. Detroit managed to pull it together in the campaign debut, slamming out 15 hits and getting timely pitching from Ray Francis in a 9–6 victory.[35] The team repudiated claims that the offense was in disarray by taking three of four from the Browns, and closing the series out with a 16–1 blowout on April 21. The club streaked to win eight of ten into early May, powering into first place, and the previously established pitching problems were almost nonexistent. Fans in Detroit were ecstatic by the showing, and with capacity increased at Navin Field due to a new upper deck on the grandstand, crowds grew to more than 40,000.

Despite the support, the Tigers endured a poor homestand in May and slipped to fourth. Howard Ehmke and Boston delivered a loss during their slump on May 18, and the ex-Tiger wasn't in a forgiving mood. He clearly remembered all of his difficulties in Detroit and renewed hostilities by dinging Cobb with a pitch in the seventh inning.[36] Cobb insisted it was purposeful, and Ehmke didn't deny it. After the game, the dispute bubbled over into what *The Sporting News* called a "fistic argument," and Ty was credited with "a couple of knockdowns." He was said to have had the "better of matters" at the conclusion of the fight, as players separated the combatants.[37] Their feud was far from over, and in fact, Ehmke made an ugly accusation, alleging that his issues with Cobb originated because he wouldn't "dust off" or hit batters when directed from the bench.[38] Essentially, Cobb was being charged with dirty ball.

The player harmony that Cobb once bragged about was rapidly disappearing and journalists were citing dissension in the ranks. Writers, relying on so-called insider reports, revealed a brewing anger by the men toward Cobb for his verbal abuse. One particular story claimed Cobb fought with his 230-pound outfielder, Bob Fothergill, and the result "was not just to the liking of the manager."[39] The team chemistry was off, pitchers were overworked, veterans were struggling, and Cobb was at a loss to fix the mounting crisis. Justifiably, a failure to be competitive was the fault of leadership, and fans in Detroit let him know their disapproval in June, booing Cobb with a passion.[40]

The lack of roster stability was a significant hindrance and Cobb was forced to make a slew of adjustments to make up for inept performances.

Even more disruptive to the club's success were the injuries to Bobby Jones, Topper Rigney, and Lu Blue, and it seemed that Cobb was lost in a never-ending search for a steady combination. On July 7, the Tigers were slated for a doubleheader against Philadelphia, and Cobb was, once again, very willing to throw a few punches in defense of his honor. The situation developed in the eighth inning of the second game when Cobb, working to advance to third on a sacrifice, spiked Harry Riconda sliding into the bag. Riconda threw the first punch and Cobb retaliated, but before their brawl could escalate any further, umpires broke things up. Cobb had the last laugh as the Tigers won both games and briefly solidified third place.[41]

Later in the month, Cobb went out with a back and shoulder strain, believed to be connected to an old injury, and received treatment from an osteopathic doctor. He was on the sidelines for a doubleheader in Chicago on July 24, 1923, and watched Rip Collins get roughed up for three hits and two runs in the first inning. The Tigers rallied in the second, scoring two runs, and Collins readied himself for his turn at the plate. However, Cobb was already peeved by Collins's sloppiness on the mound, and dashed from the first baseline—where he was coaching—back to the dugout, calling for the pitcher to return to the bench at the same time. Cobb tore off his sweater and seized a bat, and it was clear that in spite of his ailed condition, he was heading into the game as a pinch hitter. But that's when things really got interesting.

In rare form, Cobb gestured with his bat at the pitcher and said a few taunting words. He then brazenly waved to the outfielders, motioning them to move back toward the Comiskey Park wall to handle what he was about to serve up, and sportswriter H. G. Salsinger called it the "finest physical demonstration of confidence we have seen." Cobb was feeling absolutely invincible, and let the pitcher and defense know that something special was about to happen. And it did. He tripled to left-center, scoring a run in the process.[42] Historically, this was the closest Cobb would ever get to the splendor of Babe Ruth's legendary called shot, nine years before the "Bambino" pointed to center field and homered to the same location. Cobb wasn't a home run hitter, nor was this a moment of reckoning akin to Ruth's famous feat, but it was one of the finest displays of self-assuredness Ty had ever exhibited.

Rebounding, the Tigers fought to stay within arm's reach of third place and began to win the type of close games they were losing earlier in the season. In the home stretch, Detroit moved into second and won 11 of their final 13 games to beat out Cleveland for the coveted runner-up spot, finishing with an 83–71 record.[43] Second place was a proud accomplishment for Cobb, his players, and the City of Detroit, but in the overall race, the Tigers were 16 games behind the pennant-winning Yankees. New York's team was far too superior for the rest of the league and went on to beat the New York Giants in the World Series, four games to two.

The ironical story of the year involved Cobb and Ray Francis, the fiery pitcher he so direly wanted to bring to the Tigers after mixing with him the season prior. Cobb was jovial that he was able to obtain him in a trade for a lesser caliber player and truly felt he made out like a bandit in the deal.[44] Clark Griffith of the Senators was just as contented with the departure of Francis, and didn't see a future for the left-hander. By late May 1923, the shine was off Cobb's hopeful, and the manager was provoked to not only suspend Francis, but issue a $400 fine for "breaking training rules."[45] Cobb was less happy by the work of Francis in September, and during a game at Cleveland, the two volatile personalities exploded into combat on the Tigers bench. Each landed a blow before players and police interrupted in what undoubtedly would have been a brutal scrap.[46] Cobb wanted a fighter and he got one, but unfortunately for him, Francis's aggression was directed internally at his own manager and not oppositional hitters.[47]

As expected, Cobb surpassed Honus Wagner to become the all-time hits leader, breaking the record of 3,430 on September 20, 1923, at Fenway Park in Boston.[48] Another of Wagner's records fell when Cobb achieved his eighteenth-straight season with a .300 or better average, and his .340 was more than adequate to cinch that honor. In November, Cobb drew the attention of writers by declaring, "After next year I guess I'll quit baseball. They've been telling me for so long that I'm old that I'm beginning to believe it."[49] He backtracked from that notion a short time later, reiterating his anxiousness to win a championship as manager. He told syndicated columnist John B. Foster that capturing a title would wrap up his career "nicely," but, in trying to strengthen the Tigers, he was having a tough time finding a suitable second baseman.

"Give me a second baseman who can play, and I'll give the Yanks a fight they won't forget!" Cobb proclaimed with confidence.[50] Pitching still remained a question, and the inability of Rip Collins and Herman Pillette

to play consistent ball were a detriment.[51] But the showings of George
Dauss, Bert Cole, and Sylvester Johnson were definite positives, and Cobb
planned to test a number of recruits at spring camp in Augusta, intending
to bolster his rotation. Many pundits weren't surprised to hear that Bobby
Veach, a twelve-year veteran of the Tigers, was sold to the Boston Red Sox
in January 1924. Detroit's outfield was the least of Cobb's problems, and the
recent purchase of left fielder Al "Red" Wingo from Toronto of the International League added yet another powerful youngster to the roster.[52]

Over the winter, Cobb did plenty of hunting, first in Canada with Dan
Howley and well-known conservationist Jack Miner as their guide, and then
throughout the Southeast. His work as manager was never done, though,
and many preparations for spring training had to be made. Foremost, he
needed to straighten out an accommodation plan for the Tigers, and Cobb
decided that rather than renting private houses like he had the previous
two years, he'd book the newly constructed Richmond Hotel in Augusta.
The elegant structure began receiving Detroit upstarts in late February, and
twenty-year-old Charlie Gehringer of Fowlerville, Michigan, a small town 57
miles northwest of Detroit, was one of the first to arrive.[53] Being that he was
a second baseman with incredible potential, his progression in camp was
going to be watched with great interest.

More than thirty-five athletes ventured to Augusta, looking for a regular
berth on the club, and Cobb closely scrutinized each of them. Of the eleven
pitchers available, left-hander Earl Whitehill was a standout. He had
debuted for the club in late 1923, and appeared in 33 innings over eight
games. Right-hander Lil Stoner was another up-and-comer, and was making
his return to Detroit after 17 showings in 1922. He spent the year prior in
the Texas League, and the added experience convinced Cobb he was major
league ready. There were a few other prospects, joining old faces George
Dauss, Rip Collins, Ken Holloway, and the rest, and Cobb wanted his hurlers to improve upon the combined 4.09 ERA achieved in 1923.

Unfortunately for Cobb, the plight of the infield never ceased. This was
realized when Topper Rigney was forced to break from camp early to visit
the Mayo Clinic in Rochester, Minnesota, for a thorough examination of his
injured hip.[54] Doctors luckily didn't find a serious cause for concern, and
Rigney was able to resume his important role as shortstop. The Tigers plod-
ded through preseason games against Toronto and Cincinnati, and were in
pretty good condition entering the campaign opener at home versus Cleveland on April 15, 1924. Plugging the hole at second base was Del Pratt, who

had been seen as expendable, but delivered in spring exhibitions and remained with the team. As for Gehringer, he possessed surefire inborn talent, but was "green to a fault," according to the *Detroit Free Press*, and Cobb sent him to London in the Michigan-Ontario League for development.[55]

Detroit set off on the right foot, defeating the Indians in the opener, 4–3, before more than 30,000 spectators. Local fan support was at the highest level it had ever been, and 1924 would present club owners with its first total attendance of more than one million. Cobb was enthusiastic and showed amazing pep, stealing home twice in April and batting over .400 for the month. Sportswriters, in reporting on his daily exploits, reminded readers that he was playing his twentieth season in the big leagues, and some of his feats would have been extraordinary for a man in his prime. On May 10, he was regaled by friends in Congress in Washington, DC, and honored for his "outstanding example as a good citizen and good sportsman" on the field and in a special party that night.[56]

In a very Ty Cobb-like fashion, it only took a few days for an incident to occur, drawing into question—at least in some minds—his badge of "good citizen." At Shibe Park in Philadelphia, prior to a game on May 16, he left the clubhouse in search of a telephone under the grandstand. There, he located a set of phone booths, but only one was in operation with the other being occupied. Determined to make his call, Cobb waited for the man to leave and, as he did, the two spoke briefly. According to Harry Bullion of the *Detroit Free Press*, the conversation was innocuous, and Ty "was not the aggressor." In fact, Bullion claimed Cobb was sucker punched behind his right ear as he walked forward into the booth.[57] S. O. Grauley, in the *Philadelphia Inquirer*, noted that Cobb made a "remark" as the two passed, and the man, an African American, was insulted by Cobb's words. His comment prompted the initial blow and kick-started their fight.[58]

Both versions of the story said that Cobb unleashed a barrage of punches and "dropped" his foe in quick time. He likely proceeded to make his call, and later entered the ballgame, going 1-for-4 against the Athletics in a 3–1 victory. The African American's name was not revealed, and his side of the story was seemingly not recorded. W. Rollo Wilson of the *Pittsburgh Courier* added more details to the tale, claiming that Cobb struck the man first, and that the latter, who worked at the park, was fired after officials heard Ty's explanation of events. Wilson called Cobb an "insufferable cracker," and said: "For all of his education and training, he is even worse than Shoeless

Joe Jackson and Shufflin' Phil Douglas, both members of the United Order of Hillbillies. He is just as much a disgrace to our national game as those White Sox who sold out to the gamblers in 1919."[59]

For most of the summer, Detroit lingered between first and third place in a consistent battle with the Yankees and Senators for the top spot. Emotions were riding high as New York appeared at Navin Field for a June series and captured three of four games. On June 13, the vitriolic tempers were unable to be contained and all hell broke loose. Babe Ruth was blamed by the Detroit press for sparking things when he strong-armed Bert Cole in the seventh inning during a play at first base. It was alleged that Cobb directed Cole to throw at both Ruth and Bob Meusel in the ninth inning as retribution, but only Meusel was hit by a pitch. And immediately after being nailed, Meusel started toward the mound. Not wasting a second, Cobb ran from center field with Ruth heading him off. Their years of "smack" talk were about to culminate in a battle for the ages, but officials and police prevented a single punch from being thrown. The long-awaited fight between baseball's top two superstars was delayed once again.[60]

Cobb denied telling his pitcher to "dust off" any of the Yankees players. He challenged Meusel to a fight under the grandstand after the game. Meusel was prepared to fight Cobb, but was stopped by his manager, Miller Huggins. The Yankees were given the game by forfeit after Detroit patrons overloaded the field and prevented the game from continuing. Cole and Meusel were both later suspended for their actions.[61]

Winning hard-fought ballgames, Detroit gained significant momentum and Cobb's crew of pitchers, including Earl Whitehill, Rip Collins, Lil Stoner, and newly designated reliever George "Hooks" Dauss, were performing admirably. The Tigers fought their way into first a number of times in June and July, but by August, Detroit was losing steam. They fell five games out by August 29, and although the team rested comfortably in third, Cobb's "Tygers" were unable to reemerge as a contender. They did win seven of nine to close out the season, and finished with an 86–68 record. The Washington Senators, with Walter Johnson leading the way, beat out the Yankees down the stretch and won the American League title. Shortly thereafter, they also conquered the New York Giants to win the World Series in seven games.

In 1924, Cobb was indestructible. He appeared in 155 games—his most since 1915—and set personal records for plate appearances (727) and at-bats (625) in a single season. He batted .338, garnered 211 hits, and stole

23 bases, which was firm evidence that he was still to be reckoned with on the diamond, even with twenty years in the business. His legs were functioning, his eyes and timing were on target, and there was no reason for him to step away from an active part in the game any time soon. Plus, as the recent season demonstrated, Cobb was full of vim and vigor, and retained the same world-class fighting spirit that made him famous.

15

FADING FROM CONTENTION

Of all the relationships Ty Cobb enjoyed over the course of his baseball career, few were more persistently turbulent than his association with Babe Ruth. Their on-field confrontations of previous years were incredible fodder for sportswriters and rarely could an article be written on the state of baseball without mentioning their latest achievements. Animated games featuring Detroit and New York always left open the possibility of a run-in between the superstars, and they were consciously aware of the other's presence at all times. They feuded vocally on occasion, and Cobb, as it was known (and to no surprise), was the louder instigator. It often did not take much for his barbs to reel Ruth in and draw his complete and total ire. That was his primary goal, and if his words were able to fluster "The Great Bambino," hindering his performance on the diamond in any way, Cobb was thoroughly pleased.

Being two of the most recognizable names and faces in the game, Cobb and Ruth had certain public responsibilities, and sometimes they were summoned to appear at the same event. It usually was an awkward situation, with both men refusing to speak to one another and averting their eyes to avoid contact. On May 12, 1923, such an incident occurred at Navin Field in Detroit, as Cobb and Ruth stood on a special platform over home plate to help celebrate the annual "College Day." Joined by Baseball Commissioner Judge Kenesaw M. Landis and famed football coach Walter Camp (known as the "Father of American Football"), the duo were to partake in a light-hearted college skit that was expected to delight the crowd. A reporter for the *Detroit News*, who was paying specific attention to Ruth, seemed to think the latter was wholly annoyed by the shenanigans, writing that he "favored the announcements with nothing but inattention."[1]

Cobb and Ruth were given honorary degrees and went through the motions of the ceremony. At one point, they were asked to grab hold of opposite sides of a cloth banner that read 1923 across the front, and then raise it up for the enthusiastic spectators. The journalist on hand wasn't any more convinced that the home run king was taking pleasure from his surroundings, and wrote, "Mr. Ruth showed a deplorably listless attitude." The Yankee, in a culmination of his participation on the makeshift stage, literally yanked most of the cloth from the hands of Cobb in what only can be imagined was an improvised tug-of-war.[2] To the joyous recent graduates and alumni in the audience, the bitterness displayed by the ballplayers was puzzling. But the underlying atmosphere was thick with tension and neither wanted to be that close to their natural adversary.

Newspaper syndicate impresario Christy Walsh went out of his way to ensure that Cobb and Ruth were on his roster of "writers" covering the 1924 World Series between the Washington Senators and New York Giants.[3] At first, they played their old game, refusing to communicate even though only feet separated them. At Washington, however, they found common ground when both were verbally accosted by a couple of rambunctious fans. By the time the Senators gained a victory in seven games, the two were passing each other cigars and bantering, not in a hostile way, but on friendly terms. Several newspapers boldly declared that they had buried the hatchet altogether.[4] There still was plenty of room for teasing, and Cobb couldn't resist reminding Ruth how Detroit knocked New York from first place the September before, which helped Washington secure the pennant.[5]

Headed into that winter, Cobb's future was a prime subject for discussion. He freely admitted that he was slowing up a bit, and wanted to cut back the total number of games he was to play in the upcoming season. New York Giants manager John McGraw felt the Georgian's days were numbered and, in fact, told a reporter, "If I were Cobb, I would never again put on a uniform. Cobb is still good today, better than the average. But Cobb is a long way from the Cobb pictured in the minds of the fans. Why not let that picture stand? Why dim it by failures that are bound to come to him because of slowing down? Cobb cannot possibly improve on his record as it stands. He has won more honors than any man that ever played baseball. Nature has to be reckoned with, and Cobb has reached that stage where muscles stiffen quickly and where they respond slowly. The longer he plays the more he will hurt his record."[6]

The truth was that Cobb, amazingly, *could* improve on his career statistics, distancing himself as the leader of many categories from his contemporaries. There was also the little thing of finally achieving a World Series championship, a thought that never left his mind. Pitcher extraordinaire Walter Johnson won his first title in 1924 at thirty-six years of age, and, for Cobb, the added element of being a manager and leading his warriors to the top of baseball's hierarchy was an exhilarating proposition. He had no intention of listening to the words of McGraw or anyone else. At the same time, he was working in the final year of a three-year contract valued at $40,000 annually, and while his status for 1926 was unsettled, he was fully committed to produce for Detroit through the forthcoming season.[7]

Hot stove chatter regarding the Tigers was mostly negative, especially after team ownership departed the league meetings in December without a single acquisition. The club had enough reserve players to work a trade and strengthen the known weaknesses on the mound and infield. Instead, Cobb was venturing back into spring training with more inexperienced rookies up from the minors. Those circumstances weren't ideal, and *The Sporting News* indicated that three of Detroit's leading rivals, New York, St. Louis, and Washington, had sufficiently benefited from deals during the offseason.[8] In comparison, Detroit wasn't keeping pace in the highly competitive environment, making it a lot harder to churn out a winner. Cobb anticipated another year of challenges.

Visiting a restaurant at Union Station in Atlanta on February 26 with Tigers coach George McBride, Cobb was involved in a forgettable melee that did nothing but highlight his own stubbornness. This time, however, his mulish behavior was flaunted in the face of authority—meaning an Atlanta police officer—and Cobb was subsequently arrested. The story, which received national attention, had two versions: one pieced together by a journalist based on statements from the officer and perhaps witnesses, and the other provided by Cobb himself. The reporter's account appeared in the *Atlanta Constitution*, and claimed that the argument was initiated between Cobb and a waitress over a discrepancy in the check. Once the dispute grew in volume and foul language was used, the officer, W. C. Hardy, was called upon. Hardy later reported that Cobb "had been drinking," and refused to leave the establishment when ordered.[9]

The officer ended up forcibly removing him from the eatery and called a paddy wagon to take him to police headquarters on a charge of disorderly conduct. The most sensational part of the tale, aside from the assertion that Cobb had been drinking, was the allegation that an unnamed woman had smashed Cobb in the head with a heavy dish during the noisy quarrel. Such a thing never happened, according to Cobb. "The statement that I was hit over the head with a glass by the wife of the restaurant manager is preposterous," he explained. "There was no woman concerned except the cashier." He admitted that he was told to leave, but felt the "restaurant was a public place and that [the officer] had no right" to force him to depart when he wasn't yet ready. He believed the patrolman wanted to get his name in the newspaper at his expense, and insisted that he didn't resist when finally corralled outside.[10]

To lessen the embarrassment, Cobb agreed to pay for a taxi to the station rather than be subjected to the back of a police wagon, and promptly paid an $11 bond to secure his release. He told a reporter, in talking about the odd affair, "I was never so humiliated," and said that the officer involved hadn't "heard the last of this."[11] McBride backed Cobb up on his version of events, and George Conklin, one of Ty's Augustan neighbors, wrote to the *Atlanta Constitution* in defense of the ballplayer's good name. "Ty Cobb is an orderly citizen," the man wrote. "He is not a drunken brawler, in fact, no one in this town ever heard of him being intoxicated or under the influence of strong drink. We do not believe he was drinking or that he did any 'cussing' in the presence of a lady or that he acted in any other than a proper manner."[12]

Over thirty veterans and recruits trickled into Augusta for spring camp beginning in early March, and the Tigers went to work shedding their winter weight. Cobb, personally, was interested in dropping ten pounds and, during workout sessions, led by example. He was adamant that the club follow a slowly intensifying conditioning program and didn't want his men throwing out their weakened arms during the first week of camp. Detroit benefitted greatly from optimal weather and didn't miss a day of practice, allowing for a significant amount of improvement. Cobb was clued into the needs of his athletes, and after grievances were lodged about the food at the Richmond Hotel where the team was staying, he moved the club to the Partridge Inn, ensuring a better quality of chow.[13]

Heinie Manush presented another problem. He was peeved with a stipulation in his contract calling for a bonus only if Cobb agreed that his play warranted the money at season's end. Manush furiously disagreed with the clause and engaged in "verbal combat" with his manager, stressing the need for its removal. He didn't want Cobb's opinion deciding the fate of that money, and offered to sign if the bonus hinged on a certain batting percentage. Cobb needed Manush available, and the two sides eventually agreed but the terms were not revealed.[14] With Manush in the fold and a host of others locked in, Cobb was pleased to have a good starting lineup, plus backups at every infield position. That meant, in the case of injury or slump, he could rotate between Lu Blue and Johnny Neun at first, Frank O'Rourke and Leslie Burke at second, Jackie Tavener and Topper Rigney at short, and Bobby Jones and Fred Haney at third.

In the outfield he had Harry Heilmann in right, Red Wingo in left, and he'd play center with Manush and Bob Fothergill able to step in whenever needed. Behind the plate, Cobb relied on dependable Johnny Bassler and used Larry Woodall as a backup. Incidentally, veteran Tigers backstop Oscar Stanage was also part of the Detroit contingent as a coach. The pitching department offered another wide assortment of individuals of varying degrees of skill. George "Hooks" Dauss, at thirty-five, was just a few years younger than Cobb, and still a potent right-hander. Mainstays Earl Whitehill, Ken Holloway, Lil Stoner, and Rip Collins were surrounded by a handful of others, most notably Dutch Leonard, who returned to Detroit for nine games in 1924 after two years on the periphery of Organized Baseball. Leonard became estranged from the Tigers after a pay squabble, joining the California outlaws before clearing his name with the powers-that-be.

The flexible options all over the diamond were just to Cobb's liking, and his mind was always cooking up a strategy considering the use of all the players at his disposal. While participating in preseason exhibitions, Cobb became ill, but decided to push forth anyway, exerting himself when he should have been resting. By April 9, his condition worsened and he was battling full-fledged influenza.[15] Told by doctors to scale things back, he managed from the bench five days later when the season opened at Navin Field, where 40,000 fans saw Detroit beat Chicago, 4–3. It wasn't until April 20 that Cobb made his 1925 debut, entering a game against Cleveland as a pinch hitter in the seventh inning, and walked in a 5–4 loss. Heckled from the Indians dugout about the so-called deterioration of his vision due to old age, Cobb defiantly pointed to his eyes, ready to prove everyone wrong.[16]

The Tigers were abysmal on the field in April, the losers of seven-straight, and began May in last place. A chief concern was the pitching staff, which was out of sorts mostly because of Cobb's deliberately unrushed condition-ing program in the spring, leaving many hurlers without the stamina neces-sary to work a complete game. Cobb didn't have the patience for anyone not producing; during the string of losses, he benched players, rearranged the batting order, and generally turned things upside down in an attempt to get some semblance of results. His constant use of substitutions created an unbalance that hurt the club more than it helped. For instance, his first-string infielders were not appearing long enough together as a singular unit to gain traction, failing to develop timing and squandering what were routine double-plays for other clubs. The topsy-turvy environment reduced confidence and, in turn, errors were commonplace.[17]

Cobb joined the regulars on April 27, 1925, going to right field for the ailing Heilmann, and hit a double in his first at bat. Over the next week, he appeared superhuman on several occasions, batting 4-for-5 on May 1 and 3-for-6 on May 2 against Cleveland. He was in the mindset of trying to sin-glehandedly break the Tigers from their slump, performing the antiquated delayed steal at one juncture, and hoping his aggressive play would be con-tagious with the rest of the team. Detroit was 4–14 going into its game against the St. Louis Browns on May 5, and there wasn't much positivity surrounding the franchise. In fact, Harry Bullion of the *Detroit Free Press*, usually a cheerleader for the Tigers, couldn't contain his frustrations the day before, writing a headline that read, "Stupid Play Causes Defeat of Cobbman," and harped on the mental mistakes that cost the team yet another agonizing loss.[18]

Despite the team's struggles, history was made by Cobb on May 5 at Sportsman's Park in St. Louis that came in a highly unexpected fashion. According to a report by Sid Keener, a journalist who sat with the Tigers manager prior to the game, Cobb talked about Babe Ruth and the massive slugging displays the "Bambino" had put on in the past. He then said, "I'll show you something today. I'm going for home runs for the first time in my career."[19] Cobb proceeded to hit three homers, a double, and two singles in six times to the plate—a masterful effort—and quickly labeled by experts as the greatest accomplishment of his career. As far as modern-day achieve-ments went, he broke the total bases mark with 16 and tied the single-game home run record. The next day, Cobb added to his unparalleled streak by adding two more homers to his credits, and, in total, went 9-for-12 over the course of two days, with five round trippers and 25 bases. His batting average was up over .500 on the season and, once again, Cobb was the toast of the baseball universe.[20]

The record books had to be adjusted again and, this time, Cobb went to the top of the list for home runs on consecutive days in the modern era, tying Cap Anson's old National League mark set in 1884. Sportswriters went haywire lauding his remarkable play and words of praise and congratulations were offered via telegram from innumerable friends, including Detroit Mayor John W. Smith.[21] The way Keener explained Cobb's attitude prior to his onslaught and even the tone of Ty's words explaining the situation in his autobiography, there was a terrific sense of individualism in his motivation. It was almost as if Cobb was out to prove something and put himself on the same plateau of slugging as Ruth.

But, in 1925, the press expressed a more team-oriented tenor to Cobb's work on May 5–6, which had nothing to do with individual home run achievements or proving his value as a power hitter. A journalist for the *Detroit Free Press* wrote that Cobb was focused on breaking the Tigers "jinx," and had "announced his determination to do anything short of suicide" to turn the club's losing habit around.[22] Harry Bullion added, "Cobb bears his new laurels lightly. He seemed more pleased with the way his club performed in the two uprisings with the bats here."[23]

With Cobb leading the way, Detroit won both games versus St. Louis, 14–8 and 11–4, and there was widespread hope amongst Tigers fans that it was the dawn of a new day for the team as a whole.

The Tigers didn't win their tenth ballgame until May 19, and remained at the tail end of the league through the end of the month. Finally, Detroit launched a massive push, and won nine-straight between June 16 and 27, fighting into fourth place. At Boston on June 19, Cobb resumed his long-standing feud with Howard Ehmke, flustering the Red Sox pitcher with his excitable words from the coach's box. Disjointed by the disruptive behavior, Ehmke balked and, in retribution, placed one high and inside when Cobb was at the plate later in the game. Ducking out of the way, Cobb naturally reacted, stepping toward the mound in a rage. Although the game resumed without a brawl, gossip circulated that Cobb and Ehmke were going to participate in an organized fight of some sort. This story was denied by both parties.[24]

Perhaps ending their dispute in the ring was a better alternative than tangling nearly every time Ehmke took the mound when Detroit played

Boston. They went at it again in the third inning of a game at Navin Field on July 8, after Cobb smacked a liner off the glove of first baseman Phil Todt. As Todt went after the ball, Ehmke judiciously ran over to cover the bag. Cobb, of course, doing whatever he could to reach first safely, slid hard, and one of his spikes grinded into Ehmke's heel. The latter promptly offered a kick to the baserunner and the two were prepared to lock horns, only to have the umpire break things up.[25]

Despite some optimism, Detroit was proving to be a fourth or fifth place team, and Cobb admitted that his club was overrated.[26] Batting was the team's principal bright spot, but the Tigers suffered from a sincere inability to hit in the clutch. And this wasn't a new problem for Cobb's athletes. The 1925 season was shaping up to be the third year in a row that Detroit led the majors in men left on base, and a total of 1,232 would ultimately be stranded.[27] Regardless of how much Cobb tried to persuade his men to bunt, sacrifice, and hit scientifically to drive in runs, his players were faltering in a big way. But if the perspective was adjusted a little bit, it could be that Cobb himself was the one failing to provide the necessary leadership to mold his club into a winner. It appeared that either his players weren't listening or he was unsuccessfully managing them.

Cobb's friends were undismayed by the league standings and arranged a special "Ty Cobb Day" event at Navin Field on August 29, plus a banquet that night at a ritzy Detroit hotel. Acknowledged as a celebration in honor of his twentieth anniversary in the majors, the happening was actually being commemorated during his twenty-first season. However, since he only played briefly in his first year (1905), 1925 did mark his twentieth full season in the big leagues. That afternoon, Cobb went 2-for-4 with a double, two runs, and an RBI in a 9–5 defeat of Philadelphia. An estimated 20,000 people attended the festivities, in addition to several bands, and Cobb "cheerfully" shook hands with more than three hundred fans near the Detroit dugout prior to the contest.[28] In the evening, he was regaled by speeches from American League President Ban Johnson, Tigers President Frank J. Navin, Philadelphia manager Connie Mack, umpire Billy Evans, and a few others.

Mayor John W. Smith presented Cobb with a grandfather clock, a testimonial gift on behalf of the City of Detroit. To make the purchase, he actually appropriated public funds in the amount of $1,000, and sold the concept to the city council by explaining, "Two names alone in Detroit history are associated with the supreme degree of achievement in their respective fields. They are those of Henry Ford and Tyrus Cobb."[29] The councilmen wholeheartedly agreed and authorized the gift. The legendary Honus Wagner, whose all-around baseball accomplishments were just as revered as Cobb's, sent a note to be read during the banquet, stating: "I have always had great respect for Ty both as a man and as a ball player. He has been a credit to the game and his sterling work on the diamond has been the means of making many a fine young ball player."[30]

The season concluded with the Tigers finishing in fourth place, 16.5 games behind the pennant-winning Washington Senators, and in possession of an 81–73 record. Attendance at home fell off by more than 190,000 patrons versus 1924 totals, and while Cobb was well regarded, fan support had clearly waned in response to the club's struggles. In his own plight, Ty dealt with a number of issues from hip trouble to lingering pain in his lower extremities. He fought off a summer slump and was even suspended for a handful of days after a vigorous argument with umpire Clarence Rowland. At his lowest point, he even benched himself to get Heinie Manush in a game. Always searching for a way to gain an advantage, Cobb adjusted his batting stance from a crouch to a more upright position and found steady success.[31] He hit .378 in 121 games, and was fifth in the majors in average. His prodigy, Harry Heilmann, won the league title with a .393 average.

On October 7, 1925, Cobb returned to Pittsburgh for Game One of the World Series between the Pittsburgh Pirates and Washington Senators. He buried the hatchet with John McGraw and mingled with Babe Ruth again in the press box, and appeared at home plate for a photo op with Honus Wagner and Babe Adams as recollections of the 1909 Series were shared.[32] Interested in escaping the hubbub of baseball, Cobb ventured into the Northern Ontario woods to hunt moose. He ended up missing Pittsburgh's title victory in seven games, but preferred his own achievement, bagging a moose head trophy with an antler width of more than 45 inches.[33] From Canada, he ventured to Shreveport, Louisiana, in early November, to duck hunt.

Spending his birthday and the holidays with family, Cobb had to cope with the sudden illness of his youngest child, four-year-old Jimmy, who wrangled with a bout of pleurisy before recovering.[34] More disheartening news emerged in February 1926, after it was alleged that Iola Williams, a housekeeper at the Cobb residence for five years, had been stealing from the family. Cobb and an Augusta police officer located a number of items taken from his home in the custody of Williams; both Iola and her husband Robert were subsequently arrested. Reporter J. Raiford Watkins of the

Augusta Chronicle noted that Cobb "expressed much regret" at the situation, particularly because Williams had been such a "trusted" employee.[35]

To sporting press syndicates, the idea of running an in-depth biography of Cobb as a series in newspapers from coast-to-coast during the offseason was nothing more than brilliant. His life story was a fascinating one, and editors believed readers would be enthralled by the accomplishments, conflicts, and personal details of his rise to superstardom. Christy Walsh, later acknowledged as the first baseball agent, saw the interest in the concept and wanted to run an authorized account of Cobb's history under his syndicate byline. He guaranteed Cobb $10,000 for the narrative and planned to roll the articles out for a period of months between late 1924 and into early 1925. Things were forcibly changed when Harry G. Salsinger of the *Detroit News*, one of the closest sportswriters to Cobb, came out with his own multipart biography on the Georgian. Walsh patiently waited until December 1925 and finally released *Twenty-Years in the Line-Up, Ty Cobb's Own Story*.[36]

As the members of the Tigers began to report for the commencement of spring training at Augusta on March 1, 1926, Cobb was not in his customary position to receive them. Instead, Coach George McBride welcomed the squad and initiated the formalities of camp. On that same day, Ty underwent an operation by William H. Wilmer, an acclaimed specialist at Johns Hopkins Hospital in Baltimore, Maryland, to remove a growth from his left eye.[37] Cobb had been bothered by this problem for some time, and the mass was said to be a build-up of dirt and dust particles. The procedure was a success and, although he experienced a considerable amount of pain during a two-week recuperation period and had to wear dark glasses to shield his eyes, the sacrifices were advantageous in continuing his career. He even displayed his revitalized vision by lifting a ball into the center-field stands in his first appearances at the plate upon returning to Augusta.[38]

The personnel of the Tigers changed noticeably heading into opening day. Twenty-two-year-old third baseman Jack Warner and pitcher Clyde Barfoot were picked up in a high-priced deal with the Vernon Tigers of the Pacific Coast League, Fred Haney and Topper Rigney were sent to Boston, and Cobb embraced second baseman Charlie Gehringer as a regular. Right-hander Sam Gibson was also brought in from the Toronto Maple Leafs of the International League, while Jess Doyle, Owen Carroll, and Carl Hubbell were farmed back in the other direction to the Maple Leafs. A famous story circulated years later about how Cobb tried to convince Hubbell to drop the screwball from his repertoire, telling him, "You will never get anybody out with it."[39] Hubbell went on to have great success with the pitch for the New York Giants and was elected to the National Baseball Hall of Fame in 1947.

Cobb planned to step further away from an active, day-to-day role with the team, telling a reporter: "There is one thing that I have found out as manager, and that is that the most successful method is managing from the bench. I used to think that I could direct better while playing in the field, but I know now that psychologically the bench method is best."[40] His eyes remained bothersome, but he stepped in to play a spring exhibition between Detroit and Augusta, donning the uniform of the latter against his own club at Warren Park on April 3, 1926. He went 2-for-4 with a run, but the local franchise was toppled, 12–3.[41] In Atlanta two days later, the Tigers helped the Disabled American Veterans organization by raising awareness for a fund-raising campaign, and Cobb, in a stunt, dropped baseballs from the eighteen-story Hurt Building, with players on the ground trying to catch them.[42]

Bearing in mind the team's additions, the Tigers were still fundamentally weak. Cobb liked the offensive power and the depth at various positions, but wanted "two or three steady, dependable pitchers" to eliminate many of the questions that still lingered.[43] On paper, the infield appeared stronger with Jack Warner and Charlie Gehringer, but after years of disappointments, he wasn't ready to guarantee a thing. The season kicked off at home on April 13, 1926, with a 2–1 loss to Cleveland, and Cobb entered the game briefly as a pinch hitter. He'd sporadically play off the bench, along with Gehringer and Manush—each of them future Hall of Famers—until breaking into the starting lineup on April 27, after the Tigers had dropped five-straight. Cobb went 3-for-4 with a double and triple, driving in four runs, and snaring an incredible catch in an 8–7 victory over Chicago.[44] Both Gehringer and Manush became essential regulars as the year progressed.

At St. Louis on April 30, Cobb got into a verbal spat with Browns catcher Wally Schang, and Ty made one of his old-time promises: if he got on, he'd promptly steal second. In the seventh inning, Cobb walked and tried to make good on his boastful declaration. However, the thirty-nine-year-old Cobb wasn't the indomitable force he was in the early 1910s, and Schang threw him out. Cobb hadn't missed a step in terms of talking trash, and could easily get under the skin of rivals, no matter how peace-loving the individual was. Lou Gehrig was a perfect example. The New York Yankees first baseman, in his fourth season, was already known as a class act. He was a gentleman, good-natured, and a true asset to the game of baseball. But Cobb knew how to turn his pleasant attitude into anger, using simple badgering, and in doing so, Ty hoped to frustrate the youngster into making mental blunders during a game.

Before sportswriters, Cobb rejected any claim that the two detested each other, and Gehrig did similarly. "Last year Ty gave me tips on batting," Gehrig explained. "We've always been good friends, and the first thing he did when he saw me this season was to come up and shake hands with me on winning the first base job."[45] In the heat of the battle, however, admiration and familiarity disappeared, and that was definitely the case on May 8, 1926, at Yankee Stadium. New York was sitting pretty in first place at the time and didn't want to lose a big Saturday afternoon game to the sixth place Tigers before 30,000 spectators. Gehrig struck out twice and Cobb was probably antagonizing him a bit, adding to the growing volatility. With two outs in the ninth and the Yankees down two runs, Earl Whitehill hit Gehrig on the hand with a pitch.[46]

Deeming the act deliberate, Gehrig exploded into rage—a completely uncharacteristic behavior—and wanted to fight the pitcher. Umpires separated the two, but that didn't end the hostilities. "I'll meet you right after the game and give you a good beating," Gehrig shouted. Whitehill agreed, and the next batter, Babe Ruth, grounded to second to conclude the contest. New York baseball writer Joe Vila described the scenario in his column in *The Sporting News*. He indicated that just minutes after the game, Whitehill and Gehrig were set to duel in the tunnel leading to the clubhouse. Cobb then turned up, and instead of looking to square things with Whitehill, Gehrig changed his focus to him, telling Ty, "You've been riding me for a long time, and now I'm going to fix you." Vila said that Cobb and Gehrig brawled "rough and tumble" on the ground until Gehrig accidentally hit his head on a wall and was knocked unconscious.[47]

The story continued, as Vila added that Cobb and Ruth "swung harmless blows" at each other as well, prior to the calamity being broken up. Interestingly, another version of this tale was reported in *The Sporting News*, but didn't mention anything about Cobb and Gehrig battling in a "rough and tumble." It confirmed that Gehrig and Whitehill were the primary battlers, and claimed that Ruth dragged his teammate away from the scene. En route to the Yankees locker room, Gehrig was indeed knocked out, and the unnamed journalist who wrote the article seemed to think it came from a "punch." Ruth was also irate because he had been kicked during the skirmish, and teammates told him that Cobb was the culprit. Fred Merkle, Yankees backup first baseman disagreed, and told Babe that it hadn't been Ty. Ruth chose not to believe him.

Blinded by his anger, he raced to the Detroit clubhouse and surprisingly found that Cobb was uninterested in fighting. Ty said he didn't do it, but noted, "If you make me very angry, I may take a kick at you."[48] There are several other versions of the Gehrig-Whitehill-Cobb-Ruth saga, including one told by Cobb in his autobiography. In that edition, he said he pulled who he thought was Whitehill from underneath Gehrig, but it turned out to be Ruth instead, and that started their conflict.[49] Yet another explanation stated that Gehrig went after Cobb in the dugout of the Tigers, and was knocked out when he swung wildly, lost his footing, and bashed his head against the wall.[50] As with many things in baseball history, the truth and sensationalized legends often become entangled, and this story was no different.

The day after the brouhaha, Cobb went 4-for-4 and Al Munro Elias, the noted statistician, revealed that he had upped his lifetime batting average to .370.[51] He wasn't playing every day, but when he did, he was as hard-nosed as ever. During one June game, he turned his ankle and was obviously in a lot of pain. Rather than put in a substitute, he had it bandaged and was right back in the action the next inning.[52] Back problems also bothered Cobb for a stretch. With the issues to Cobb's back and other bumps and bruises, the team faced another crisis when catcher Johnny Bassler went out with a broken ankle in late May. There was no question that Detroit had talent, but the constant good work of a handful of players was being constantly reversed by costly errors and overall bad luck.

On June 19, 1926, the Tigers presented "Ty Cobb Day" at Navin Field, and Cobb was celebrated for being league MVP in 1911, an honor that didn't receive specific acknowledgment at the time. The players of Detroit and Philadelphia formed a circle around home plate and Cobb was showered with adoration from Ban Johnson, Frank Navin, and Detroit Mayor John Smith.[53] The following month at Washington, Cobb was treated with anything but adulation. He was hassled constantly by Senators fans, had items thrown at him, and was openly challenged to fights by members of the audience. Despite informing stadium authorities to remove certain individuals, he was ignored even though that was the way league officials had instructed him to handle such occasions.[54] The Senators complained that the ever-animated Cobb was holding up the game by invoking delay tactics and fans around the Detroit dugout protested Ty's alleged foul language.

When a segment of the Washington press jumped on the anti-Cobb bandwagon, *Baltimore News* sportswriter Rodger H. Pippen came to his defense, declaring: "What baseball needs is more managers and more players [like Cobb] who rave and rant and at least give the impression they are doing more for their money than going through the motions. Give us more Cobbs!"[55] Going into the stretch, there was an outside chance Detroit could compete for as high as second place, but with Cleveland, Philadelphia, Washington, and Chicago coming on strong, their chances quickly faded. Outside a few hopeful runs, the team experienced nearly every bad break possible, and slowly fell from the first division, landing in sixth place in September. Behind the scenes, plans for 1927 were taking shape in the form of player recalls and purchases. Frank Navin was also working to reestablish spring training camp at San Antonio, Texas.

Finishing the season with a 79–75 record and in sixth place was depressing for team management and fans back home. Heinie Manush gave the club a tremendous lift by achieving the highest batting average in the majors, .378, and Bob Fothergill and Harry Heilmann (both at .367) were in the top five. For Cobb, he played only 79 games and batted a respectable .339. In six seasons as manager, he'd put up a record of 479–444 (.519) and finished no worse than sixth place. His second place ranking in 1923 was commendable, and under the right circumstances, a legitimate pennant contender was probable somewhere in his managerial future. Headed for a hunting trip in Wyoming with Tris Speaker, he informed the press that he was going to return in 1927 and try his hand again.[56] But secretly, there were major happenings in the baseball world, and not only was Cobb's good name threatened, but his career as well. The same went for Speaker, and the next few months were going to present serious adversity and test the fortitude of both men.

16

OLD MAN COBB

As the baseball community was busily preparing for the commencement of the World Series in late September 1926, Ty Cobb quietly escaped to the fresh air and mountains of the West. Having initially departed Chicago with several friends, Cobb set off for Omaha, where the group met Tris Speaker, now the manager of the Cleveland Indians, on September 28. They planned to continue their jaunt on the Chicago, Burlington, and Quincy Railroad for a big game hunt near Cody, Wyoming.[1] During his brief stay in Omaha, Cobb was interviewed by a local reporter, Frederick Ware, and spoke favorably about Heinie Manush, the celebrated young outfielder for Detroit. Manush played for the Omaha Buffaloes of the Western League in 1922 just prior to jumping to the majors, and Cobb's comments were of great interest. "I am pretty certain," Cobb explained, "that a career of stardom is ahead of him."[2]

Cobb added that he planned to play in 1927. "I'm going to get in the lineup off and on for next season, at least," Cobb told the reporter. "The lure of the game is still strong, but fully as strong is the delight I get in helping a youngster to develop. You can see that I've frequently been delighted during the past seven months, for I've had a team of rookies—able rookies, too, lacking chiefly only experience. Bringing them along is greater compensation to me now than money. We didn't finish any higher because we had a kid infield and our pitchers weren't dependable enough. But next year . . ."[3] Rumors were circulating that Cobb's days at the helm of Detroit were numbered, but to Ware and the newspaper readers in Omaha, there was no evidence in the interview that he was through in any form or fashion. It seemed pretty much guaranteed that he was returning to lead the Tigers in their next campaign.

But things weren't so cut and dry. Cobb was well aware of the brewing firestorm festering behind closed doors that endangered his future in baseball. His difficulties with club owner Frank Navin were more complicated than ever; a segment of Detroit fans had lost confidence in his ability as a manager and attendance was dropping. Truth be told, he was under the impression that he likely would've been fired at the end of the 1925 season, but was only saved by the fact that the City of Detroit honored him with a special banquet, celebrating his tremendous baseball achievements and contributions to the local community. Navin apparently realized that it would've been in incredibly bad taste to pay such tribute to Cobb one month, and then hand him his walking papers the next.[4] The sorrowful recent pennant run added to Navin's desire for change, and the budding storm on the horizon seemed to seal Cobb's fate.

The controversy itself was initiated with malice in June 1926 by Dutch Leonard, a veteran of eleven years of big league ball, including five with Detroit from 1919 to '21 and from 1924 to '25. Leonard posted a career record of 139 wins and 114 losses and was Cobb's most reliable pitcher in 1925, winning five-straight in June and July, before losing the strength in his arm. It wasn't until after the ball was rolling on the scandal in 1926 that he divulged a highly venomous version of events from the year prior. He claimed that Cobb reneged on a promise to work him every fifth game, allowing him four days to rest, and that overwork was the central reason for his downfall. "I beat Cleveland," Leonard said. "Two days later, [Cobb] made me pitch against St. Louis. I beat them. Then I beat Chicago. Still I knew I was killing myself in winning these games for him. I complained to him. I reminded him of his promises."

According to Leonard's charges, it was a game against Philadelphia on July 14, 1925, that really displayed the weakened condition of his arm. He never even expected to pitch that afternoon. He explained to Cobb how he physically couldn't, and Ty responded by saying, "Yes, you are going to pitch, whom do you think you are, manager of this team? Get out there on the field. Don't you dare turn Bolshevik on me, I am the boss here." Leonard did what he was told and went out to the mound. "Philadelphia made 23 hits against me," he said, offering his memory of the event. "Still Cobb kept me in the box. Connie Mack himself, I learned later, said during the game that it was not right to let me stay in the box. 'You are killing that boy,' Mack said. Cobb only laughed and made me stay in. Then the fans themselves took it up. They could see I was being punished. They booed Cobb. They could see he was trying to break me."[5]

Against the Yankees on July 19, Leonard was called upon again, and he went five innings, giving up four runs on seven hits. A little over a week later, he joined the Tigers on a road trip to Philadelphia, and visited a local physician. He was informed of the seriousness of his injury and it was estimated that he'd need three weeks to recover. However, it soon became apparent that his arm wasn't bouncing back despite the ample rest, and with the intention of beefing up the team's infield, Detroit packaged Leonard into a deal with Vernon of the Pacific Coast League for Jack Warner, a promising third baseman.[6] Leonard was "astounded" to learn of the transaction, and his devaluation from being one of the most talked about pitchers in the league in July to clearing waivers in September, was simply remarkable.

Closer scrutiny of exactly how Cobb utilized Leonard in June and July 1925 offers a starkly different impression than the one Leonard provided in 1926. Between June 14 and July 19, Leonard worked eight games, and Cobb provided him with at least four full days of rest in-between appearances in all but one. The latter was on three days' rest on June 29, and never did Cobb ask him to pitch one day and then again two days later like he claimed. Leonard did throw six-straight complete games and went 65 innings over the course of his eight showings. During that run, he provided Cobb with the kind of dependability the Tigers longed for and was a great asset to the club before the demise of his potency. But at the time, notably, Leonard didn't cite any so-called pressure by Cobb to work on little rest as the cause of his sudden ineffectiveness.

Instead, Leonard blamed the lively ball. "In the old days," he explained, "I used to regularly pitch a high, fast one that the batter had to hit into the air. The result usually was a high fly and an easy out. I could go along inning after inning in this fashion and there was little strain on my arm. Only in a pinch did I have to curve the ball, and the old ball would curve much easier than the one they now have. The high flies that were easy outs then would be home runs now. The result is that a pitcher has to 'bear down' in every inning and on almost every pitch. He has to keep the ball low, so the batter will hit it on the ground and everybody knows that it is harder on the arm to pitch a low ball than a high one." Additionally, it was mentioned that Leonard was using "six times" as many curve balls than he threw earlier in his career, and his arm suffered significant damage as a consequence.[7]

The grievances addressed by Leonard against Cobb weren't made public until well after "Dutch" had been sent packing from the major leagues. He decided against reporting to Vernon, and did a lot of thinking about the injustices surrounding his demotion. Finally, he concluded that his ex-manager was at fault for his fall from grace, and dredged up a memory bank of purported ill-treatment, figuring he'd gotten a "bum deal" all around. "I could not figure how Cobb could turn on me as he did," he declared, taking it extremely personally.[8] Tris Speaker, his former friend, was also in the wrong for not grabbing him when offered on waivers. Leonard, burning with fury, wanted vengeance and knew the best way to go about it. He departed his ranch eight miles east of Fresno, California, and ventured to Chicago in June 1926, ready to shatter the purity of Cobb and Speaker as baseball players.

Leonard desired a meeting with American League President Ban Johnson first and foremost, but after being ignored, caught up with Washington manager Bucky Harris in Chicago for a series against the White Sox. He showed Harris copies of two letters he possessed, one from Cobb and the other written by Boston and Cleveland alumni "Smoky" Joe Wood, who retired from Organized Baseball in 1922, and was the current baseball coach at Yale University. The missives were sent to Leonard seven years before in 1919 and, based on a cursory examination, Harris quickly notified Senators business manager Ed Eynon. Eynon was so blown away by the contents of the letters that he went directly to Johnson's Chicago home and shared the information. Johnson undoubtedly regretted his earlier disregard for Leonard and, infused with a maddening urgency, sought the ex-ballplayer for a meeting.[9]

Unsuccessful in his attempt to find him, Johnson raced to Cleveland for a one-on-one discussion with Tris Speaker. He proceeded next to Detroit, and discovered that Leonard had also been in town trying to sell the letters to the *Detroit News*. The newspaper apparently declined to purchase the correspondence for their $20,000 to $30,000 sales price.[10] Leonard revealed the letters to Harry Heilmann during his brief stay in the "Motor City," and Heilmann didn't waste any time presenting the information to Cobb.[11] Being the author of one of the documents in question, Cobb was aware of what it contained, and for that reason, he had cause to be concerned. With the right kind of negative spin, the contents of his letter could be misconstrued to show him as a willing participant in the fixing of a baseball game.

Even a hazy notion of him being tied to crookedness was enough to tarnish his reputation.

That's precisely what Leonard was striving for. When he ultimately met Johnson in Chicago, he was uncompromising in his language, charging Cobb, Wood, and Speaker with malfeasance, and used the 1919 letters as evidence. He asserted that the three men had joined him in a conspiracy on September 24, 1919, to give Detroit a victory over Cleveland the following day. The agreement was made with the idea that Cleveland had already captured second place in the league, thus garnering a share of World Series money and, with a Tigers win, would help them in their fight for third place. Meaning the game was inconsequential to Speaker and Wood; thus, they were allegedly willing to throw it to help Cobb and Leonard. Additionally, since they already knew who was going to win on September 25, they decided to place a bet on Detroit to garner a little extra money from the deal.[12]

Putting up $1,500, Leonard was all for the idea. He, however, left Detroit before the September 25 game was played. As far as he knew, Cobb was placing $2,000 on the contest, while Speaker and Wood were both contributing $1,000 to the pot.[13] As expected, Detroit was victorious, winning by a score of 9–5. Several weeks after the 1919 season closed, October 23, 1919, to be exact, Cobb sat down at his Augusta home and penned a letter to Leonard. It read, in part:

Wood and myself were considerably disappointed in our business proposition, as we had $2,000 to put into it and the other side quoted us $1,400, and when we finally secured that much money, it was about two o'clock and they refused to deal with us, as they had men in Chicago to take the matter up with and they had no time, so we completely fell down and of course we felt badly over it.

Everything was open to Wood and he can tell you about it when we get together. It was quite a responsibility and I don't care for it again, I can assure you.[14]

Wood also mailed correspondence to Leonard, but his message contained more details of the transaction than Cobb had. He also included a certified check for $1,630 that was Leonard's original $1,500, plus a third of the winnings ($130). The message read, in part:

The only bet [Fred] West could get up was $600 against $420 (10 to 7). Cobb did not get up a cent. He told us that and I believe him. Could have put some at 5 to 2 on Detroit, but did not, as that would make us put up $1,000 to win $400.

We won the $420. I gave West $30, leaving $390, or $130 for each of us.

If we ever have another chance like this we will know enough to try to get down early.[15]

In his letter, Wood affirmed that Cobb hadn't put any money down on the game, a crucial fact. But taking into consideration what Cobb printed in his document, he still had a lot of explaining to do. One of the most interesting portions of the Wood letter stated, "I gave West $30, leaving $390, or $130 for each of us." The $390 was apparently being split three ways, "$130 for each of us," as he explained. But other than Wood and Leonard, who admittedly had been part of the deal, who was the third individual involved? There was sufficient reason to wonder about improprieties by both Cobb and Speaker, and they were possibly complicit at the very least.

Threatening to go public with the story and initiate a lawsuit for money he believed was owed to him by the Detroit Tigers, Leonard convinced Johnson in June 1926 to make financial reparations in the reported amount of $20,000.[16] He agreed to throw in the original copies of the Cobb and Wood letters to complete the deal. Johnson, through American League attorney Henry Killilea, worked out the details and the agreement was finalized. Had Leonard taken the matter to the press, the league would have suffered greatly, Johnson felt, as would have Frank Navin, an important friend. To a lesser degree, he was concerned about protecting managers Cobb and Speaker. Altogether, obtaining the letters and sending Leonard back to California content was seen as the best way to keep the story suppressed until an internal league investigation could bear further results.

While Leonard was adamant about gaining revenge, his motivation might have been dual-faceted. For years, disseminated reports claimed he was a wealthy man, but what Ed R. Hughes of the *San Francisco Chronicle* uncovered in his research challenged that assumption. He found that Leonard was in debt because of the ranch he purchased in 1922 and had to borrow the money he used to travel to Chicago in June 1926. Things quickly changed though, and after confirming with the Fresno County Courthouse, Hughes wrote: "Whatever happened in Detroit and Chicago last June when

Leonard was there, he came back and paid off that mortgage on July 17, 1926." The amount was $15,000.[17]

The American League Board of Directors held a secret meeting in Chicago on September 9, 1926, and the two letters were presented for review. Understanding the heavy implications of their move, the directors voted to issue unconditional releases to Speaker and Cobb, ousting them from the league. With regard to Cobb, Johnson later said that Ty "couldn't explain the letter [he wrote] satisfactorily," and "on that letter alone the American League was forced to let Cobb go."

The directors spoke about protecting the two superstars, and Johnson added, "They had done a lot for baseball. We had to let them out, but we saw no reason for bringing embarrassment upon their families. We wanted to be decent about it."[18] A coordinated effort was made to give dignity to Cobb and Speaker, and allowing them to resign with the appearance of doing so on their own terms was concocted.[19]

Justifiably, Cobb was enraged by the maneuvering of Leonard. Johnson described him as "heartbroken," and said he "maintained his innocence" when they met just prior to Cobb's hunting trip in October. Johnson informed him that "whether guilty or not he was through in the American League."[20] Navin notified him of his release as well, according to *The Sporting News*, a few days before the season concluded, but the public wasn't made aware of it until early November.[21] That meant his public comments, including the interview he gave in Omaha en route to Wyoming, when he discussed his future in baseball, were specifically curtailed and not forthcoming. Cobb withheld the information about his dismissal from the Tigers, not only as a manager but as a player. As stunning as it was, he was unemployed in Organized Baseball for the first time in over twenty years.

"I hate to leave baseball," Cobb told the Associated Press. "You know I am going to be forty years old December 18. I am about as good as I ever was, but the time has come for me to quit taking chances, and that means that it is time for me to get out."[22] It clearly appeared that Cobb was stepping out on his own terms, and if things continued to proceed smoothly, there were hopes that the entire scandal would blow over without any public knowledge at all. He didn't stray too far from baseball, attending the minor league annual meetings at Asheville, North Carolina on December 5. Fighting off a cold, he told inquisitive reporters, "I said when I left Detroit that I had swung my last bat in a competitive game, and I meant just that."[23] Journalists were sure he was taking charge of a minor league team, and the Atlanta Crackers of the Southern Association seemed to be his club of choice.

Another rumor tied both Cobb and Speaker to positions in the Boston Red Sox franchise. But on December 21, 1926, the Commissioner of Baseball, Judge Kenesaw M. Landis, released 100 pages of documentation from his investigation into the alleged fixed game involving the two men, effectively ruining any future for them in Organized Baseball.[24] The revelation rocked baseball, tarnishing Cobb and Speaker before the public, and dropped them into the same heap as the crooked "Black Sox." Once reporters had a chance to review the evidence, there were questions why Landis would destroy the reputations of two celebrated superstars on the word of just one man, Leonard, especially when acknowledging his dubious motives.

Cobb went into self-preservation mode, offering a lengthy explanation to Bert Walker of the *Detroit Times*. "Is there a God?" he asked. "I am beginning to doubt it. I know there is no gratitude. Here I am, after twenty-two years in hard, desperate, and honest work, dismissed from baseball in disgrace without ever having a chance to face my accuser. It is enough to try one's faith. I am branded as a gambler on ball games in which my club took part. I have never in the twenty-two years I have been in baseball made a single bet on an American League game. These vague accusations that have driven me out of baseball come from a man who is nothing short of a blackmailer. I was not surprised at my dismissal [from the Tigers], but I do think that this manner in which I was dismissed was nothing short of a conspiracy to oust me."[25]

At the center of the conspiracy, Cobb believed, was Frank J. Navin, his boss since 1905. He razed what was left of their relationship with his comments, claiming that he would've won a championship if he'd gotten any cooperation from the owner, and frankly announced, "I do not believe Mr. Navin wanted me to win a pennant for Detroit." Cobb explained that the Tigers had opportunities to sign Paul Waner, Alphonse "Tommy" Thomas, and others, but that Navin blocked each and every acquisition. Major criticism was directed at Navin's so-called "gift" of $10,000 presented during the August 1925 banquet for Cobb. Ty denied it was a gift at all, stating that the money was part of his salary, but that Navin pawned it off as a big bonus to honor him. "The ball club never gave me a red cent," Cobb declared, "and when I left Detroit after the last game, the club owners did not even express the slightest word of appreciation."[26]

In the fight of his life, Cobb's strength and passion were visible to reporters, but his emotions got the best of him. A correspondent for the

United Press couldn't help but notice tears flowing from his eyes during one interview in Augusta.[27] Responding to questions about the infamous letter he wrote to Leonard, Cobb did his best to clarify himself. He confessed that his use of the words "business proposition" was his way of shrouding his comments because he knew how they might be interpreted if in the wrong hands. He denied being part of any conspiracy with Leonard, but admitted that he knew "Dutch" was betting on the game in 1919. In fact, Cobb agreed to do him a favor, and that tied to the "responsibility" he mentioned in the missive.

Cobb explained that Leonard, because he was leaving Detroit early, had asked him to convey the amount wagered on the September 25 ballgame, and that was the overall purpose of his October 23 letter. Cobb insisted he never bet on the game, nor did he ever intend to. Speaker said likewise. *The Sporting News* indicated that "As far as the evidence shows, Cobb and Speaker did not put up any money," seemingly absolving them.[28] There was also significant backlash to the claim that the September 25, 1919, game was "thrown" to Detroit, with several of the game's participants not remembering anything specifically amiss about the affair. Amongst those to comment were Pep Young, Jack Graney, Bill Wambsganss, and Bernie Boland.[29]

Proactive in their defense, Cobb and Speaker hired attorneys and were preparing a lengthy legal strategy to restore their reputations. They received a stunning amount of support throughout the sporting world, and on a personal level from friends, colleagues, and admirers. Late in December 1926, the ostracized duo went to Washington, DC, to consult officials, and there was speculation that a few of their allies in the US Senate were considering a public hearing to get to the bottom of the controversy.[30] Cobb and Speaker welcomed such an event, and particularly wanted to face Leonard who had yet to step before them at any point since the accusations were made.[31] The scope of Judge Landis's probe grew when further allegations of corruption were made separate from the Cobb-Speaker situation, and the political wrangling between the commissioner and Ban Johnson intensified going into 1927.

Opposite all the support bestowed upon Cobb by individuals maintaining his innocence, there was still much criticism. As a matter of fact, the harshest censure appeared in W. Rollo Wilson's column in the *Pittsburgh Courier*. It read: "Somehow or other, I do not feel that Tris Speaker is guilty of the charges launched against him by Dutch Leonard. But when I remember about Ty Cobb beating and kicking that colored chambermaid in a

Cleveland (sic) hotel, I would not put anything down as being too low for him to do. And do you recall that he tried to lick a colored employee at Shibe Park a couple years since because he would not discontinue a phone call so that he, the mighty Cobb, could use the instrument? That's how I feel about Master Cobb."[32]

Nevertheless, Landis, at the conclusion of his investigation, exonerated Cobb and Speaker of all charges on January 27, 1927, declaring in a statement: "These players have not been, nor are they now, found guilty of fixing a ball game."[33] With the announcement, they were restored to the reserve lists of their former teams, Detroit and Cleveland respectively, and then given their freedom by those clubs to shop their services around the American League as free agents. Cobb, hunting in South Carolina at the time, was relieved by the news, but had expected to be cleared of the damaging allegations. However, he felt the totality of the entire case besmirched his standing with the public and a lawsuit for defamation against the league was not off the table.[34] He did welcome the chance to play again, saying that he was "honor bound" to make his return.

"Words fail to express my happiness over my vindication," he explained. "I have suffered deeply, but never lost hope that eventually right and justice would prevail. I wish to thank from the bottom of my heart the baseball fans, the newspapers, sporting writers, and all my friends for their wonderful confidence in me. For twenty-two years, I have given my all to baseball. I am supremely happy to know that what I gave was not given in vain."[35] Several teams put out feelers for Cobb's rights for the upcoming season, including St. Louis Browns, New York Yankees, and Brooklyn Dodgers, and Connie Mack was so enthusiastic about signing him that he went to Augusta to meet with him personally.[36] Mack also wanted Speaker for Philadelphia, but Tris worked a deal with the Washington Senators instead. Cobb displayed restraint in his negotiations but Mack was persistent, finally offering him a sum of money that just couldn't be refused.

During a banquet of the Philadelphia Sportswriters Association at the Hotel Adelphia on February 8, Cobb publicized his decision to join the Athletics. The next day, he formally endorsed a contract in the office of Mack at Shibe Park, but the details of the agreement were withheld. Experts guessed it was as high as $75,000, while Cobb denoted a $70,000 figure, plus 10 percent of gate receipts for exhibition games, in his 1961 autobiography.[37] According to records held by the National Baseball Hall of Fame at Cooperstown, New York, he made $50,000 for 1927, but the document didn't specifically outline a bonus figure.[38] Altogether, his total income from Philadelphia was believed to supersede that of Babe Ruth and once again make him the highest paid player in the game.

A certain amount of irony existed in Cobb's signing with the Athletics. Billy Evans, the longtime umpire and writer, recalled that some of his greatest battles were against Philadelphia and, in a syndicated article, referenced his infamous spiking of Home Run Baker. Philadelphia was also the scene of immense fan demonstrations against Cobb and where death threats were levied, making it mandatory for special police units to guard the player from bodily harm. He had fond moments in the city as well. One of the most personal occurred on June 12, 1915, when he was warmly honored by Philadelphia fans during an on-field ceremony organized by the Masons and given an expensive double-barreled hammerless shotgun.[39] Cobb knew the fans were a loyal bunch, and gaining their favor earlier in his career had been a chore, but now that he was in the fold; things were going to be much different.

Feeling physically good and motivated to "show the public that [he could] still reach dizzy heights in baseball," he joined the Athletics at their Fort Myers, Florida, camp on March 7, 1927.[40] Mack's club featured a striking mixture of youthful talent and veterans, and Cobb, Eddie Collins, Zach Wheat, and Jack Quinn—each hovering around the forty-year-old mark—made up the senior contingent. Adding the experience of Mack and the wisdom of coach Kid Gleason, Philadelphia was privy to an unparalleled baseball intellect. Cobb acquainted himself with the players he didn't already know, worked with the rookies, and bonded with his new roommate, outfielder Al Simmons. In just three seasons, Simmons had displayed the makings of a superstar, and would glean much from Cobb's teachings.[41]

The press jumped on the story of Cobb's ejection at St. Petersburg on March 17 for aggravating umpire Frank Wilson in the fourth inning of an exhibition against the Boston Braves, and affirmed that he was up to his old, rebellious tricks.[42] And Cobb certainly was. He was doing what he always had, shouting disparaging remarks at opposing players from the dugout and employing psychological warfare. Interestingly, even though he was in full rebel mode, he refrained from showing any sign of dissension toward Mack, and completely trusted the latter's leadership. He was in his twenty-third year of major league ball and had been a manager himself, but still didn't second-guess Mack for a second. His respect for him was too great. The 1927 season opened with Cobb in right field at New York on April 12 before a massive crowd of 60,000, but Philadelphia was turned back, 8–3.

Cobb got off to a flying start, doing everything imaginable to prove his critics wrong. He was batting at a terrific clip and amazingly stole home twice in April, both within a week's time. Sportswriter James C. Isaminger wrote that Ty was playing "as if he shed ten years."[43] Despite the perception that he was quick to temper, Cobb displayed a mellower personality on the field. In a game against Washington at Shibe Park, an obnoxious fan got on his case, recklessly shouting from the crowd. Unhesitant, Cobb was ready to interact with the spectator, but rather than issuing a challenge to fight, he asked, "Do you think it is fair to yell at us in such a manner when we are trying our best to bring a pennant to Philadelphia? What have we done to deserve it? Give us encouragement and not abuse." The man was humbled by Cobb's mild-mannered and logical response. He walked down, apologized and shook the player's hand.[44]

While Cobb was doing his best to keep his temper in check, journalists weren't buying the composed Cobb in any shape or form. For them, he'd forever be the maniacal madman of the basepaths, and the spin surrounding an incident on May 5 at Philadelphia highlighted the kind of sensationalism that normally followed him. In that game, he drove a ball over the right-field fence in the eighth inning, seemingly tying the game at three apiece against Boston. Umpire Red Ormsby decided that the ball had veered foul and called Cobb back to the plate to continue his at bat. The audience reacted loudly and Simmons's wordy protest earned him a first class ticket to the clubhouse. Cobb was surprisingly calm in the matter and returned to the box, where he "accidently" brushed against Ormsby. The latter deemed the move hostile and ejected him.[45] The national press painted the story as yet another of Cobb's long line of rowdy shenanigans, claiming that Ty had incited thousands of Philadelphia fans to riot. Cobb denied all of it and felt the entire tale was "grossly over colored" for effect.[46]

Upon his return to Detroit on May 10, Cobb was roundly welcomed and honored with a special luncheon, an on-field ceremony, and dinner. More than 27,000 fans turned out for a weekday game at Navin Field to pay tribute, and Cobb was given several nice gifts, including an automobile. He told the audience at the luncheon that he was moved by their show of affection. "I am grateful to all of you," he explained. "I am out today in another uniform, but I can't work up that competitive spirit against Detroit. You can't be sold on a town and its people for twenty-two years and then go against them in a competitive way all of a sudden. I have only friendship and gratitude in my heart for the Detroit players and the Detroit fans."[47]

Cobb was enjoying a remarkable run, hitting safely in 21-straight games in May, and briefly pushed his batting average over .400. A Philadelphia writer noted that Detroit regretted his departure, stating, "The Michigan city never realized just how great he was until they let go of him. Now they know he can never be replaced."[48] It was appropriate, though, that Detroit fans were witnesses to the history he made on July 18, 1927, when he became the first major leaguer in history to achieve 4,000 career hits.[49] A few days later in Cleveland, he flashed great agility in working the delayed steal in the sixth inning. After the catcher mistakenly threw the ball into center field, Cobb raced to third in a full stride with no intention of stopping. In a glimpse of the Cobb of old, he rounded the bag, and with the ball sailing in from the outfield, slid safely underneath the tag to score.[50]

The season wasn't always picturesque, and Cobb sustained a handful of injuries. The worst was a severe charley horse, suffered during an exhibition at Buffalo in early May. He slumped at times and New York sportswriter Joe Vila offered an unsubstantiated report that he had been "playing for an individual record," and not for the team. Vila was sure that he wouldn't play for Mack in 1928.[51] As a club, the Athletics were one of the hottest teams in baseball during the second half, and ordinarily, the kind of play Philadelphia demonstrated would have been enough to win a pennant. But the Yankees were even hotter. Led by Babe Ruth, Lou Gehrig, and Waite Hoyt, New York sauntered to a league title and then won the World Series over the Pittsburgh Pirates in four-straight games. The A's finished with a 91–63 record, good for second place, and were 19 games behind the Yankees.

With permission from management, and since the pennant race was decided, Cobb broke from the team early on September 21 to attend his annual expedition to Wyoming. Before he left, he told reporters that Mack had invited him to return in 1928 at the same salary, but he declined to make any decisions.[52] However, upon his homecoming to Philadelphia following his western hunting jaunt, Mack informed him of his release on November 2. Facing a downturn in attendance, the Athletics were economizing, and Cobb's tremendous paycheck was too much of a burden. Mack was not happy about the decision, telling him, "Ty, you meant a whole lot of us, and I am sorry that you will not be with us again. Your aid to us cannot be exaggerated."[53] Cobb accepted the news with dignity, and embraced the thought of spending more time with family. "I am still a young man in everything except baseball," the forty-year-old said. "What I will do in the future is something I cannot tell."[54]

Charlie Cobb was "glad" about her husband's imminent retirement, and the couple talked about a sightseeing trip to Europe. Over the subsequent weeks and months, Ty remained busy and rumors sprouted up connecting him to the Atlanta minor league franchise, much like they had in late 1926. After the first of the year, Mack revealed his change of heart and wanted Cobb back. The two exchanged correspondence, and although Cobb told the newspapers he wanted to leave baseball behind, he was swayed by Mack's "kind persistence."[55] On March 1, 1928, he announced that he signed a contract for the upcoming campaign in a deal valued at $35,000, and told a reporter that he planned to do his best "to help the team win."[56] The Athletics were significantly enhanced by the signing of Cobb's recent partner-in-arms, Tris Speaker, and Mack was pretty well convinced the team was headed for a championship.

At Augusta, Cobb did a little training with the New York Giants and joined Philadelphia when his teammates arrived for an exhibition at Warren Park on March 16. In the camps of both teams, he proved an influential coach, working extensively with younger players. He ventured with the Athletics to Fort Myers—their spring headquarters—but was forced to return to Augusta after Charlie became sick. Her condition was such that she needed an operation, but mended quickly.[57] Cobb dispelled the story that he'd cleaned up in the stock market and was retiring, and made the trek to Philadelphia. There, he aided the Athletics in their win over the Phillies for the local city title.[58] The season opened on April 11, 1928, but Philadelphia wasn't as strong as it appeared and lost its first four games. The absence of Al Simmons because of rheumatism in his legs was a crucial reason for the team's slow start.[59]

Cobb's batting eye was sharp in the early going, and his average was over .350 for the first month. His fielding and base running were subpar on occasion, and it was obvious that his legs were tired. Columnist Westbrook Pegler remarked, "It was both inspiring and depressing to see Ty hobble around the baseball field." Other journalists called him "grandpa" or "old man" in their reports, and crowds razzed him, but the criticism likely served to motivate him all the more. He ran into a cocky twenty-two-year-old in Leo Durocher, an infielder for the Yankees, who was verbally aggressive toward just about everyone, and showed no fear against Cobb. As legend has it,

Durocher told him, "Don't flash your spikes at me or I'll show you how to really spike a guy."[60] That kind of repartee never impressed Cobb, and he was all too willing to exchange barbs or even punches if need be, but their bickering never developed that far.

On June 21, 1928, at Yankee Stadium, a game was contested in which thirteen future Hall of Famers took part. That included managers Connie Mack and Miller Huggins, plus Cobb, Speaker, Simmons, Eddie Collins, Lefty Grove, Jimmie Foxx, and Mickey Cochrane from the Athletics. For New York, there was Babe Ruth, Lou Gehrig, Earle Combs, and Tony Lazzeri.[61] The Yankees won the game, 4–0, and were essentially steamrolling over the American League for the third year in a row. For Cobb, his play was somewhat erratic, and he slumped pretty badly in late May and into June. He managed to rebound, but his slowing agility left him susceptible to injury. In the outfield against Boston in early July, a ball glanced off the side of his head after a tricky hop. On July 18 against Detroit, he took a pitch on his right wrist and exactly a week later, he was struck by a ball again, suffering a bad bruise.

Cobb started his final game on July 26, 1928, at Comiskey Park in Chicago, and went 2-for-5 with a double in a 5–1 victory. While nursing his wounds, Cobb watched as Mack lined his outfield with Simmons, Bing Miller, and George "Mule" Haas, moved Ossie Orwoll from the mound to first base and placed Jimmie Foxx at third, initiating a brilliant period of winning for the A's. In fact, the team won 10-straight from July 25 to August 2 and advanced from eleven games behind the Yankees to only 4.5. New York's lead diminished more in the days that followed and, at one juncture, the Athletics briefly moved into first place. Notably, the turnaround for Philadelphia was done without Cobb or Speaker in the regular lineup. Their leadership and influence from the sidelines were valuable to the club, nonetheless.

Sportswriter Frank G. Menke wrote, "Cobb is something of a bench warmer now, but he never became such until he had established every existing durability record, and bench warmer that he is, he still possesses a walloping record of around .333 for this season."[62] On September 3, 1928, at Washington's Griffith Stadium, he appeared as a pinch hitter in the first game of a doubleheader, and smashed a double off Washington's Bump Hadley. This would mark Cobb's final major league hit. Ironically, twenty-three years before, he doubled in his first major league hit, that one was off Hall of Famer Jack Chesbro. Cobb played his final game on September

11 at Yankee Stadium before 50,000 people, and was unsuccessful in a pinch-hitting role for Jimmy Dykes in the ninth inning. The moment wasn't acknowledged as historic at the time because nobody knew whether Cobb would perform again or not.

But days later, on September 17 in Cleveland, Cobb made a decision about his future. He issued a statement to reporters, announcing that"Never again, after the finish of the present pennant race will I be an active player in the organization to which I have devoted twenty-four seasons of what for me was hard labor." Acknowledging that it had been a "privilege" to play for Mack, he was retiring for good, and explained his intention to be around his family. "I scarcely know my children," he told a reporter, and he hoped to change that.[63] The pennant race remained tight until the end, but the Athletics couldn't upend New York, finishing in second place with a record of 98–55 and 2.5 games back. Cobb and his family, who maintained a residence in Bala Cynwyd, on the western border of Philadelphia, soon packed up their belongings and headed back to Augusta.

Entering a world post-baseball was both exciting and frightening for Cobb. He had expressed a desire to play twenty-five seasons during interviews, but the ninety records that he had established, the amazing .367 lifetime batting average he attained, and the 54 steals of home plate, spoke volumes about his commitment to the national pastime. He had nothing left to prove. Ed R. Hughes of the *San Francisco Chronicle* reflected on his accomplishments, and wrote that Cobb was "one of the truly greats and those who saw him at his best will never forget him."[64] An editorial in the *Philadelphia Inquirer* stated that his retirement would "be heard with regret by tens of thousands of fans who were always sure of good entertainment when Cobb was in the game." Considering his great financial stability, the newspaper added that Cobb "deserves all he has because he has given all that he had to the patrons of the game."[65] It is true, and it is arguable that any man ever loved baseball more than Ty Cobb.

17

IMMORTALIZED IN BRONZE

The departure of Ty Cobb from the major leagues was inevitable, and baseball was going to enter the 1929 season without him on an active roster for the first time in nearly a quarter century. Of course, a significant void was going to be left in his wake, and although the national game was bigger than one man, his contributions and achievements wouldn't be forgotten anytime soon. For Cobb, he was walking away from the sport on his own terms, and that was important to him. As early as 1913, he had expressed a desire to eventually retire from baseball while still exhibiting some semblance of success on the diamond.[1] The forty-one-year-old batted .323 in 95 games in 1928, and later said, "There was nothing wrong with my eyes or the upper part of my body," when he retired. "I could throw and hit with the rawest rookie," but his legs "couldn't stand the strenuous exercise."[2]

Washington Senators star Clyde Milan, a speedster who fought Cobb for stolen base honors in the early 1910s, spoke with the Georgian around 1928. He recalled Cobb telling him that he was leaving baseball "simply because playing was getting to be work for him."[3] The wear and tear, plus his extraordinary mental and physical exertion—continuous for over two decades—had finally exhausted the seemingly infinite boundaries of Cobb's endurance. He told a reporter in 1931, "During my twenty-five years in the game, I had become its slave. And that is why I got doggoned tired of it."[4] He wanted other things out of life, far from the constant demands and the grueling hassle of baseball. His love for the sport unquestionably remained, but he was ready to sever his arterial ties once and for all . . . or so he believed at the time.

It is arguable how productive Cobb would have been in 1929 had he elected to continue his career. As a part-time player, mostly used in pinch-hit situations, he would have been an asset in the crunch, and his veteran perspective would've been a major aid to younger athletes. Having Cobb on the bench was a positive in many ways, but his days as a regular outfielder were long gone. Cognizant of his deterioration, Cobb was protective of his image. He knew that he could no longer steal multiple bases in a game, race in from center field to snag a tough fly, and fleetly proceed from first to third on a bunt. He figured that playing in a reduced state of ability was altering his standing in the eyes of baseball fans. "I didn't want to, at my age and weight, disillusion a lot of people," he explained with surprising candor.[5]

Cobb appeared convinced he was doing the right thing and he had plenty of ideas for the near future, but was he mentally equipped to live without baseball? Was he ready to watch his fellow major leaguers report for spring training and stand idly on the sidelines for the first time in his adult life?[6] Financially stable, he didn't need any form of employment and without a job or a schedule dictating his plans, he was facing an extended period of leisure. To some that would be an exciting prospect. But for a person of Cobb's high strung nature, it was disconcerting. "He shouldn't have retired at forty-one," Cobb's daughter Shirley later told biographer Don Rhodes. "A man with that much energy shouldn't retire at that age."[7]

Concerns over inactivity were not necessarily a problem for Cobb in late 1928. He was booked to tour Japan with several other American ballplayers by the Osaka *Mainichi Shimbun* newspaper for a series of games and baseball demonstrations. Cobb had always wanted to travel, and, in fact, planned to honeymoon with his wife Charlie in Asia following the 1908 season. The offer to barnstorm, including a nice guarantee, came at just the right time and Cobb wasn't about to pass it up.[8] Since he was able to bring his wife and three of his children on the journey abroad, it was altogether a special opportunity, and the Cobbs looked forward to the venture with great optimism.

The legendary "Big Train" Walter Johnson, winner of 417 games, was scheduled to join the party headed overseas, but backed out at the last minute after accepting a managerial job for the Washington franchise.[9] Ex-major leaguers Bob Shawkey, Fred Hofmann, and Herb Hunter, along with National League umpire Ernie Quigley were confirmed for the tour, as was Cobb's friend, George "Putty" Putnam, co-owner of the San Francisco Seals Pacific Coast club. The Cobb family arrived in Seattle on October 18 and Ty participated in a farewell exhibition the following afternoon at the Coast League Park. Sportswriter Ken Kay Kelso noted that Cobb played "with all the enthusiasm of a rookie" in the contest, teamed with the American Mail Line squad against the West Seattle Athletic Club, going 3-for-5 with three runs in a 12–5 victory.

Kelso interviewed Cobb and took specific notice of his disposition. He wrote: "You've read in the papers of the many mix-ups Ty Cobb has been in, haven't you? And you got the idea he was a rather tough hombre didn't you? Well, you're wrong. He isn't. He's the softest spoken, most courteous and gentlemanly ball player in the game—a fitting person to be the idol of every youngster in America." He explained how Cobb accommodated auto-graph hounds, was jovial when lightheartedly ribbed from the audience, and added, "No finer emissary could have been selected for a goodwill tour of Japan." On October 20, Cobb, his family, and associates boarded the American Mail Liner *President Jefferson* and sailed from Smith Cove terminal at the Port of Seattle, beginning its voyage across the Pacific.[10]

For years, college teams from Japan and the United States had barn-stormed in each other's countries, and Herb Hunter was experienced in ventures to Asia, leading a noteworthy tour of major leaguers in 1922.[11] Baseball's popularity was astonishingly robust in Japan and the arrival of superstar Cobb was momentous. Thousands turned out for the nine exhibi-tions, including a crowd of 22,000 at Tokyo, and scores more appeared to see Cobb deliver training sermons on the fundamentals of the game and good sportsmanship.[12] Attendance was believed to have been curtailed by the ceremonies surrounding the coronation of Hirohito as the Emperor of Japan, also taking place in November 1928 but die-hard baseball fans demonstrated their enthusiasm, and Cobb was followed on the streets by kids awestruck by his presence. Had Cobb been able to tour with an All-American ballclub instead of just a handful of countrymen with Japa-nese college players filling in the gaps, there would have been an even greater response.

Stopping in Honolulu on the way back, Cobb and his family were pho-tographed wearing Hawaiian leis, and completed their journey on the *Pres-ident Jefferson*, arriving in San Francisco on December 12. The "trip was a successful one," it was reported, and much was accomplished in the way of further escalating interest in the sport.[13]

Cobb didn't completely shun baseball in 1929, and he briefly worked out with the St. Louis Browns in Florida and Baltimore Orioles in Geor-gia during the spring.[14] His real focus was on a continued global explora-tion, venturing first to Cuba in late March and then a more pronounced expedition to Europe beginning in June. His journey, accompanied by Charlie and their children, Shirley, Herschel, Beverly, and Jimmy, launched from Hoboken, New Jersey, on June 15 on the *S.S. President Roosevelt*, and would encompass several months of sightseeing.[15] The Cobbs trekked from Germany to Scotland and absorbed all of the landmark attractions along the way. Ty, an avid reader of ancient European culture, not only appreciated the aesthetic beauty but the historical importance as well, particularly the Appian Way in Rome. Italy, overall, was his favorite location and he later told a reporter that evening time at St. Mark's Square in Venice was "too wonderful to describe."[16]

Cobb also enjoyed the iconic architecture of Paris, and the lack of thorough baseball coverage in Europe did a great deal to stifle his natural impulse of following every little detail related to the sport.

On September 10, 1929, the RMS *Majestic* arrived at New York and five members of the Cobb Family debarked. The sixth, Ty himself, remained in Europe for a few additional weeks, really maximizing his vacation to the fullest, while Charlie was compelled to return to get their kids ready for school.[17] The divide at the end of the family retreat wasn't really surprising. Charlie was the primary caregiver to the Cobb children and Ty usually was caught up in baseball, hunting, or some other occupation, away from home for weeks and months at a time. His prolonged absences, aloofness, and irregular disposition made the relationship between Ty and his wife and kids unique, and the Cobb Family structure, like everything else in his life, was utterly complex.

Things had changed significantly for Ty and Charlie over the years. As newlyweds in 1908, an onlooker, after seeing them shopping, said, "You couldn't see a better looking couple in Detroit than Ty Cobb and his cute little bride."[18] They were joyous, stylish, and inseparable, representing young love at its finest with nothing but brightness in their future. Cobb was ever conscious of his wife's feelings through the years, as demonstrated in 1916 when filming the movie *Somewhere in Georgia*. The film called for him to perform close to his costar Elsie MacLeod, but he was exceedingly bashful because he was concerned what Charlie would think.[19] Years later, daughter Shirley read letters that Ty had sent Charlie from the road during his baseball career, and was taken aback by the sweetness of her father, indicative of his pure adoration for his wife.[20]

But on the other side of the coin, Cobb was known for his harsh discipline, and there were allegations of abuse—both mental and physical—to Charlie and the Cobb children. From his perspective, aside from being the breadwinner, he was responsible for ensuring that the family lived up to his high standards when it came to work, schooling, and household management. His personality and temper were overbearing to say the least, and in trying to convey his message, he was more like a drill sergeant than a compassionate father. He commanded respect, and through an "atmosphere of fear," as Shirley later explained, Ty received it.[21]

In terms of his expectations, Cobb demanded unreasonable and unrealistic productivity from those closest to him. He wanted his wife and children to put the same kind of pressure on themselves that he placed on himself to be successful, exhausting every inch of their being to thrive in whatever endeavor they were engaged in. It was difficult to understand and, unfortunately, there was no one alive who could ever measure up to his standards. Being a man of the public, too, he wanted only favorable press about the success of his youngsters, especially anything involving his namesake, Ty Junior. Journalists loved to bring up the sons of baseball stars, assessing their athletic abilities, and although Junior wasn't following his father's footsteps, he was fostering a good name as a tennis player.[22] Ty undoubtedly wanted his son to be a winner.

Cobb also wanted his children to be tough. In 1916, a writer for *Baseball Magazine* conveyed a story about Ty Junior, explaining how he was confronted by an older boy and insulted. His father heard the argument and insisted that "Junior" stand up for himself, telling him, "If you don't go out and lick him, I will lick you." Needless to say, the youth did what his father ordered.[23] So concerned about their fighting abilities, Cobb hired veteran professional boxer Kid Beebe, a bantamweight from Philadelphia, to train two of his sons, presumably Ty Junior and Herschel, in 1928. "I think everyone ought to be able to handle his dukes," Cobb explained. "You know, I got into plenty of tight places during my baseball career, and it is always better to be prepared."[24]

Of his boys, Herschel was the most inclined toward physical athletics. He told Grantland Rice that he liked a sport that was "rougher" than tennis, golf, or baseball, and was a particular fan of football.[25] But his brother Jimmy figured Herschel was the only son with "natural ability" on the baseball diamond. However, he noted that Herschel's chances to advance as a ballplayer diminished "when he injured an eye."[26] Shirley Cobb was athletically proficient in her own right as a competitive equestrian rider. Amongst her achievements was the blue ribbon prize in the ladies' horsemanship class at the 1928 Augusta Horse Show. Notably, the Cobb family talent wasn't limited to sports, as both Shirley and Beverly were gifted pianists, and Jimmy would later gain national recognition after saving the life of a drowning fellow cadet at a New Mexico military school.[27]

Ty's European adventure ended aboard the SS *Bremen*, sailing from Southampton, England, and arriving in New York on October 1, 1929. During the voyage, he bonded with a fellow traveler, Dr. Royal S. Copeland, a US Senator originally from Michigan but elected in New York, and the two "talked about everything." Copeland, in a syndicated article, revealed their discussion about eating habits, and explained how Cobb stressed a two-meal-a-day limit.

Having listened eagerly to the ex-ballplayer's theories, Copeland stated that Cobb was a "philosopher" and was mighty impressed by his intellect.[28]

The press fervently awaited Cobb's arrival home, yearning for his World Series pick and any news about his suspected return to baseball. Cobb was supportive of his old manager Connie Mack and predicted Philadelphia to win over Chicago. He told reporters that he was more interested in the executive side of the game than anything else. "I am not ready to say that I would not manage a club again, although, of course, I shall never play again," he said. "The idea of a major league connection with the player production part of it, appeals to me most. Tentative offers have been made and I believe I will be back in the game next year."[29] Ever since his retirement, the rumors of his reemergence had been constant. Stories tied him to jobs from the Southern Association to the majors and everywhere in between. The Brooklyn Robins and Cincinnati Reds were often mentioned in the gossip, but Cobb denied any dealings.[30]

Cobb joined Christy Walsh's troupe of syndicated writers, sitting alongside former rivals Babe Ruth and John McGraw, and covered the Series.[31] Mack and the Philadelphia Athletics were dominant and, without the aid of Cobb and Tris Speaker, accomplished in 1929 what they weren't able to do the year before by winning the American League pennant and World Series championship in five games over the Chicago Cubs. Before the end of October, economic prosperity and stability came to a crashing halt when the stock market plummeted, destroying the wealth of millions including a number of Cobb's peers in the baseball world. The commencement of the Great Depression was jarring, but not crippling to Cobb, and he'd survive the financial calamity with the bulk of his wealth safely intact.

The unceasing energy Cobb was known for on the field transferred seamlessly to the country club, and his new passion was actually an old one: golf. He broke back into the sport he disavowed during his baseball career at the Forrest Hills–Ricker Hotel course in Augusta, enjoying his first game in two years in the spring of 1929, and when he wasn't traveling, he was on the links.[32] Cobb was addicted to the personal challenge presented by golf; the intrigue of mind over matter and, after resuming play, his handicap was well over 90. But he was determined to improve, and worked at it every chance he had. He hobnobbed with fellow Georgian and golfing sensation-Bobby Jones, and even staged a party at his home after Jones won the 1930 Southeastern Open. Photos of the two shaking hands circulated in the papers, and Cobb was quoted as saying Jones was "the greatest competitive athlete" he'd ever seen.[33]

Hunting remained a hobby, and in the early part of 1930, Cobb welcomed two of his former Philadelphia teammates, Eddie Collins and George Earnshaw, to join him on an outdoor excursion into Burke County, Georgia. He also made arrangements to return to Detroit and see another friend, businessman John Roesink, owner of the Detroit Stars Negro League club, and helped inaugurate the new stadium in Hamtramck by throwing out the first pitch.[34] On September 8, 1930, Cobb teamed with an all-star aggregation against a squad of all-stars from Boston in the latter city during an old-timers contest for charity. Amongst those he teamed with were Honus Wagner and Home Run Baker, while Boston featured Cy Young and Tris Speaker. Cobb, incidentally, played for both teams, pinch-hitting for the local favorites late in the game, and going 0-for-4 in total. Boston won, 8–4, before 22,000 appreciative fans.[35]

Invited to San Francisco to help open the brand new Seals Stadium by his pal George Putnam, Cobb agreed and was joined by Harry Lea, a golfing and hunting companion from Virginia for the journey. On April 7, 1931, Cobb stood at the plate and became the stadium's first batter, merrily swinging at a wild pitch thrown by Mayor Angelo Rossi and displaying great enthusiasm. Eight days later his festive vacation was interrupted by an upsetting report flashing across the news wire services. His wife Charlie had hired an attorney and filed a divorce suit in Augusta Superior Court, requesting custody of their three young children, plus temporary and permanent alimony. In addition to the startling notice was the damning "cruel treatment" allegation against Cobb, but little other documentation was provided to support her claims. Nonetheless, a hearing was scheduled, and the suit was pressing forward.[36]

"I do not know what to say except that I have always loved my wife, my children, and my home," Cobb said in response to the news. "I am sorry such apparently hasty action as this was taken in my absence from home and without having consulted me in the matter. A family is an institution where the children's interests should come first and even now I say that Mrs. Cobb and I should think of our children and not bring them into any court procedure."[37] A writer for the *Greensboro Daily News* noted that Charlie "probably got along with him well until he began to stay at home," and it was likely very true.[38] The nearly constant presence of Cobb's domineering attitude was no doubt a contributing factor in their dispute. The *Macon Telegraph* added that local sympathy in Augusta was "with Mrs. Cobb," but there was a general belief that their troubles would be mended "without a court trial."[39]

Within a few days, Cobb returned to Augusta and began the task of reconciliation. His efforts were fruitful, and the divorce suit was withdrawn. In an official statement, it was stated that Charlie "took this step on her own initiative, and that no further comment [was] to be made on account of the sacredness relating to her decision."[40] By June 1931, Ty was headed back to San Francisco via automobile, and Bay Area writers were frequently declaring that the Cobbs were soon to make California their home. On the surface, it appeared that Ty was the only one interested in making it a reality. Charlie, during the family crisis, had proven her independence by relocating with her kids from their family home on Williams Street in Augusta to a new place at 1122 Greene Street. She remained steadfast as he left for California, and although there was not going to be a divorce, the couple was firmly stationed on separate coasts.[41]

To Ty, though, he loved the weather in San Francisco. His first trip to the city in 1920 etched an indelible impression on his mind and of all the places in the United States to live, Northern California was his choice. He clearly intended for his children to join him, as shown by a 1939 explanation of his big move, when he criticized Georgia schools weakened by the Depression. California, he felt, offered a better education, and he wanted his kids to receive the best opportunities possible. He also candidly stated that he hated the summers in the South.

Jack Troy of the *Atlanta Constitution* responded to Cobb's comments: "It does seem that one of the immortals of baseball could have used a little tact in his explanation. Certainly such a blunt declaration is not calculated to boost his friendship rating at Augusta."[42]

Expecting an eventual reunion with his family, Cobb became accustomed to life in San Francisco. He immersed himself in the culture, venturing to resorts, relaxing, and when in the mood, traveled out to Seals Stadium to watch and occasionally work out with the local team. On August 15, 1931, he was the recipient of a welcome party tendered by ex-major leaguer Bill Lange at his Millbrae area home. Hall of Famer Johnny Evers and Ira Thomas, a teammate in Detroit, were on hand.[43] The following month, he went out to San Quentin prison and helped arrange a special track and field event, a vivid example of his commitment to the entire community. Cobb was always busy, lending his name to various causes, attending luncheons and dinners, and was more sociable than he'd ever been in his life. Reborn, in fact, and his new, outgoing attitude was not temporary.

Bill Leiser of the *San Francisco Chronicle* wrote, "A loner? Not the Ty Cobb of today. He smiles in a friendly way, and he remembers you. The boys who told me of Ty Cobb of long ago must have been telling me of some other guy. Or is it that, long ago, he *was* some other guy. Maybe, in those old days of every man for himself in baseball, he was."[44] Cobb was still adjusting to his new lifestyle, but there was absolutely no outward evidence of the rowdy player he once was accused of being. He was maturing, and as organizations up and down the coast beckoned for his involvement, he settled into a nice routine of golf and fraternization with a legion of new friends.

Cobb and several others were invited to the cabin of vaudeville comedian Clarence Kolb along the McKenzie River in Oregon in June 1932 to fly fish, and Ty took him up on his offer. Meanwhile, back in Augusta, an accident involving his fifteen-year-old son Herschel critically injured Tommy Hankins, a "popular local entertainer," according to the *Augusta Chronicle*. The two were filling a gas can outside the Cobb residence when a match, lit by Herschel, ignited, setting Hankins on fire. His burns were severe and Tommy died a couple days later.[45] Herschel wasn't injured, but the tragedy was disheartening, and Charlie was inspired for a change of scenery, both to give her youngest a father figure and improved schooling. Ty told the press in July that he anticipated his family joining him "within the next month or so," and made arrangements for a property in Atherton on the San Francisco peninsula.[46]

Of the five Cobb children, Ty Jr. was the only one not to move west. The twenty-two-year-old had proven to be the most like his father, high-strung and driven. He was also a little defiant, wanting to distinguish himself as his own man. But there was no way for him to escape the shadows created by his father's fame, especially when sharing the same name. "The people think you ought to be as good as your dad," he told a reporter in 1930, "and that's tough. You see, I don't want the people to think of me as Ty Cobb's son. I want to be on my own. I want to do things myself."[47] Going back to his earliest days at Summerville School and Richmond Academy in Augusta, he devoted only a limited amount of time to baseball, instead preferring football, swimming, and, above all else, tennis. Aware of the tremendous energy his father brought to baseball, Ty Jr. still said that the national pastime lacked the "pep" required by tennis.[48]

In 1927, Ty Jr. was enrolled in the Hun School of Princeton, a college prep school, and it didn't take long for coaches to recognize his athletic abilities. He was named captain of the tennis squad and helped capture interscholastic tournament honors. Two years later, he entered the exclusive Hill School at Pottstown, Pennsylvania, and then advanced to Yale University in 1930, where he continued to play both tennis and football. Standing better than six feet and weighing around 185 pounds, he was a natural sportsman in every endeavor. James C. Isaminger of the *Philadelphia Inquirer* wrote about him, stating, "Ty is a clean cut, fine-looking and quick-spoken young man, who is a real credit to his father and mother." And in terms of looks, "he does not look unlike his distinguished father."[49]

But the similarities between father and son caused them to clash repeatedly until the final straw was broken in 1933. The argument was about money, according to *The Sporting News*, and as a result, Senior stopped paying tuition, causing Junior to drop out of Yale. The latter remained in New Haven and began working for a coal and coke organization, all too prepared to finance his own way through college.[50] The two severed all ties, refusing to talk to one another, and Senior blamed Charlie for the unruly behavior of their children. However, it has been alleged that Cobb spitefully sold all of the stock he'd saved up for Junior after their falling out, but that wasn't true. He kept 1,005 shares of General Motors, 200 of Coca Cola, and 170 of Kelsey Wheel, and although he maintained power of attorney to get rid of the stock, Cobb held on to the shares for his namesake despite their quarrel.[51]

While Cobb retained a sense of stubbornness, an old characteristic, toward his son, he continued to evolve. Before a gathering of baseball folks in San Francisco on February 5, 1934, he delivered a speech, and was surprisingly reflective. "You know, I may have had the wrong idea when I was a kid," he explained. "My single purpose was to win ball games and I was willing to fight to win them. But as I look back now I can see many grand characters, many loveable fellows whose friendship I would cherish now. I guess I won a lot of ball games all right, but I wish they had been friends instead. If I had it to do all over again, I think I would be different."[52] The news corps immediately picked up on the story, adjusting his quote to read, "If I had it to do over again, I wouldn't take baseball so seriously."[53]

His comments drew plenty of response, including Bill Dooley of the *Philadelphia Record*, who said: "It required Ty a long time to see the light and it is a little pathetic that he didn't get wise to himself until he was out of the game. The blame for Ty's unpopularity in the profession was not due in any very large way to his actions on the field, where he stood head and shoulders above all competitors, both in ability and thinking. It wasn't envy of his ability that begrudged him friendship. Ty made his enmities in exchanges of personalities in the clubhouses and off the field. He was as careless of the feelings of others as he was jealous about his own being hurt. Ty went out of his way so often to sow dislike that it was beyond understanding."[54]

Cobb wrote a letter in reply to the commentary and provided a lengthier explanation of his thoughts. He said that there was a segment of the baseball populace, guys who were lazy, critical, and intolerant to religion, plus those in harmful cliques, that he never got along with. But he made plenty of lasting relationships. "Yes, I even can claim some intimate friends," he explained, "and I think you will agree one usually is rich in friends if he can claim as many as he has fingers on one hand. I don't feel I fail to have a single friendship in baseball that I regret not having. I have never been jealous toward any player. If I had to go over my career again, I don't believe I would take the game as seriously as I did, for, no doubt, in my last few years, when the more easy-going players came into the game, they could not understand my style and, no doubt, had their feelings hurt and thought me different than I really felt. I find life very agreeable and I am not at all lonely for friendship."[55]

During the summer of 1934, Ty took his two youngest children, Beverly and Jimmy, to Detroit so he could show them his old stomping grounds at Navin Field. He was welcomed by Tigers fans and cheered as he threw out the ceremonial first pitch for a game there. Detroit, led by Mickey Cochrane and Charlie Gehringer, were on their way to winning the club's first American League pennant since 1909, but would ultimately lose in the World Series against St. Louis, 4–3. Also on the trip, Cobb journeyed back to Atlanta to see his mother Amanda, who had moved from Royston to 38 Orme Circle in the late 1910s.[56]

Always youthful looking, Amanda was very proud of Ty's accomplish-
ments, but was equally proud of her other two children, Paul and Florence.
Her life had been strained by the loss of her husband and, in 1912, she said,
"When Ty was making good, I couldn't appreciate it much, because
Mr. Cobb died then and I was so grief stricken Ty's success was secondary."[57]
Denver Post writer Fay King met the Cobb family and described Amanda as
having a "shower of fluffy brown hair" and "pretty dimples." Amanda doted
on her grandchildren and was active in the community until illness slowed
her down in the mid-1930s. She passed away on October 19, 1936. Florence
lived with her mother, and was called "one of the most attractive, dainty
little brunettes" King had ever seen. She didn't expect her to be single for
long, but Florence never married. She later moved in with her brother Paul
in Sarasota, Florida, and passed away in 1944.

The membership of the Baseball Writers' Association of America (BBWAA)
began voting to determine the inaugural class for the National Baseball Hall
of Fame, the day before Christmas in 1935. Less than two months later, the
results were in, and Cobb received the highest vote total, 222, and was only
four short of unanimous.[58] There were detractors to Cobb being number
one, particularly individuals who criticized his weak outfield performance
in comparison to the likes of Tris Speaker, and the fact that he arguably
"flopped" three times in the World Series (hitting only .262 with nine RBIs
and seven strikeouts in 17 games).[59] Nevertheless, Cobb's statistics and legacy were well-known and the writers with the responsibility of picking the
original entrants to the Hall concurred in support of his recognition.

Over the next three years, the glorious shrine to honor baseball's legends was constructed at Cooperstown, New York, and in June 1939, the
anticipated dedication ceremony was held with old-time luminaries coming
in from all parts of the nation. Cobb wasn't about to miss it. Accompanied
by Beverly and Jimmy, Cobb made the trip cross country from California,
stopping in Detroit en route to see the Tigers beat Washington on June
11.[60] They continued their venture to Utica, New York, and planned to drive
down to Cooperstown to make the 12:15 p.m. start time on Monday, June
12. But timeliness was never Ty's strong suit, and even though he arrived in
town with a little time to spare, he couldn't find a hotel room. "I passed the
mob coming in," he explained. "Still, I thought I had time to wash up."[61]

Cobb finally found lodging at nearby Knox College and was readying himself to head over when he heard the "Cavalcade of Baseball" exercises officially commence on the radio. He was not on the platform with his fellow immortals when Master of Ceremonies Charles J. Doyle, president of the BBWAA, announced the inductees one-by-one. Doyle exclaimed: "Ty Cobb, who won the heart of fans by playing the brand of baseball called, 'reckless, daring and devil may care!'"[62] The crowd reacted respectfully, but Cobb was nowhere to be seen. To record the historic moment, photographers snapped pictures of the Hall of Fame group, including Babe Ruth, Connie Mack, Honus Wagner, Walter Johnson, and Cy Young—ten individuals in total. The eleventh man, and technically Hall of Fame member number one, Cobb, was absent.

Missing in action for the introductions, Cobb quickly joined the festivities, talking with fans and reporters, and getting reacquainted with old friends. He joked about his absence, stating that he was "called out on strikes, I guess," but his tardiness more than likely stuck in his craw.[63] All during his playing career, he was known for being late to spring training and sometimes appeared just moments before game time during the regular season. Occasionally, he arrived after scheduled contests had already begun. Running late was just part of his makeup, but missing the grand stage at the inaugural Hall of Fame ceremony was an embarrassing gaffe, and writers claimed two separate reasons for his delay. One was that he had been held in California to see his daughter's graduation, and the other cited a case of ptomaine poisoning suffered in Utica. His condition reportedly required medical attention prior to his journey to Cooperstown.[64]

Cobb was in good spirits and remained that way while in New York City the days following, sightseeing with his kids and touring the World's Fair. He was more than willing to discuss the current state of the sport, telling Paul Sann of the *New York Post* that "As a spectator, I can take baseball or leave it."[65] He wanted more inside ball, and decried the numerous home runs being hit on a yearly basis. "The lively ball has destroyed the value of the run," he proclaimed.[66] Before returning to California, he wanted to squeeze in a golf game with Babe Ruth at St. Albans Country Club in Queens. "Babe probably is a better golfer," Cobb said, "but I'll nettle him. I always could get the Babe mad. He was the greatest long hitter in baseball. He belts a golf ball a mile. But brain can always beat brawn."[67] The plans fell through after Cobb was called out of town, but Ty looked forward to getting another chance to prod the "Bambino"—just like old times.

18

THE DEPRESSED PHILANTHROPIST

During the heyday of Ty Cobb's ball playing career, experts spent a lot of time searching for the "next Cobb," a player of similar ability and style. Every spring, managers and club owners touted their new acquisitions, comparing their speed and hitting ability to the man who stood at the top of the pyramid. Detroit had the real "Georgia Peach," and other teams desperately wanted a comparable athlete. Interestingly, each league and organization had their own version of "Ty Cobb" as well, meaning that the individual designated was the preeminent star in their specific field. For instance, Benny Kauff was the "Ty Cobb" of the Federal League, Edd Roush was often said to be the "Cobb" of the National League, and Oscar Charleston and Spottswood Poles were considered the "Cobbs" of the Negro Leagues.

Journalists took it all directions, too. Harry Yost was the "Ty Cobb of Football"; Clare Caldwell, nineteen years of age in 1923, was the "Female Georgia Peach" of women's baseball in Detroit; and Dr. James W. Kramer, an evangelist, was the "Ty Cobb of Preachers."[1] In addition, legendary tough guy Eddie Shore was "frequently referred to as the 'Ty Cobb' of ice hockey," according to *The Sporting News*.[2] In baseball circles, the tendency to compare players to Cobb faded in the 1920s and '30s, particularly when managers began moving away from "small ball" and focused on heavy hitting. Slick base stealing and technical batting became a lost art, and only once in a while did someone rise up through the ranks with the same kind of approach to the game which Ty exhibited. Those rarities were generally regarded as a throwback to a bygone era, and purists of the game were thrilled.

Suspected to be a millionaire going back to his days in Detroit, Cobb was long fascinated with the stock market and money. He mingled with leaders of industry, picking up tips of the trade, and gained firsthand insight from trips to various commodities exchanges and even the National Treasury.[3] Finding friends and advisors in all walks of life, he developed his simple interest in stocks and bonds into great proficiency. By the late 1930s, Cobb was highly active in the market, and occasionally a writer ventured to guess the value of his estate. Bill Corum of the *New York Journal American* estimated that Cobb was worth $3 million in 1938, holding 12,000 shares of Coca-Cola and 5,000 shares of General Motors stock.[4] Cobb wasn't the type of man to reveal his net worth, but didn't deny the reports floating around about his wealth.

A shrewd investor, Cobb was protective of his money and avoided unnecessary risks. He found around fifteen companies that he liked and purchased shares for himself to include his two core stocks. Others were Gillette, Nash-Kelvinator, Westinghouse Electric, Chase National Bank, Atlas Powder, Rustless Iron and Steel, and Studebaker. Wanting to ensure financial security for his wife and children, he also purchased stock in their names, investing in a wide range of businesses. As of 1941, the Cobb family, as a whole, owned just more than 7,000 shares of Coca-Cola and nearly 4,500 General Motors. Cobb personally had 2,500 shares of Rustless Iron and Steel and 1,000 of Gillette. He had money in over a dozen banks from New York to California and kept in close touch with his investment banker, Joseph Hauck, of Schwabacher and Company in San Francisco.[5]

Living in Northern California, Cobb had a front row seat to the rise of baseball prodigy Joe DiMaggio, a product of local Bay Area schools and a prominent member of the San Francisco Seals during the 1933–35 seasons. DiMaggio entered the majors in 1936 for the New York Yankees and was an immediate superstar. Cobb was a fan, and offered advice whenever he had the opportunity. In October 1937, at a luncheon to honor local participants of the recent World Series that was won by Yankees, Cobb was joined by Joe's younger brother Dominic at the microphone in front of the crowd. Dominic asked him, simply, "What does a young fellow have to do to be a good ball player?" Ty replied, "Just ask your brother, Joe."[6] "Joltin'" Joe played big league ball for thirteen years, amassing over 2,200 hits and a career average of .325. Although Ty was never credited with improving his batting, Joe did acknowledge his suggestions about signing contracts and getting enough pregame rest.[7]

Cobb returned to Augusta to attend the annual Masters Golf Tournament in late March 1941, and again brought up the possibility of meeting Babe Ruth on the links, this time for charity. "Maybe we could raise some money for bundles for Britain or some other war relief," he explained. "Anyway, it would be a lot of fun. I have been hankering to take a shot at the Babe ever since I started playing golf."[8] PGA tournament director Fred Corcoran loved the idea and went to work bringing the sides together for best two out of three series beginning on June 25 at the Commonwealth Country Club outside Boston. The event drummed up sensational press, and Cobb was reported to have gone into "seclusion" to work on a "pressure shot" to unnerve Ruth.[9] The initial match was going to be staged for the benefit of the Golden Rule Farm for Boys in New Hampshire, and actress Bette Davis was donating a special cup to the winner.

Ruth predictably hit the ball harder from the tee, but Cobb was a better putter and used his skill to win the first contest. Their struggle featured some awkwardness, and certainly neither man was headed for the pro tour, but it was still entertaining to the 2,000 in attendance. Cobb said he was "fortunate" to win, telling a reporter, "The Babe is a darn nice fellow to play with. He was polite, and I tried to be."[10] Continuing, Cobb admitted that he'd never been under such pressure, accentuating the competitiveness between the two individuals. "In my twenty-five years of baseball, I never had to bear down as hard as I did in that match. Well, I beat Ruth and so I have something good to tell my children. I have finally beaten the Babe at something."[11] Cobb appeared much more humble next to Ruth, and in a mutually respectful environment, was comfortable sharing the spotlight. Any of the previous hostilities were long gone, but their passion to win remained.

The public's interest in the Cobb-Ruth golf battle dropped off almost immediately, at least in New York, where their second round was held at the Fresh Meadow Country Club in Flushing. A reporter for the *Brooklyn Eagle* claimed that there were about 100 paid admissions to see the affair and a guesstimate by the *New York Sun* was only a little more generous, stating that attendance was closer to 200 people. Either way, the event was a "financial flop," according to George Trevor of the *Sun*, and the USO, the charity benefitting from the proceeds, was not in for a windfall.[12] The match itself ended with a victory for Ruth, setting up a third and final contest to be held at the Grosse Ile Country Club near Detroit on July 29, 1941.

Two days before their match, Cobb and Ruth stopped in Cleveland and were joined by Tris Speaker for a big appearance during the local Amateur

Day celebration, an event attended by 15,000 baseball fans. Sporting a Detroit uniform, Cobb signed autographs and was more than happy to offer tips to the youngsters on the field. But by the time the golf series was resumed, both men were out of sorts and playing drearily. Ruth disliked traveling and, according to Cobb, had been drinking overnight, leaving him a little worse for wear.[13] He sweated profusely during the four-hour matchup and was ultimately defeated. Cobb said afterward, "I'm mighty proud to have won and I'm very glad we put up such a good match in the town where I used to play ball."[14] The crowd was back up over 2,000 for the occasion, and the ex-ballplayers were satisfied to see the USO receive a nice check.

The recognition of Cobb's career continued. In 1942, six years after writers deemed him the top choice going to the Hall of Fame at Cooperstown, the players and managers themselves voted him the greatest of all-time. The balloting was arranged by *The Sporting News*, and Cobb received 60 of the 102 votes cast by former contemporaries. The next highest vote getter, Honus Wagner, was picked by only 17 individuals, and Ruth had but 11 supporters. *The Sporting News*, as a sidebar to the results, published the quotes of voters, briefly explaining their endorsement. For example, Walter Johnson stated that Cobb "could do everything better than any player I ever saw." Tris Speaker said he had "great competitive spirit and the willingness to take chances at all times." Connie Mack, with all of his experience, declared that Cobb "surpassed all the players that I remember," and Eddie Collins simply said that the choice of Cobb was "obvious."[15]

Upon hearing the news, Cobb responded by saying, "I feel very much flattered and honored to have so many fine things relative to me appear in *The Sporting News*, also to know of the vote from those who are so highly qualified. It is very highly satisfying. I have been amply rewarded for all that I worked for, and deprived myself of, in order that I might be fit for the game. This honor from those who voted, and coming from *The Sporting News*, the baseball publication, is the capstone, in my estimation. I wish I could say more."[16]

The war raging overseas was on the mind of all Americans and Cobb was ever the patriot, doing whatever was asked of him in the way of serving the cause. Mostly, he donated his time and used his notoriety to sell war bonds, and autographed balls to be auctioned off. Away from the public's eye, he was equally vigilant. Around March 1942, he contacted the San Francisco office of the Federal Bureau of Investigation and "reported several items of interest and of value . . . in connection with Internal Security and Espionage." He expressed his thorough support of Director J. Edgar Hoover and the FBI organization as a whole, leading N. J. L. Pieper, the Special Agent in Charge of the local office, to notify Hoover, and suggest a personal letter to Cobb in response.[17]

Director Hoover replied to Pieper and proposed that he contact Cobb "with the view to developing him as a Special Service Contract." The position would allow Ty to cooperate with the Bureau on a regular basis and, according to Hoover's letter, might prove invaluable "in furnishing information concerning individuals associated with organized baseball."[18] Hoover wrote Cobb as well, thanking him for his "commendatory remarks concerning the work being done by this Bureau and me." He added, "I want you to know that I sincerely appreciate your assistance . . . and your willingness to continue cooperating" with the San Francisco office.[19]

Acting on the guidance offered by Hoover, Special Agent John A. Cost interviewed Cobb at length on June 5, 1942, and Ty again said he would "give his wholehearted cooperation to the Bureau in any way." According to a summation of the discussion prepared by Agent Pieper for Hoover, "Cobb advised that he did not believe that there was any subversive element at work among the organized baseball players, and he stated that from his long study and observation that the baseball players and managers as a whole are a loyal and patriotic American group." He would, however, "be vigilant for any type of subversive activity and would immediately advise the San Francisco Field Division should he detect such."[20] Thus, Cobb was acknowledged as a "Special Service Contact" for a period during the war. Around the same time, an alleged distant family member of Cobb's was investigated for pro-Nazi beliefs, but an FBI investigation failed to substantiate any claims or locate "any active connection or association" to Cobb himself.[21]

Cobb's ties to the war became more personal after his youngest son, James Howell, joined the US Army at twenty-one years of age in 1943. He was inducted into service at the Fort Bliss Reception Center in El Paso after graduating from the New Mexico Military Institution, and was stationed at Fort Riley, Kansas, where his father visited him at least twice in 1943 and '44.[22] James was shipped overseas to fight in the Pacific campaign in May 1945. Of Ty's other children, his daughter Shirley was the only

other volunteer for overseas service. She enlisted in the Red Cross and
helped support the Fifth Army in Italy in 1944. Incidentally, she ran into
her father's old rival, Leo Durocher, as the latter toured through as part of
the USO, and the two talked baseball for a spell.[23] Both of Cobb's children
returned home safely.

Similar to 1917 and '18, during the First World War, pundits questioned
whether baseball should continue in spite of the destabilized conditions.
On his soap box, Cobb was adamant about the sport carrying on unmo-
lested. "Baseball deserves the right to operate," he declared. "It's a great
American institution."[24] In another interview, he asserted that he wanted
baseball to have "some official recognition that is essential to morale," and
announced that, "If worst came to worst, I'd get back into harness myself to
help preserve it."[25] Cobb was fifty-seven years old at the time. Additionally,
he was defensive of players in the military, especially against those con-
demning athletes in noncombat positions, saying that it was "unfair." The
same kind of accusations cropped up when he was in the service. "Not one
player could, if he wanted to, ask for some soft assignment or one where he
plays baseball," he said. "It's not done."[26]

Cobb's compassion for the military extended even further. He united
with fellow baseball alumni from the Northern California region and visited
wounded veterans at area hospitals from the naval facility at Mare Island to
Letterman General at San Francisco. His crew of traveling companions
included Tony Lazzeri, Lefty O'Doul, Oscar Vitt, and Bill Lange.[27] During a
trip to Denver in April 1945, Cobb and Vitt specifically planned to visit two
health care centers to spend time with wounded warriors.[28] A special part of
their routine was to visit bedridden soldiers recently returned from overseas, and their presence undoubtedly did much to raise their spirits.

The sizable San Francisco sporting community, plus the vast surrounding area, was never at a loss for social events, and Cobb was busy attending
dinners, on the golf course, and hosting friends at his Atherton home. Away
from California, he often returned to Detroit and circulated with friends
old and new. He loved to talk baseball, and although watching the on-field
action made him nervous, he had a gold lifetime pass to enter any major
league ballpark and attended games when he had a chance.[29] On July 14,
1943, he saw a game in Detroit featuring military and essential work personnel as the Great Lakes Bluejackets, managed by US Naval officer Mickey
Cochrane, beat the Ford League All-Stars, 6–2. Cobb was joined in the
stands by Tris Speaker and Wally Pipp.[30] During the summer of 1944, he

attended a benefit in Seattle and planned to make the Connie Mack 50th anniversary celebration in Philadelphia, but caught poison oak and was forced to miss the affair.[31]

In May 1945, Cobb graciously accepted the managerial position of a western squad of high school all-stars headed to New York for an August 28 battle against their eastern counterparts. Babe Ruth signed on to lead the eastern team, and their rivalry was rekindled to a degree in the press. The entire affair, organized by *Esquire* magazine, was masterfully promoted, and Cobb talked up the contest with Harry Wismer on ABC radio beforehand.[32] The game itself was witnessed by 20,000 people, and Cobb's team held a solid lead going into the ninth inning. But in a similar fashion to his days in Detroit, his pitchers crumbled, giving up three runs, and his youngsters were defeated.[33] Cobb, Ruth, and Speaker were reunited again at Cleveland for an Indians game versus the White Sox on August 18, 1946, and fans respectfully honored the trio with a prolonged applause.

One aspect that Cobb never really had to contend with earlier in life was his health. He was always in tip-top shape, and his body remained strong regardless of the strain he put it through. After his retirement, Cobb settled into a new lifestyle, and was a lot less active than he used to be. Golf was no substitute for baseball, and he gained weight steadily. Following exposure to rain during a hunting trip in 1946, he developed a severe case of bursitis in his limbs and he became more inactive than usual. His weight jumped to 230 pounds and he began experiencing a loss of appetite, weakness, and bouts of itching. After an examination by a doctor in Reno in 1947, it was found that Cobb was suffering from gall bladder trouble, an enlarged liver, and the early stages of jaundice. Likely caused by a virus, his ailment required immediate attention, and he was placed on a very strict low-calorie diet.[34]

It wasn't coincidental that his health began to fail during a time of extreme stress. His wife, Charlie, who moved into her own residence at 84 Princeton Road in nearby Menlo Park in 1939, wanted a divorce and reaching a compromise in light of the family's widespread financial holdings was proving difficult.[35] The suit, initiated by Charlie in March 1947, unleashed a stream of bad publicity his way, including the charge that he was responsible for a "continued course of extreme cruelty from the date of the marriage [in 1908] to the present time." She asked for half of the Cobb fortune, a total amount she believed to be greater than $7 million, and other monetary stipulations. Ty denied their estimated wealth, asking, "Would you reporters like to place a little wager on it? I'll give you everything over $7 million." Strangely, he said he didn't know his wife's Christian name, saying, "Why don't you ask her?"[36]

Known to be exceptionally persuasive, Ty convinced Charlie to drop her suit in San Mateo County, and she did on March 15. He told his investment banker Joe Hauck that he had proposed settlement terms three times, but she turned him down.[37] Finally, the Cobbs severed legal ties after thirty-eight years of marriage on June 17, 1947, agreeing to conditions that were much different than those originally asked by Charlie. The arrangement allowed her to keep all stock in her name and joint custody of their Atherton home, amongst other things, but the majority of Ty's money remained his and his alone.[38]

Ever since his separation from Charlie in 1939, Cobb reveled in his private sanctuary at Cave Rock, Nevada, a home he purchased that year on the eastern shore of Lake Tahoe. The residence, over 230 miles from Atherton on US Highway 50, provided a needed getaway during the summer months, and he enjoyed the scenic outdoor recreation.[39] While visiting the nearby Glenbrook Inn, an upscale hotel for vacationers, in June 1949, Cobb met Frances Fairbairn Fusca, a twice-married thirty-nine-year-old from Buffalo, New York, in town with her teenage daughter, Geraldine. Over the next few weeks and months, Ty and Frances endured a whirlwind courtship and Cobb was infatuated by her. "She is the most unusual woman I have ever met," he told Joe Hauck by letter. "She knows more about more subjects, so diplomatic and delicate and more form and etiquette, etc. She waits on me hand and foot, thinks for me. She is a wonder."[40]

Bonded by similar interests—particularly golf and traveling—the couple was married on September 24, 1949, at a private ceremony in Buffalo. They attended the World Series in New York City as part of their honeymoon, and watched the Yankees dismantle the Brooklyn Dodgers in five games.[41] Hobnobbing at the Stork Club in Manhattan and the Brown Derby in Hollywood, the Cobbs were highly visible on the social scene and seemingly couldn't be happier. In terms of making public appearances, few were larger than the celebration oilman Dick Burnett was planning for the Texas League opener of his Dallas Eagles on April 11, 1950. Burnett extended invitations to Cobb and eight other baseball legends to attend as special attractions, and offered to pay all their expenses. Cobb was so enthusiastic about the affair that he told Burnett that he'd pay his own way to Dallas.[42]

The superstars participated in a luncheon promotional gig the day of the game and offered commentary on the radio. They each were asked about their favorite moments in baseball and many had the crowd in stitches. Cobb stepped up when it was his turn and was setting up a potentially off-color punch line involving his old Tigers teammate, Davy Jones. As he was proceeding, someone close to him leaned in and informed him about the radio broadcast. "Oh," Cobb said, "I've just been told that we're on the air and I'd better not tell that story. Guess I'd better retreat from that one." The audience got a big chuckle out of it. That evening, more than 53,000 individuals packed the Cotton Bowl for the event, and a few of the legends on hand, including Tris Speaker, performed a batting exhibition before the contest. In old form, Cobb dropped down a few bunts, and even slashed one over second base.[43]

Cobb remained busy, and journeyed to innumerable dinners, dedications, and reunion events across the country. He mingled with fellow Hall of Famers and swapped stories with friends he hadn't seen in years. The financial security he'd built up over the decades gave him and his wife the freedom to travel when they wanted, and all Cobb needed was a heads-up about the next essential get-together. He was comfortable knowing that his business investments were on autopilot and needed only slight attention. For instance, his Coca-Cola Bottling Company at Twin Falls, Idaho, had been run by his son, Herschel, since it was initially purchased in 1940, and Ty left the management up to him.[44] When he trekked to Idaho, he was usually more interested in visiting with his grandchildren and hunting than he was in overseeing the day-to-day business operations.

Physically imposing, Herschel Cobb had lived a turbulent life going back to his teenage years. In 1935, he faced assault charges on a nineteen-year-old girl in San Mateo County, California, but was later acquitted.[45] He was up against an even more serious charge in Idaho in 1949, after the drowning death of a man who had been riding on a boat Herschel was driving. The boat actually capsized after a sharp turn, and Glenn Linzy succumbed while in the water. Hauled into court on an involuntary manslaughter charge, Herschel claimed the accident was caused by a power failure, and a jury found him not guilty.[46] In early 1950, a damage suit by the man's family was settled out of court. Around that same time, Herschel returned to California and became the Coca-Cola distributor for San Luis

Obispo County and Northern Santa Barbara County, doing business from Santa Maria.[47]

The relationship between father and son was always special to Ty Cobb, and recollections of his own dad were heartwarming. He was a regular at the organized annual Father and Sons gatherings, staged by the Elks in Northern California, and made a conscious effort to be a better father in his old age than he was as a younger man. But he was everlastingly stubborn, and arguments came quickly in the Cobb household. In a lot of ways, Herschel was a darker and more exaggerated version of his father, especially in the way he related to his wife and kids. His venomous personality was highlighted in the 2013 book *Heart of a Tiger*, written by his son of the same name.[48] On April 13, 1951, at the age of thirty-three, Herschel passed away unexpectedly of a heart attack, leaving his wife and three small children. Ty was crushed by the loss of his son.

Further sadness was ahead. The rift that alienated Cobb from his son, Ty Jr., was longstanding and compounded by other quarrels. They remained estranged for years with Junior on one coast and his father on the other. In 1915, Ty told a journalist that he didn't want his namesake entering the athletic world, instead, he hoped he'd become a lawyer or a "good doctor."[49] Junior followed through and graduated with his medical degree in obstetrics and gynecology in the early 1940s. He formed a practice at Dublin, Georgia, and with a wife and three children, was proving to be a laudable father and provider. Things took a shocking turn when, in 1952, it was found that he had a malignant tumor in his brain. Ty Jr. underwent surgery at Columbia-Presbyterian Medical Center in New York, but his condition never improved. He passed away on September 9 at the age of forty-two.[50]

Over the previous years, and considering the progression of the elder Cobb's own health problems, it was presumed that his condition deteriorated in part by the stresses in his life. Joe Hauck wrote a letter to Ty Jr. in 1948, suggesting the same thing. He wrote, "I personally think [Ty Sr.] has been brooding over his troubles and his nervous system has borne the brunt of this. I feel that his unhappy mental condition is to a large extent due to the lack of understanding which exists between you."[51] The anxiety caused by being estranged was agonizing, but the loss of two sons in two years created an intolerable suffering for Cobb. The internal guilt and pain was manifesting into an unmanageable struggle that would continue to sap his health. His reliance on alcohol was also contributing to his growing number of personal tribulations.[52]

Still greatly respected by the mainstream, Cobb was called before the US House of Representatives Judiciary Subcommittee investigating baseball in Washington, DC, on July 30, 1951. He discussed his long history in baseball starting at age seventeen in Augusta and, in defense of baseball against antitrust charges, supported the reserve clause. He said that the national pastime was a "sport," not an "industry," and clearly expressed his opinions. "Baseball has made it possible for hundreds of young men from small towns, like myself, to improve their lot in life and become useful members of their communities," he explained. "I revere baseball. I'm loyal to it for what it has done for me."[53]

But Cobb's loyalty wasn't always clear-cut. In two separate articles featured in *Life* magazine in March 1952, he took a number of heavy-handed swings at modern baseball, asserting that contemporary players didn't learn the fundamentals of the game, run the bases well, or match-up with the athletes from his generation. The title of the series, "They Don't Play Baseball Any More," summed up his sentiment and he didn't hold a thing back, hitting upon the weaknesses of Rogers Hornsby, Ted Williams, and Joe DiMaggio with authority. His controversial remarks, spread out over eighteen total pages, were eye-opening to say the least, and generated a wealth of conversation.[54] Needless to say, most of the comments were critical toward Cobb and in defense of the current status of the game. Bucky Harris called him "nuts," and Dizzy Dean declared that Cobb was "making himself mighty unpopular."[55]

And that was certainly true. The articles did significant damage to Cobb's reputation, and years of goodwill to fellow players, both in the press and on tour to stadiums across the majors, crumbled around him. Hornsby, who idolized Cobb and always recognized him as one of his all-time heroes, renounced that distinction as a result of the *Life* article, replacing him with Joe Jackson. He also offered a full rebuttal in *Look* magazine.[56] Fiery Billy Martin of the New York Yankees took a more direct tact. During a speech in California, he specifically turned to Cobb and said, "No matter what some people tell you, this game of baseball is still being played for keeps." At that same event, Cobb announced that he was done writing articles, stating that it "caused too much of a turmoil and got too many people mad at me. From now on I'm taking life easy out here in California and leaving that sort of thing to other people."[57]

Little did people know, but significant good came from the *Life* magazine articles, as Cobb diverted the $25,000 he received as payment to the newly established "Ty Cobb Educational Foundation." Announced on November 27, 1953, the organization was created to help qualified college students from Georgia with financial assistance, and planned to offer scholarships on an annual basis.[58] Recalling the importance his father placed on education, Cobb had long been inspired to develop such a program, and was keenly enthusiastic about its growth.

Cobb's philanthropy didn't end there. In 1945, he first publicly revealed his intentions of erecting a progressive hospital in his hometown of Royston. He discussed the project with local powerbrokers and personally donated $100,000 to ensure that his dream would become a reality.

The moment finally arrived on January 22, 1950, when the doors of the Cobb Memorial Hospital swung open for the first time, and Ty couldn't have been prouder. The building was dedicated to his parents, and during the dedication ceremony, Cobb became justifiably choked up. "This hospital belongs to all you people here where I used to live," he announced, "and it's for you people whom I've always had in my heart."[59]

While Cobb was known for his temperamental attitude, he managed to avoid hairy legal situations for the most part during his post-baseball existence. In fact, he was entangled with the law only here and there, and several of the incidents involved an automobile. On a highway south of San Jose in August 1935, his car accidentally hit a pedestrian, and Cobb immediately rushed the man to a medical facility. The police absolved him of any blame.[60] Twelve years later, in Placerville, California, he was taken into custody for drunkenness on a public road. Infuriated by the matter, Cobb made things worse by speaking "too freely" to the judge and was jailed for a couple of hours, then released on bail. The situation was resolved after he paid a $25 fine.[61] In 1954, he became the defendant in a lawsuit after an alleged drunken spat with a friend.

Elbert D. Felts, a sixty-two-year-old former minor league ballplayer, was now a former friend of Cobb's, and was pushing forward with a $100,000 civil suit, filed in Butte County (CA) Superior Court. He charged that Cobb, sixty-seven, "willfully and intentionally" assaulted him in the back of an automobile in April, causing "severe bodily injuries" to include swelling, lacerations, contusions, and nervous shock. Cobb denied the claims, maintaining that he only defended himself from Felts's aggressiveness. The case played out over the next year; in November 1955, a jury issued a verdict for Cobb after seven hours of deliberation.[62] But things were far from over. Lawyers for Felts wanted to file an appeal and feature startling new testimony from Cobb's wife Frances, who, for the second time in 1955, was pursuing a divorce. Her first attempt in January was settled amicably, but the relationship stalled out again by the summer.[63]

Although the Felts's appeal was denied, a detailed twenty-four-page statement of charges by Frances against Ty for their divorce proceedings was submitted into the record. Notably, the documents were reflective of only one side of the argument, but nonetheless provided a disturbing look inside their personal troubles. The reoccurring theme was Cobb's drinking, and Frances revealed many broken promises to quit during the length of their marriage. When he was drunk, he was verbally abusive, cruel, and used vile language at the drop of a hat. He was suspicious and defensive, and at times, made horrid threats. Gentleman-like behavior was lost as he argued with women and men equally, and displayed his insecurities with a glaringly obvious jealous streak.[64]

Cobb's inner turmoil seeped into the letters he wrote, and he was a prolific correspondent with people all over the map. In an August 21, 1954, letter to Dr. Daniel Elkin, chairman of his educational fund, he divulged that he was "very prone to depressionist feelings" and that he tried hard not to inflict his "dark moments upon others." He wrote about his alcoholic consumption, mentioning that Frances had helped him "wonderfully" in his ongoing battle.[65] But with Frances now out the door, whatever assistance she provided was all but gone. Plus, his children were routinely estranged from him to some degree, leaving him lonelier than ever. His forlorn feelings were more prevalent at his large seven-bedroom home in Atherton than anywhere else, and he concluded that a significant change was necessary.

"I'm going home," he announced, signaling his intention to leave California for his birth state. "All my interests are on the other side of those mountains. My heart is in two things, the Cobb Educational Fund, with headquarters in Atlanta, and the Cobb Memorial Hospital, which I built in Royston. I have no business of any kind out here, and with my children married, I have no use for this big house. I want to go back to my own Georgia, back to my Georgia people, back to my Georgia relatives. I want to build a house, hunt birds, and just visit."[66] Cobb admitted that he hated to leave California, but things were much too fast for him nowadays. He wanted quiet and peacefulness.[67] In the summer of 1957, he scouted potential

properties and found a nice bit of land on Chenocetah Mountain, outside
Cornelia, Georgia.[68] From his towering vantage point, he could see the area
in which he was born at Narrows and, upon realizing that, was taken by the
sentimentality of the location, and shed a tear.[69]

Unquestionably, Cobb still lingered in the consciousness of the public,
but he was more known by name and accomplishment than by sight. He
reportedly entered Yankee Stadium twice without being recognized and
during an appearance on the popular game show *I've Got a Secret* in 1955,
he managed to avoid being identified altogether, that is until the host
revealed his name.[70] In turn, the audience roundly applauded the baseball
legend. Cobb always loved public fanfare. In Baltimore on August 24, 1956,
he had to be impressed when he was given the loudest applause of the
night during an appearance with eight other superstars prior to an Orioles
game. He continued to be highly active, attending reunion events at Kansas City and New York, and made a sincere effort to return to Cooperstown
on a yearly basis.

Enjoying the nostalgia, he was showered by affection from Augusta baseball rooters on August 27, 1957, and the entire gate was donated to his
educational fund. A speaker told the crowd that the venue they were in,
Jennings Stadium, was just two miles from where Cobb slashed his first professional hit in 1904. Cobb was bowled over by the emotional response to
his presence, and remarked, "I can't tell you how deeply I feel about all
this."[71] In July 1959, he made his way back to Navin Field (now known as
Briggs Stadium) in Detroit, and his old haunts dredged up plenty of memories. He snuck down to the Tigers bench during a game against Washington and shook hands with players and manager Jimmy Dykes.[72] Incidentally,
Cobb never figured major league ball would make it to the California coast,
but certainly relished attending the 1959 World Series between the Los
Angeles Dodgers and the Chicago White Sox.

As illustrated in Chapter One, the progression of Cobb's cancer was swift
and he shuttled back and forth between hospitals, enduring a massive treatment schedule. He wasn't incapacitated by his health and did the things he
wanted to do—visiting casinos, attending spring training at Arizona, and
made his final trip to Cooperstown in late June 1960. Acting out on occasion and drinking to excess, Cobb refused to curtail his behavior despite

the circumstances. He persistently battled away at whatever issue was in front of him, no matter how trivial, and fought for his own set of principles. In May 1960, he filed a lawsuit against the Pacific Gas and Electric Company that served his Atherton home, for inaccurate recording of his utilities and purposely went without power at his residence as a demonstration of his stubbornness.[73]

A true track and field aficionado, Cobb was delighted to share a stage with four-time Olympic gold medalist Jesse Owens for an event in Boston. The two ran into each other again at the airport the next day and Cobb put his arm around Owens and complimented his "great speech." After a group of children came over to get an autograph, Cobb told them, "You want this man's autograph, Sonny. Why boy, I'm just a ball player, this man is one of the great gentlemen of sports." As Owens was leaving, Cobb said, "Jesse, take care of yourself. Come see me, please." Cobb then told sportswriter Bill McSweeney, "There goes a great man, Bill, a great man."[74] Having taken great pleasure from attending the 1932 Olympics in Los Angeles, Cobb made hasty plans to venture to Rome for the 1960 Summer Games with a friend from Georgia. He spent seventeen liberating days overseas and continued to test his so-called health limitations.[75]

The work on his autobiography was a heartening project for Cobb in his last months, and he truthfully believed he was going to straighten out the jumbled record of his career. Writing his memoirs was a dream of his, and had been on his mind for years. From what he was seeing so far, he was happy about the way it was coming together and the idea of submitting his version of history to the public was personally gratifying. On April 27, 1961, he turned up at the home opener for the debuting Los Angeles Angels, and to old friends like Fred Haney and J. G. Taylor Spink, it was evident that Cobb was in the advanced stages of his illness. According to *The Sporting News*, Cobb "received a tremendous reception" from the crowd, and that same day, attended a gathering at the famous Brown Derby in Beverly Hills. Comedian Groucho Marx was one of the notables to greet him, and hit the mark when he said, "Ty, many people think there have been greater outfielders, but in my book, you were the best."[76]

Cobb was admitted to Emory University Hospital in Atlanta several different times between 1960 and '61, and employees who dealt with him remembered their encounters. Dr. Joseph E. Hardison was hammered by Ty's irritable personality, and told that he was a "rank incompetent amateur" because he wouldn't give him pain medication without an examination.

But after his agony was reduced, the two talked baseball and "became friends."[77] Nurse Alice Kierspe said Cobb was "very charming to me," but Dottie Wills admitted that he was "ornery."[78] Nevertheless, Ty signed baseballs for both and did likewise for others at the hospital. Medical student Rex Teeslink joined Cobb as his caregiver from May to July 1961, and witnessed Ty's "hair-trigger temper." No one could override his forceful personality when he was set in his ways, but Teeslink was exposed to the softer side of him as well. "All I want people to realize is that he was a fair and meaningful guy," he later said.[79]

When Cobb was hospitalized for good on June 5, his mountaintop home hadn't yet been built and the strained relationships in his life were still to be mended. However, time was running out, and his family knew it. His two daughters, son Jimmy, and first wife Charlie raced from California to be by his bedside. Beverly expressed her father's sentiment at the time, saying that "he recognized that he drove everyone very hard and he was sorry for the unhappiness that had gone on before."[80] In that regard, a level of peace had been made in a family who'd suffered unbearably for decades. Surrounded by his loved ones, Ty died on July 17, 1961. He was seventy-four.

Condolence messages streamed in from across the baseball world, many with personal anecdotes about Cobb, and his reach as an influential player and mentor went farther than imagined. The Associated Press and United Press International, in reporting on his passing, specifically denoted that "private funeral services" were to be held, nixing any mass display of respect from the baseball community. A few close friends, including Ray Schalk and Mickey Cochrane, did make the journey, joining 150 others in Cornelia for the services at the McGahee Funeral Home chapel. Over two dozen cars entered in the procession headed for Royston, where Cobb was laid to rest in the family mausoleum next to his parents and sister.[81]

Fittingly, the Hillerich & Bradsby Company, producer of the bats Cobb used to secure a majority of the record 4,100 hits during his career, fashioned a poetic tribute in his honor. It featured an image of Cobb in all his baseball glory and read:

> This was Ty Cobb.
> America has lost a great American.
> The World of Sport has lost its most spirited competitor.
> Baseball has lost its most brilliant player.
> We have lost a true friend.[82]

19

"I LOVED THE GUY"

Of all the prevailing suppositions that have endured about Ty Cobb throughout history—and there have been many—the belief that he was a volcanic scrapper, itching to brawl at a moment's notice, is certainly at the forefront of his reputation. Today's representation of Cobb portrays him as one of the rowdiest rowdies of old-time baseball and a guy who apparently sought confrontation in each and every one of the 3,035 games he participated in. No one in the modern era can take credit for developing the fantastic notion of Cobb the pugilist, as Ty actually dealt with the allegation during his playing career. Sportswriters extended his willingness to fight to basically anyone in the majors, including his teammates, and exaggerated stories for maximum effect. Their efforts created a mythical aura around "Ty Cobb," much like dime novelists did for Jesse James in the nineteenth century. The legend of Cobb was created on paper but, unfortunately, it read more like fiction than fact.

Before baseball fans realized it, Cobb was bigger than life, and because of this had lost any say or control over his own reputation. It was a living, breathing entity all its own, and journalists ensured that it thrived within the spectrum of any given baseball season. In 1921, he addressed the libel commentary, stating, "A pet subject for writers has been to elaborate on my readiness to get into fisticuffs with other ball players." He went on to explain that he'd been in a total of three scuffles since joining the majors in 1905, and two of them were in the infancy of his career against Ed Siever and Charley "Boss" Schmidt, with the third versus Buck Herzog in 1917.[1] From his account, he hardly possessed an overpowering resume of warfare. However, there were many close calls, perhaps a thrown punch here or there, and rumors of clashes with George Moriarty and even Sam Crawford, but nothing demonstrating the fiendish storybook warrior he was made out to be.[2]

In the years following Cobb's statements, he had a well-known fracas with umpire Billy Evans, altercations with Howard Ehmke and Ray Francis of the Tigers, and near exchanges with Babe Ruth, which were perfect to keep to the narrative of his combativeness alive. Cobb, in 1946, told a reporter, "It's a funny thing. People always want to talk about the fights I had in baseball. They seem to forget that I took time off from fighting to play a little baseball."[3] But Cobb did himself no favors. His reaction during the unfortunate Claude Lucker situation in 1912 played into the storyline flawlessly and also took its toll on his reputation. It didn't take long for rival fans to go out of their way to antagonize him. They howled, yelled epithets, and intentionally worked to provoke him; all in the hopes of seeing the "hot head" explode. In a way, it was introducing a colorful vaudevillian aspect into the baseball realm, and to fans drinking in the bleachers, they wanted nothing more than to see an action scene break out before them.

Cobb was perceived to be the kind of man who could be cracked by taunts and abuse, and, admittedly, his pride could only take so much. "Walking along the street, would a citizen allow another to call him vile and vulgar names?" he asked a reporter in 1916. "No, you bet he wouldn't. Must the ball players allow the fans to hurl vulgar remarks at him? For one, I won't." Cobb acknowledged that there was little he could do under the rules, but said he'd rather leave baseball than tolerate the cruelty anymore. "I'll quit the game; I'll throw away the uniform and go back to my Georgia home before I will put up with this stuff. It isn't in me." He finally asked, "Do you ever see me abusing the fans?"[4] At his weakest point, pushed beyond control, he had the ability to literally explode into an uncontrollable rage. He eventually learned to better control himself in those tense moments, preventing a slew of Lucker-like occurrences.

The hostility of fans wasn't limited to talking trash from the stands. For instance, outside Shibe Park in Philadelphia, Cobb was accosted by hostile thugs in 1913. Sensing the danger of the situation, he rushed onto a moving streetcar but his aggressors managed to halt the progress of the vehicle, yearning to continue their assault. It was only through the diligence of the conductor to get the vehicle moving again that Ty escaped harm.[5] His fame brought other kinds of uninvited schemes as well, including the infamous "badger game," which was perpetrated by a couple at a Philadelphia hotel. The ruse began when Cobb ran into a woman in need of assistance in the hallway near his room. He asked her inside, intending to summon a doctor by phone, but rather quickly, the woman's husband burst in. She yelled, causing a scene, but Cobb was wise to things. He didn't wait around to be blackmailed and simply punched the man, threw the woman from his room, and called it a night.[6]

Cobb absorbed a lot of peculiar responses from audiences, including being booed on the road for not hitting, and then cheered once he got on base. Those same fans might also applaud if he was struck out, creating the oddest dichotomy in baseball. Sportswriters occasionally commented on the strangeness of Cobb being booed without any kind of trigger incident. Babe Ruth was treated similarly from time to time, though, and it seemed to be a kind of symbolic ritual for some fans toward baseball's cream of the crop. In all honesty, people paid their hard-earned money to see Ruth power out home runs and Cobb run the bases with reckless abandon. Anything less was a disappointment. Tongue in cheek, Rogers Hornsby said in 1935 that fans went out to see Cobb "because they figured he'd be good for a couple of fights during the afternoon."[7]

The excitement that was generated by his hard play improved box office sales across the American League and, without a doubt, Cobb was a natural showman. He played to win at all times, never giving an inch and, to outsiders, his approach to the game appeared remarkably flamboyant. While spectators were thrilled by his furious antics, opposing teams were often embarrassed and, as a result, considerable bad feelings developed. Billy Evans wrote in 1916, "Any player who is a success, who is the big star that Cobb is, naturally must make a good many enemies," and Ty positively didn't have any trouble aggravating opponents to the point of dislike.[8] He butted heads with other loud personalities in the league and traded insults with whoever wanted to engage him. His voice boomed from the dugout as he chided rivals, but on the field, he ably backed up his snarky arrogance.

Tris Speaker and Connie Mack coached their players not to irritate Cobb during a ballgame, convinced that Ty's skills were wholly improved when he was heated. In fact, Tris wanted to keep the Detroit outfielder laughing, and plied him with humor in an attempt to throw him off his game.[9] Seeing that Cobb was accused of having very little or no sense of humor, it probably took some work on Speaker's part. But nevertheless, the understanding of Ty's basic psychological programming was studied by the intellects of the game, just as Cobb did to his opponents. Knowing how to avoid getting under the Georgian's skin was precious information.

The old-time dime novelists would've been proud how baseball writers romanticized the notion of "Cobb the Terrible," a spike-wielding demon of the diamond. Stories about his so-called flying-steel added much to his long-term reputation, and most of it was critical. The central argument involved the claim that he purposefully slid into bases with his spikes pointed upwards at opponents with the intent of hurting them. In 1915, Frank P. Sibley of the *Boston Daily Globe* disagreed that his actions were deliberate, but stated, "It is part of his creed, apparently, that if he is entitled to the baseline, he will take no precautions to save the man in his way."[10] That meant the defender was supposed to respect the runner's rights and protect his own well-being at the same time because Cobb surely wasn't going to do it.

"Ty Cobb is not such a villainous villain as he is painted," infielder Bobby Wallace explained. "The base runner has the right of way and Cobb only demands that his rights be respected. If you get in the baseline you are in danger of being cut down for Cobb comes in determined to make the bag. If the baseman takes his proper position, Cobb will never cut him."[11] Jimmy Dykes added, "You know, I played a lot of games against Ty and I was never cut once. As for the charges that he deliberately spiked his opponents, its hogwash."[12] Moreover, two men who feuded with Cobb, teammates Sam Crawford and Davy Jones, also denied the charges in a report to the UPI (United Press International) in 1962. Their statement read: "Cobb never spiked anyone deliberately in his life. He did only what was expected of him as a player and when he was running the bases, he rightly felt the path belonged to him."[13]

"I would not willingly harm any player except in retaliation or to protect myself," Cobb once said, and all of the rampant accusations grated on his conscience.[14] It got to the stage that he began doing research and maintaining a special log listing the American League players who had spiked more individuals than he had. In 1911, there were ten players who'd committed the act more than him, he revealed to columnist Bozeman Bulger.[15] Notably, the most famous spiking incident of Cobb's life, the Frank "Home Run" Baker episode in 1909, was routinely brought up by history buffs whenever the opportunity presented itself. For Baker, though, it was water under the bridge. He said, in 1955, that the entire affair "received far too much publicity." Additionally, he not only rated Cobb the greatest player of all-time, but stated that Ty was one of his "best friends in the baseball world."[16]

All of the rotten tales about Cobb went a step further by insisting that he sharpened his spikes to achieve better results in slashing rivals on the base-paths. Davy Jones again stepped up to defend Cobb despite their turbulent history. "Cobb never filed his spikes," he said. "Poor Ty, because of his aggres-siveness, always got the blame for anything that looked like rough play." Jones told a story from around the time of the Baker incident, revealing that Tigers' players did use files on their spikes in an effort to frighten their rival Athletics. He said that Cobb wasn't willing to join them, "but because he was sitting on the bench and because everybody seemed anxious to pin some-thing on him, he was made the brunt of the charge of spike-filing."[17]

Surprisingly, Cobb came clean in 1952. He admitted in *Life* magazine that there were two instances in his career that he actually did try spiking someone, and Harry Bemis and Dutch Leonard were the intended victims. He said that he was provoked to do so in both cases.[18] A few months later, Cobb told the California Grid Club in Sacramento that he partook in filing his spikes with teammates at least once. "It was a gag, partly," he said. "It happened in New York and we figured it might intimidate some of the younger players on the opposing team. It didn't bother the old-timers, but I believe it may have put a little fear in the hearts of the rookies."[19] The tactic was not a common practice, and Cobb, in 1910, even proposed that league umpires check the shoes of players before games to ensure they were well within the rules. He didn't mind because he had nothing to hide.[20]

St. Louis Browns physician Dr. Robert F. Hyland, in an article for *The Sporting News*, made a statement about a highly overlooked factor in Cobb's dashing style. "One often hears about Cobb being a reckless base-runner, who insisted on the right of way and didn't care whom he cut down," Hyland explained. "Well, I can testify that Ty never saved himself, and he took plenty of spikes without crying. From his hips down, his legs were a succes-sion of spike wounds and 'strawberries.'"[21] And Cobb bore the scars to prove it. He pulled up his pant legs during an Oakland event in 1951 and displayed so many blemishes that it appeared like "a map of the Mississippi River basin with the Missouri, Ohio, Tennessee, and contributory streams flowing through," Jack McDonald of the *San Francisco Call-Bulletin* wrote. Cobb added, "I didn't spend half my life spiking people as some think. I spent some of my time getting spiked."[22]

The press did Cobb few favors and rarely gave him the benefit of the doubt. For that reason, he felt the stories about him were always magnified, and whenever another player did something similar, they received a much softer blow. Occasionally, journalists just made up lies. At the 1947 World Series in New York, Grantland Rice introduced him to perennial batting champion Ted Williams of the Boston Red Sox. Williams asked Cobb a baseball-related question and the latter offered words of guidance. A reporter later claimed that Williams was irritated by the response and gestured angrily as he walked away. The yarn infuriated Cobb. He said it was all nonsense and Williams agreed. "Cobb is correct," he said. "It never happened. I never even thought of such a thing. His advice was sound and I appreciated it."[23]

When discussing Ty Cobb in modern times, it is impossible to avoid the question of whether Cobb was racist against African Americans. Supporters of Cobb have tried to rebuke the charges by listing his black friends, citing his post-1950 avocation of blacks in the majors, and the fact that he had colored housekeepers and other employees around him his entire life. These details, while important, cannot explain away the question in any shape or form. Of Southern heritage and with a pro-Confederate belief system, Cobb was undoubtedly influenced by his surroundings growing up. His father, though liberal, didn't altogether sway his son toward free thinking in racial subject matter. In 1908, after a couple years in the "North," Cobb was still holding onto his Southern philosophies. He told the *Detroit Free Press*, "Course being from Georgia, I think different about Negroes from what they do up here."[24]

From all accounts, his mindset didn't evolve much in the years that followed, at least as far as baseball was concerned. Appearing in an exhibition at Putnam, Connecticut, on October 8, 1916, Cobb performed at first base for the New Haven Colonials. He was already a bit antsy after a dispute over money with promoters before the game, but managed to get through five innings. After that, he unceremoniously left the contest when Putnam inserted black pitching sensation "Cannonball" Dick Redding on the mound.[25] Columnist Otto Floto of the *Denver Post* wrote, "One can't blame Cobb, however, for his action. He comes from the South, where such things are not possible, and he has only lived up to the tradition of his section of the country."[26] Alfred J. Roy of the *Chicago Defender* remarked on Cobb skipping out on a 1923 series between the Tigers and American Giants, stating,

"Ty Cobb, Georgia Peach, would not play of course, but the rest of the play-ers were glad to mix with their darker brothers."[27]

It must be clarified that Al Stump and other sportswriters did not initiate the campaign to vilify Cobb as a racist in the last fifty years. Pundits were openly questioning his prejudices in the 1920s, mostly in African American newspapers. Al Monroe in the *Chicago Defender*, W. Rollo Wilson and Wen-dell Smith in the *Pittsburgh Courier*, and Orrin C. Evans of the *Philadelphia Tribune* were amongst those to remark about his apparent racist views. In 1949, Lucius Harper called Cobb "a rabid race-baiter with very pro-nounced prejudices against Negroes."[28] These perceptions were not invented out of thin air but based on a track record of events, including several notable physical altercations between Cobb and African Americans during his lifetime. That aside, Cobb wasn't consumed with an all-encom-passing hatred for all people of color. There was a middle ground for friend-ship, compassion, and respect.

Growing up, he was influenced by several African Americans. A black acquaintance taught him how to swim and, working on his father's planta-tion, he labored alongside people of all types of backgrounds. He expressed sincere empathy after a home run ball he hit at Mobile in 1915 struck a black child, rushing to his aid, and generously doled out baseballs to Phila-delphia youngsters in 1928.[29] Alexander Rivers, a mascot for the Tigers in 1917 and credited with aiding Cobb during his 35-game hit streak, became Ty's personal assistant for a number of years.[30] Charles M. Ridley, a tailor in Augusta, was also a close friend, and Cobb reportedly helped put singer Arthur Lee Simpkins through college.[31] Later in life, Cobb supported the eradication of the color barrier in the majors and publicly praised Jackie Robinson, Roy Campanella, Willie Mays, and Hank Aaron.

Cobb clearly acknowledged skin color, and had expectations from African Americans to respect and adhere to a subservient doctrine he accepted as normal. He didn't automatically hate on first sight, but pre-sumed all blacks would conform to the tenets he grew up on. He gave respect where he felt it was deserved, but the moment anyone talked back to him, regardless of their color, he was fuming with wrath. The several moments of physicality against African Americans during his life cannot plausibly be explained other than conceding that he let his madness rage out of hand. They weren't targeted events, but played out in impulsive fashion, leaving behind an embarrassing stigma that haunts his legacy to this day. But his standing in history was further hurt by misleading and irresponsible information, particularly the notion put forth by Fred Lieb, that Cobb might have been a member of the Ku Klux Klan.[32]

Turning to baseball itself, Cobb left behind ninety records when he retired in 1928. He set high marks for batting average (.367), hits (4,191), runs (2,246), games played (3,035), times at-bat (11,429), stolen bases (892), and years leading league in batting (12). The inevitable thing about marks in baseball was that no matter how exceptional, they were liable to fall over time. Cobb was asked if he was concerned or upset about that, and he replied, "Truthfully, no. The important thing to me is that I played as hard as I could to be the best man on the field. If somebody comes along later and does the same thing better, I know at least that I gave him something to shoot at."[33]

The sports world was electrified in 1985 as Pete Rose chased Cobb's all-time hit record. Finally, on September 11, 1985, "Charlie Hustle" scored hit number 4,192 and stood alone at the top of the pyramid. Ty's single-season stolen base record of 96 was broken by Maury Wills in 1962, and a number of his other records have since fallen. His lifetime batting average of .367 seems untouchable. To put it into perspective, Rogers Hornsby finished his career with .358, Ted Williams .344, and Babe Ruth .342. Some of the greatest hitters of the last thirty years, Tony Gwynn (.338), Wade Boggs (.328), and Rod Carew (.328) had stellar careers (yet not anywhere close to Cobb), while current stars Miguel Cabrera (.320 through the 2014 season) and Albert Pujols (.317 through the 2014 season) sit around 50 points lower than the "Georgia Peach." Achieving anything close to .367 is next to impossible nowadays, especially for a career lasting over two decades.

Interestingly, Cobb's batting average has been affected by the diligent research of baseball statisticians. In 1981, it was revealed in *The Sporting News* that a discrepancy in his records reduced his overall average a point to .366. Additionally, the new findings gave Napoleon Lajoie the 1910 American League batting championship with a .383 to Cobb's .382. The information was embraced to a certain degree, but Major League Baseball leaders opposed any sanctioned decree altering the record books.[34] To this day, his official batting average remains .367, although some prominent sources acknowledge the .366 figure.[35] By the way, while on the topic of stats, Ty's numbers have been crunched in almost every way possible.

Using advanced metrics, statisticians have tabulated his WAR (wins above replacement), "an encompassing metric" that considers multiple elements.[36] Cobb ended up with a 151, fourth amongst hitters in MLB history after Babe Ruth, Barry Bonds, and Willie Mays.[37]

Of all the outsiders to have an actual effect on the legacy of Ty Cobb, no one was more effective than Al Stump. He was the ghostwriter of Cobb's 1961 autobiography, he penned *Cobb: A Biography* (1994), and was depicted by Robert Wuhl in the film version *Cobb*, starring Tommy Lee Jones. His link to the ballplayer was so important that when Stump passed away in 1995, the *New York Times* prominently highlighted the information, denoting that he was the "chronicler of Ty Cobb's life."[38] His projects garnered widespread attention, but as historians and fact-checkers analyzed material in the study of the Hall of Famer's life, certain inaccuracies came to light. In fact, many things pointed to a specific attempt to foster an unseemly perception about the Georgian, in line with the dime novelist-like sportswriters of yore.

Later, things were exposed to be even far more insidious than that. Beginning with his 1961 *True—The Man's Magazine* article, Stump had attempted to reframe the Cobb legacy, using his inside-track to Ty himself as his gateway to storytelling. Because he worked closely with Cobb on his autobiography, he was privy to firsthand accounts that no one else possessed or could possibly substantiate. It was a license to develop a stunning portrait of the legend, and Stump went all out. The most explosive allegation of the *True* piece was the claim that Cobb had admitted to killing a man after being assaulted in 1912. The incident, which happened in Detroit and was related in Chapter 10, was undeniably violent, but absolutely no evidence corroborated the statement.

Doug Roberts, a baseball historian, conducted an exhaustive investigation in the mid-1990s, working to either prove or invalidate the story, challenging the subject from all sides. After studying Detroit Medical Examiner's records, newspapers, and other available sources, he determined that "Ty Cobb Did Not Commit Murder," and wrote a laudable article under that headline in the 1996 publication of *The National Pastime*.[39] If Cobb did tell Stump that he killed a man, it was pure exaggeration, a fable shared during the hazy, booze-infested last days of a terminal cancer patient. Instead of acknowledging the possibility that the statement was hyperbole, the writer took the comment as truth, and delivered it to the public without any kind of asterisk, footnote, or follow-up explanation. Similar to Lieb's comment that Cobb could have been affiliated with the KKK, the entire thing was riddled with irresponsibility.

In 2010, William R. Cobb (no relation to Ty) presented a separate dissection of Stump in his article, "The Georgia Peach: Stumped by the Storyteller," featured in the 2010 edition of *The National Pastime.* He too called attention to unverifiable statements in the *True* magazine story, and questioned the validity of a shotgun Stump said was used in the murder of Ty's father by his mother in 1905. In his thorough evaluation of the facts, Cobb outlined a number of instances in which memorabilia Stump tried to sell was proven forged, including numerous letters and signed baseballs. There was a Cobb diary as well and, after FBI analysis, was deemed a fake.[40] Altogether, the negligence of Stump as an investigative researcher, plus his attempt to saturate the baseball market with fraudulent Cobb merchandise, left an unmistakable tarnish on his reputation akin to the blemishes his work caused Cobb.

There were other items in the *True* article that could've been better explained, had there been any attempt. Stump professed that Cobb used stamps sent in by people requesting autographs for his own postage needs and burned the letters, indicative of a callous and tightfisted man.[41] But this wasn't true. Cobb cared about his fans, but realized decades earlier that it was impossible to respond to everyone. "I have the feeling that I am always neglecting someone," he told *Baseball Magazine* with regret in 1916.[42] Following Cobb's death, readers to *The Sporting News* sent in stories of their personal correspondence with the ballplayer, refuting the allegation that he was completely heartless toward enthusiasts. As for the stamps themselves, Cobb wanted to send over whatever he had in surplus to his granddaughter Shirley McLaren, who was collecting them. He also asked his friend Joe Hauck to do likewise, "particularly any foreign ones," as requested in an undated letter found in the Hauck Collection at Berkeley, California.[43]

An overly paranoid sensibility was reflected in the "high-voltage wires" Cobb used to protect his property at Atherton, and Stump quoted Ty as saying that "detectives" had broken in looking for documents to use against him in a divorce action. If that wasn't reason enough, his home had been robbed at least one other time, in 1947, and thieves made off with a number of valuable belongings.[44] Bearing in mind that he was away from the residence for long periods of time, it only made sense to safeguard it in the best way possible. Lastly, Stump said Cobb was "suffering from megalomania, or acute self-worship."[45] On the contrary, as Cobb didn't show the least bit of conceitedness when asked by journalists to convey his all-time all-star team, and over and over through the years, left himself off the list. John Kieran of the *Boston Herald* stated that it was "sheer modesty."[46] Cobb named Eddie Collins the best player of all-time, while designating "Shoeless" Joe Jackson as the greatest hitter.

Responding to the profuse vilification of his father, Ty's son James told a reporter in 1995 that it was "like a vendetta." The comments of Stump "hurt the family very much," he admitted, and twisted the perception of Cobb into that of a villain.[47] But all things considered, Cobb didn't quite qualify as a scoundrel. In fact, some of the positive things he did might surprise even his most ardent critics. As a teammate, he was the kind of guy who'd go months without talking to someone he was at odds with, but the moment he saw one of his brethren being abused on the field by an opposing team, he was there with fire in his eyes. Oscar Vitt was a perfect example. The two didn't speak for reportedly three years, but the instant Vitt had trouble with catcher Les Nunamaker, Cobb interjected, running full force into the backstop and nearly sending him from the game on a stretcher.[48]

As a mentor, Cobb was determined to share his knowledge and experiences, and his guidance was helpful to innumerable ballplayers. He personally impacted four future Hall of Famers—Harry Heilmann, Heinie Manush, Charlie Gehringer, and Al Simmons—and continued to assist players well after his retirement. He sent insightful messages to the likes of Mickey Mantle and Casey Stengel; had Eddie Joost to his home for specialized baseball sermons during dinner; and was a relentless advisor to others. There were days when Cobb could be found behind the grandstand working with young boys on the proper way to toss a ball or giving lectures to up-and-comers, preaching teamwork and inspiring them to give their all. He donated his time to visiting hospitals and other causes, giving back to the community in any way he could.

Cobb pushed for the inductions of Sam Crawford and Harry Heilmann into the National Baseball Hall of Fame, but didn't necessarily want public acknowledgement for his actions. He gave financial advice to players up and down the baseball ranks, from rookies to executives, and later sent checks to friends in need without a second thought. One of his most striking gestures of goodwill came in 1952 when, at sixty-five years of age, he ventured to the Missouri Ozarks in incredible heat to coach at a small base-ball camp. He could've gone anywhere in the world, but was determined to teach the youngsters at the school the tricks of the trade. As a role model, he lived up to the expectations of a baseball hero, and his generosity was palpable.

Cobb, "The Georgia Peach," got that nickname from sportswriter Joe Jackson in the infancy of his career, and was a legend in his home territory. A reporter for the *Atlanta Constitution* wrote, "Every Georgia adult knows the story of Ty Cobb and youngsters in every community in the state learn about him before they can read."[49] Today, fans can admire a statue depict-ing Cobb sliding at the home of the Atlanta Braves, Turner Field, alongside those of Hank Aaron and Phil Niekro. Many people don't realize that there were two significant events in Cobb's youth in Georgia that could have robbed baseball from his services altogether. The first happened when he was just a boy, not even a teenager. Carelessly handling his .22 rifle, he was accidentally shot in the collarbone. Taken to a hospital in Atlanta, physi-cians couldn't locate the bullet, but he luckily survived the ordeal with nothing more than a bit of pain.[50]

The other was Cobb's choice of another path entirely and focusing on college instead of baseball like his father had wanted. He once said that if he could do it all over again, he'd choose medicine, and forgo the concerns of the diamond.[51] Being a surgeon would've eliminated the worries over rowdy audiences, insults, and public scorn. But at the same time, he would have lost the international acclaim, the thrill of thousands cheering his name, and missed rising to the top of a profession in such a way that his legacy on the field remains significant a century later.

The national pastime was his true calling, and, in 1948, he told a crowd in California, "I am supremely proud that I happened to be a ball player."[52]

For all the wicked narratives and condemnation, there are an equal num-ber of tales describing his baseball feats and accomplishments. Cobb was an imperfect man, and his missteps make interesting reading, but to compre-hend his full legacy, the entire story has to be taken into consideration. That includes the death of the most important person in his life, his father, the painful bullying he endured in his youth, and the loneliness he inter-mittently experienced. Often feeling isolated from the world around him, baseball was his savior, and had he stepped into another occupation, one can only wonder how he would've progressed. Baseball, as an outlet, gave him the opportunity to run, slash, and scrap his way into the record books. His personality needed that kind of avenue to channel his immense energy. He spent his days and nights laboring to improve his mental and physical skills, and worked immensely hard to gain the advantages necessary to be successful.

His personal finances blossomed much the same way. Taking the time to learn about stocks and bonds, the small-town athlete with no formal higher education developed his baseball income into a multimillion dollar estate. When he passed away, according to probate records, he left behind a net worth of more than $4 million, including his personal effects, furnishings, and stock holdings.[53] His biggest investment was Coca-Cola, of course, and he possessed 18,320 shares of common stock valued at $1.3 million, and another 380 shares of Coca-Cola International, also worth 1.3 million. He bequeathed 75 percent of his estate to his family and the other 25 to the Ty Cobb Educational Fund.[54] The fund, as a result of its strong financial standing, remains a pivotal organization today and has issued over $15 million in scholarships to the students of Georgia.[55] Ty's father would have been proud.

The Cobb Memorial Hospital matured as well, developing from a one-building structure into a "system" of facilities in both Royston and Hartwell, Georgia. In 2012, the two facilities united into a singular health care venue in Lavonia, known as the Ty Cobb Regional Medical Center. At Royston, the Ty Cobb Museum, which celebrates the career of the "Peach," is open to visitors and enthusiasts can observe a wealth of memorabilia.[56] Taking into consideration that 2015 is the 110th anniversary of Cobb's major league debut, there is much to commemorate. The evolution of his reputation in the modern era continues to progress as fans of baseball learn and embrace the totality of his life story. No longer is it acceptable to pawn off the tired, sensationalistic notions as the truth, and the simple adjectives used to describe Cobb in the past are archaic. They certainly work in the tabloid environment, but not in the respected culture of baseball history.

Reflecting on his career, Cobb delivered many exciting moments to the sporting world. His inner drive to be the best was unceasing and the generation that watched him in motion was privileged to see a one-of-a-kind ballplayer who could never be duplicated in mind, heart, or spirit. Babe Ruth, the great slugger of 714 home runs and Cobb's most natural adversary, said:

"Ty Cobb is my idea of the greatest ball player that ever lived. Most guys are dangerous only when at bat. Cobb was dynamite at the plate, and when he got on base, he was plenty worse. Nobody ever could figure out what he was going to do."[57] Ray Schalk, a Hall of Famer for the Chicago White Sox, saw no limits of Cobb's athleticism, especially being a catcher. The two were good friends for many years, and in 1961, a few months after Cobb's passing, he said: "The great things he did on the field probably will never be forgotten. I loved the guy."[58]

In all his years, Cobb never lost sight of baseball's most crucial element, the lifeblood of the sport, and he was always cognizant of who really paid the bills. At the tail end of a series of articles he contributed to in 1927, he wrote, "In closing, I want to take this opportunity to express my appreciation to every baseball fan in the country. Without them there wouldn't be any game."[59] There is little doubt that baseball would have endured had Cobb chosen to go into medicine, but it is hard to imagine the sport without the massive footprint he left behind. His contributions to the game are still being felt a century after some of his greatest achievements, and will unquestionably be felt for as long as the game is played.

ENDNOTES

INTRODUCTION:

1 *The Sporting News*, February 13, 1936, p. 4. Cobb achieved a vote percentage of 98.23. In the seventy-eight years since 1936, only three players in history have been acknowledged by greater vote margins: Tom Seaver in 1992 (98.84), Nolan Ryan in 1999 (98.79), and Cal Ripken Jr. in 2007 (98.53).

2 *New York Times*, February 3, 1936, p. 23.

3 *The Sporting News*, February 16, 1939, p. 4.

4 The 1910 batting championship has been in dispute for decades. Read more about it in Chapter 8.

5 *The Sporting News*, September 21, 1939, p. 1.

6 Cobb admitted to trying to spike only two players in his career. *The Sporting News*, March 2, 1955, p. 20.

7 *Boston Daily Record*, September 22, 1959, p. 38.

8 *The Sporting News*, September 2, 1959, p. 1.

9 *New York Times*, April 17, 1959, p. 33.

10 Letter from Cobb to Joseph Hauck dated April 4, 1959, Joseph Hauck Papers (1914–1965), Bancroft Library, University of California, Berkeley, California.

11 *San Diego Union*, November 9, 1959, p. 26. Cobb reportedly saw physicians attached to the Scripps Medical system.

12 *Boston Evening American*, December 17, 1959, p. 62. Two photos of Cobb in the hospital were sent across the Associated Press wire, and in both pictures, Cobb was smiling. One appeared in this *Boston Evening American* edition and the other in the *New York Times*, December 18, 1959, p. 38; in this one he was holding a baseball.

13 *The Sporting News*, December 16, 1959, p. 21.

14 *Otsego Farmer & Republican*, July 20, 1961, p. 1.

15 *The Sporting News*, February 10, 1960, p. 6.

16 *Boston Daily Record*, December 19, 1959, p. 16.

17 *The Sporting News*, February 10, 1960, p. 6, 16.

18 *The Sporting News*, June 22, 1960, p. 11.

19 *The Sporting News*, May 5, 1938, p. 4.

20 *The Sporting News,* February 17, 1960, p. 10.

21 Ibid.

22 *Cleveland Plain Dealer,* February 13, 1960, p. 23.

23 *The Sporting News,* March 18, 1953, p. 22.

24 *Ty Cobb: Safe at Home* by Don Rhodes, 2008, p. 162.

25 *The Sporting News,* June 22, 1960, p. 11.

26 *New York Times,* December 18, 1995.

27 *Portland Oregonian,* June 26, 1946, p. 21.

28 Stump's version of events was chronicled in *True—The Man's Magazine,* December 1961, p. 38–41, 106–115. The article was entitled "Ty Cobb's Wild, 10-Month Fight to Live."

29 Cobb's drinking was corroborated by his friend Pope Welborn, in his interview in *Ty Cobb: Safe at Home* by Don Rhodes, 2008, p. 171–179. Also by Stump in his article, plus in the court documentation for *Elbert D. Felts v. Tyrus R. Cobb,* Case No. 29889, Superior Court of the State of California, County of Butte, 1954–56.

30 *Evening Star,* Washington, DC, July 18, 1961, p. 21.

31 *Omaha World Herald,* July 21, 1961, p. 21.

32 *Omaha World Herald,* September 24, 1961, p. 49.

33 *Evening Star,* Washington, DC, September 24, 1961, p. 43.

34 Gregory also wrote, "By long odds, it's the best, most interesting, most informative baseball book ever written." *Portland Oregonian,* October 8, 1961, p. S1, S4.

35 Ibid.

36 *Springfield Republican,* October 1, 1961, p. 4D.

37 *The Seattle Times,* November 25, 1954, p. 62.

38 *The Sporting News,* January 3, 1962, p. 18, 22.

39 Ibid.

40 *The Sporting News,* December 6, 1961, p. 15.

41 *Jamestown Post Journal,* February 6, 1960, p. 18.

42 *Fort Wayne News and Sentinel,* September 17, 1918, p. 3.

43 *Evening Star,* Washington, DC, July 8, 1962, p. 37.

44 *St. Louis Post Dispatch,* May 9, 1909, p. 1S.

CHAPTER ONE: "DON'T COME HOME A FAILURE"

1 Genealogical information provided by the Cherokee County Historical Museum, Murphy, North Carolina. Sarah Ann Elizabeth Waldroup was originally from Macon County, North Carolina, which was just east of Cherokee County. Cobb's enlistment may have been tied to the First Conscription Act, which was passed by the Confederate Congress in April 1862.

2 U.S. Civil War Soldier Records and Profiles, 1861–1865, ancestry.com.

3 Genealogical information provided by the Cherokee County Historical Museum, Murphy, NC.

4 The county seat in Cherokee County was Murphy and by 1870, just over 8,000 people lived in the area. The region was considered part of the Southern Appalachian Mountains. Notla Township was spelled "Notala" in the 1880 Census.

5 *Ty Cobb: My Life in Baseball* by Ty Cobb with Al Stump, 1993, Bison Books edition, p. 34.

6 *Greensboro News and Record,* January 13, 1985, p. E3.

7 1880 U.S. Federal Census, ancestry.com.

8 *The Herald and News,* Newberry, South Carolina, August 16, 1921, p. 2.

9 U.S. Civil War Soldier Records and Profiles and Civil War Prisoner of War Records, 1861–1865, ancestry.com.

10 The actual Cobb-Chitwood marriage document is featured in the Georgia Marriage Records, ancestry.com. In publications circulating for the past few decades, there have been a few discrepancies surrounding her age, including a completely erroneous claim that they were married around 1882 when she was twelve years of age. Unfortunately, this mistake was initially published and then continued to be referenced in succeeding books without any evidence proving its credibility. None of the authors who attributed the information cited any verifiable source. According to the 1880 U.S. Federal Census, her age was cited as eighteen, which was another error, and an examination of the actual census document appears to show her age to be either sixteen or ten. Ancestry.com. The birth date of "January 15, 1871" was printed on the wall of the Cobb Family mausoleum.

11 *Ty Cobb: My Life in Baseball* by Ty Cobb with Al Stump, 1993, Bison Books edition, p. 34.

12 *Atlanta Constitution,* May 21, 1944, p. A1.

13 *Ty Cobb: My Life in Baseball* by Ty Cobb with Al Stump, 1993, Bison Books edition, p. 32. *New York Times,* December 18, 1983, p. A96.

14 Correspondence with Mark McCoy from July 2014.

15 North Georgia Agricultural College annual catalogues were reviewed from 1887 to 1892. digitalcommons.northgeorgia.edu/collegestate_collections.

16 The article claimed Cobb graduated as the adjutant, meaning he was the assistant to the senior officer, but no corroboration was found in the college catalogues. Cobb was said to have been a "first honor man." *Atlanta Constitution,* June 12, 1892, p. 18.

17 *Macon Telegraph,* July 4, 1891, p. 3.

18 *Atlanta Constitution,* February 23, 1913, p. 7.

19 *The Athens Banner,* September 12, 1893, p. 6.

20 John Paul was born on February 23, 1889, and Florence Leslie on October 29, 1892.

21 *Franklin County Press,* March 10, 1900, p. 1. *Franklin County Press,* September 29, 1899, p. 3.

22 Carnesville High School bulletin, 1891–92, *History of Franklin County, Georgia,* The Franklin County Historical Society, 1986, p. 185.

23 A modern two-story schoolhouse was built in Royston in 1895. *History of Franklin County, Georgia,* The Franklin County Historical Society, 1986, p. 373.

24 *Franklin County Press,* June 16, 1899, p. 3.

25 *Athens Weekly Banner,* February 7, 1919, p. 2.

26 *Ty Cobb: My Life in Baseball* by Ty Cobb with Al Stump, 1993, Bison Books edition, p. 37.

27 *Ty Cobb: My Life in Baseball* by Ty Cobb with Al Stump, 1993, Bison Books edition, p. 280.

28 *Atlanta Constitution,* February 23, 1913, p. 7.

29 *New Orleans Times-Picayune,* July 28, 1912, p. 46. Also *Ty Cobb: My Life in Baseball* by Ty Cobb with Al Stump, 1993, Bison Books edition, p. 37.

30 *Atlanta Journal,* October 25, 1907, p. 18.

31 *Baseball Magazine,* March 1912, p. 1–5. *Ty Cobb: My Life in Baseball* by Ty Cobb with Al Stump, 1993, Bison Books edition, p. 39.

32 *Baseball Magazine,* March 1912, p. 1–5. *Ty Cobb: My Life in Baseball* by Ty Cobb with Al Stump, 1993, Bison Books edition, p. 32.

33 *Ty Cobb: My Life in Baseball* by Ty Cobb with Al Stump, 1993, Bison Books edition, p. 37–38.

34 *The Rotarian Magazine,* July 1947, p. 10–12.

35 *Atlanta Constitution,* August 3, 1899, p. 4.

36 The 31st District included Franklin, Habersham and Hart Counties. The newspaper indicated there was a large turnout to vote. *Atlanta Constitution,* July 28, 1900, p. 3.

37 *History of Franklin County, Georgia,* The Franklin County Historical Society, 1986, p. 373, 382.

38 *Toccoa News,* June 11, 1886.

39 *Hartwell Sun,* July 6, 1900.

40 *Augusta Chronicle,* August 7, 1904, p. 5.

41 *Boston Herald,* February 11, 1912, p. 34.

42 *Brooklyn Daily Eagle,* August 13, 1908, p. 21.

43 *New York Evening World,* August 12, 1911, p. 7.

44 *Baseball Magazine,* March 1912, p. 1–5.

45 *New York Evening World,* August 12, 1911, p. 7.

46 *Ty Cobb: My Life in Baseball* by Ty Cobb with Al Stump, 1993, Bison Books edition, p. 39–40.

47 Some historians, like Fred Lieb have referred to the team Cobb played with while a teenager as the "Royston Rompers." *Baseball As I Have Known It* by Fred Lieb, 1977, p. 49. Cobb called the team, the Royston "Reds." *Ty Cobb: My Life in Baseball* by Ty Cobb with Al Stump, 1993, Bison Books edition, p. 38, 41. The "Rompers" may have been a secondary squad made up of younger players, a team Cobb was a member of prior to joining the senior "Reds," but the names of the two teams have often been interchangeable in historical pieces on Cobb.

48 *Atlanta Constitution,* February 23, 1913, p. 7.

49 Ibid.

50 *Ty Cobb: My Life in Baseball* by Ty Cobb with Al Stump, 1993, Bison Books edition, p. 38.

51 *Atlanta Constitution,* February 23, 1913, p. 7.

52 *Ty Cobb: My Life in Baseball* by Ty Cobb with Al Stump, 1993, Bison Books edition, p. 38–39.

53 In December 1904, Ginn became Ty's uncle when he married Eunice Chitwood, his mother's sister. Because of the close proximity of ages, Ginn (born in 1882) and Ty were close friends. *Hartwell Sun*, July 10 and July 17, 1903.

54 *Nashville Tennessean*, March 19, 1909, p. 7. Another source stated that Cobb had to walk six miles to participate in his first paying gig and made $1.25. *Outing Magazine*, September 1909.

55 *Ty Cobb: My Life in Baseball* by Ty Cobb with Al Stump, 1993, Bison Books edition, p. 43–44.

56 *New Orleans Times-Picayune*, July 28, 1912, p. 46.

57 *New York Evening World*, August 12, 1911, p. 7.

58 *Atlanta Journal*, August 12–13, 1903. No box scores for these games were available.

59 He was known mostly as "Van Bagwell," and his family had lived in Elbert, Franklin, and Madison Counties. He was back with the Royston team in 1906 and a photo of him with the Reds was featured in the *History of Franklin County, Georgia*, The Franklin County Historical Society, 1986, p. 378. Amongst the others on the club were Paul Cobb, Stewart Brown, and Joe Cunningham.

60 *Dallas Morning News*, January 15, 1926, p. 8.

61 Ibid.

62 *Atlanta Constitution*, March 2, 1913, p. 7.

63 *Ty Cobb: My Life in Baseball* by Ty Cobb with Al Stump, 1993, Bison Books edition, p. 144.

64 *Atlanta Constitution*, March 2, 1913, p. 7.

65 *Ty Cobb: My Life in Baseball* by Ty Cobb with Al Stump, 1993, Bison Books edition, p. 45.

66 *Rotarian Magazine*, July 1947, p. 10–12, *Dallas Morning News*, January 15, 1926, p. 8. Amanda Cobb said: "His father and I were very much opposed to his playing professional ball at first, but his mind was so set on it that I relented. I felt that a man should go into whatever walk of life his heart was set upon." *Athens Weekly Banner*, February 7, 1919, p. 2.

67 *Augusta Chronicle*, April 10–24, 1904.

68 *Augusta Chronicle*, April 13, 1904, p. 3.

69 *The Sporting News*, December 8, 1910, p. 4.

70 Ibid.

71 See *Augusta Chronicle*, April 27–28, 1904.

72 Ibid. Also *Dallas Morning News*, January 15, 1926, p. 8.

73 *Atlanta Constitution*, February 18, 1912, p. D5.

74 Hays knew George "Dad" Groves, the manager of the Anniston club (known as the Noblemen), whom he played with in Tampa in 1903. Interestingly, Cobb maintained his friendship with Groves for several decades, as demonstrated by a letter to "Dad" for sale on eBay in November 2014. In the letter, dated March 7, 1928, he also mentioned Hays.

75 *Rotarian Magazine*, July 1947, p. 10–12.

76 A copy of his Anniston contract was printed in the *Atlanta Constitution*, January 2, 1927, p. A2. The Dardens were originally from Cave Spring, GA, and Edna ran a boarding house in Anniston. According to the 1900 U.S. Federal Census, 10 individuals lived in the Darden home at 1010 Quintard Avenue, ancestry.com.

77 *Anniston Star*, August 18, 1968, p. 1D, 4D and *Atlanta Constitution*, June 27, 1904, p. 7.

78 *Anniston Star*, July 19, 1961, p. 13. Lindsay L. Scarbrough, a prominent Anniston businessman and associated with the club behind-the-scenes, said: "I remember several fistic encounters that he engaged himself in, growing out of jibes from the older players on the club. The old heads found soon, however, that they could not bluff the youth. I found him a strictly honest and straightforward youth, ready to back up his own convictions with his fists." *Atlanta Constitution*, January 2, 1927, p. A2.

79 *Anniston Star*, July 19, 1961, p. 13.

80 *Atlanta Constitution*, July 12, 1904, p. 10.

81 Anniston newspapers from 1904 were not available for research through Interlibrary Loan or at the Public Library of Anniston-Calhoun County in Anniston, AL. *Anniston Star*, August 18, 1968, p. 1D, 4D.

82 *Augusta Chronicle*, September 11–12, 1904.

83 Roth said he corresponded with Cobb prior to the 1905 season before signing him to a "fairly good salary." *Charleston Evening Post*, November 17, 1911, p. 3.

84 The first game against Detroit occurred on March 20 and the Tigers won 6–0. Cobb played right field and went 1-for-3. Amongst the Detroit players in the game were Sam Crawford, Herman Schaefer, and Bill Donovan. *Augusta Chronicle*, March 21, 1905, p. 3.

85 *Augusta Chronicle*, March 24, 1905, p. 3.

86 *Augusta Chronicle*, March 26, 1905, p. 11.

87 *Augusta Chronicle*, April 26, 1908, p. 13. At one point during the problems between Roth and Cobb, Roth tried to sell Ty to the Charleston Sea Gulls for $25, but the deal was scrapped at the last minute. *Biloxi Daily Herald*, April 12, 1939, p. 2.

88 *San Antonio Light*, December 29, 1926, p. 10.

89 *New York Evening World*, August 12, 1911, p. 7. The "peanut taffy" was also referred to as popcorn in subsequent stories, including in Cobb's autobiography, *Ty Cobb: My Life in* Baseball by Ty Cobb with Al Stump, 1993, Bison Book edition, p. 50.

90 *Atlanta Constitution*, November 29–30,1924. *Ty Cobb: My Life in Baseball* by Ty Cobb with Al Stump, 1993, Bison Books edition, p. 51.

91 *Augusta Chronicle*, August 1, 1905, p. 8.

92 No mention of his status was provided by the *Augusta Chronicle*.

93 *Washington Post*, August 11, 1905, p. 3.

94 All reviewed reports cited a "pistol" as the murder weapon. For more information on whether an alleged shotgun was used by Amanda Cobb, please review William R. Cobb's important historical article, "The Georgia Peach: Stumped by the Storyteller." sabr.org/research/georgia-peach-stumped-storyteller.

95 Amanda sent Clifford Ginn for a doctor and John O. McCrary, who lived next door, was the first physician to attend to Professor Cobb. *Atlanta Journal,* August 9–10, 1905. It was believed Cobb was hit by the bullets sometime around midnight. He was declared dead around 1:30. *Atlanta Constitution,* August 10, 1905, p. 1. *Washington Post,* August 11, 1905, p. 3. Please note that the *Royston Record* newspaper, of which Professor Cobb was editor since early 1905, is not currently available for research through Interlibrary Loan, through the Georgia Newspaper Project managed by the University of Georgia, or at institutions in Franklin County. Not having this primary resource leaves many details of Mr. Cobb's death in question.

96 The paper reported Cobb had returned to his Royston home after touring his county schools. *Columbus Ledger,* August 9, 1905, p. 1.

97 *Atlanta Constitution,* August 9–12, 1905.

98 Comments in an interview were attributed to Ty's siblings Paul and Florence Cobb. *Augusta Chronicle,* August 13, 1905, p. 1.

99 *Augusta Chronicle,* August 10, 1905, p. 8.

100 Cobb was sold by Augusta President Charles D. Carr. *Augusta Chronicle,* August 20, 1905, p. 13. Jack Horner, another scout for the Tigers, was also credited with "discovering" Cobb. *Detroit Free Press,* July 15, 1910, p. 8. During spring training, the Tigers arranged to give pitcher Eddie Cicotte to Augusta as a form of payment for training costs, and made a deal that would provide them with a first option of any Augusta player. It was suspected that the Tigers would take Clyde Engle, but because of the club's need for a good hitting outfielder, Detroit picked Cobb. *Ty Cobb: My Life in Baseball* by Ty Cobb with Al Stump, 1993, Bison Book edition, p. 53. Cobb tried to hold out for some of his purchase money, creating an unnecessary stink, but was paid around $150 to resolve the issue. *Augusta Chronicle,* August 26–27, 1905.

101 *Ty Cobb: My Life in Baseball* by Ty Cobb with Al Stump, 1993, Bison Books edition, p. 21.

CHAPTER TWO: NOT A BORN BALLPLAYER

1 As of 1898, Detroit was rated second in the United States as a port entry, behind Vermont, and had an annual trade of $14 million. According to the Municipal Manual of Detroit (1897–98), the city covered 29 square miles and featured near complete water works, widespread electric lighting, and over 230 miles of paved roadways. *Jackson Citizen Patriot,* February 9, 1898, p. 5.

2 Charles B. King drove the first auto, a four-cylinder car with a top speed of 20 mph, on the streets of Detroit in 1894. With aid from King, Henry Ford built his version a year later. However, Ransom Olds was credited with creating the very first motorcar in 1886 while in Lansing, Michigan. *The City of Detroit, Michigan, 1701–1922, Volume 1.* Clarence M. Burton, 1922, p. 562-595.

3 Population information found at www.census.gov.

4 Baseball historian Fred Lieb chronicled the early history of baseball in Detroit, and especially the success of the "Big Four" in the 1887 championship season, in his 1946 book, *The Detroit Tigers*.

5 *Rocky Mountain News*, October 26, 1893, p. 3

6 *Evansville Courier and Press*, February 20, 1894, p. 1

7 *Detroit Free Press*, February 7, 1908, p. 1.

8 *The City of Detroit, Michigan, 1701–1922, Volume 3*. Clarence M. Burton, 1922, p. 772–775

9 The corporate name of the Tigers was the Detroit Baseball and Amusement Co. There were reportedly two other minority shareholders, Edward Barrow and A.L.C. Henry, with stock valued at a couple thousand dollars. *Detroit Free Press*, December 1, 1903, p. 10. Only days earlier, on November 23, 1903, Yawkey suffered the loss of his father, William Clyman Yawkey, and inherited a multi-million dollar empire. His business holdings included interests in timber and iron mines. *Detroit Free Press*, November 24, 1903, p. 1.

10 *Detroit Free Press*, January 23, 1904, p. 7.

11 *Detroit Free Press*, February 7, 1908, p. 1.

12 *The Sporting News*, December 24, 1904, p. 2.

13 *The Sporting News*, August 6, 1904, p. 4.

14 *The Sporting News*, March 4, 1905, p. 3.

15 *Cleveland Plain Dealer*, September 9, 1904, p. 8.

16 *The Sporting News*, September 24, 1904, p. 6.

17 *Detroit Free Press*, September 20, 1904, p. 3.

18 *Detroit Free Press*, October 9, 1904, p. 11.

19 *The Sporting News*, October 22, 1904, p. 4.

20 *The Sporting News*, November 5, 1904, p. 5.

21 *The Sporting News*, December 10, 1904, p. 5.

22 *The Sporting News*, February 25, 1905, p. 2.

23 *The Sporting News*, January 7, 1905, p. 3.

24 Washington picked for last place. *The Sporting News*, April 1, 1905, p. 2.

25 *The Sporting News*, July 15, 1905, p. 3.

26 Barrett's injury occurred in the ninth inning and he was replaced by Dick Cooley. *Detroit Free Press*, April 27, 1905, p. 10.

27 *The Sporting News*, May 19, 1906, p. 3. Barrett was in his fifth year as a member of the Tigers. He began his career with Cincinnati, where he first developed a friendship with Sam Crawford, a teammate in 1899 and 1900. A biography of Barrett appeared in the *Detroit Free Press*, April 6, 1905, p. 10.

28 *The Sporting News*, August 12, 1905, p. 3.

29 *Detroit Free Press*, August 2, 1905, p. 9.

30 *New York Times*, May 2, 1905, p. 2.

31 *Atlanta Constitution*, December 2, 1924, p. 11.

32 Letter to Cobb from Armour dated August 25, 1905, Ernie Harwell Collection, Burton Historical Collection, Detroit Public Library, Detroit, Michigan.

33 A report in *The Sporting News* stated that veterans of the South Athletic League believed Cobb was "the fastest youngster that ever broke into professional ball." *The Sporting News*, September 2, 1905, p. 2.

34 Cobb reportedly left Georgia on Saturday, August 26, and arrived in Detroit on Tuesday night, August 29. The usually 30-hour trip was extended by missed train connections at Atlanta and Cincinnati. *Detroit Free Press*, August 30, 1905, p. 9.

35 *Ty Cobb: My Life in Baseball* by Ty Cobb with Al Stump, 1993, Bison Books edition, p. 21.

36 *The Sporting News*, November 18, 1926, p. 7.

37 The paper included a photo of young Cobb. *Detroit Free Press*, August 27, 1905, p. 11.

38 *The Sporting News*, October 17, 1918, p. 8.

39 *The Sporting News*, July 1, 1905, p. 5.

40 Crawford would play 19 years in the majors and end up with 2,961 hits, 458 doubles, an all-time record 309 triples, 97 homers, and a .309 lifetime batting average. www.baseball-reference.com/players/c/crawfsa01.shtml.

41 Around 1903, Crawford became a "choke-style" batter, more along the lines of Willie Keeler, but he admitted in early 1906 that he was discontinuing that effort and returning to the long swing. *Sporting Life*, April 7, 1906, p. 7.

42 *Chicago Daily Tribune*, March 18, 1911, p. 17.

43 *Ty Cobb: My Life in Baseball* by Ty Cobb with Al Stump, 1993, Bison Books edition, p. 22.

44 *Atlanta Constitution*, December 3, 1924, p. 13. *y Cobb: My Life in Baseball* by Ty Cobb with Al Stump, 1993, Bison Book edition, p. 21.

45 *Detroit Free Press*, August 31, 1905, p. 11.

46 Ibid.

47 *Detroit Free Press*, August 30, 1905, p. 9.

48 *Ty Cobb: My Life in Baseball* by Ty Cobb with Al Stump, 1993, Bison Books edition, p. 19.

49 *The Sporting News*, September 16, 1905, p. 8. Cooley played 13 seasons in the majors and ended with over 1,500 hits and a .294 lifetime batting average. He played 97 games for Detroit in 1905. www.baseball-reference.com/players/c/cooledu01.shtml. Cooley made history as a rookie on September 30, 1893, when he recorded six hits in a nine-inning game as a member of St. Louis against Boston. *The Sporting News*, January 19, 1933, p. 5.

50 *The Sporting News*, September 23, 1905, p. 3.

51 *Detroit Free Press*, September 6, 1905, p. 9. McIntyre was a much more polished fielder than Cobb in 1905. At Washington on September 21, Cobb was so adversely affected by the sun that he dropped two fly balls. Armour then moved Cobb to left and put McIntyre in center. *Detroit Free Press*, September 22, 1905, p. 10.

52 *Detroit Free Press*, September 5, 1905, p. 8.

53 *Detroit Free Press*, September 13, 1905, p. 9.

54 *The Sporting News*, October 14, 1905, p. 4.

55 *Detroit Free Press*, January 20, 1906, p. 10.

56 *The Sporting News*, August 26, 1905, p. 4.

57 *The Sporting News*, November 11, 1905, p. 7.

58 Cobb's batting average was also given as .242. *The Sporting News*, October 28, 1905, p. 7. Cobb was also certified as the leader of the South Atlantic League for 1905. He played 103 games for Augusta and ended with a .326 batting average, 134 hits, and 40 stolen bases. *The Sporting News*, November 11, 1905, p. 7.

59 *Ty Cobb: My Life in Baseball* by Ty Cobb with Al Stump, 1993, Bison Book edition, p. 20, 23.

60 *Detroit Free Press*, October 9, 1905, p. 8 and *Detroit Free Press*, October 10, 1905, p. 9.

61 *Sporting Life*, October 21, 1905, p. 11.

62 The paper Cobb spoke with was the *Atlanta Journal*. He also complimented Armour as a topnotch manager. *Augusta Chronicle*, December 4, 1905, p. 8. Georgia Tech won the football game, 17–10.

63 *Flint Journal*, August 29, 1905, p. 2. Jones played 128 games for Minneapolis in 1905 and hit .346 on the year.

64 *The Glory of Their Times*, Lawrence S. Ritter, 1966, p. 38.

65 Letter to Cobb from Armour dated January 6, 1906, Ernie Harwell Collection, Burton Historical Collection, Detroit Public Library, Detroit, Michigan.

66 Letter to Cobb from Armour dated January 20, 1906, Ernie Harwell Collection, Burton Historical Collection, Detroit Public Library, Detroit, Michigan. Also *Detroit Free Press*, January 20, 1906, p. 10.

67 *The Sporting News*, February 10, 1906, p. 6.

68 *Detroit Free Press*, March 5, 1906, p. 10.

69 *Detroit Free Press*, March 18, 1906, p. C2.

70 Letter to Cobb from Armour dated January 20, 1906, Ernie Harwell Collection, Burton Historical Collection, Detroit Public Library, Detroit, Michigan.

71 *The Sporting News*, February 10, 1906, p. 6.

72 It was said that the school principal asked Armour to give Cobb a few extra days and the latter seemingly agreed with no hard feelings. *Detroit Free Press*, March 5, 1906, p. 10.

73 *Detroit Free Press*, March 9, 1906, p. 10.

74 *Sporting Life*, March 24, 1906, p. 7.

75 *Sporting Life*, February 17, 1906, p. 7. Crawford would later say that Jones was the "greatest leadoff man" he ever saw. *Reno Evening Gazette*, February 5, 1957, p. 12.

76 *Detroit Free Press*, March 10, 1906, p. 10.

77 Crawford and Mullin did likewise. *Detroit Free Press*, March 27, 1906, p. 10.

78 More information on the friendship of Crawford and Barrett was included in the *Detroit Free Press*, March 24, 1906, p. 10.

79 *Baseball As I Have Known It*, Fred Lieb, 1977, p. 54.

80 Davy Jones said that Cobb "didn't have a sense of humor." *The Glory of Their Times*, Lawrence S. Ritter, 1966, p. 41.

81 *Fort Wayne News and Sentinel*, September 21, 1918, p. 12.

82 It was mentioned that Cobb's play had been "uncertain" leading up to the trial "due to the nervous strain." *Detroit Free Press*, April 1, 1906, p. 13.

83 A number of newspapers, including the *Atlanta Journal, Macon Telegraph, Columbus Ledger, Danielsville Monitor*, and *Athens Banner* all cited the trial (*State v. Amanda Cobb*) as occurring in Carnesville. The *Atlanta Constitution, Augusta Chronicle*, and *Savannah Tribune* stated it was held in Lavonia. No central newspaper source from Franklin County exists for this time-period to search for additional trial information. An extremely limited amount of case information was available in the Franklin County Superior Court Minutes. Minutes, Superior Court, Franklin County, RG 159-1-58, Georgia Archives. This data is available online as part of the Ad Hoc Digital Collection at the Georgia Archives website.

84 *Atlanta Journal*, March 31, 1906, p. 1.

85 *Detroit Free Press*, April 1, 1906, p. 13.

86 *Athens Banner*, April 6, 1906, p. 5.

87 A photograph of Amanda Cobb appeared on the front page as well. *Atlanta Journal*, April 1, 1906, p. 1. *Detroit Free Press*, April 1, 1906, p. 13.

88 *New Orleans Times-Picayune*, July 28, 1912, p. 46.

89 *Detroit Free Press*, April 4, 1906, p. 9. Apparently other players asked Baldwin about Detroit's place finish and got the same answer. *Detroit Free Press*, April 7, 1906, p. 10. A description of her performance was offered in the *Augusta Chronicle*, March 29, 1906, p. 6. Baseball writer Joe Vila disagreed with Baldwin's prediction, pegging the Tigers for sixth place instead. *The Sporting News*, March 31, 1906, p. 3.

90 *Detroit Free Press*, April 12, 1906, p. 10.

91 *Ty Cobb: My Life in Baseball* by Ty Cobb with Al Stump, 1993, Bison Books edition, p. 54–55.

92 *Detroit Free Press*, April 14, 1906, p. 9.

CHAPTER THREE: WAITING FOR THE COBB TO CRACK

1 *Ty Cobb: My Life in Baseball* by Ty Cobb with Al Stump, 1993, Bison Books edition, p. 20.

2 Sam Crawford stated that had Cobb not possessed the severe "persecution complex," perhaps he would not have become the "great ballplayer he was." *The Glory of Their Times*, Lawrence S. Ritter, 1966, p. 62.

3 *Ty Cobb: My Life in Baseball* by Ty Cobb with Al Stump, 1993, Bison Books edition, p. 23.

4 *Detroit Free Press*, June 26, 1906, p. 9.

5 *The Sporting News*, April 7, 1906, p. 3–6. Barrett ultimately spent most of 1906 in the Eastern League for Rochester, but performed in five games for Cincinnati of the National League. He returned to the American League and played for Boston in 1907 and '08 prior to landing back in to the minors, where he finished his career in 1911. He died on October 25, 1921, in Detroit. www.baseball-reference.com/players/b/barreji01.shtml.

6 *Detroit Free Press*, March 18, 1906, p. 14.

7 Detroit won the game over Chicago, 4–3. *Philadelphia Inquirer*, April 22, 1906, pg. 15. Detroit opened the season on April 17, at home versus the White Sox. Crawford reportedly had an injured leg. *The Sporting News*, April 28, 1906, p. 6. Another report claimed he strained his side.

8 *Detroit Free Press*, April 26, 1906, p. 10.

9 *Detroit Free Press*, April 29, 1906, p. 17.

10 The man on first was catcher Charley "Boss" Schmidt. He scored on Chris Lindsay's sacrifice. *Detroit Free Press*, May 1, 1906, p. 9.

11 *Detroit Free Press*, May 15, 1906, p. 10.

12 *Detroit Free Press*, May 18, 1906, p. 9. Waddell, a 6'1" pitcher from Pennsylvania, would amass a career win-loss record of 193–143 and was inducted into the National Baseball Hall of Fame in 1947.

13 *Detroit Free Press*, May 27, 1906, p. 19.

14 The headline was "Saved by Cobb." *Detroit Free Press*, May 23, 1906, p. 9. The Boston Americans were in the midst of a horrendous run and already had upwards of 25 losses on the season. They would finish with a 49–105 record. Incidentally, *Detroit Free Press*, May 22, 1906, p. 9.

15 *The Sporting News*, May 12, 1906, p. 1.

16 *The Sporting News*, September 29, 1906, p. 3.

17 *Sporting Life*, February 17, 1906, p. 7.

18 *Sporting Life*, September 22, 1906, p. 19.

19 Armour was credited with developing Cobb, first baseman Chris Lindsay and catchers Fred Payne and Charley "Boss" Schmidt. *Cleveland Plain Dealer*, August 11, 1906, p. 6. He was previously known as a producer of baseball talent while boss in Cleveland. A local paper credited him with fostering the growth of Addie Joss, Harry Bemis, Otto Hess, and Harry Bay. *Cleveland Plain Dealer*, September 9, 1904, p. 8. *Sporting Life*, June 2, 1906, p. 2.

20 *Detroit Free Press*, June 24, 1906, p. 14.

21 *The Sporting News*, April 1, 1905, p. 2.

22 *Ty Cobb: My Life in Baseball* by Ty Cobb with Al Stump, 1993, Bison Books edition, p. 144.

23 *Ty Cobb: My Life in Baseball* by Ty Cobb with Al Stump, 1993, Bison Books edition, p. 23.

24 *The Glory of Their Times*, Lawrence S. Ritter, 1966, p. 62.

25 Cobb claimed his verbal quarrel with Crawford occurred in 1907, but finding an accurate date for such an event is impossible. *Ty Cobb: My Life in Baseball* by Ty Cobb with Al Stump, 1993, Bison Books edition, p. 59. There were other claims that Cobb and Crawford actually fought one time, but it was never verified.

26 *The Glory of Their Times*, Lawrence S. Ritter, 1966, p. 41.

27 *Evening Star* (Washington, DC), June 23, 1906, p. 8.

28 *Detroit Free Press*, June 26, 1906, p. 9.

29 Cobb was mentioned as having complained to management about McIntyre, but that information was later refuted. A report stated that he had continued to do his best throughout the controversy. *Detroit Free Press*, June 27, 1906, p. 9.

30 See *Detroit Free Press*, June 24 and June 26, 1906. The latter edition called McIntyre a "Horrible Example," and noted that he would receive no pay during his suspension.

31 *The Sporting News*, June 30, 1906, p. 1.

32 Prior to Cobb taking over left field, he had been sitting on the bench as a result of Armour's reorganization plan of June 18. His demotion was in spite of his impressive .330-plus batting average. The entire shift was as a result of the injury to second baseman Herman Schaefer (broken thumb). Initially, Armour moved Chris Lindsay from first to second base, and then had Crawford cover first. Cobb covered right. But the new set-up had Bobby Lowe on second, Lindsay back on first, and Crawford in right. Thus, Cobb was benched. *Detroit Free Press*, June 18–19, 1906.

33 *The Sporting News*, July 7, 1906, p. 4.

34 *Sporting Life*, July 28, 1906, p. 12.

35 Ibid.

36 More of an explanation of Cobb's battle with various members of the Tigers is provided in *The Tiger Wore Spikes*, John McCallum, 1956, p. 45–46. McCallum's book also perpetuates the belief that the cliques of the Tigers who tormented Cobb "converted him from a keen, cheerful youth into a lone wolf who felt that the rest of the world was against him." This may not be true. Even with Augusta in 1905, Cobb didn't display the disposition of a chummy ballplayer and one that was especially "cheerful." It might be easier to say that the torment suffered in 1905–06 did more to ostracize Cobb than any other time in his baseball career, and forcibly altered his mindset from a shy but volcanic kid into an even more isolated and maniacally angry man. Of course, all of the other factors in Cobb's life contributed to the evolution as well.

37 *Ty Cobb: My Life in Baseball* by Ty Cobb with Al Stump, 1993, Bison Books edition, p. 58.

38 *Detroit Free Press*, June 27, 1906, p. 9.

39 *Detroit Free Press*, July 8, 1906, p. 12.

40 The Tigers won, 4–3. *Detroit Free Press*, July 14, 1906, p. 9.

41 *Detroit Journal*, July 18, 1906, p. 7.

42 *Detroit Times*, July 31, 1906, p. 7.

43 Alexander, in his 1984 biography of Cobb, stated that the Detroit outfielder experienced "some kind of emotional and physical collapse." *Ty Cobb* by Charles C. Alexander, 1984, p. 45.

44 *Detroit Journal*, July 20, 1906, p. 11. This was likely the same venue Cobb mentioned in his autobiography as having a procedure done on his wounded legs, caused by the strain of continuous sliding. *Ty Cobb: My Life in Baseball* by Ty Cobb with Al Stump, 1993, Bison Books edition, p. 55. The Detroit Sanitarium closed in 1914.

45 *Detroit Times,* July 31, 1906, p. 7.

46 Cobb said he regained fifteen pounds of his lost weight. *Detroit Times,* August 15, 1906, p. 9. Also see *Detroit Journal,* August 15, 1906, p. 6. Leith played with an independent franchise out of Seville, Ohio, and would go on to become Director of Athletics at Adrian College in Adrian, Michigan. *Augusta Chronicle,* August 1, 1906, p. 3.

47 *Detroit Times,* July 27, 1906, p. 9.

48 *Detroit Journal,* July 31, 1906, p. 7.

49 *Detroit Journal,* August 28, 1906, p. 6.

50 Thompson was inducted to the National Baseball Hall of Fame in 1974.

51 McClure and Kelsey were business partners in the lumber industry. Kelsey would also thrive in the automotive field with the Kelsey Wheel and Kelsey Auto Body companies. Later, he would become an owner of the Detroit Tigers. The McClure and Cobb Families were tight-knit, evidenced by the fact that Albert's daughter Dorothy visited Georgia in 1918 and spent several months visiting with Ty's wife, mother, and sister. *Detroit Free Press,* May 24, 1918, p. 7.

52 *Detroit Free Press,* September 3, 1906, p. 10.

53 *Detroit Journal,* August 23, 1906, p. 8.

54 Statistics from www.baseball-reference.com/players/j/jennihu01.shtml. A biography about Jennings claimed his 1895 average was .386, and in 1896, it was .397. *The Sporting News,* March 7, 1935, p. 7.

55 *Detroit Journal,* September 3, 1906, p. 7.

56 *Detroit Free Press,* September 4, 1906, p. 10.

57 *The Sporting News,* March 7, 1935, p. 7.

58 Chicago won the pennant over the New York Highlanders by three games. www.baseball-reference.com/leagues/AL/1906.shtml. *The Sporting News,* September 22, 1906, p. 5.

59 *Sporting Life,* September 29, 1906, p. 25.

60 *Detroit Free Press,* September 23, 1906, p. 11. Warner ended his 14-year career in the majors in 1908.

61 *Detroit Free Press,* October 7, 1906, p. 11.

62 *St. Louis Post-Dispatch,* October 7, 1906, p. A12.

63 *Ty Cobb: My Life in Baseball* by Ty Cobb with Al Stump, 1993, Bison Books edition, p. 26.

64 *Detroit Free Press,* October 7, 1906, p. 11.

65 *Ty Cobb: My Life in Baseball* by Ty Cobb with Al Stump, 1993, Bison Books edition, p. 27.

66 Ibid.

67 *Detroit Free Press,* October 14, 1906, p. 14. Cobb played in 98 games and had 113 hits. Crawford ended the season with a .295 average. (www.baseball-reference.com/players/c/cobbty01.shtml)

68 *Ty Cobb: My Life in Baseball* by Ty Cobb with Al Stump, 1993, Bison Books edition, p. 27.

69 *Detroit Journal,* May 30, 1906, p. 7.

70 *Atlanta Constitution*, December 7, 1924, p. B3.

71 *Detroit Free Press*, May 31, 1906, p. 10.

72 *The Sporting News*, August 18, 1954, p 9.

73 *Atlanta Constitution*, December 8, 1924, p. 7.

74 *Detroit Free Press*, September 6, 1906, p. 9. White had a career record of 189–156. www.baseball-reference.com/players/w/whitedo01.shtml.

75 *The Tiger Wore Spikes*, John McCallum, 1956, p. 220.

76 The ash timber bats were likely created using Joe Cunningham's father's tools in Royston. *The Tiger Wore Spikes*, John McCallum, 1956, p. 14.

77 *The Sporting News*, January 13, 1954, p. 14. *Ty Cobb: My Life in Baseball* by Ty Cobb with Al Stump, 1993, Bison Books edition, p. 24.

78 Cobb quote from the *Atlanta Constitution*, June 1, 1934, p. 17.

79 *Sporting Life*, January 6, 1912, p. 11.

80 *The Sporting News*, April 6, 1939, p. 9.

CHAPTER FOUR: A HUMBLED BATTING CHAMPION

1 *The City of Detroit, Michigan, 1701–1922, Volume 3*. Clarence M. Burton, 1922, p. 772–775.

2 *The Sporting News*, November 17, 1906, p. 2.

3 *The Sporting News*, October 13, 1906, p. 2.

4 See *The Sporting News*, November and December 1906.

5 *Detroit Free Press*, February 5, 1907, p. 8.

6 *Detroit Free Press*, December 23, 1906, p. 13.

7 *Detroit Free Press*, November 8, 1906, p. 9.

8 Flick ended his major league career with Cleveland in 1910 and finished with a .313 lifetime batting average. He was inducted into the National Baseball Hall of Fame in 1963. www.baseball-reference.com/players/f/flickel01.shtml.

9 *Cleveland Plain Dealer*, December 14, 1906, p. 8.

10 *The Sporting News*, December 29, 1906, p. 2.

11 *Augusta Chronicle*, November 2, 1906, p. 12.

12 *Augusta Chronicle*, December 4, 1906, p. 10.

13 *Sporting Life*, December 8, 1906, p. 11.

14 *Augusta Chronicle*, December 4, 1906, p. 10.

15 Cobb would earn $2,400 in salary for 1907.

16 Letter to Cobb from Navin dated February 11, 1907, Ernie Harwell Collection, Burton Historical Collection, Detroit Public Library, Detroit, Michigan.

17 *Augusta Chronicle*, February 2, 1907, p. 10.

18 *The Sporting News*, February 2, 1907, p. 6.

19 Expounding on the difficulties seen by a young player in the majors, legendary Pittsburgh Pirate Honus Wagner explained that he was in the National League "several years" before a member of an opposing team talked to him. *Atlanta Constitution*, March 10, 1936, p. 18. 1975 Hall of Fame inductee Bucky Harris told a story of once being in a Detroit Tigers training camp very early in his

baseball career, and said that he was ignored by practically everyone, including by Cobb, adding, "When they sent me home, I was glad to get away." *The Sporting News*, March 5, 1952, p. 19.

20 *Ty Cobb: My Life in Baseball* by Ty Cobb with Al Stump, 1993, Bison Books edition, p. 23, 29. As mentioned previously, Davy Jones also endeavored to understand Cobb, but few others made the effort.

21 Ibid, p. 24.

22 Schaefer and O'Leary were close friends. O'Leary once told a story about getting rides to Bennett Park in "Crazy Hank's" automobile. Hank, in this instance, was Henry Ford, who offered O'Leary and Schaefer in on the ground floor of what would ultimately be a massive auto conglomerate. However, the two ballplayers didn't see any value in the opportunity and refrained from investing. *The Sporting News*, February 1, 1956, p. 18.

23 Schaefer said old-timer Jimmy Ryan originally coached him on the "old Chicago slide." Additionally, regarding Cobb, he noted that he wasn't a proficient slider when he became a member of the Tigers. *Wilkes-Barre Times Leader*, September 16, 1909, p. 14. Cobb confirmed that Schaefer taught him how to slide. *The Sporting News*, November 3, 1910, p. 4.

24 Jennings described Schaefer's importance in 1907. *Atlanta Constitution*, December 31, 1925, p. 7.

25 Cobb arrived at camp in Augusta on the afternoon of March 12. *Detroit Free Press*, March 13, 1907, p. 9. Cobb was expected to meet up with the team in Atlanta on March 11, but missed a connection. *Augusta Chronicle*, March 12, 1907, p. 8.

26 Cummings was listed as "Henry Cumming" in the 1910 U.S. Federal Census and his occupation was listed as "Janitor; Warren Park." His wife was named Savannah. His nickname has been spelled "Bungy" and "Bungey."

27 The newspaper called it the "most sensational incident" of Detroit's spring training. *Detroit Free Press*, March 17, 1907, p. 17. Also, ancestry.com.

28 *Detroit Free Press*, April 1, 1906, p. 13.

29 *Detroit Free Press*, March 17, 1907, p. 17.

30 *Detroit Free Press*, March 17, 1907, p. 17.

31 Details about Schmidt's toughness were offered in the *Milwaukee Journal*, November 27, 1932, p. S2.

32 *The Detroit Tigers*, Frederick G. Lieb, 2008, Kent State University Press edition, p. 82–83.

33 *Detroit Free Press*, March 17, 1907, p. 17.

34 Ibid.

35 *Augusta Chronicle*, February 14, 1908, p. 10.

36 *Augusta Chronicle*, August 27, 1907, p. 4.

37 *Detroit Free Press*, March 26, 1907, p. 9.

38 *Detroit Free Press*, March 21, 1907, p. 8. One of five famous baseball brothers, Frank Delahanty played six seasons between the American and Federal Leagues and ended his career with a .226 batting average. www.baseball-reference.com/players/d/delahfr01.shtml.

39 *Ty Cobb: My Life in Baseball* by Ty Cobb with Al Stump, 1993, Bison Books edition, p. 60–61.

40 *The Sporting News*, April 6, 1907, p. 6.

41 *Atlanta Constitution*, April 2, 1907, p. 9.

42 *Detroit Free Press*, March 25–26, 1907.

43 *Detroit Free Press*, March 22, 1907, p. 9.

44 *The Sporting News*, April 6, 1907, p. 2.

45 *Atlanta Constitution*, January 6, 1926, p. 6.

46 *Ty Cobb: My Life in Baseball* by Ty Cobb with Al Stump, 1993, Bison Books edition, p. 25.

47 *The Sporting News*, June 19, 1941, p. 5.

48 *The Sporting News*, April 6, 1907, p. 4.

49 *Atlanta Constitution*, January 6, 1926, p. 6.

50 *The Sporting News*, January 16, 1908, p. 2.

51 *The Sporting News*, June 19, 1941, p. 5.

52 *The Sporting News*, April 27, 1907, p. 6.

53 Over 6,000 fans attended the game in brisk weather at Bennett Park. *Detroit Free Press*, April 12, 1907, p. 1.

54 *Detroit Free Press*, May 9, 1907, p. 8.

55 *Detroit Free Press*, May 15, 1907, p. 9.

56 *Detroit Free Press*, June 11, 1907, p. 8.

57 Cobb committed two errors before a large crowd in Detroit on June 22. The newspaper indicated that Cobb's three doubles would normally have won the game, but was hurt by the established ground rules that limited what would have normally been triples to two-baggers. Detroit lost to Chicago, 4–3. *Detroit Free Press*, June 23, 1907, p. 17.

58 *The Sporting News*, May 18, 1907, p. 3.

59 The Detroit report claimed Bemis had the ball when Cobb was only "three steps" from the plate, while Cleveland sportswriter Ed Bang in *Sporting Life* noted that Cobb was "20 feet" out when Bemis caught the throw from third baseman Bill Bradley. *Detroit Free Press*, June 30, 1907, p. 17 and *Sporting Life*, July 13, 1907, p. 2.

60 *Detroit Free Press*, June 30, 1907, p. 17. Ibid and *The Sporting News*, July 11, 1907, p. 3. Stump's assertion, *Cobb*, Al Stump, 1994, p. 148.

61 The steal of home was part of a double steal with Rossman. Ibid.

62 *Sporting Life*, July 13, 1907, p. 2.

63 *Detroit Free Press*, July 13, 1907, p. 6.

64 *Detroit Free Press*, July 21, 1907, p. 13.

65 *Detroit Free Press*, July 31, 1907, p. 7.

66 *The Sporting News*, December 18, 1946, p. 4.

67 Detroit team owner Bill Yawkey was given an inside tip about Johnson from a friend in Idaho, and passed the information on to Navin. Navin doubted the information and neglected to follow up. *Detroit Free Press*, August 3, 1907, p. 6.

68 *Ty Cobb: My Life in Baseball* by Ty Cobb with Al Stump, 1993, Bison Books edition, p. 65.

69 *The Sporting News*, December 18, 1946, p. 4.

70 *Detroit Free Press*, August 9, 1907, p. 6.

71 *The Sporting News*, August 22, 1907, p. 1. After the season, Fogel made the assertion that the Washington Senators purposefully lost games to the Tigers, aiding Detroit in their pennant win. *The Sporting News*, November 14, 1907, p. 5.

72 *The Sporting News*, September 5, 1907, p. 3.

73 Cobb went 3-for-3 in a Detroit win. *Detroit Free Press*, August 9, 1907, p. 1.

74 *Detroit Free Press*, August 15, 1907, p. 6.

75 *Detroit Free Press*, September 4, 1907, p. 6.

76 *The Sporting News*, September 26, 1907, p. 3. This injury caused him to miss his first game of the season on September 16 and Wade Killifer played right field.

77 *The Sporting News*, September 19, 1907, p. 1.

78 *Detroit Free Press*, October 1, 1907, p. 1.

79 Ibid.

80 *The Sporting News*, July 27, 1944, p. 11.

81 *The Sporting News*, June 19, 1941, p. 5.

82 *Detroit Free Press*, October 4, 1907, p. 8.

83 The race was basically settled after Detroit beat St. Louis on October 5. They would lose the final two games at St. Louis, but played half-heartedly with numerous substitutes. Cobb missed both games. The Tigers finished with a 92–58 record.

84 *Ty Cobb: My Life in Baseball* by Ty Cobb with Al Stump, 1993, Bison Books edition, p. 73.

85 *Detroit Free Press*, October 10, 1907, p. 1.

86 *Detroit Free Press*, August 18, 1907, p. 14.

87 *Detroit Free Press*, October 11, 1907, p. 1.

88 *Detroit Free Press*, October 12, 1907, p. 1.

89 *Detroit Free Press*, October 13, 1907, p. 17. A detailed breakdown of the 1907 World Series was offered in *The Detroit Tigers*, Frederick G. Lieb, 2008, Kent State University Press edition, p. 94–104.

90 *Detroit Free Press*, October 13, 1907, p. 1.

91 *Detroit Free Press*, October 17, 1907, p. 1.

92 *The Sporting News*, October 24, 1907, p. 6.

93 The Jennings-led barnstorming squad played the Logan Squares in Chicago on October 19–20, and Cobb was one of the top performers, working the bases, fielding strong, and hitting to all parts of the field. They also went to Racine, Wisconsin, on October 21 and Cobb again played remarkably well. See *Detroit Free Press*, October 20–22, 1907.

94 *Atlanta Journal*, October 25, 1907, p. 18.

CHAPTER FIVE: "UP HERE, THEY DON'T UNDERSTAND ME"

1 In 1907, Cobb resided at 2384 Woodward Avenue. The Brunswick Hotel was at the corner of Grand River and Cass Avenues. Cobb talked about players staying

at the Brunswick in his autobiography, *Ty Cobb: My Life in Baseball* by Ty Cobb
with Al Stump, 1993, Bison Books edition, p. 23–24.

2 *Detroit Free Press,* March 24, 1907, p. 17.

3 *Detroit Free Press,* March 8, 1907, p. 8. He was said to be shorter than his brother
and differed greatly in his batting style. *Detroit Free Press,* May 16, 1907, p. 8. Paul
Cobb would finish 1907 in the Western Association as a member of the Leaven-
worth, Kansas team.

4 *Cleveland Plain Dealer,* November 3, 1907, p. 27. Also see *San Diego Union,* November 3, 1907, p. 7.

5 *The Sporting News,* December 31, 1908, p. 6. *Sporting Life,* May 16, 1908, p. 11.

6 Amongst the 100-plus contributors to the "Ty Cobb Fund" were leading businessmen and politicians. $30 was donated by Cobb's home city of Royston and
Governor Hoke Smith added $5. The original plan was to buy him a medal, but
with the increase in funds, the idea switched to a pocket watch crafted by Schaul
and May. *Atlanta Journal,* October and November 1907.

7 *Atlanta Journal,* October 25, 1907, p. 18.

8 *Atlanta Journal,* October 16, 1907, p. 20.

9 *Atlanta Journal,* November 13, 1907, p. 14.

10 Additional articles in the "Ty Cobb Edition" were about Detroit trainer Tom
McMahon, Rube Waddell, Bob Lowe, and Jim McGuire. *Atlanta Journal,* December 22, 1907, p. 13. *Atlanta Journal,* December 22, 1907, p. S1–S4. Cobb reportedly worked on the articles over the course of a month. Paul Bruske circulated
blurbs from the articles in the *Detroit Times.*

11 *Atlanta Constitution,* August 5, 1907, p. 7.

12 *Ty Cobb: My Life in Baseball* by Ty Cobb with Al Stump, 1993, Bison Books edition,
p. 76. Notably, several times during Cobb's short career, the press alluded to him
getting poor or foolish advice from southern associates. An example of this was
when he was originally signed by the Tigers and wanted half of his purchase
price in the transaction between Detroit and Augusta, an uncustomary request.
Detroit Free Press, March 10, 1906, p. 10. Joe S. Jackson mentioned this problem
again, *Detroit Free Press,* March 7, 1908, p. 7.

13 *Detroit Free Press,* January 10, 1908, p. 6.

14 Letter to Cobb from Navin dated January 9, 1908, Ernie Harwell Collection,
Burton Historical Collection, Detroit Public Library, Detroit, Michigan.

15 *Atlanta Journal,* November 11, 1907, p. 14.

16 Navin reportedly offered $3,500, the same amount given to Crawford.

17 Cobb's point of view and Navin's response was covered in-depth by *Sporting Life,*
February 8, 1908, p. 10. Cobb explained an earlier medical situation in his
career in which he had to cover the costs himself, rather than the team paying
for it. *Ty Cobb: My Life in Baseball* by Ty Cobb with Al Stump, 1993, Bison Books
sedition, p. 55. However, the club did cover his medical bills in the summer of
1906. *The Sporting News,* January 30, 1908, p. 2. Cobb wasn't the only player of
note in the majors holding out. Bobby Wallace, Tommy Leach, Nick Altrock,
Jack Pfiester, and the great Honus Wagner each had their own reasons for delay-
ing signature to a new contract, and waited for the right conditions to present

themselves. Even Claude Rossman haggled with Navin, citing his terrific play in the World Series as reason for a bump in salary.

18 *Detroit Free Press,* January 25, 1908, p. 6.

19 *Augusta Chronicle,* February 2, 1908, p. 8.

20 Apparently, he told the youngster about an incident that occurred during his own career, when he forced Baltimore Orioles owner Ned Hanlon to pay what he asked through a holdout-type situation. *Augusta Chronicle,* February 9, 1908, p. 12.

21 *Augusta Chronicle,* March 16, 1908, p. 8. The Logan Squares were operated by former major leaguer, Jimmy Callahan. *Augusta Chronicle,* March 1, 1908, p. 10.

22 *The Sporting News,* February 13, 1908, p. 2. The same issue discussed a National Agreement amendment to shield owners from player extortion.

23 *Detroit Free Press,* February 15, 1908, p. 7.

24 *Detroit Free Press,* March 15, 1908, p. 13.

25 See *Detroit Free Press,* March 19–21, 1908. An odd comment appeared in the *Lansing State Republican,* which said: "Perhaps the long uncertainty over the signing of Ty Cobb helped to increase the prevalence of the cocaine habit in Detroit." *Detroit Free Press,* March 25, 1908, p. 4.

26 *Augusta Chronicle,* March 26, 1908, p. 10. Other sources have his salary affixed at $4,500. www.baseball-reference.com/players/c/cobbty01.shtml. One rumor claimed his salary was as high as $6,500 and that he received part of it from prominent Detroit rooters. *Detroit Free Press,* March 22, 1908, p. 17.

27 *Detroit Free Press,* March 21, 1908, p. 1, 6.

28 *Detroit Free Press,* March 31, 1908, p. 6.

29 *Atlanta Constitution,* December 5, 1924, p. 13 and January 6, 1926, p. 6.

30 *Detroit Free Press,* May 22, 1906, p. 9.

31 *The Sporting News,* April 9, 1908, p. 6.

32 *Current Literature,* November 1911. *The Sporting News,* November 16, 1911, p. 4. Cobb participated in a field day exhibition on October 18, 1908 at Chicago and circled the bases in 13.8 seconds, ran to first after a bunt in 3.2 seconds, and beat Jones in a 100-yard dash with a 10.4. *Detroit Free Press,* October 19, 1908, p. 6. Two years later, Hans Lobert reportedly circled the bases in 13.8 seconds, the same as Cobb, but his time was established as the official world record. Maurice Archdeacon broke that mark with a 13.4, and later, Evar Swanson broke that record with a 13.3 in 1931. *The Sporting News,* February 1, 1950, p.6.

33 *Detroit Free Press,* April 15, 1908, p. 1.

34 *Detroit Free Press,* April 18, 1908, p. 9.

35 *Brooklyn Daily Eagle,* April 27, 1908, p. 22.

36 *Detroit Free Press,* May 2, 1908, p. 6.

37 *Fort Wayne News and Sentinel,* September 17, 1918, p. 3.

38 *Detroit Free Press,* June 6, 1908, p. 6.

39 The Pontchartrain Hotel rested at the southwest corner of Cadillac Square at 660 Woodward Avenue. It opened on October 29, 1907. historicdetroit.org/building/hotel-pontchartrain. The hotel was east of Bennett Park along Michi-

gan Avenue, and street car lines were available for transit to and from the ball field.

40 *Detroit Free Press*, June 7, 1908, p. 10. The crew of at least six workers was under the management of foreman Peter J. Breen.

41 Ibid.

42 Ibid. Collins was listed as a "paving worker" in the World War I Draft Registration Records at ancestry.com. The press made sure it was known that Collins was wearing eyeglasses when the confrontation started.

43 Ibid. Detroit lost to Boston, 10–5. Cobb wasn't the only member of the Tigers to fight with a member of the public. A Toronto visitor to Detroit named Archibald Tark vocally criticized players at the Brunswick Hotel, and was trounced by Herman Schaefer. *Detroit Free Press*, June 10, 1908, p. 16.

44 *St. Louis Post Dispatch*, June 7, 1908, p. A10.

45 *Detroit Free Press*, June 7, 1908, p. 10.

46 *Atlanta Constitution*, July 9, 1900, p. 2.

47 *Atlanta Constitution*, June 13, 1896, p. 3. Details about the hanging of Ware were featured in multiple papers, including *Augusta Chronicle*, September 19, 1904, p. 1. Ware, who was accused of murdering a white man, was taken from authorities by a lynch mob, killed, and shot 50 times in the vicinity between Royston and Carnesville.

48 *Franklin County Press*, July 28, 1899, p. 1.

49 *Franklin County Press*, January 5, 1900, p. 1.

50 *Savannah Tribune*, December 7, 1901, p. 2.

51 *Detroit Free Press*, June 10, 1908, p. 4.

52 *Ty Cobb: My Life in Baseball* by Ty Cobb with Al Stump, 1993, Bison Books edition, p. 94.

53 *Washington Post*, June 9, 1908, p. 8 and the *Daily Illinois State Register*, June 21, 1908, p. 14.

54 These incidents occurred in games between June 21 and June 30, 1908.

55 *Detroit Free Press*, June 28, 1908, p. 17.

56 Ibid.

57 *Ty Cobb: My Life in Baseball* by Ty Cobb with Al Stump, 1993, Bison Books edition, p. 27.

58 *Detroit Free Press*, July 26, 1908, p. 17.

59 *Detroit Free Press*, September 22, 1907, p. 17.

60 *The Sporting News*, January 30, 1908, p. 4.

61 *Ty Cobb: My Life in Baseball* by Ty Cobb with Al Stump, 1993, Bison Books edition, p. 27.

62 Wright's comments in *The Sporting News*, September 5, 1907, p. 3. Bruske's remarks in *Sporting Life*, October 5, 1907, p. 7.

63 *The Sporting News*, October 10, 1907, p. 6.

64 *The Sporting News*, November 21, 1907, p. 4.

65 *The Sporting News*, January 16, 1908, p. 3.

66 *Wilkes-Barre Times-Leader*, May 18, 1910, p. 11.

67 *Detroit Free Press,* April 4, 1909, p. 19. Also see *Muskegon Chronicle,* March 25, 1908, p. 3.

68 *Cleveland Plain Dealer,* July 5, 1908, p. 8D.

69 Ibid.

70 *Detroit Free Press,* July 18–19, 1908.

71 Cobb wrote a letter to Paul Bruske and notified him of his engagement. It was erroneously reported that she was an "Atlanta girl." *Sporting Life,* December 14, 1907, p. 3.

72 Charlie Lombard was reportedly born on July 3, 1890, however, the 1900 U.S. Federal Census listed her birth year as 1891, which would have made her 17 at the time of her wedding. Lombard was part of a commencement ceremony at St. Mary's in 1907. See *Augusta Herald,* June 7, 1907, p. 7.

73 *Augusta Chronicle,* August 7, 1924, p. 5.

74 Alfred O. Lombard was a soldier in Company K (known as the Olglethorpes), Third Infantry, Georgia National Guard.

75 *Detroit Free Press,* July 23, 1908, p. 9.

76 *Detroit Free Press,* July 26, 1908, p. 17.

77 Clifford Ginn was married to Cobb's mother's sister, Eunice, and was four years older than Cobb.

78 Wedding coverage found in the *Augusta Chronicle,* August 4–7, 1908. *Augusta Chronicle,* August 22, 1908, p. 5.

79 *Detroit Free Press,* August 10, 1908, p. 8.

80 *Detroit Free Press,* August 11, 1908, p. 6.

81 *Detroit Free Press,* August 21, 1908, p. 9.

82 *Detroit Free Press,* August 15, 1908, p. 6. Read more about the Morgan-Cobb incident at sabr.org/bioproj/person/dfafa3e0. Also see *The Sporting News,* September 3, 1908, p. 6.

83 *Detroit Free Press,* October 7, 1908, p. 1. For that reason, the team would elect to give him a full slice of the World's Series cut, even though he was unable to play due to National Commission rules preventing late season additions from participating.

84 During the August eastern jaunt, Cobb was allowed to miss an exhibition at Newark to spend time with Charlie in Washington, DC Mrs. Cobb also attended road games of the World Series in Chicago.

85 *Detroit Free Press,* November 16, 1908, p. 8.

86 *The Sporting News,* October 17, 1907, p. 1.

87 *Detroit Free Press,* October 11, 1908, p. 1, 17.

88 *Detroit Free Press,* October 12, 1908, p. 1.

89 *Detroit Free Press,* October 13, 1908, p. 1.

90 See *Detroit Free Press,* October 14, 1908, p. 1, and *The Sporting News,* October 22, 1908, p. 4. In an interesting sidebar to the Series, before one of the games, Cobb briefly acted as a catcher for Cubs' Mordecai Brown in warm-ups. Ibid.

91 *Detroit Free Press,* October 15, 1908, p. 1.

92 A full breakdown of the 1908 World Series was offered in *The Detroit Tigers,* Frederick G. Lieb, 2008, Kent State University Press edition, p. 109–117.

93 The trip to the Orient was cancelled because Charlie Cobb was battling a lengthy illness.

94 Cobb's terms for 1909 were the same as for 1908. *Detroit Free Press*, January 1, 1909, p. 9.

CHAPTER SIX: THE LUCKY STIFF

1 *Atlanta Constitution*, December 6, 1924, p. 9.

2 *The Sporting News*, September 24, 1931, p. 4.

3 *The Sporting News*, April 16, 1908, p. 4.

4 *Atlanta Constitution*, December 6, 1924, p. 9.

5 *Chicago Defender*, July 22, 1911, p. 5.

6 An entertainer named "Zalla, Queen of Dancers" performed for the crowd on the passenger steamer *Sappho* at the event. Also in attendance were Ed Willett, Ira Thomas and team trainer Harry Tuthill. *Detroit Free Press*, June 17, 1908, p. 10.

7 These instances occurred on September 2 at the Gayety Theater in Detroit and on September 4 at the American Theater in St. Louis.

8 *Detroit Free Press*, October 9, 1908, p. 8.

9 *Atlanta Constitution*, October 29, 1908, p. 11.

10 Cobb's team beat the Bernhardt club before a large crowd. *New Orleans Times-Picayune*, November 15, 1908, p. 15. *New Orleans Times-Picayune*, November 16, 1908, p. On December 12, 1908, Cobb acted as referee for a boxing match at New Orleans' Southern Athletic Club and allowed the fight to continue despite Kid Greaves's domination over Charley Fury. Police finally stepped in to halt the contest, and Cobb later said he was just abiding by Marquis of Queensberry rules by allowing the battle to continue. He was supposed to referee the main event between Young Corbett and Phil Brock as well, but was pulled from the job. *New Orleans Times-Picayune*, December 14, 1908, p. 10. Cobb wanted to be paid in full, including for the main event job, but finally accepted partial pay before leaving New Orleans with a bad taste in his mouth. *Detroit Free Press*, December 16, 1908, p. 9.

11 Multiple reports located in the *Detroit Free Press*, January 1909.

12 *Detroit Free Press*, February 14, 1909, p. 17.

13 *Augusta Chronicle*, March 2, 1909, p. 4.

14 *Augusta Chronicle*, March 10, 1909, p. 5 and *Detroit Free Press*, March 12, 1909, p. 10.

15 *Augusta Chronicle*, March 11, 1909, p. 5.

16 Cobb's pitching ambition was talked about in *The Sporting News*, June 8, 1907, p. 6.

17 *Atlanta Constitution*, November 25, 1924, p. 8.

18 Ernie Harwell Collection, Burton Historical Collection, Detroit Public Library, Detroit, Michigan. He told Cobb to "be more careful of your arm."

19 *Detroit Free Press*, March 29, 1909, p. 8.

20 *The Sporting News*, June 24, 1943, p. 5.

21 *St. Louis Post-Dispatch*, March 7, 1909, p. 2S.

22 *Detroit Free Press*, March 18, 1910, p. 10.

23 *St. Louis Post-Dispatch*, May 9, 1909, p. 1S.

24 *Detroit Free Press*, May 1–2, 1909.

25 *Detroit Free Press*, September 6, 1909, p. 7. After a game on June 26 at Bennett Park, Detroit sportswriters really got after Criger for a "bonehead play" they felt he made. The catcher had a poor inning and was taken out of the game with an injured knee. *Detroit Free Press*, June 27, 1909, p. 17. He mistakenly wrote that Criger was still a teammate of Cy Young at Boston at the time, but really Criger was with St. Louis and Young was playing for Cleveland. The claim that Cobb stole three bases on Criger went back a lot earlier than Cobb's autobiography, however.

26 *Ty Cobb: My Life in Baseball* by Ty Cobb with Al Stump, 1993, Bison Books edition, p. 161–163.

27 *The Sporting News*, April 23, 1936.

28 *The Sporting News*, May 1, 1941, p. 14.

29 *Los Angeles Times*, March 9, 1951, p. C1.

30 Ibid. *The Sporting News*, November 9, 1955, p. 13. A variation of this story was told in Cobb's autobiography, and the player who noticed his "tell" was Boston's Larry Gardner. *Ty Cobb: My Life in Baseball* by Ty Cobb with Al Stump, 1993, Bison Books edition, p. 163.

31 Ibid. Mike "King" Kelly, who played in the majors from 1878 to '93, was said to be an "earlier edition" of Cobb for his "color and the audacity of his base-running." Kelly was inducted into the Hall of Fame in 1945. *The Sporting News*, May 3, 1945, p. 7.

32 *Detroit Free Press*, May 12, 1909, p. 1.

33 *Detroit Free Press*, July 16, 1909, p. 8.

34 *Detroit Free Press*, July 23, 1909, p. 9.

35 *Philadelphia Inquirer*, August 26, 1909, p. 8. *Philadelphia Inquirer*, August 27, 1909, p. 6.

36 The spiking of Baker was mentioned, but the story didn't receive headline press the day after it happened. There was no immediate riot at the scene as it has been claimed. *Detroit Free Press*, August 25, 1909, p. 9.

37 *Philadelphia Inquirer*, August 25, 1909, p. 6. Also see *Ty Cobb: My Life in Baseball* by Ty Cobb with Al Stump, 1993, Bison Books edition, p. 114–116.

38 *Boston Journal*, August 3, 1909, p. 8.

39 *St. Louis Post-Dispatch*, May 9, 1909, p. 1S. Bradley was spiked on the hand by Cobb in the eighth inning of a contest on April 17.

40 *The Sporting News*, February 18, 1953, p. 10.

41 *The Sporting News*, September 2, 1909, p. 1, 4.

42 *Harrisburg Patriot*, August 28, 1909, p. 10.

43 Players were "heartbroken" by the trade. Red Killefer was also sent to Washington in the Schaefer deal. *Wilkes-Barre Times-Leader*, August 17, 1909, p. 13. In another trade, Claude Rossman went to St. Louis for first baseman Tom Jones.

44 *Wilkes-Barre Times-Leader*, September 16, 1909, p. 14.

45 *Wilkes-Barre Times-Leader*, September 7, 1909, p. 10.

46 *Detroit Free Press*, August 31, 1909, p. 8.

47 *Detroit Free Press*, August 28, 1909, p. 8.

48 *Cleveland Plain Dealer*, September 8, 1909, p. 8.

49 *Cincinnati Post*, October 21, 1909, p. 6.

50 *Cleveland Plain Dealer*, September 8, 1909, p. 8.

51 *Detroit Free Press*, September 8, 1909, p. 9.

52 A photo of the penknife was displayed in the paper. *Cincinnati Post*, October 21, 1909, p. 6. The knife had a blade one and one-sixteenth inches long. *Cleveland Plain Dealer*, October 21, 1909, p. 5. Ironically, only days before the Cleveland incident, G. E. Schwab of Detroit's G. E. Schwab Chandelier Company fashioned "pocket knives" for each of the members of the Tigers with the likeness of Hugh Jennings and others on the outside casing. It isn't known whether this knife was the weapon used by Cobb. *Detroit Free Press*, August 28, 1909, p. 8.

53 *Cleveland Plain Dealer*, September 8, 1909, p. 8.

54 *Detroit Free Press*, September 8, 1909, p. 9.

55 Stanfield had hired the law firm of Hidy, Klein and Harris. *Cleveland Plain Dealer*, September 8, 1909, p. 8. A doctor listed his injuries, including "three deep cuts," one to his scalp, his shoulder, and left hand. *Cleveland Plain Dealer*, September 6, 1909, p. 12.

56 *Cleveland Plain Dealer*, September 5, 1909, p. 1C.

57 *Detroit Free Press*, September 6, 1909, p. 7.

58 *Cobb: My Life in Baseball* by Ty Cobb with Al Stump, 1993, Bison Books edition, p.116. *Washington Post*, August 31, 1909, p. 8.

59 *Fort Wayne News and Sentinel*, September 19, 1918, p. 3.

60 Ibid.

61 *Detroit Free Press*, September 17, 1909, p. 8.

62 *The Sporting News*, September 23, 1909, p. 1. Additional reports in the *Detroit Free Press*, September 18–19, 1909 and *Philadelphia Inquirer*, September 18, 1909, p. 1, 10. Baker and Cobb shook hands during the September 17 game after Cobb stole third. 27,814 were present to see the important historical moment of sportsmanship. Jimmy Dykes called Baker an "extremely awkward" third baseman, giving a sort of reasoning for why he was spiked. *The Sporting News*, May 13, 1953, p. 21. During the 1911 World Series, New York Giants outfielder Fred Snodgrass spiked Baker, and the Cobb incident, of course, was remembered. Cobb believed that it demonstrated Baker's ill-advised blocking techniques on the baselines and vindicated him in his own case. *Omaha World Herald*, October 29, 1911, p. 23. Famous pitcher Christy Mathewson explained in another article how Cobb and Snodgrass were guiltless in their run-ins with Baker. *Lexington Herald*, June 16, 1912, p. 5.

63 *Philadelphia Inquirer*, September 21, 1909, p. 10. Cobb told a story of accidently breaking a fan's straw hat during this series and giving the man $5 for it, which undoubtedly earned him some new admirers. *Cobb: My Life in Baseball* by Ty Cobb with Al Stump, 1993, Bison Books edition, p. 117.

64 Ibid. The series ended with Philadelphia winning three of four games and a total of 117,208 fans witnessed the important contests. However, despite the

results, the Tigers would never relinquish first place to their rivals. Connie Mack would lay blame for his team's inability to win the pennant squarely on the injury to Barry, as the shortstop would miss the remainder of the season because of the spiking by Cobb. *Denver Post*, October 1, 1909, p. 11.

65 *Detroit Free Press*, October 1, 1909, p. 1, 8.

66 *Detroit Free Press*, October 3, 1909, p. 1.

67 *Detroit Free Press*, October 5, 1909, p. 4.

68 Cobb's bat, interestingly, was auctioned off and purchased by cartoonist Tad Dorgan for $50. *Detroit Free Press*, October 7, 1909, p. 8.

69 Bourke was a junior partner in the law practice of Navin, Sheahan, and Bourke. Navin, in this instance, was Thomas J. Navin, brother of Detroit Tigers owner Frank Navin. He handled much of the legal duties for the club. Tom Navin died unexpectedly in December 1910 and Cobb was quick to send a message of sympathy to Frank. It was mentioned in a letter to Cobb from Navin dated December 21, 1910, Ernie Harwell Collection, Burton Historical Collection, Detroit Public Library, Detroit, Michigan.

70 Mintz said the settlement amount between Cobb and Stanfield was "so small that I would be ashamed to tell you." *Cleveland Plain Dealer*, September 10, 1909, p. 9.

71 Wagner would win eight National League batting championships during his career, including four in a row from 1906 to '09.

72 *Detroit Free Press*, November 21, 1909, p. 19.

73 *Detroit Free Press*, October 9, 1909, p. 1. A photo of Wagner and Cobb's initial meeting appeared in the newspaper. *Detroit Free Press*, October 10, 1909, p. 23. Bat expert Henry Morrow of the J.H. Hillerich Company, manufacturers of the Louisville Slugger, once claimed Cobb began his career using a 44-ouncer, and then went to a 38-ounce later on. *The Sporting News*, January 21, 1953, p. 17. The same resource stated Wagner used a 38-ounce bat. *The Sporting News*, May 6, 1953, p. 3. For that reason, it isn't known how much of a dramatic difference in the bats of Cobb and Wagner were observed in 1909.

74 *Detroit Free Press*, October 9, 1909, p. 1.

75 In his recollection, Wagner said he tagged Cobb out. *The Sporting News*, April 13, 1944, p. 17.

76 *The Sporting News*, November 11, 1909, p. 4.

77 *The Sporting News*, November 13, 1941, p. 2.

78 *Detroit Free Press*, October 11, 1909, p. 8. Amanda Cobb, R.O. Lombard, and the latter's brother were also in Pittsburgh on October 9 and likely attended Series games. *Detroit Free Press*, October 10, 1909, p. 23.

79 *Detroit Free Press*, October 12–13, 1909.

80 *Detroit Free Press*, October 13, 1909, p. 10.

81 *Detroit Free Press*, October 14, 1909, p. 1.

82 *Detroit Free Press*, October 17, 1909, p. 17.

83 A full breakdown of the 1909 World Series was offered in *The Detroit Tigers*, Frederick G. Lieb, 2008, Kent State University Press edition, p. 125–137. Detroit players earned $1,274.76 for their work.

84 Wagner had eight hits and six stolen bases during the Series. Cobb had six hits, three of them being doubles, and two stolen bases.

85 *Bismarck Daily Tribune*, October 24, 1909, p. 6.

CHAPTER SEVEN: DETROIT'S PRIMA DONNA

1 Comiskey wrote a lengthy article explicitly lauding Cobb's baseball skills. *Denver Post*, April 17, 1910, p. 30.

2 *Augusta Chronicle*, December 27, 1908, p. 9.

3 *Detroit Free Press*, September 19, 1909, p. 19.

4 *Ty Cobb: My Life in Baseball* by Ty Cobb with Al Stump, 1993, Bison Books edition, p. 178–180. It is altogether likely that Cobb also mingled with fans at the Pontchartrain Hotel. He reportedly found "delight in fanning with the local bugs," and "bugs" in this sense was baseball-speak for enthusiasts. *The Sporting News*, April 16, 1908, p. 6.

5 It was said he was going to invest in "Georgia timberlands." *The Sporting News*, October 24, 1907, p. 2.

6 Cobb also owned property outside Brunswick, Georgia. *Detroit Free Press*, March 21, 1909, p. 17. Another report stated his property was two miles from Hazlehurst and that he bought it in 1908. *Boston Herald*, December 13, 1909, p. 4. Hazlehurst is 169 miles south of Royston and west of Savannah. Brunswick is directly south of Savannah, along the Atlantic coast.

7 Cobb's new investment was in the southern part of Jeff Davis County. Ibid. An article located in the *Macon Telegraph* said that George W. Evans lived on the "Ty Cobb place" in Hazlehurst and was growing cotton. He was evidently a renter on Cobb's property. *Macon Telegraph*, June 11, 1912, p. 4.

8 *St. Louis Post-Dispatch*, May 9, 1909, p. 1S. The property was also known as the "Booker T. Washington Heights subdivision."

9 *Atlanta Constitution*, November 9, 1932, p. 20.

10 Notably, Cobb's advertisement for Coca Cola coincided with his first batting championship and with Detroit's initial showing in the World Series in 1907. *The Sporting News*, September 26, 1907, p. 8. Coca Cola was an Atlanta-based organization, originally introduced in 1886, and Cobb would later have a lengthy association with the company.

11 See *Grand Rapids Press*, October 17, 1907, p. 6 and *Muskegon Chronicle*, March 25, 1908, p. 3.

12 Wagner was the first to sign a deal with Hillerich on September 1, 1905, then Lajoie on September 12, 1905. Following Cobb was Eddie Collins (1910) and Frank Baker (1911). Henry Morrow was the central bat contact for players at the company. *The Sporting News*, June 22, 1939, p. 6B.

13 *Detroit Free Press*, April 18, 1908, p. 10.

14 *Cleveland Plain Dealer*, October 16–19, 1909. McKisson served as Cleveland Mayor from 1895 to 1898. He was part of a law firm with William E. Minshall, working out of the Williamson Building.

15 The newspaper called the night watchman, "Frank Stanfield," and said he was "formerly a park policeman." No other information was provided about Stanfield or his background. *Cleveland Plain Dealer*, October 21, 1909, p. 5.

16 "Old Reliable" had been driven to Mexico City and other locations, adding up a mileage of 40,000 prior to the "Good Roads" journey. *Harrisburg Patriot*, November 3, 1909, p. 8.

17 *Detroit Free Press*, October 27, 1909, p. 9. *Wilkes-Barre Times-Leader*, October 27, 1909, p. 12.

18 *Charlotte Observer*, October 31, 1909, p. 7.

19 *Augusta Chronicle*, November 3, 1909, p. 5. The tour itself ended in Atlanta at the headquarters of the *Atlanta Journal*. The *New York Herald* was the other sponsor of the event. Cobb sent a telegram to the Chalmers-Detroit Company, extolling the virtues of the vehicle he drove, and made a point to say that he "arrived first" at the destination. *Augusta Chronicle*, November 7, 1909, p. 12. A few days later, he was involved in a car accident in Atlanta with another member of the Good Roads excursion, but wasn't injured. *Augusta Chronicle*, November 6, 1909, p. 5. Cobb was always a fan of vehicles and speed. He raced around Augusta on a motorcycle on New Year's Day 1909. *Augusta Chronicle*, January 2, 1909, p. 5. A few months later, he was in Texas for spring training, and went for a ride in Murray Raymond's Apperson automobile along with teammates Crawford, Bush, Summers, and Rossman. Raymond apparently was showing off and sped beyond 50 miles per hour before Crawford told him to slow it down. An accident, the Detroit paper noted, would have destroyed the Tigers ballclub. *Detroit Free Press*, April 2, 1909, p. 8.

20 Butt called Cobb and set the meeting up. The Cobb-Taft conversation lasted about twenty minutes. *Augusta Chronicle*, November 8–9, 1909. Butt, a hero in every sense of the word, would later perish in the sinking of the RMS Titanic. Cobb and other members of the Tigers first met President Taft during a visit to the White House on June 14, 1909. *Detroit Free Press*, June 15, 1909, p. 9. The Augusta Country Club, where Taft and Cobb met, is not to be confused with the Augusta National Golf Club, established in the early 1930s.

21 *Daily Capital Journal*, November 5, 1909, p. 1.

22 See *Cincinnati Post*, November 22, 1909, p. 1 and *Cleveland Plain Dealer*, November 23, 1909, p. 10.

23 Letter to Cobb from Navin dated February 24, 1910, Ernie Harwell Collection, Burton Historical Collection, Detroit Public Library, Detroit, Michigan.

24 Ibid.

25 *Detroit Free Press*, October 24, 1909, p. 17. *Detroit Free Press*, March 30, 1910, p. 11. Transaction Card Collection, National Baseball Library, Cooperstown, New York.

26 *Detroit Free Press*, March 30, 1910, p. 11.

27 *Augusta Chronicle*, November 28, 1909, p. 7.

28 *Detroit Free Press*, December 7, 1909, p. 8.

29 *Augusta Chronicle*, December 29, 1909, p. 7.

30 *Detroit Free Press*, December 29, 1909, p. 9. The silver trophy stood about two feet tall and a photo of the prize was featured in the *Detroit Free Press*, October 5, 1909, p. 10.

31 *Augusta Chronicle*, January 15, 1910, p. 10.

32 *Macon Telegraph*, February 1, 1910, p. 7. The Cobbs sent out announcements about their newborn to friends and reporters. *Macon Telegraph*, March 5, 1910, p. 7.

33 *Detroit Free Press*, April 10, 1910, p. 15.

34 Charlie and Ty Jr. joined Cobb in Detroit in May. Charlie joined other Tigers' wives as chaperones for "Blue Star Day," collecting money in the fight against Tuberculosis, at Bennett Park on June 9. *Detroit Free Press*, June 9, 1910, p. 1.

35 Cobb's garage was on Broad Street in Augusta.

36 Letter to Cobb from Navin dated March 29, 1910, Ernie Harwell Collection, Burton Historical Collection, Detroit Public Library, Detroit, Michigan.

37 *Detroit Free Press*, March 24, 1910, p. 8. *Detroit Free Press*, March 29, 1910, p. 8.

38 *Detroit Free Press*, April 4, 1910, p. 4.

39 *Detroit Free Press*, April 9, 1910, p. 9.

40 *Sporting Life*, June 4 and June 25, 1910.

41 *Sporting Life*, June 4, 1910, p. 5.

42 Cobb was late and pitcher Bill Donovan covered for him in center field. *Detroit Free Press*, June 8, 1910, p. 9.

43 *Atlanta Constitution*, January 6, 1926, p. 6.

44 Jones was educated to be a lawyer, and when he got into it with Cobb, displayed his excellent arguing skills.

45 *Fort Wayne Journal Gazette*, February 5, 1918, p. 24. Cobb's hounding of Bush may have started in 1908, when the latter was first breaking into the majors at twenty years of age. Bush played 20 games that year. *Charlotte Observer*, March 14, 1911, p. 2.

46 Bush batted .262 in 1910 with 130 hits, a .365 OBP, and 82 strikeouts.

47 Jones, incidentally, demonstrated his physicality when he fought with Washington Senators manager Jimmy McAleer after a game in June. *Detroit Free Press*, June 9, 1910, p. 9.

48 *The Glory of Their Times*, Lawrence S. Ritter, 1966, p. 42.

49 *Boston Journal*, August 3, 1910, p. 1.

50 *The Glory of Their Times*, Lawrence S. Ritter, 1966, p. 42. Moreover, other sources have claimed the Cobb-Jones hit-and-run argument occurred in the ninth inning, during an important rally. This appears false, as neither Jones nor Cobb went to bat in that inning. Batters four through nine in the line-up went to the plate in the bottom of ninth, and Crawford and George Simmons scored. *Detroit Free Press*, August 3, 1910, p. 9.

51 *Detroit Free Press*, August 7, 1910, p. 15.

52 The Tigers beat Boston, 4–2 on August 4, and New York on August 5, 9–6. *Sporting Life*, August 20, 1910, p. 7.

53 *Detroit Free Press*, August 6, 1910, p. 8.

55 *Detroit Free Press*, August 7, 1910, p. 15. Boston reportedly offered to send Harry Lord and Tris Speaker to Detroit for Cobb, but Navin refused.

56 Detroit won 5–0. When Cobb and Jones went to bat the first time around, the crowd gave them a nice ovation. Additionally, Cobb hit a sacrifice fly to score Jones in the opening inning, which was a "very neat touch to the reconciliation sketch." *Detroit Free Press*, August 7, 1910, p. 15.

57 Ibid.

58 *Detroit Free Press*, June 19, 1910, p. 15.

59 *Detroit Free Press*, August 12, 1910, p. 9.

60 *Detroit Free Press*, July 24, 1910, p. C4.

61 *Detroit Free Press*, September 8, 1910, p. 9. *Ty Cobb: My Life in Baseball* by Ty Cobb with Al Stump, 1993, Bison Books edition, p. 95–96, 101.

62 See *Chicago Daily Tribune*, October 9, 1910, p. C1 and *Detroit Free Press*, October 13, 1910, p. 9.

63 *Cleveland Plain Dealer*, October 10, 1910, p. 1.

64 Detailed coverage appeared in most major American newspapers. Amongst the sources used were the *St. Louis Post-Dispatch, Cleveland Plain Dealer*, and *Detroit Free Press*, October 10–12, 1910. St. Louis journalists were amongst the most fierce in response to the actions of the Browns. R. E. McLaughlin, a St. Louis businessman, was part of a movement to collect money to purchase Cobb his own automobile, if Lajoie was awarded the Chalmers. *St. Louis Post-Dispatch*, October 10, 1910, p. 12.

65 Corriden played 26 games for St. Louis in 1910, including 14 games at shortstop and 12 games at third.

66 *St. Louis Post-Dispatch*, October 11, 1910, p. 15. Lajoie said Cobb wrote a "blistering letter" to Corriden following the incident. *The Sporting News*, February 26, 1942, p. 7.

67 *Detroit Free Press*, October 12, 1910, p. 9.

68 *St. Louis Post-Dispatch*, October 14–16, 1910. While it is difficult to prove either way, it is not unlikely, particularly because Lajoie was well-liked across the majors. Shortly after Lajoie was pronounced the unofficial winner, eight-members of the Detroit Tigers wired congratulations to Lajoie for winning the championship. The classy move was common in those days, and might not have been purposefully done to show preference over Cobb, despite the impression it gave. The names of the eight members of the Tigers who signed the telegram were not revealed.

69 *The Sporting News*, February 26, 1942, p. 7.

70 *Cleveland Plain Dealer*, October 11, 1910, p. 1.

71 *Detroit Free Press*, October 16, 1910, p. 15.

72 *Boston Herald*, October 16, 1910, p. 1.

73 *Canton Repository*, October 27, 1910, p. 6.

74 *The Sporting News*, April 18, 1981, p. 3, 10–11. Amongst the historians to work on the new 1910 Cobb-Lajoie research were Leonard Gettelson, Pete Palmer, and Clifford Kachline, with additional help from the Society for American Baseball Research (SABR). Today, many sources have updated the stats to reflect .384 for Lajoie and .383 for Cobb.

75 MLB.com lists Cobb ahead of Lajoie in the 1910 race with a .385, compared to the latter's .384.

76 *Wilkes-Barre Times-Leader*, September 28, 1910, p. 14.

77 *St. Louis Post-Dispatch*, September 25, 1910, p. 1S.

78 *New York Evening World*, August 12, 1911, p. 7.

79 *Detroit Free Press*, March 27, 1911, p. 10.

CHAPTER EIGHT: THE PSYCHOLOGICAL ADVANTAGE

1 *Detroit Free Press*, September 5, 1908, p. 9.

2 *Detroit Free Press*, June 24, 1910, p. 9.

3 *Washington Post*, September 13, 1914, p. S2.

4 *Atlanta Constitution*, May 20, 1934, p. SM3.

5 *Boston Daily Globe*, June 13, 1915, p. 53.

6 *New York Tribune*, November 7, 1920, p. 9.

7 *Atlanta Constitution*, July 5, 1939, p. 14. It isn't known when Cobb adopted this particular routine. Stambaugh, from Demorest, GA, was a newsreel cameraman and lived for a time in Cleveland. When Cobb would tour through Cleveland with the Tigers, he'd often meet up with Stambaugh, who Cobb saw as a trusted Southern friend.

8 *The Sporting News*, June 19, 1941, p. 5.

9 *Detroit Free Press*, July 22, 1911, p. 8.

10 Other substances were used as well to create the spitball.

11 *Detroit Free Press*, February 19, 1908, p. 7. Joss was injured in 1910 and was set to make his triumphant return when he took ill in April 1911. A short time later, at thirty-one years of age, he passed away. Cobb played in the Addie Joss Benefit Game for his family on July 24, 1911 at League Park in Cleveland, joining Tris Speaker, Eddie Collins, Sam Crawford, Hal Chase, Frank Baker, and many other All-Stars. The latter contingent beat Nap Lajoie and the Cleveland squad, 5–3 and Cobb went 2-for-4. Over 15,000 people were in attendance. *Cleveland Plain Dealer*, July 25, 1911, p. 7. Additionally, Cobb purchased a $100 box at the event, and wrote an organizer to say, "Please don't use my name in the papers," with regard to his donated money. "I want to do all I can for Addie's family, but I don't want to attract any notoriety." The organizer convinced Cobb to agree to use his name and the story became public. *Detroit Free Press*, July 21, 1911, p. 9.

12 *Philadelphia Inquirer*, November 30, 1910, p. 10.

13 *St. Louis Post-Dispatch*, September 25, 1910, p. 2S

14 *Detroit Free Press*, October 19, 1910, p. 9.

15 *The Sporting News*, November 3, 1910, p. 4.

16 A race between Cobb and Rucker was to be held daily from November 3 to November 5, 1910. *Detroit Free Press*, October 20, 1910, p. 10.

17 *Detroit Free Press*, November 4–5, 1910.

18 *Indianapolis Star*, April 5, 1911, p. 10.

19 Matty McIntyre, who had led previous tours of Cuba, was a member of the Detroit contingent. Notably, he was dealt to the Chicago White Sox in January 1911.

20 Habana was also billed as the Habana or Havana "Reds" and Almendares was dubbed the "Blues" in some reports.

21 *Detroit Free Press*, November 8, 1910, p. 9.

22 *Detroit Free Press*, November 28, 1910, p. 8.

23 *Sporting Life*, December 31, 1910, p. 8. Jose Mendez, a noteworthy Cuban pitcher, ·was said to have struck Cobb out "four times in succession" during this tour. *Sporting Life*, November 18, 1911, p. 6. However, according to the December 31, 1910 edition of the same publication, Cobb only struck out once during the series. *Augusta Chronicle*, December 18, 1910, p. 8.

24 *Augusta Chronicle*, December 21, 1910, p. 10.

25 Petway was said to have caught Cobb on the basepaths three times in a single game. *Atlanta Daily World*, August 9, 1939, p. 5. Lloyd and Hill are members of the National Baseball Hall of Fame.

26 *The New York Age*, September 28, 1911, p. 6.

27 Ex-world heavyweight boxing champion James J. Corbett was in attendance. *Augusta Chronicle*, January 13, 1911, p. 4. The trophy was valued at $600.

28 Letters to Cobb from Navin dated February 9, February 23, and March 6, 1911, Ernie Harwell Collection, Burton Historical Collection, Detroit Public Library, Detroit, Michigan. The University of Alabama ballclub refused to play the Tigers unless Cobb was in the game. *Detroit Free Press*, February 7, 1911, p. 9. Cobb's delay was said to be caused by his desire to bring his wife and son to Detroit and set them up in a comfortable residence prior to the launch of the season. *Detroit Free Press*, February 25, 1911, p. 9.

29 *New Orleans Times-Picayune*, March 16, 1911, p. 13. Cobb went 0-for-3 with a walk and a run. Cobb made his first hit of the spring the following day in an 8–0 Detroit win over New Orleans.

30 A Detroit businessman traveling through Charlotte told a local newspaper he had firsthand knowledge that Cobb was ostracized by the entire Tigers franchise and not speaking to anyone. Players were reportedly happy when he failed. *Charlotte Observer*, March 14, 1911, p. 2. The validity of this information cannot be substantiated.

31 *Sporting Life*, April 1, 1911, p. 3.

32 *Sporting Life*, May 6, 1911, p. 1.

33 See *Sporting Life*, April 22 and May 6, 1911.

34 *New York Daily Tribune*, Friday, March 31, 1911, p. 8.

35 *Evening Star*, Washington, DC, April 3, 1911, p. 13. It isn't known if these shoes were the ones he had lead weights implanted in, as mentioned in Chapter Six.

36 *New York Sun*, April 10, 1911, p. 5.

37 The Tigers won 21 of its first 23 games.

38 Detroit beat Cleveland 5-4. *Detroit Free Press*, May 1, 1911, p. 1.

39 *Detroit Free Press*, May 13, 1911, p. 9.

40 *The SABR List & Record Book*, 2007, p. 8.

41 *Detroit Free Press*, May 23–24, 1911.

42 *Philadelphia Inquirer*, June 9, 1911, p. 10. A Detroit report stated Baker wasn't touched by Cobb's spikes in the sixth inning. *Detroit Free Press*, June 9, 1911, p. 9.

43 What Baker did exactly is up for question. There are reports claiming that he successfully booted Cobb, another saying he kicked and missed, and a claim that both men kicked at each other, but didn't make contact. One newspaper stated they stomped on each other's feet.

44 Detroit beat the Athletics, 8–3 and Cobb went 3-for-3. *Detroit Free Press*, June 9, 1911, p. 9.

45 *Evening Star*, Washington, DC, June 9, 1911, p. 14.

46 Willie Keeler and Bill Dahlen had longer consecutive game hit streaks, 45 (over two seasons) and 42, respectively.

47 *Detroit Free Press*, July 26, 1911, p. 12. *Detroit Free Press*, July 5, 1911, p. 9.

48 Cobb had lost sleep for 4–5 evenings. *New York Evening World*, July 20, 1911, p. 12.

49 *New Orleans Item*, August 15, 1911, p. 6.

50 See *Detroit Free Press*, July 29, 1911, p. 8 and *Boston Journal*, August 13, 1911, p. 8.

51 *Harrisburg Patriot*, August 16, 1911, p. 8.

52 *Washington Post*, August 10, 1911, p. 8.

53 *Detroit Free Press*, August 26, 1908, p. 9.

54 *Chicago Defender*, August 12, 1911, p. 5.

55 *The Sporting News*, November 20, 1941, p. 7. Yet another explanation of the Cobb-Jackson situation was offered in *The Sporting News*, September 10, 1936, p. 4. It was reported that Cobb was jealous of Jackson. *Trenton Evening Times*, August 14, 1911, p. 11.

56 Cobb received 64 out of 64 votes by the eight writers representing the different American League cities. Frank Schulte won the National League Award. *Detroit Free Press*, October 12, 1911, p. 10. Cobb and Schulte were given Chalmers "36" models. Cobb's play in 1911 also set a new major league record for hits in a single season, topping Jesse Burkett's 1896 effort of 240.

57 *Cleveland Plain Dealer*, October 13, 1911, p. 7. On September 17, Cobb used his Sunday in New York City to play for a semi-pro "All Star" aggregation against the Metropolitans at the Lenox Oval. Although his team was defeated, 6–4, Cobb went 4-for-5 at the plate and played both first base and pitched. *Jersey Journal*, September 18, 1911, p. 9. Notably, Sunday baseball was outlawed in New York. Cobb's actions of playing for a team outside the Tigers violated National Commission rules and he was fined $100. *Detroit Free Press*, September 30, 1911, p. 9.

58 Cobb's guarantee was rumored to be anywhere from $10,000 to $25,000, but the amount cannot be verified.

59 *Trenton Evening Times*, October 31, 1911, p. 7. *Evening Star*, Washington, DC, November 6, 1911, p. 14.

60 *Trenton Evening Times*, October 31, 1911, p. 7. MacManamy was a Michigan-born actress and had made her stage debut only weeks before joining "The College Widow." *Boston Herald*, May 5, 1918, p. 43. She became Mrs. Sue Kruger and

continued her acting career into the 1930s. Also starring in the play were Martin Woodworth, Howard Teachout, and Robert Hill.

61 As it was described, the widow was "not a widow at all," but an "attractive young girl." MacManamy's character's name was "Jane Witherspoon" and she was daughter of the Atwater College President. Further explanation can be found in the *Cleveland Leader,* January 7, 1912, p. 28. Cobb recalled the play's debut being in Newark. *Baseball Magazine,* March 1912, p. 53–56.

62 *Richmond Times Dispatch,* November 6, 1911, p. 10.

63 *Cleveland Leader,* January 9, 1912, p. 11. As part of his media blitz in Cleveland, he agreed to be "sports editor" of the *Cleveland Plain Dealer* for a day, appearing at the offices of the newspaper on January 10, 1912. A series of articles and comments by Cobb, including his time hanging out with Cleveland's new catcher Paddy Livingston, were printed in the following day's paper. *Cleveland Plain Dealer,* January 11, 1912, p. 10.

64 *Detroit Free Press,* December 24, 1911, p. 13.

65 *Detroit Free Press,* December 18, 1911, p. 8.

66 *Duluth News-Tribune,* December 19, 1911, p. 10.

67 *Detroit Free Press,* December 24, 1911, p. 13.

68 Shirley Marion Cobb was born on June 2, 1911, weighing nine pounds. *Bellingham Herald,* June 4, 1911, p. 13.

69 *Detroit Free Press,* January 1912.

70 *Atlanta Constitution,* December 14, 1924, p. B2.

71 *Detroit Free Press,* May 1, 1912, p. 10.

72 *Detroit Free Press,* July 5, 1918, p. 14.

73 *Sporting Life,* January 6, 1912, p. 11.

74 *Atlanta Constitution,* March 19, 1912, p. 10.

75 *Detroit Free Press,* April 12, 1912, p. 1.

76 *Detroit Tribune,* June 21, 1914, p. 1. *Detroit Free Press,* April 18, 1912, p. 10.

77 Cobb left for Detroit on the 10:40 p.m. train. See the *Chicago Daily Tribune* and *Detroit Free Press,* April 16, 1912.

78 *Detroit Free Press,* April 21, 1912, p. 17.

79 *Detroit Free Press,* April 22, 1912, p. 8.

CHAPTER NINE: BRAWLS AND STRIKES

1 *Fort Wayne News and Sentinel,* September 16, 1918, p. 14.

2 *The Sporting News,* April 16, 1908, p. 6.

3 *Detroit Free Press,* July 3, 1910, p. 13.

4 During the first game of the series, Cobb was awarded the George "Honey Boy" Evans trophy, his third such honor. *New York Times,* May 12, 1912, p. C7. Cobb would also win the 1912 "Honey Boy" Evans trophy, the final year the prize was awarded, on August 25, 1913 at the Detroit Opera House. *Detroit Free Press,* August 26, 1913, p. 10.

5 Cobb claimed he was verbally attacked by Lucker, specifically, as soon as he stepped on the field for batting practice. *The New York Sun*, May 17, 1912, p. 10. Lucker told the press he didn't get to the game until "after the first inning." *New York Evening World*, May 18, 1912, p. 2.

6 U.S. World War I Draft Registration Cards, ancestry.com. Lucker's last name was often misspelled "Lueker," "Lucher," and other variants. Phelon claimed that Lucker was from Georgia and that he actually knew Cobb dating back to their time in the south together. *The Sporting News*, February 27, 1913, p. 4. Nothing further about that assertion could be located. Lucker worked in the headquarters of politician Thomas F. "Big Tom" Foley at 112 Centre Street.

7 *New York Sun*, May 17, 1912, p. 10.

8 Hugh Jennings told a reporter that he heard Cobb called a "half-nigger." *New York Press*, May 16, 1912, p. 1. Lucker stated he heard someone sitting near him call Cobb a "half-coon," and it was yelled while Cobb was still in the field during the bottom of the third inning. *New York Evening World*, May 18, 1912, p. 2.

9 *Fort Wayne News and Sentinel*, September 17, 1918, p. 3.

10 *New York Evening World*, May 18, 1912, p. 2.

11 Ibid. A Detroit report stated Lucker's face was "hamburger" and that he needed a doctor, but added that he wasn't seriously injured. *Detroit Free Press*, May 16, 1912, p. 10.

12 *The Saratogian*, May 20, 1912, p. 3.

13 *Detroit Free Press*, May 16, 1912, p. 10.

14 Ibid.

15 *The Sporting News* stated: "It is significant that New York newspaper sympathy seems to be all with Cobb." *The Sporting News*, May 23, 1912, p. 4.

16 Ibid, p. 1.

17 Ibid, p. 2.

18 Ironically, Johnson was in attendance in New York and witnessed the hubbub personally. He sent Jennings a telegram on the morning of May 16, informing him of Cobb's suspension. *Detroit Free Press*, May 17, 1912, p. 14. Sportswriter I. E. Sanborn wrote: "I don't think Ty Cobb will find a great many sympathizers outside the confines of his own team, for the punishment inflicted on him." *The Sporting News*, May 23, 1912, p. 1.

19 *Detroit Free Press*, May 18, 1912, p. 1.

20 The Tigers players, as part of their telegram to Johnson informing him of their potential strike, stated: "If players cannot have protection, we will protect ourselves." Ibid. If a prolonged strike was to occur, the athletes were considering a barnstorming tour. *New York Evening World*, May 18, 1912, p. 2.

21 Paddy Baumann played center field for Cobb. *Philadelphia Inquirer*, May 18, 1912, p. 10.

22 *Philadelphia Inquirer*, May 19, 1912, p. 15. Before the game, Jennings consulted with John Nolan of the *Philadelphia Bulletin* and the latter reached out to a friend, Aloysius Stanislaus Travers of St. Joseph's College, to help locate a group

of amateurs to take the field. Each of the neighborhood boys would be paid $25 for their participation. Philadelphia manager Connie Mack lambasted the Tigers for their strike, calling them a "bunch of rank quitters." *The Saratogian,* May 20, 1912, p.3.

23 *Washington Evening Star,* May 19, 1912, p. 2.

24 *Philadelphia Inquirer,* May 27, 1912, p. 10.

25 Cobb was said to be a "natural insurrectionist," and that he was "ever predisposed to take the law into his own hands." *The Sporting News,* May 23, 1912, p. 4.

26 Better relations between Cobb and his teammates were fostered by the series of events. After the strike was settled, Cobb made an effort to go to each of his fellow players, and personally thanked them what they had done for him. *Detroit Free Press,* July 19, 1912, p. 12.

27 Cobb was eligible to play at Chicago on Sunday, May 26. *Detroit Free Press,* May 26, 1912, p. 17. The other Detroit players were fined $100 apiece and owner Frank Navin agreed to pay $1,800 to settle things up. *Detroit Free Press,* May 22, 1912, p. 10.

28 *New York Sun,* July 9, 1912, p. 5.

29 Cobb mentioned being followed by a "shadow" and confronting the individual in the New York subway. *Detroit Free Press,* January 25, 1914, p. 20.

30 *Detroit Free Press,* July 10, 1912, p. 10. There was speculation that Lucker would go forward with a charge of assault and have Cobb arrested, and also file a civil suit, but neither occurred.

31 *Detroit Free Press,* August 13, 1912, p. 10. The men reportedly spoke a foreign language. *Cleveland Leader,* August 13, 1912, p. 7. In spite of his knife wound, a knee problem, and an illness, Cobb played in the Syracuse game on August 12, going 2-for-4 with two singles.

32 *Detroit Free Press,* August 13, 1912, p. 10 and *Detroit Tribune,* June 21, 1914, p. 1.

33 *Philadelphia Inquirer,* July 20, 1912, p. 8.

34 Detroit finished the 1912 season with a 69–84 record. Cobb was seventh in league voting for the Chalmers automobile, receiving 17 votes. Tris Speaker and Larry Doyle, representing the American and National Leagues respectively, were recognized as the MVPs. *Detroit Free Press,* October 4, 1912, p. 12.

35 *Ty Cobb: My Life in Baseball* by Ty Cobb with Al Stump, 1993, Bison Books edition, p. 104.

36 *Detroit Free Press,* October 28, 1912, p. 8.

37 *Detroit Free Press,* October 28, 1912, p. 8.

38 *Augusta Chronicle,* March 25 and March 30, 1913.

39 *Detroit Free Press,* February 25, 1913, p. 10.

40 *Spartanburg Herald,* July 28, 1961, p. 14.

41 Ibid.

42 Cobb demanded an apology from Osborne, according to the latter's statement, but he refused. He said Cobb "acted cowardly and overbearing." *Spartanburg Herald,* April 11, 1913, p. 6. One of the reports claimed that Cobb pointed the pistol at Osborne's teammates, asking them if they "had enough." *Spartanburg Herald-Journal,* July 30, 1961, p. C1.

43 *Detroit Free Press*, April 14, 1913, p. 8.

44 *Augusta Chronicle*, April 17, 1913, p. 4.

45 *Augusta Chronicle*, April 20 and April 22, 1913.

46 *The Sporting News*, April 24, 1913, p. 1.

47 Glaser was in Detroit at the time, performing at a local theater when he decided to intervene in the matter. *Detroit Free Press*, April 25, 1913, p. 12.

48 *Detroit Free Press*, April 26, 1913, p. 10. Cobb made $2,000 per month for five months beginning on May 5, 1913, equaling $10,000. Transaction Card Collection, National Baseball Library, Cooperstown, New York. That tied Honus Wagner for the most paid a ballplayer. The Congressional threats to investigate baseball were believed to have influenced Navin to settle the holdout swiftly and amicably.

49 *Detroit Free Press*, May 2, 1913, p. 13.

50 *Detroit Free Press*, July 6, 1913, p. 13.

51 *Detroit Free Press*, July 13, 1913, p. 17.

52 *Sporting Life*, September 27, 1913, p. 2.

53 *Detroit Free Press*, September 1, 1913, p. 8.

54 *Cleveland Leader*, July 5, 1913, p. 10.

55 *New York Sun*, November 2, 1913, p. S2.

56 *Atlanta Constitution*, December 12, 1913, p. 8.

57 *The Sporting News*, May 26, 1938, p. 7.

58 *Detroit Free Press*, November 11, 1913, p. 12. Transaction Card Collection, National Baseball Library, Cooperstown, New York. Cobb, sometime in 1914, caught Navin reading his private telegrams out of fear that he was going to jump to the Federals. *Ty Cobb: My Life in Baseball* by Ty Cobb with Al Stump, 1993, Bison Book sedition, p. 108–111.

59 *Denver Post*, August 27, 1913, p. 8.

60 *Detroit Free Press*, January 19, 1914, p. 10.

61 *Elkhart Progressive Democrat*, March 17, 1914, p. 3.

62 *Gulfport Daily Herald*, March 20, 1914, p. 1, 8. While in Jackson, Mississippi, Cobb addressed the state legislature and attended a reception at the governor's mansion. *Detroit Free Press*, March 27, 1914, p. 12.

63 *Detroit Free Press*, March 25, 1914, p. 10.

64 *Detroit Free Press*, April 15, 1914, p. 1.

65 *New York Sun*, May 15, 1914, p. 5. As a book, *Busting 'Em* was called a "symposium of baseball stories, mostly concerning well-known managers and players of the two big leagues." *Rockford Republic*, July 20, 1914, p. 6.

CHAPTER TEN: BUTCHERING PENNANT CHANCES

1 *Detroit Free Press*, May 21, 1914, p. 10.

2 *Detroit Tribune*, June 21, 1914, p. S3. The Tigers would ultimately beat Washington, 1–0.

3 Ibid.

4 The Cobb Family lived at 164 Longfellow Avenue. They had previously resided in a home at 103 Commonwealth in Detroit.

5 Cobb was aware of the problem with the spoiled fish prior to the game that afternoon. One version of the story had Charlie Cobb ordering the fish a week before on June 13, and, after the three perch were delivered, calling back to complain about their poor condition a few days later. It wasn't until June 20 that she made a third phone call and asked why she was charged 20 cents for the spoiled perch. *Detroit Tribune*, June 21, 1914, p. 1, 2.

6 This was according to Cobb's version. Ibid. Carpenter adamantly denied apologizing to Mrs. Cobb when he spoke with her on the phone. He didn't think there was anything to be sorry for. *Detroit News*, June 22, 1914, p. 1.

7 Ibid. Several Cobb biographers have identified Howard Harding as a black man, but according to information found in the 1900, 1920, and 1940 U.S. Federal Census Records, plus the U.S. World War I Draft Registration Cards, Mr. Harding was a Caucasian. Howard Gerry Harding was born on January 13, 1894 in Warehorn, Massachusetts, the son of William and Clara Harding. He lived with his brother-in-law William Carpenter and his sister Clara at 134 Rosedale throughout the 1920s, and was a veteran of World War I.

8 In a unique sidebar to the series of events, the man Cobb handed his weapon to, decided to run off with it, only to be tracked down by police. *Detroit Tribune*, June 21, 1914, p. 1, 2.

9 Ibid.

10 Ibid.

11 Ibid.

12 Gillespie arrived at the station with Cobb's friend, W. J. Chittenden of the Pontchartrain Hotel. *Detroit Free Press*, June 21, 1914, p. 1.

13 *Detroit News*, June 25, 1914, p. 1.

14 *Detroit Tribune*, June 21, 1914, p. 2.

15 *Detroit Free Press*, August 8, 1914, p. 10.

16 *Evening Star*, Washington, DC, August 25, 1914, p. 12.

17 *Detroit Free Press*, August 26, 1914, p. 10.

18 *Chicago Daily Tribune*, September 8–9, 1914. Cobb took a lot of heat in the Chicago press. He later said that Breton "apologized [to him], saying he wasn't responsible for the stuff that appeared in the news columns." *St. Louis Post-Dispatch*, October 2, 1914, p. 18.

19 *Charleston Evening Post*, February 1, 1915, p. 3.

20 *Detroit News*, June 26, 1914, p. 1. Cobb said he was offered a $100,000 deal by the Federal League to jump sides in the war. *Ty Cobb: My Life in Baseball* by Ty Cobb with Al Stump, 1993, Bison Books edition, p. 107–108. He had a lengthy meeting with Federal League President James A. Gilmore on June 29, 1914, at Buffalo. *Detroit Free Press*, June 30, 1914, p. 12.

21 *Detroit Free Press*, August 12, 1914, p. 10. Transaction Card Collection, National Baseball Library, Cooperstown, New York. The newspaper mistakenly claimed the new three-year deal encompassed only 1915–17, when, in fact, it extended

through 1918. It also erroneously stated that Cobb didn't get a raise. According to the research of Michael Haupert, who compiled a listing of the highest paid players between 1874 and 2012, Fred Clarke was the highest paid in 1915 ($15,050), indicating that Cobb's $20,000 salary didn't kick in until 1916. sabr.org/research/mlbs-annual-salary-leaders-1874-2012. This information disputes the data found on his transaction card.

22 *Macon Telegraph*, December 18, 1914, p. 1, 7.

23 One of his hunting excursions included trap shooting champion James M. Barrett and Vaughan Glaser. *Sporting Life*, September 18, 1915, p. 27.

24 *Macon Telegraph*, May 17, 1914, p. 8.

25 *Baseball Magazine*, April 1916, pgs. 47–58.

26 *Detroit Free Press*, March 21, 1915, p. 17.

27 *Detroit Free Press*, May 2, 1915, p. 17.

28 *Detroit Free Press*, June 4, 1915, p. 14.

29 *Syracuse Post-Standard*, June 4, 1915, p. 14.

30 *Detroit Free Press*, June 10, 1915, p. 11 and *Boston Herald*, June 11, 1915, p. 6.

31 *Evening Star*, Washington, DC, June 19, 1915, p. 8.

32 *Detroit Free Press*, June 20, 1915, p. 15B.

33 *Detroit Free Press*, July 18, 1915, p. 20.

34 Crawford and Veach led the American League in RBIs in 1915, each with 112. Cobb (208), Crawford (183) and Veach (178) were also the top three in hits.

35 *Detroit Free Press*, August 25, 1915, p. 10.

36 *Boston Journal*, September 17, 1915, p. 1, 9.

37 Ibid. At one point during the game, Cobb turned to the center-field rowdies and pointed at the scoreboard, which displayed a comfortable Detroit lead. *Boston Herald*, September 17, 1915, p. 1, 6.

38 Ibid.

39 Ibid. Sportswriter T. H. Murnane of the *Boston Globe* cited the "language" of Detroit players as the central provoking factor in the game. He also wrote that fans "had considerable fun" with Cobb at the conclusion of the contest. *Boston Globe*, September 17, 1915, p. 1, 5.

40 Detroit completed the 1915 season with a 100–54 record, second in the American League, and trailed Boston by 2.5 games. Boston had a 101–50 record and would ultimately defeat the Philadelphia Phillies in the World Series, four games to one. Cobb turned journalist once again and wrote syndicated articles about the Series for the *Baltimore Sun* and, it is believed, other papers. During one of the games, he made a "sensational catch" of a foul ball in the press area. *Detroit Free Press*, October 9, 1915, p. 10.

41 *Detroit Free Press*, September 1, 1915, p. 10. Cobb set a new major league stolen base record.

42 *Detroit Free Press*, January 7, 1916, p. 14.

43 *Detroit Free Press*, September 12, 1915, p. 17.

44 *Augusta Chronicle*, March and April 1916.

45 *Philadelphia Inquirer*, December 23, 1915, p. 12.

46 *Detroit Free Press*, April 3, 1916, p. 10–11 and *New York Sun*, April 3, 1916, p. 8. Cobb and Kauff were said to have had a "friendly" meeting in the hotel. *Fort Worth Star Telegram*, April 2, 1916, p. 14. The Tigers won the series over the Giants, three games to two.

47 *Evening Star*, Washington, DC, May 14, 1916, p. 56.

48 *Detroit Free Press*, May 16, 1916, p. 17 and *Evening Star*, Washington, DC, May 16, 1916, p. 18. Cobb's trip to Washington also included a game on May 13 in which he didn't arrive to Griffith Park until the third inning, apparently unaware of the correct starting time. J. Ed Grillo noted that Cobb was "much chagrined" by the error and upset that he "disappointed" fans and his teammates. *Evening Star*, Washington, DC, May 14, 1916, S1.

49 Heilmann went to center field after Cobb was thrown out. It was said that fans seated in the area where Cobb's bat landed were absent because of an earlier rainfall. The Sox won in the 12th inning, 1–0. *Chicago Daily Tribune*, July 3, 1916, p. 11. The Tigers, in this run of games, lost six-straight.

50 *Detroit Free Press*, July 4, 1916, p. 13.

51 *Brooklyn Daily Eagle*, July 26, 1916, p. S2.

52 Cobb was batting champion in the American League for nine-straight seasons (1907–15). Amongst his achievements for 1916 was his becoming the youngest player in baseball history to record 2,000 hits on June 20, 1916. *The SABR List & Record Book*, 2007, p. 8. He led the majors in stolen bases (68), runs scored (113), and was third in hits (201) behind Speaker and Jackson.

53 Cobb initially agreed to a $350 guarantee to play for the Colonials, but Weiss ended up giving him $800. *Baseball in New Haven* by Sam Rubin, 2003, p. 27.

54 Cobb was fined $50. *Detroit Free Press*, December 9, 1916, p. 11.

55 The film was the first produced by the newly established Sunbeam Motion Picture Company of Cleveland. *Cincinnati Post*, October 26, 1916, p. 3.

56 *Boston Sunday Post*, December 3, 1916, p. D1.

57 Of all his scenes, Cobb was most "bashful" about displaying intimacy with costar Elsie MacLeod. *Boston Sunday Post*, December 3, 1916, p. D1. The movie required four weeks of filming. *Portland Oregonian*, November 22, 1916, p. 10. The movie appeared in theaters during the following spring and summer. *Variety* noted that it had "a good, wholesome atmosphere and a real, live-blooded, clean-limbed athlete for a hero." It added that the story didn't "matter much as Cobb's actions are always closely followed." *Variety*, unknown date in 1917. It has been claimed that Cobb in "Somewhere in Georgia" was the first time a professional athlete starred in a motion picture.

CHAPTER ELEVEN: ALWAYS EXPECT THE UNEXPECTED

1 Cobb did the best against Joe Bush of the Philadelphia Athletics, batting .474 in 11 games. He batted only .253 against the late Addie Joss of Cleveland. *Boston Herald*, December 17, 1916, p. 14.

2 *Boston Daily Globe*, June 13, 1915, p. 53.

3 Sibley wrote that Cobb joshed pitchers from the batter's box, and once he was on the bases, was known to instigate balks because of the frustrations he caused. Ibid.

4 Ibid.

5 *Detroit Free Press*, February 24, 1918, p. 17.

6 *Colorado Springs Gazette*, February 11, 1917, p. 19.

7 *Augusta Chronicle*, January 4, 1917, p. 6.

8 *Dallas Morning News*, March 31, 1917, p. 15. Cobb reportedly played golf at the River Crest Country Club prior to the March 30 game at Fort Worth. He was about 45-minutes late to arrive at the park, and a loudmouth fan got on his case from the audience, shouting that the outfielder had a swelled head and was running on his own time clock. Cobb offered to have a few words with the man in private, but the hostilities quickly ceased. *Fort Worth Star-Telegram*, March 31, 1917, p. 6.

9 *Charleston News and Courier*, April 9, 1917, p. 6.

10 *The Sporting News*, February 22, 1950, p. 12.

11 *Charleston News and Courier*, April 9, 1917, p. 6.

12 "Among other things Herzog insinuated that I was yellow, that I'd be afraid to try to steal second with him on the job," Cobb explained later. *Fort Wayne News and Sentinel*, September 18, 1918, p. 10.

13 *Dallas Morning News*, April 1, 1917, p. 8. A few days after the incident, Cobb told journalist Jack Ryder of the *Cincinnati Enquirer*, "It was not an accident, but if you knew the vile names [Herzog] had been calling me, you would consider it excusable." *Charleston News and Courier*, April 9, 1917, p. 6. However, in 1918, Cobb explained that the spiking was altogether unintentional. "I wouldn't have spiked him even accidentally if he had stayed where he belonged. But he didn't. So I had no other choice than to go into him." *Fort Wayne News and Sentinel*, September 18, 1918, p. 10. Cobb admitted that he wasn't out to hurt Herzog. *Trenton Evening Times*, April 6, 1917, p. 21.

14 Newspaper reports from Dallas, Detroit, and New York City, April 1, 1917.

15 *Dallas Morning News*, April 1, 1917, p. 8. Interestingly, the Detroit press reported that fans were angry when Cobb was ejected. *Detroit Free Press*, April 1, 1917, p. 22. Cobb, playing right field, was replaced by Sam Crawford and New York won the game, 5–3. According to Fletcher, Cobb made numerous threats after being thrown out. *The Sporting News*, February 22, 1950, p. 12.

16 *Trenton Evening Times*, April 6, 1917, p. 21.

17 *Charleston News and Courier*, April 9, 1917, p. 6. Not shockingly, New York papers supported McGraw and the Giants, while Detroit writers backed Cobb. The *Brooklyn Daily Eagle* asserted that Cobb was "responsible for the start of the trouble," and noted that "only the diplomacy of McGraw" stopped any additional fighting between the clubs. *Brooklyn Daily Eagle*, April 1, 1917, p. S1.

18 *Kalamazoo Gazette*, November 7, 1914, p. 6.

19 *The Sporting News*, March 28, 1946, p. 2.

20 *Fort Wayne News and Sentinel*, September 18, 1918, p. 10. Due to the endless number of variations of the Cobb-Herzog fight, there are untold discrepancies

between the stories. Versions include information claiming that Benny Kauff, not Zimmerman, accompanied Herzog to Cobb's room, one that had Eddie Ainsmith as referee, another that had Zimmerman as the official, and yet another with Tigers infielder Donie Bush also in the room as a witness. A more farfetched tale stated that the Cobb-Herzog hotel scrap lasted a half-hour. Needless to say, a half-hour of "rough and tumble" fighting would have likely ended with both men in need of dire medical assistance. *Sporting Life* reported that the scuffle went on for about five minutes. *Sporting Life*, April 7, 1917, p. 6.

21 *The Sporting News*, March 28, 1946, p. 2.

22 *Dallas Morning News*, April 2, 1917, p. 7. The "bad blood" between the two teams was visible outside the Cobb-Herzog scrap. Art Fletcher knocked down Detroit third baseman Bob Jones at one point in the second game, and also had an ongoing rift with Harry Heilmann. Zimmerman and Stanage had a few words as well. *Bay City Times*, April 19, 1917, p. 12. The series ended in a 4–4 tie. *Toledo News-Bee*, April 9, 1917, p. 12.

23 *The Sporting News*, April 5, 1917, p. 1.

24 *Trenton Evening Times*, April 6, 1917, p. 21. Herzog told a reporter in 1919, "We settled our troubles in Dallas and I regard that tiff as a thing of the past. It was man to man, and I don't think that Cobb harbors any hard feelings toward me anymore than I do towards him." *Detroit Free Press*, January 17, 1919, p. 13.

25 *The Sporting News*, January 21, 1953, p. 4.

26 *The Sporting News*, January 14, 1932, p. 4.

27 *Trenton Evening Times*, April 6, 1917, p. 21.

28 *Cincinnati Post*, April 5–6, 1917.

29 *Toledo News-Bee*, April 7, 1917, p. 12.

30 *Toledo News-Bee*, April 9, 1917, p. 12.

31 *Detroit Free Press*, March 30, 1917, 17.

32 *Detroit Free Press*, May 26, 1917, p. 12.

33 Syracuse Journal, May 24, 1917, p. 12.

34 Cobb hit .537 (29-for-54) in a 14-game span. *Detroit Free Press*, June 20, 1917, p. 15.

35 His 35-game hit streak began on May 31 and ended on July 6 and he achieved 64 hits in that stretch. *Detroit Free Press*, July 7, 1917, p. 9. In the game that ended his streak, he faced Red Faber three times and Jim Scott once. It was said that of all active pitchers, Faber, a right-hander, gave Cobb the most difficulty. *Detroit Free Press*, September 9, 1917, p. 20.

36 *Detroit Free Press*, July 6, 1917, p. 11.

37 *Detroit Free Press*, July 31, 1917, p. 9–10.

38 *Detroit Free Press*, July 14, 1917, p. 10.

39 Burns's run in the bottom of the ninth won the game, 2–1, over Washington. *Evening Star*, Washington, DC, August 20, 1917, p. 10 and *Detroit Free Press*, August 20, 1917, p. 9.

40 *Wilkes-Barre Times-Leader*, May 18, 1910, p. 11. *Wilkes-Barre Times-Leader*, June 7, 1910, p. 13.

41 *St. Louis Post-Dispatch*, December 22, 1911, p. 20 and *Detroit Free Press*, May 23, 1915, p. 20.

42 *Boston Journal*, August 24, 1911, p. 5.

43 *The Sporting News*, September 3, 1942, p. 4.

44 It was claimed that neither Cobb nor Jennings joined the rest of the Tigers on the field to honor "Wahoo" during the special ceremony in August, indicative of the bad relations. *The Sporting News*, November 22, 1917, p. 6.

45 *The Sporting News*, January 24, 1918, p. 5.

46 *Fort Wayne News and Sentinel*, September 21, 1918, p. 12.

47 *Springfield Union*, July 18, 1961, p. 23.

48 Interestingly, when Sisler was a member of the University of Michigan baseball team, Cobb went to Ann Arbor and watched him play on May 6. *Detroit Free Press*, May 7, 1913, p. 13.

49 *Detroit Free Press*, December 23, 1917, p. 15.

50 Cobb's third child, a son, was born in Augusta, GA on September 29, 1916. He was named Roswell Herschel Cobb after his grandparents, Roswell Lombard and William Herschel Cobb. *Augusta Chronicle*, September 30, 1916, p. 5. He would go by the name Herschel, however. Most genealogical sources incorrectly list his birth year as 1917.

51 He was the ninth man to register in Augusta. His order number was 1368 and his serial number was 1209. *Augusta Chronicle*, December 28, 1917, p. 5. Also see *Augusta Chronicle*, January 19, 1918, p. 5.

52 In response to the trade rumors, Navin said: "I have often said that Cobb will complete his major league career in a Detroit uniform, and I will reiterate that statement. Cobb will never be sold, traded or released." *Augusta Chronicle*, February 17, 1918, p. 5.

53 *Cincinnati Post*, April 15, 1918, p. 3.

54 *Cleveland Plain Dealer*, April 17–18, 1918. Cobb told a reporter, "It is nothing serious, but I feel so weak that I couldn't play if the doctor gave me permission to." *Detroit Free Press*, April 16, 1918, p. 13.

55 In the opener, Cleveland beat the Tigers, 6–2.

56 *Detroit Free Press*, May 27, 1918, p. 11. Cobb was also injured at New York in July.

57 *Detroit Free Press*, June 9, 1918, p. 15.

58 Cobb entered the game, held on June 3, 1918, to hit for pitcher George Cunningham. *Boston Herald and Journal*, June 4, 1918, p. 4 and *The Sporting News*, June 1, 1933, p. 4.

59 Cobb was said to have made 41 hits in 19 games. *Detroit Free Press*, July 14, 1918, p. 15.

60 *Evening Star*, Washington, DC, July 14, 1918, p. 48.

61 *Detroit Free Press*, August 25, 1918, p. 13.

62 The last game of the season on September 2 marked the final major league contests for "Wild" Bill Donovan, who pitched five innings for Detroit, Hugh Jennings, and Davy Jones. In addition to playing center field and pitching, Cobb also played third base briefly.

63 Cobb received his commission on August 27 in Washington, DC *Detroit Free Press*, August 28, 1918, p. 9. Cobb's official enlistment date into the U.S. Army was September 5, 1918. Georgia World War I Service Cards, 1917–1919, ancestry. com.

64 *Detroit Free Press*, October 10, 1918, p. 13.

65 Ibid.

66 *Fort Wayne News and Sentinel*, September 16, 1918, p. 3. Corbett lauded Cobb's abilities, saying that he was "greater than any of the past generations, the greatest of this; a ballplayer whose like probably never [would] be seen again." *Fort Wayne News and Sentinel*, September 26, 1918, p. 12. There were ten parts to the Corbett-Cobb series.

CHAPTER TWELVE: PATHWAY TO RICHES

1 He called Napoleon, a "remarkable man," and that he never grew tired of "digging up something about his life." *Baseball Magazine*, April 1916, p. 53–54.

2 *Detroit Free Press*, April 2, 1914, p. 10. Ty's mother Amanda also took great pride in the actions of the south during the Civil War and was involved in the United Confederate Veterans organization. *Atlanta Constitution*, May 22, 1925, p. 5.

3 *The Sporting News*, February 12, 1942, p. 10.

4 The newspaper stated that Cobb was the "first Tiger to go overseas for the great cause of democracy." *Detroit Free Press*, October 29, 1918, p. 11.

5 Cobb and Mathewson were joined by Bill Donovan and Hugh Jennings to pitch Third Liberty Loan war bonds at Fort Smith, Arkansas. *Rockford Republic*, April 10, 1918, p. 7.

6 *Ty Cobb: My Life in Baseball* by Ty Cobb with Al Stump, 1993, Bison Books edition, p. 189–192. Research was conducted in effort to substantiate the information provided by Cobb relative to the eight deaths in the training accident, but no independent evidence was located. Cobb indicated that Mathewson's lung injuries were sustained in a singular incident, claiming, "I saw Christy Mathewson doomed to die." Ibid. However, Jane Mathewson, Christy's wife, said his illness developed because he was repeatedly exposed to "lethal gas shells" as an instructor at the camp. Additionally, he suffered from a bad case of influenza around that same time frame, and the combination contributed to his health deterioration in subsequent years. *San Francisco Chronicle*, November 14, 1920, p. 51. Mathewson died at 45 years of age on October 7, 1925 of tuberculosis.

7 *New York Sun*, December 17, 1918, p. 3.

8 Cobb was officially discharged from the army on December 30, 1918.

9 *Baseball Magazine*, April 1916, p. 53–54.

10 *Sporting Life*, October 8, 1910, p. 18.

11 *Detroit Free Press*, October 13, 1912, p. 21.

12 Cobb and Jennings both owned 12.5 percent of the club, Frank Van Dusen, a businessman from Detroit, owned 25, and Navin and Yawkey possessed the remaining 50. *Jersey Journal*, January 13, 1912, p. 9. In February 1922, Cobb

became a part owner of the Augusta baseball franchise with five partners. *Augusta Chronicle,* February 27, 1922, p. 1.

13 One advertisement read, "Bevo is a great favorite in the Army canteens," and "For the boys in Khaki." Underneath was information about Cobb's business. It stated, Ty Cobb Beverage Co., Wholesale Dealers, 313 Leonard Bldg., Augusta, GA. *Augusta Chronicle,* October 5, 1917, p. 5.

14 *Detroit Free Press,* October 20, 1917, p. 12.

15 Cobb's two partners were Bill Sanford and Frank "Shorty" Bussey, hunting buddies, and the business location was 662 Broad Street. Various *Augusta Chronicle* articles September-November 1919.

16 See *Augusta Chronicle,* July 24, 1929, June 16, 1933, and November 14, 1933, for more details about his Augusta holdings.

17 Cumming Street is also 10th Street in Augusta, and the address for the apartments is 1001 Greene Street. The United Apartment Company sold the Shirley Apartments in 1944 to Ways and Means for the Blind for an estimated $46,000, according to the newspaper report. *Augusta Chronicle,* November 21, 1944, p. 9. In his Detroit real estate ventures, Cobb was involved with the William S. Piggins Building Corporation. *American Builder,* March 1, 1927, p. 152.

18 General Motors Corporation Transcript of Stock Account, February 10, 1944, Joseph Hauck Papers (1914–1965), Bancroft Library, University of California, Berkeley, CA. Cobb claimed in his autobiography that he purchased 50 shares in United Motors much earlier than 1918 and that his stock rose to $180 per share. *Ty Cobb: My Life in Baseball* by Ty Cobb with Al Stump, 1993, Bison Books edition, p. 181.

19 Ibid.

20 *Detroit Free Press,* March 6, 1919, p. 5.

21 *The Sporting News,* March 29, 1945, p. 3.

22 The 10-day clause was eliminated from the contract. Transaction Card Collection, National Baseball Library, Cooperstown, New York. Cobb was scheduled to meet the team for a game at Florence, South Carolina on April 8, but missed a train connection, and caught up with the club at Columbia that evening.

23 *Detroit Free Press,* April 10, 1919, p. 14. Cobb played in five games of the Tigers-Boston Braves exhibition series lined up by the latter's business manager, Walter Hapgood, and batted .500. *Detroit Free Press,* April 17, 1919, p. 16. The Braves were managed by Cobb's friend, George Stallings.

24 Detroit led the American League in attendance in 1919 (643,805).

25 *Cleveland Plain Dealer,* April 26, 1919, p. 14.

26 *Chicago Defender,* May 3, 1919, p. 1. The *Detroit New Era* also believed there was an "air of secrecy and suppression in this case." *Cleveland Gazette,* May 17, 1919, p. 2.

27 Ibid, *Chicago Defender,* June 7, 1919, p. 1.

28 Notice of the suit was reportedly served during the ball game against Cleveland on April 26. *San Antonio Evening News,* June 3, 1919, p. 8. An article in the *Chicago Defender* displayed frustrations about a lack of criminal prosecution toward Cobb, and alluded to a possible payoff to keep the matter quiet. Morris was

contacted by a group of lawyers and ministers, trying to offer assistance in what could have been an exceptionally high-profile legal matter. She was said to have refused the help. *Chicago Defender*, May 10, 1919, p. 1.

29 *New Orleans Times-Picayune*, May 30, 1919, p. 14.

30 *Cleveland Press*, November 22, 1909, p. 1.

31 *Chicago Defender*, June 21, 1919, p. 1.

32 Hundreds of sources were searched trying to find a follow-up report to the civil suit, but nothing was located.

33 Cobb battled a midseason left leg injury that hampered his play, and because of the pain, missed some action. One report stated that it was a "large and feverish boil." *Philadelphia Inquirer*, June 19, 1919, p. 14.

34 *The Sporting News*, September 11, 1919, p. 3 and *Detroit Free Press*, September 5, 1919, p. 12.

35 *The Sporting News*, September 11, 1919, p. 3.

36 Detroit finished 1919 with an 80-60 record. A dispute arose between Detroit and New York over the distribution of third place prize money, but after a meeting in Chicago, the Yankees were awarded the funds. *Tucson Daily Citizen*, February 11, 1920, p. 5.

37 *San Francisco Chronicle*, December 24, 1926, p. 19.

38 Cobb's nearest rival for batting honors was his teammate, Bobby Veach, who was 29 points behind with a .355 average. 1919 marked the final time he'd win a batting title. Both Cobb and Veach achieved 191 hits and led the majors. It would be 55 years before another American League player won three consecutive batting titles; Rod Carew accomplished the feat in 1972–73–74. He added fourth title in 1975, and also led the majors in hitting from 1973[replace with en dash]75.

39 *Detroit Free Press*, June 20, 1915, p. 21 and *Baltimore Sun*, October 14, 1915, p. 10.

40 *Evening Star*, Washington, DC, October 1, 1919, p. 23.

41 *Boston Herald*, October 25, 1919, p. 8.

42 *Montgomery Advertiser*, November 30, 1919, p. 7.

43 *Riverside Daily Press*, November 8, 1919, p. 8.

44 *Augusta Chronicle*, October 19, 1919, p. 29. Cobb was also the Georgia, Alabama, and South Carolina distributor for the Peerless Starter, operating out of his Broad Street business. *Charleston News and Courier*, November 2, 1919, p. 17.

45 *Augusta Chronicle*, January 4, 1920, p. 19.

46 *Augusta Chronicle*, March 7, 1920, p. 39.

47 *Greensboro Daily News*, April 1, 1920, p. 8. The series against Boston was another tour scheduled by Walter Hapgood, which was panned for its poor accommodations in backwater towns. *The Sporting News*, January 20, 1921, p. 5. Cobb said his sickness was caused by a diet of milk and cornbread. *Detroit Free Press*, April 4, 1920, p. 21.

48 *Detroit Free Press*, June 7, 1920, p. 12.

49 *Augusta Chronicle*, June 25, 1920, p. 10. But after the gossip began about Cobb's career being finished, Detroit Tigers team physician Dr. William E. Keane

announced that the player had suffered no torn ligaments, and that it was just a bad wrench. *Evening Star*, Washington, DC, June 25, 1920, p. 25.

50 The deal was brokered by Charles H. "Doc" Strub of the San Francisco Seals (Pacific Coast League).

51 Detroit went 8–19 with Cobb out of the lineup. *Detroit Free Press*, July 9, 1920, p. 13–14. Cobb's batting average had improved to .316, although reporters cited that it had taken him two months to reach .300.

52 *Detroit Free Press*, July 16, 1920, p. 12.

53 Chapman, twenty-nine years of age, died at St. Lawrence Hospital. *New York Evening Telegram*, August 17, 1920, p. 6.

54 When he first stepped onto the field, Cobb bowed to the New York audience and motioned toward the newspaper writers, seemingly holding them accountable for the way the entire story was spun. *Detroit Free Press*, August 22, 1920, p. 21.

55 *New York Evening Telegram*, August 21, 1920, p. 6.

56 The show reportedly aired on March 4, 1942. *The Sporting News*, March 12, 1942, p. 12.

57 *Richmond Times-Dispatch*, December 1, 1919, p. 4.

58 The reporter was Scoop Latimer. *Augusta Chronicle*, June 5, 1942, p. 17.

59 *Detroit Free Press*, October 16, 1920, p. 13.

60 Cobb explained that Jennings asked him about the managerial position in 1919. *Portland Oregonian*, October 16, 1920, p. 13. His belief that a player shouldn't also carry the manager's burden went back to, at least, 1912. *Sporting Life*, January 6, 1912.

61 *Denver Post*, June 14, 1920, p. 10.

62 *San Francisco Chronicle*, October 17, 1920, p. S10.

63 *San Francisco Chronicle*, October 23, 1920, p. 7.

64 *San Francisco Chronicle*, October 21, 1920, p. 10. Finn played in the California State League from 1883 to 1888 and managed the San Jose club in 1891–92 when Cobb's friend George Stallings was a member.

CHAPTER THIRTEEN: MICROMANAGER

1 *Boston Herald*, February 10, 1920, p. 9.

2 Ruth was the major league leader in home runs, on-base percentage, slugging percentage, RBIs, runs scored, and a number of other categories. George Sisler of the St. Louis Browns also had a career year in 1920, becoming the first man since Cobb to hit over .400 (.407) and breaking Cobb's single-season hit record with 257.

3 The Dead Ball Era, which arguably began around the turn of the century, ended with the arrival of the Lively Ball Era.

4 *Kalamazoo Gazette*, June 23, 1920, p. 9.

5 *The Sporting News*, February 25, 1943, p. 4.

6 *The Sporting News*, August 25, 1938, p. 4.

7 *Springfield Republican*, April 22, 1920, p. 14.

8 *Collyer's Eye*, October 16, 1920, p. 1.

9 *Detroit Free Press*, October 20, 1920, p. 15.

10 *Salt Lake Telegram*, December 6, 1920, p. 16.

11 *The Detroit Tigers*, Frederick G. Lieb, 2008, Kent State University Press edition, p. 82–83.

12 *The Sporting News*, January 6, 1921, p. 2.

13 *Detroit Free Press*, December 19, 1920, p. 23. Transaction Card Collection, National Baseball Library, Cooperstown, New York. It was reported that Cobb's salary was in excess of $30,000. Ruth's salary for 1921 was $20,000.

14 *Detroit Free Press*, November 18, 1920, p. 16.

15 *Detroit Free Press*, February 2–3, 1921.

16 Ibid.

17 Harry Bullion of the *Detroit Free Press* wrote that Cobb handed out candy and cigars to his players and guys who'd been with him for years, had gotten to know him more than at any time prior. *Detroit Free Press*, March 9, 1921, p. 11.

18 *The Sporting News*, February 10, 1921, p. 3. Also *Ty Cobb: My Life in Baseball* by Ty Cobb with Al Stump, 1993, Bison Books edition, p. 197–198.

19 *San Diego Evening Tribune*, January 19, 1921, p. 14.

20 On March 14, 1921, Cobb delivered a clubhouse speech to motivate his men. According to sportswriter Harry Bullion, Cobb "pledged to fight by their side and if they must sink he would sink too." He told them he would treat them "like human beings," and take them on their honor. Bullion wrote that the entire team, in response, "jumped to their feet and cheered him roundly." Cobb was touched by their reaction. *Detroit Free Press*, March 15, 1921, p. 11.

21 *Fresno Morning Republican*, September 18, 1920, p. 17.

22 *The Sporting News*, January 20, 1921, p. 5.

23 *Detroit Free Press*, March 23, 1921, p. 14 and *The Sporting News*, January 27, 1921, p. 1.

24 A large tree stood in center field of the Brackenridge Park grounds, making play difficult for the Tigers, and Cobb later recommended moving the diamond rather than cut down the tree. *San Antonio Light*, April 7, 1921, p. 13. The Tigers moved over to League Park after the Giants left town. *Detroit Free Press*, March 23, 1921, p. 14.

25 *Ty Cobb: My Life in Baseball* by Ty Cobb with Al Stump, 1993, Bison Books edition, p. 198.

26 The tale was told by sportswriter Dan Daniel. *The Sporting News*, January 24, 1962, p. 10.

27 Stengel said the event happened in 1923, but the Tigers didn't hold spring training in San Antonio that year. In fact, in the spring of 1921, Stengel, who said he witnessed the incident, wasn't yet with the Giants. He was traded to New York from Philadelphia in July 1921. *The Sporting News*, March 30, 1955, p. 6.

28 *Kalamazoo Gazette*, April 22, 1921, p. 19.

29 *Detroit Free Press*, April 15, 1921, p. 12. Cobb delayed the announcement of Dutch Leonard as his starter in the opener until just before the game, in what would be a routine strategy throughout his tenure as manager.

30 Cobb was so disturbed by the 8–3 loss to Chicago that he was barely willing to talk after the game. *Detroit Free Press*, April 22, 1921, p. 12.

31 *Detroit Free Press*, June 13, 1921, p. 9. Ruth's boyhood nickname "Nigger Lips," and other variances, was used by many major leaguers to get under his skin on the field, and Cobb certainly was known to apply these utterances to instigate his rival. Cobb talked about getting Ruth's "goat" in his autobiography, *Ty Cobb: My Life in Baseball* by Ty Cobb with Al Stump, 1993, Bison Books edition, p. 215–218. More about Cobb's nickname can be found in *Pueblo Chieftain*, June 30, 1918, p. 17 and also *The Big Bam: The Life and Times of Babe Ruth* by Leigh Montville, 2007, p. 21, 155.

32 *Brooklyn Standard Union*, June 14, 1921, p. 12.

33 Cobb was said to have spiked himself sliding into second base and needed five stitches. *Detroit Free Press*, July 1, 1921, p. 13.

34 *Detroit Free Press*, July 10, 1921, p. 17.

35 As a result of the controversial umpire decisions, a riot nearly broke out. Fans surrounded umpires Billy Evans and Brick Owens after the game, but no violence occurred. *Detroit Free Press*, July 14, 1921, p. 12.

36 *Detroit Free Press*, September 25, 1921, p. 25.

37 *The Sporting News*, August 15, 1935, p. 4.

38 *The Sporting News*, July 11, 1951, p. 9. Evans's challenge was also acknowledged in the *Philadelphia Inquirer*, December 17, 1921, p. 14.

39 Griffith Stadium groundskeeper James O'Dea was reportedly the "self-appointed referee" for the fight. *Evening Star*, Washington, DC, September 25, 1921, p. 30.

40 *The Sporting News*, August 15, 1935, p. 4. Evans later said: "That Cobb not only is the world's greatest ball player, he could have been a champion in the ring. I thought I was pretty good, but he had it on me all the way." *The Sporting News*, February 1, 1956, p. 21. Cobb only agreed to fight if American League President Ban Johnson wasn't notified and Evans kept his word. Johnson found out about the battle through the press and suspended Cobb for the final two games of the season. *The Sporting News*, October 6, 1921, p. 2. Cobb's eleven-year-old son, Ty Jr., was reported to have witnessed the fight.

41 After Cobb was named Tigers manager, Heilmann was asked what he thought of it. He answered, "None could be better." *Detroit Free Press*, December 26, 1920, p. A1.

42 *Miami Herald*, November 8, 1921, p. 10.

43 *Atlanta Constitution*, May 18, 1924, p. B1.

44 *Ty Cobb: My Life in Baseball* by Ty Cobb with Al Stump, 1993, Bison Books edition, p. 35–36. Also see *Atlanta Constitution*, November 27, 1924, p. 10. Cobb's Aunt Nora, who was the youngest child of John and Sarah Ann Cobb, was only about six years older than Ty, and the two were close. In fact, Nora took him into nearby Murphy and other towns to watch baseball games.

45 She was buried at Notla Baptist Church Cemetery in Murphy, NC. North Carolina Death Certificates, ancestry.com. Her husband, John Franklin Cobb, passed away on June 17, 1911 at seventy-nine years of age.

338

WAR ON THE BASEPATHS

46 *Ty Cobb: Safe at Home* by Don Rhodes, 2008, p. 66.

47 *Evening Star*, Washington, DC, December 2, 1921, p. 31.

48 *San Francisco Chronicle*, October 27, 1921, p. 15.

49 *San Francisco Chronicle*, October-November 1921. Winter League President Frank Chance fined Cobb $100 for delaying the game and $50 for abusive language. *San Francisco Chronicle*, November 21, 1921, p. 10. Another highlight happened on October 25 at Recreation Park in San Francisco when Cobb and Hornsby met on the field for the first time. *San Francisco Chronicle*, October 26, 1921, p. 14.

50 *San Francisco Chronicle*, November 16, 1921, p. 14.

51 The homes, on Carolina Avenue in North Augusta, were rented from the Jackson Family. *Augusta Chronicle*, January 11, 1922, p. 5.

52 Detroit paid $40,000 cash and eight players, equaling $100,000 in total. *Seattle Daily Times*, December 8, 1921, p. 17.

53 *Detroit Free Press*, March 7, 1922, p. 14. Ehmke reversed his negative opinion and told a reporter, "I will be out there doing my best for Ty and the rest of the boys." *Detroit Free Press*, March 31, 1922, p. 12.

54 *Augusta Chronicle*, March 7, 1922, p. 8.

55 *Augusta Chronicle*, March 15, 1922, p. 1.

56 *Detroit Free Press*, April 5, 1922, p. 11.

57 *Detroit Free Press*, May 1, 1922, p. 12.

58 *Boston Globe*, July 7, 1948, p. 11. After the contest, Cobb wrote a letter to American League President Ban Johnson and an investigation was conducted. It was determined that balls had been discolored from oil used on a screen behind home plate, but it had nothing to do with Robertson—and the pitcher was absolved of any alleged wrongdoing. *Detroit Free Press*, May 3, 1922, p. 12.

59 *Detroit Free Press*, May 21, 1922, p. 27.

60 *Detroit Free Press*, May 30, 1922, p. 13 and June 6, 1922, p. 15.

61 *New Orleans States*, May 27, 1922, p. 4 and *Tampa Tribune*, May 26, 1922, p. 8.

62 *Dallas Morning News*, May 27, 1922, p. 13.

63 Cobb went 5-for-6 on July 7, 5-for-5 on July 12, and 5-for-5 on July 17. Adding the game from May gave Cobb the honor four times in 1922, setting a new major league record. *The Sporting News*, September 29, 1948, p. 29.

64 *New York Call*, August 17, 1922, p. 7.

65 *Detroit Free Press*, August 18, 1922, p. 14.

66 *Detroit Free Press*, September 18–19, 1922.

67 The Tigers finished with a 79–75 record, 15 games out of first place. The Yankees were defeated in the World Series by the New York Giants in four straight.

68 *Detroit Free Press*, August 17, 1922, p. 13.

CHAPTER FOURTEEN: THE FIGHTING SPIRIT

1 In the premodern era, nine players bettered Cobb's single-season stolen base record in the National League and American Association.

2 *Detroit Free Press*, April 29, 1924, p. 16.

3 *The Sporting News*, September 29, 1962, p. 13.

4 *Atlanta Constitution*, December 18, 1924, p. 10.

5 *Atlanta Constitution*, October 29, 1933, p. 4B.

6 *Detroit Free Press*, March 6, 1921, p. 22. To combat the wounds he'd receive while sliding, Cobb began sewing sheepskin into his baseball pants around 1912.

7 *The Sporting News*, August 13, 1942, p. 4.

8 Various newspapers, November-December 1922. The Writers' Association voted 5–4 to back Kieran's score and wanted an asterisk on publications indicating that Cobb's average was not supported by the organization. *Baseball As I Have Known It*, Fred Lieb, 1977, p. 68–72. Kieran offered quotes about the matter in *The Sporting News*, February 8, 1940, p. 9.

9 *Detroit Free Press*, September 11, 1922, p. 13. At the time, it was reported that Cobb had passed Lajoie with 3,237 hits on September 1. Lajoie's all-time hit totals were later raised to 3,243.

10 *Detroit Free Press*, April 15, 1921, p. 12.

11 *Detroit Free Press*, May 10, 1922, p. 16.

12 A New York writer claimed that Detroit players were "rough" on the basepaths, and inspired by Cobb. *The Sporting News*, June 5, 1924, p. 4.

13 *Detroit Free Press*, April 2, 1922, p. 21.

14 When Cobb convinced Heilmann to ride Veach, he did it with the caveat that he'd explain the entire concept to Bobby after the season, and smooth matters over between the two. However, Cobb neglected to do so and Veach reportedly maintained a sour relationship with Heilmann from that point forth. *Evening Star*, Washington, DC, July 29, 1963, p. A-13.

15 *Detroit Free Press*, March 26, 1922, p. 26.

16 Jones returned to play in the second game of the doubleheader. *Detroit Free Press*, July 5, 1922, p. 12.

17 *Detroit Free Press*, July 14, 1922, p. 14.

18 *Detroit Free Press*, July 19, 1922, p. 13.

19 Cobb did not like to alter the personal hitting style of his players and didn't unless he was asked. *The Sporting News*, May 17, 1923, p. 4.

20 A local sportswriter claimed that this was only the second time Cobb had ever yielded to a pinch hitter in his career. The lone incident occurred in 1906 when catcher Freddie Payne, a righty, went in to bat against lefty "Doc" White of Chicago. *Detroit Free Press*, May 6, 1922, p. 14. Research indicates that there were at least three other instances of pinch hitters being used for Cobb. Sam Crawford did it on April 24, 1906. Babe Herman reportedly did it sometime during spring training in 1922, and George Mullin was also credited as having done it. Interestingly, for years, Payne was acknowledged as the "only man" to have batted for Cobb. See *Detroit Free Press*, April 25, 1906, February 4, 1911, and June 23, 1912 and *The Sporting News*, December 21, 1944, p. 11.

21 *Baseball As I Have Known It*, Fred Lieb, 1977, p. 72–73.

22 *Grand Rapids Press*, October 31, 1922, p. 16. Ehmke, who finished 17–17 in 1922, achieved a 20–17 record for Boston in 1923. He said, "I am winning because

[Red Sox manager] Frank Chance lets me pitch the way I want to. He never bothers me." His comment was a quip at the constant oversight Cobb gave him in Detroit. *The Sporting News*, October 4, 1923, p. 4.

23 *Evening Star*, Washington, DC, December 15, 1922, p. 30.

24 *The Sporting News*, January 4, 1923, p. 1.

25 *The Sporting News*, March 22, 1923, p. 1.

26 Howley had been Detroit's coach under Cobb's leadership since 1921 and was taking on the managerial job for Toronto of the International League.

27 *The Sporting News*, March 8, 1923, p. 1.

28 *Detroit News*, April 1, 1923, p. D1.

29 *Athens Banner-Herald*, March 1923.

30 *Augusta Chronicle*, March 28, 1923, p. 6.

31 *Detroit News*, April 5, 1923, p. 34.

32 *Augusta Chronicle*, April 8, 1923, p. A2.

33 Johnson was reportedly fired from working any other exhibitions for the Tigers by Cobb immediately after the game, only to be rehired by Ty after the latter had time to cool down. *Standing the Gaff: The Life and Hard Times of a Minor League Umpire* by Harry "Steamboat" Johnson, 1994, Bison Books edition, p. 51–54.

34 *Augusta Chronicle*, April 8, 1923, p. A2.

35 *Detroit News*, April 19, 1923, p. 36.

36 *Detroit News*, May 19, 1923, p. 14.

37 *The Sporting News*, May 24, 1923, p. 1.

38 *The Sporting News*, June 7, 1923, p. 4.

39 *The Sporting News*, June 21, 1923, p. 1.

40 The writer defended Cobb, stated that Ty had always given his best to the fans of Detroit, and wondered why he was being insulted in such a manner. *The Sporting News*, June 14, 1923, p. 1.

41 *Detroit News*, July 8, 1923, p. D1.

42 *Detroit News*, July 25, 1923, p. 29. Cobb scored that inning as well, and the Tigers won both games of the doubleheader versus Chicago. The White Sox pitcher was Sloppy Thurston. Ruth's famous called shot home run occurred during the 1932 World Series.

43 Superstition played a key role in the rally of Detroit players during the 1923 season. While in Chicago in July, a mixed breed dog wandered into the Tigers clubhouse and walked across the team's bats, which were lying on the floor. Detroit went on to win that day's game, and the players decided to adopt the good-luck animal, naming it "Victory." *Detroit News*, July 26–29, 1923. The dog went on the road with the team. Victory was mentioned again by the press at the start of the 1924 season, indicating that it was continuing on as the team's mascot. *Detroit Free Press*, April 16, 1924, p. B2. Each of Detroit's players was awarded $1,078 as part of the second place World Series money.

44 *Atlanta Constitution*, August 8, 1923, p. 8.

45 *The Sporting News*, May 31, 1923, p. 1.

46 According to the report, Cobb hit Francis twice with an open hand, and Francis returned with a punch square to Cobb's nose. The Cleveland crowd booed Cobb in the aftermath of the fight. *Cleveland Plain Dealer*, September 8, 1923, p. 14.

47 Francis went 5–8 in 33 games for the Tigers in 1923. Following the season, he was sold to Atlanta. *The Sporting News*, December 27, 1923, p. 1.

48 The record fell in the first game of a doubleheader and Cobb went 4-for-4 in the contest. *The Sporting News*, September 27, 1923, p. 1.

49 *The Sporting News*, November 22, 1923, p. 6.

50 *Charleston Evening Post*, December 28, 1923, p. 15.

51 Collins went 3–7 and Pillette had a record of 14–19. Cobb worked with Pillette prior to the 1923 season, trying to get him to add a curve ball to his repertoire. But with the new pitch, he began to suffer control problems. *Detroit Free Press*, April 13, 1924, p. 24.

52 Wingo hit 34 home runs for Toronto in 1922 and 20 in 1923. His purchase reportedly cost the Tigers $50,000. *Springfield Republican*, August 21, 1923, p. 8.

53 *The Sporting News*, February 28, 1924, p. 1. Gehringer was reportedly discovered by Bobby Veach, and, after seeing him for the first time, Cobb was more than impressed. He considered Gehringer to be the "best prospect" he'd ever seen. *The Sporting News*, April 10, 1941, p. 9. Cobb convinced Frank Navin to quickly sign him to a contract.

54 *The Sporting News*, March 27, 1924, p. 1.

55 *Detroit Free Press*, May 3, 1924, p. 15.

56 The Cobb "Day" celebration was arranged by Michigan Congressman Robert H. Clancy of Detroit. 130 members of Congress were at the game to honor Cobb and Ty was presented with a collection of books, one for each year of his baseball career. *Detroit Free Press*, May 8 and May 11, 1924.

57 *Detroit Free Press*, May 17, 1924, p. 15.

58 *Philadelphia Inquirer*, May 17, 1924, p. 20.

59 *Pittsburgh Courier*, May 24, 1924, p. 10.

60 *Brooklyn Standard Union*, June 14, 1924, p. 8.

61 *New York Sun*, June 14, 1924, p. 15 and *The Sporting News*, June 19, 1924, p. 1.

CHAPTER FIFTEEN: FADING FROM CONTENTION

1 *Detroit News*, May 13, 1923, p. D2.

2 Ibid.

3 Walsh explained the situation in *The Sporting News*, January 20, 1938, p. 5.

4 *Seattle Daily Times*, October 6, 1924, p. 19.

5 The Yankees were tied for first place on September 18, 1924, but lost their next three games at Detroit, falling to second place, where they'd remain the remainder of the season.

6 *Atlanta Constitution*, October 20, 1924, p. 7.

7 Cobb earned $35,000 for 1922, and then received a $40,000, three-year deal, in 1923. Transaction Card Collection, National Baseball Library, Cooperstown, New York.

8 *The Sporting News*, January 1, 1925, p. 1.

9 *Atlanta Constitution*, February 28, 1925, p. 1. Due to conflicting newspaper reports, there remains a question of whether the incident in the restaurant occurred on February 26 or February 27.

10 *Atlanta Constitution*, March 1, 1925, p. 14.

11 Ibid. It isn't known whether anything further transpired relative to this case.

12 *Atlanta Constitution*, March 12, 1925, p. 10.

13 *Detroit Free Press*, March 17, 1925, p. 16.

14 *Detroit Free Press*, March 12, 1925, p. 14 and *The Sporting News*, March 19, 1925, p. 1.

15 *Boston Herald*, April 10, 1925, p. 31.

16 *Detroit Free Press*, April 21, 1925, p. 16.

17 *The Sporting News*, May 7, 1925, p. 3.

18 *Detroit Free Press*, May 5, 1925, p. 18.

19 *The Sporting News*, December 27, 1961, p. 11–12. Cobb offered a version of this story in his autobiography, but claimed it happened in 1926. *Ty Cobb: My Life in Baseball* by Ty Cobb with Al Stump, 1993, Bison Books edition, p. 237.

20 *Detroit Free Press*, May 6–7, 1925.

21 *Detroit Free Press*, May 8, 1925, p. 17.

22 *Detroit Free Press*, May 7, 1925, p. 18.

23 *Detroit Free Press*, May 8, 1925, p. 17.

24 *Detroit Free Press*, June 20, 1925, p. 14 and *Detroit Free Press*, July 10, 1925, p. 15. Cobb did a fair share of boxing while a member of the Tigers, working out heavily with team trainer Harry Tuthill. *Atlanta Constitution*, December 22, 1924, p. 9.

25 *The Sporting News*, July 16, 1925, p. 1.

26 *The Sporting News*, July 2, 1925, p. 4.

27 Baseball-reference.com.

28 Two different crowd estimates were published at the time – one claiming 20,000 and the other 30,000. *Detroit Free Press*, August 30, 1925, p. 1, 21. The banquet was held at the Book-Cadillac Hotel.

29 *The Sporting News*, September 3, 1925, p. 4.

30 *Detroit Free Press*, August 30, 1925, p. 1.

31 *The Sporting News*, July 9, 1925, p. 3.

32 *Boston Herald*, October 8, 1925, p. 15.

33 *Boston Herald*, October 27, 1925, p. 20.

34 *Augusta Chronicle*, December 29, 1925, p. 3.

35 *Augusta Chronicle*, February 22, 1926, p. 5.

36 *The Sporting News*, January 20, 1938, p. 5.

37 *Augusta Chronicle*, March 2, 1926, p. 6.

38 *Augusta Chronicle*, March 17, 1926, p. 8. Cobb discussed his eye troubles in *Ty Cobb: My Life in Baseball* by Ty Cobb with Al Stump, 1993, Bison Books edition, p. 235–240.

39 *The Sporting News*, September 21, 1933, p. 4.
40 *Freeport Daily Review*, January 29, 1925, p. 5.
41 *Augusta Chronicle*, April 4, 1926, p. 3.
42 *Atlanta Constitution*, April 5, 1926, p. 3.
43 *The Sporting News*, April 15, 1926, p. 1.
44 *Detroit Free Press*, April 28, 1926, p. 19.
45 *Springfield Republican*, May 12, 1926, p. 16.
46 *Detroit Free Press*, May 9, 1926, p. 21.
47 *The Sporting News*, May 20, 1926, p. 1.
48 *The Sporting News*, May 27, 1926, p. 4.
49 *Ty Cobb: My Life in Baseball* by Ty Cobb with Al Stump, 1993, Bisons Book edition, p. 217–218.
50 *San Mateo Times*, August 18, 1931, p. 8.
51 *Detroit Free Press*, May 10, 1926, p. 17.
52 *Detroit Free Press*, June 4, 1926, p. 17.
53 *Detroit Free Press*, June 20, 1926, p. 21.
54 *Detroit Free Press*, July 24, 1926, p. 14.
55 *The Sporting News*, August 5, 1926, p. 4.
56 *The Sporting News*, October 7, 1926, p. 1.

CHAPTER SIXTEEN: OLD MAN COBB

1 Cobb's group met up with local trapping legend Max Wilde and ventured into the Thorofare Wilderness, where Cobb scored a silver-tip grizzly bear, moose, buck deer, and elk. *Cody Enterprise*, January 12, 1927, p. 5.
2 *Omaha World Herald*, September 29, 1926, p. 22.
3 Ibid.
4 *Rockford Republic*, December 23, 1926, p. 12.
5 *Winston-Salem Journal*, December 22, 1926, p. 16.
6 *Boston Herald*, September 23, 1925, p. 14.
7 *The Sporting News*, August 13, 1925, p. 2.
8 *Winston-Salem Journal*, December 22, 1926, p. 16.
9 Senators-White Sox series at Chicago was held from June 12 to June 16, 1926. *Cleveland Plain Dealer*, December 30, 1926, p. 16.
10 Cobb believed several West Coast papers had been offered the letters as well. *San Francisco Chronicle*, December 22, 1926, p. 6.
11 *Cleveland Plain Dealer*, December 30, 1926, p. 16.
12 *San Francisco Chronicle*, December 22, 1926, p. 6.
13 Ibid.
14 *The Sporting News*, December 30, 1926, p. 3.
15 Ibid.
16 Leonard claimed he was owed money for the 1922 and 1923 seasons, plus a portion of 1924, time in which he was blacklisted from Organized Baseball.

Leonard denied he was paid the money for the letters themselves, even though most people figured that was the case. *Chicago Daily Tribune,* December 29, 1926, p. 19.

17 *San Francisco Chronicle,* December 30, 1926, p. 21.

18 *Evening Star,* Washington, DC, January 17, 1927, p. 28.

19 Speaker resigned as manager of the Cleveland Indians on November 29, 1926. *Cleveland Plain Dealer,* November 30, 1926, p. 1. Cobb later said he "never resigned" from Detroit. *New York Times,* January 29, 1927, p. 11.

20 Ibid.

21 *The Sporting News,* November 4, 1926, p. 1.

22 *Boston Herald,* November 4, 1926, p. 14.

23 *New York Times,* December 6, 1926, p. 31.

24 *New York Times,* December 22, 1926, p. 1. It was stated that a newspaper wanted to break the story and told Landis that either he revealed his information, or they'd spill the beans themselves.

25 *Rockford Republic,* December 23, 1926, p. 12.

26 Cobb claimed his salary was $50,000 a year, but Navin wanted it officially recorded as $40,000. Navin agreed to give him the other $10,000 under the table, after the season. Ibid. According to the records on file at the National Baseball Hall of Fame, Cobb earned $40,000 for 1926. Transaction Card Collection, National Baseball Library, Cooperstown, New York.

27 *Riverside Daily Press,* December 22, 1926, p. 12.

28 *The Sporting News,* December 30, 1926, p. 3.

29 *Cleveland Plain Dealer,* December 22, 1926 and *Omaha World Herald,* December 23, 1926.

30 *The Sporting News,* December 30, 1926, p. 1.

31 Cobb and Speaker appeared before Judge Landis in Chicago on December 21 and offered testimony. Leonard was asked to be there, but refused. *New York Times,* December 22, 1926, p. 1.

32 *Pittsburgh Courier,* January 1, 1927, p. A7.

33 *New York Times,* January 28, 1927, p. 11.

34 *Ty Cobb: My Life in Baseball* by Ty Cobb with Al Stump, 1993, Bison Books edition, p. 248.

35 *New York Times,* January 29, 1927, p. 11. Cobb called it his "vindication year."

36 Brooklyn of the National League reportedly offered Cobb $50,000, but it was clear that he was going to remain in the American League. *Brooklyn Standard Union,* February 7, 1927, p. 10. St. Louis Browns manager Dan Howley also visited Cobb in Augusta trying to get him to sign.

37 *Ty Cobb: My Life in Baseball* by Ty Cobb with Al Stump, 1993, Bison Books edition, p. 249–250.

38 Transaction Card Collection, National Baseball Library, Cooperstown, New York.

39 *Detroit Free Press,* June 13, 1915, p. 15.

40 *New York Sun,* February 9, 1927, p. 44.

41 *The Sporting News,* March 12, 1947, p. 28.

42 *Boston Herald,* March 18, 1927, p. 22.

43 *Philadelphia Inquirer,* April 24, 1927, p. S6. Cobb stole home on April 19 and April 26.

44 *Philadelphia Inquirer,* May 1, 1927, p. S6.

45 *Philadelphia Inquirer,* May 7, 1927, p. 22.

46 *Philadelphia Inquirer,* May 9, 1927, p. 18. Both Cobb and Al Simmons were suspended and fined for the Ormsby incident, and Ban Johnson, in his statement, cited Cobb's "lack of intelligence in bumping the umpire."

47 *Philadelphia Inquirer,* May 11, 1927, p. 24.

48 *Philadelphia Inquirer,* May 22, 1927, p. S10.

49 The achievement came in the first inning when Cobb hit a double off Sam Gibson. *Philadelphia Inquirer,* July 19, 1927, p. 18.

50 *Philadelphia Inquirer,* July 22, 1927, p. 19.

51 *Philadelphia Inquirer,* September 28, 1927, p. 25.

52 *Philadelphia Inquirer,* September 22, 1927, p. 20.

53 *Philadelphia Inquirer,* November 3, 1927, p. 24. The Athletics were financially hurt by the fact that Sunday baseball was outlawed in Philadelphia.

54 Ibid.

55 *Richmond Times Dispatch,* March 2, 1928, p. 9.

56 *Augusta Chronicle,* March 2, 1928, p. 1. Also Transaction Card Collection, National Baseball Library, Cooperstown, New York.

57 *The Sporting News,* April 5, 1928, p. 1.

58 *Boston Herald,* April 8, 1928, p. 22.

59 *The Sporting News,* April 12, 1928, p. 1.

60 *The Sporting News,* April 16, 1947, p. 5.

61 *The Sporting News,* February 4, 1953, p. 8.

62 *Tampa Tribune,* September 12, 1928, p. 13.

63 *Philadelphia Inquirer,* September 18, 1928, p. 24.

64 *San Francisco Chronicle,* September 19, 1928, p. 27.

65 *Philadelphia Inquirer,* September 19, 1928, p. 12.

CHAPTER SEVENTEEN: IMMORTALIZED IN BRONZE

1 *Atlanta Constitution,* June 8, 1913, p. 7.

2 *Pittsburgh Courier,* February 16, 1946, p. 14.

3 *The Sporting News,* June 25, 1942, p. 5.

4 *Atlanta Constitution,* March 25, 1931, p. 14.

5 *Atlanta Constitution,* June 30, 1941, p. 6.

6 Artist Robert Ripley fashioned a drawing of Cobb standing with his hands behind his back, his head slightly bowed, watching the rush of players headed for spring training. It read, "For the first time in twenty-five years, Cobb is not going with them." It appeared in Associated Newspapers and *The Sporting News,* February 7, 1929, p. 4.

7 *Ty Cobb: Safe at Home* by Don Rhodes, 2008, p. 161.

8 It was said that Cobb was paid a "considerable sum" of money to venture to overseas. *San Francisco Chronicle*, December 12, 1928, p. 27. The pay might've been as high as $15,000.

9 Johnson had reservations for the ship departing Seattle on October 20. *Seattle Daily Times*, October 18, 1928, p. 30.

10 *Seattle Daily Times*, October 20, 1928, p. 9. During his time in Seattle, Cobb posed for a publicity photograph wearing an Osaka baseball uniform.

11 Hunter, based on his experience, was the tour manager, while Putnam did PR work and handled box office affairs.

12 Four games were played in Osaka, four at Tokyo, and one at Kyoto. While in Japan, Cobb wore the uniforms of the Daimai and Tokyo teams.

13 *San Francisco Chronicle*, December 13, 1928, p. 29.

14 The St. Louis Browns were managed by Cobb's friend Dan Howley and Ty made an appearance at West Palm Beach. *The Sporting News*, March 28, 1929, p. 1. The Orioles trained at Augusta. *Augusta Chronicle*, March 19, 1929, p. 8.

15 *Rockford Morning Star*, June 16, 1929, p. 39.

16 *Rockford Morning Star*, December 12, 1929, p. 16.

17 New York Passenger Lists, ancestry.com and *Dallas Morning News*, September 12, 1929, p. 21.

18 *Detroit Free Press*, October 11, 1908, p. 23.

19 *Boston Sunday Post*, December 3, 1916, p. D1.

20 *Ty Cobb: Safe at Home* by Don Rhodes, 2008, p. 66.

21 Ibid.

22 In 1912, Ty Jr. told a reporter that he didn't plan to play baseball. *Augusta Chronicle*, October 29, 1912, p. 7.

23 *Baseball Magazine*, April 1916, p. 47–58.

24 *Rockford Daily Register Gazette*, August 1, 1928, p. 16.

25 *Atlanta Constitution*, April 7, 1930, p. 16.

26 Jimmy Cobb said that his father wanted either him or Herschel "to follow baseball as a profession." *Baton Rouge Advocate*, June 20, 1943, p. 7B.

27 *The Sporting News*, May 20, 1937, p. 13.

28 *Canton Repository*, November 18, 1929, p. 17.

29 *Charlotte Observer*, October 3, 1929, p. 17.

30 McCallum claimed Cobb made a bid for the Cincinnati Reds prior to going to Europe in 1929. *The Tiger Wore Spikes*, John McCallum, 1956, p. 185. There was also talk of Cobb investing in the Philadelphia Phillies. Reynold H. Greenberg, a Philadelphia real estate magnate and Cobb's partner in the deal, explained just how close they were to making the purchase in *The Sporting News*, October 4, 1950, p. 7. Also see *Greensboro Record*, December 4, 1930, p. 20.

31 Cobb and Ruth also sat in close proximity during the 1930 World Series between Philadelphia and St. Louis.

32 *Greensboro Record*, May 22, 1929, p. 10.

33 *Augusta Chronicle*, April 2, 1930, p. 9.

34 *Chicago Defender*, May 17, 1930, p. 9.

35 Cobb wore a Philadelphia Athletics uniform during the game. *Boston Herald*, September 9, 1930, p. 30.

36 *Augusta Chronicle*, April 16, 1931, p. 2.

37 Ibid.

38 *Greensboro Daily News*, April 18, 1931, p. 6.

39 *Macon Telegraph*, April 26, 1931, p. 7.

40 *San Francisco Chronicle*, April 30, 1931, p. 7.

41 At least one article claimed that Cobb drove west with his "family" in June, however, the various reports of this trip are vague. Charlie and her children were present for her mother's seventieth birthday barbeque in Augusta in early August, and unless the family drove with Ty to California, and then took a train or flew back prior to this gathering, they never left at all. See *San Francisco Chronicle*, June 19, 1931 and *Augusta Chronicle*, August 4, 1931.

42 *The Sporting News*, July 6, 1939, p. 4.

43 *San Francisco Chronicle*, August 17, 1931, p. 21.

44 *San Francisco Chronicle*, February 15, 1937, p. 23.

45 *Augusta Chronicle*, June 28, 1932, p. 3, Georgia Death Index, ancestry.com.

46 *San Diego Evening Tribune*, July 11, 1932, p. 19. It was initially reported that Cobb had rented a property on Almendral Avenue. The paper indicated that his family still hadn't arrived from Georgia. *San Mateo Times and Daily News Leader*, October 19, 1932, p. 5. The Cobbs ultimately moved to 48 Spencer Lane, not far from Almendral, into a "Spanish style" estate.

47 *Baton Rouge Advocate*, October 14, 1930, p. 9.

48 *Charlotte Observer*, August 18, 1924, p. 13.

49 *Philadelphia Inquirer*, November 3, 1927, p. 24.

50 *The Sporting News*, December 7, 1933 and December 28, 1933.

51 Joseph Hauck Papers (1914–1965), Bancroft Library, University of California, Berkeley, California.

52 *San Francisco Chronicle*, February 6, 1934, p. 15.

53 *The Sporting News*, February 15, 1934, p. 4.

54 *The Sporting News*, April 5, 1934, p. 4.

55 *The Sporting News*, May 24, 1934, p. 4.

56 *Evening Star*, Washington, DC, August 19, 1934, p. 22. Amanda Cobb's Royston property was sold in 1925 by the Oglesby Realty Auction Company. *Atlanta Constitution*, April 19, 1925, p. 15.

57 *Denver Post*, June 27, 1912, p. 11.

58 The inaugural class (1936) included Cobb, Honus Wagner, Babe Ruth, Christy Mathewson, and Walter Johnson. See Chapter 1 for additional information.

59 *The Sporting News*, February 20, 1936 and February 27, 1936.

60 *Boston Herald*, June 12, 1939, p. 14.

61 *New York Post*, June 13, 1939, p. 2.

62 *Cleveland Plain Dealer*, June 13, 1939, p. 16. Also *Otsego Farmer and Otsego Republican*, June 16, 1939, p. 1.

63 *New York Post*, June 13, 1939, p. 2.

64 Dan Holmes offered another perspective on his tardiness: blog.detroitathletic. com/2013/01/16/the-story-behind-ty-cobbs-late-tardy-arrival-to-his-hall-of-fame-induction

65 Ibid.

66 *Augusta Chronicle*, June 14, 1939, p. 6.

67 *Omaha World Herald*, June 15, 1939, p. 21.

CHAPTER EIGHTEEN: THE DEPRESSED PHILANTHROPIST

1 *Atlanta Constitution*, January 21, 1923 and November 3, 1945.

2 *The Sporting News*, February 14, 1946, p. 22.

3 Cobb was shown around the vaults during his trip to the National Treasury in 1913 and the story gained widespread news after officials banned such tours by non-employees in the future. *Detroit Free Press*, September 24, 1913, p. 13.

4 *The Sporting News*, February 17, 1938, p. 4.

5 Joseph Hauck Papers (1914–1965), Bancroft Library, University of California, Berkeley, California.

6 *The Sporting News*, November 11, 1937, p. 3.

7 *The Sporting News*, March 25, 1937 and March 22, 1961.

8 *San Luis Obispo Daily Telegram*, April 1, 1941, p. 5.

9 *Omaha World Herald*, April 30, 1941, p. 27.

10 *Boston Herald*, June 26, 1941, p. 16.

11 *The Sporting News*, July 3, 1941, p. 10.

12 *New York Sun*, June 28, 1941, p. 30 and *Brooklyn Eagle*, June 28, 1941, p. 10.

13 Ruth turned down a cross-country golf tour with Cobb because "travelling gets me down," he said. *Boston Herald*, June 25, 1941, p. 17. Cobb talked about his series with Ruth at length in his autobiography, *Ty Cobb: My Life in Baseball* by Ty Cobb with Al Stump, 1993, Bison Books edition, p. 218–222.

14 *San Francisco Chronicle*, July 30, 1941, p. 19 and *The Sporting News*, August 7, 1941, p. 12.

15 *The Sporting News*, April 2, 1942, p. 1.

16 *The Sporting News*, April 16, 1942, p. 8.

17 Letter from N.J.L. Pieper to Director, FBI, Washington, DC, dated March 28, 1942, FBI Case File 94-4-5663 on Tyrus R. Cobb, National Archives and Records Administration, College Park, Maryland.

18 Letter from J. Edgar Hoover to N.J.L. Pieper, dated April 10, 1942, FBI Case File 94-4-5663 on Tyrus R. Cobb, National Archives and Records Administration, College Park, Maryland.

19 Letter from J. Edgar Hoover to Tyrus Raymond Cobb, dated April 10, 1942, FBI Case File 94-4-5663 on Tyrus R. Cobb, National Archives and Records Administration, College Park, Maryland.

20 Letter from N.J.L. Pieper to Director, FBI, Washington, DC, dated June 25, 1942, FBI Case File 94-4-5663 on Tyrus R. Cobb, National Archives and Records Administration, College Park, Maryland.

21 Office Memorandum, United States Government, dated January 27, 1954, FBI Case File 94-4-5663 on Tyrus R. Cobb, National Archives and Records Administration, College Park, Maryland.

22 *El Paso Herald Post*, August 30, 1943, p. 10.

23 *Augusta Chronicle*, September 27, 1944, p. 5 and *The Sporting News*, January 25, 1945, p. 4.

24 *The Sporting News*, July 15, 1943, p. 16.

25 *The Sporting News*, February 10, 1944, p. 14.

26 *The Sporting News*, January 18, 1945, p. 12.

27 *The Sporting News*, February 15, 1945, February 22, 1945, May 10, 1945.

28 *The Sporting News*, April 5, 1945, p. 4.

29 *The Sporting News*, April 30, 1936, p. 2.

30 *The Sporting News*, July 22, 1943, p. 9.

31 *The Sporting News*, September 21, 1944, p. 13.

32 *The Sporting News*, August 30, 1945, p. 14.

33 *Brooklyn Daily Eagle*, August 29, 1945, p. 17.

34 Letter from Cobb to Joe Hauck, dated May 20, 1947, Joseph Hauck Papers (1914–1965), Bancroft Library, University of California, Berkeley, California. Also see *The Sporting News*, April 7, 1948, p. 25.

35 Charlie later moved to 1210 Bay Laurel Road in Menlo Park, where she lived in 1947.

36 *San Mateo Times*, March 7, 1947, p. 1. Charlie Cobb signed the court documents, "Mrs. Tyrus Raymond Cobb." *Mrs. Tyrus Raymond Cobb v. Tyrus Raymond Cobb, et al.*, Case No. 42755, Superior Court of the State of California in and for the County of San Mateo, Filed March 7, 1947.

37 Letter from Cobb to Joe Hauck, dated May 20, 1947, Joseph Hauck Papers (1914–1965), Bancroft Library, University of California, Berkeley, California.

38 Ty filed the second suit in June 1947 in Nevada. A copy of their agreement was located in *Tyrus Raymond Cobb v. Charlie Lombard Cobb*, Case No. 46003, Superior Court of the State of California in and for the County of San Mateo, Filed June 9, 1948.

39 The physical address of his home was 1476 Highway 50, Cave Rock Cove, according to the Douglas County, NV Assessor's Office online records. The total acreage was 2.250 and the property was built in 1938. Some websites claim this address is in Zephyr Cove, Nevada. Cobb's post office was at Glenbrook, NV and that is what appeared on his personal stationery. Nevada was also his legal state of residence.

40 Letter from Cobb to Joe Hauck, dated September 27, 1949, Joseph Hauck Papers (1914–1965), Bancroft Library, University of California, Berkeley, California. Frances was the daughter of a prominent Buffalo doctor, and despite

reports, Cobb was not a friend of her father, John Fairbairn, prior to their marriage. Correspondence with Geraldine Eastler, September–December 2014.

41 *The Sporting News*, October 12, 1949, p. 18.

42 *The Sporting News*, April 5, 1950, p. 1.

43 *The Sporting News*, April 19, 1950, p. 21–22.

44 *Portland Oregonian*, July 5, 1940, p. 23.

45 *San Francisco Chronicle*, March 22, 1935, p. 1.

46 *Idaho Statesman*, December 22, 1949, p. 13.

47 *San Luis Obispo Daily Telegram*, February 10, 1950, p. 1. The Cobb Family was also tied to the Coca-Cola Bottling Company in Bend, Oregon, from the late 1940s until 1955. *Bend Bulletin*, April 29, 1955, p. 1.

48 *Heart of a Tiger* by Herschel Cobb, 2013.

49 *Salt Lake Telegram*, April 12, 1915, p. 6.

50 *The Sporting News*, September 17, 1952, p. 29.

51 Letter to Ty Cobb Jr., dated March 15, 1948, Joseph Hauck Papers (1914–1965), Bancroft Library, University of California, Berkeley, California.

52 Cobb's drinking was corroborated by his friend Pope Welborn, in his interview in *Ty Cobb: Safe at Home* by Don Rhodes, 2008, p. 171–179. Also by Stump in his article, plus in the court documentation for *Elbert D. Felts v. Tyrus R. Cobb*, Case No. 29889, Superior Court of the State of California, County of Butte, 1954–56.

53 *New York Times*, July 31, 1951, p. 1.

54 *Life*, March 17, 1952 and March 24, 1952.

55 *The Sporting News*, March 26, 1952, p. 8, 12.

56 *Atlanta Constitution*, January 8, 1929, p. 19 and *The Sporting News*, May 7, 1952, p. 2.

57 *The Sporting News*, February 11, 1953, p. 18.

58 *The Sporting News*, December 2, 1953, p. 30. For a detailed look at the entire program, read *The Ty Cobb Educational Foundation* by Jerry Atkins, 2007.

59 *The Sporting News*, February 1, 1950, p. 16.

60 *San Diego Evening Tribune*, August 30, 1935, p. 18.

61 *Sacramento Bee*, July 14, 1947, p. 1 and *The Sporting News*, September 3, 1947, p. 31. Cobb denied he was under the influence during the Placerville episode. Letter from Cobb to Dr. Daniel C. Elkin dated August 21, 1954, *The Ty Cobb Educational Foundation* by Jerry Atkins, 2007, p. 58.

62 The incident was said to have taken place originally on April 15, 1954 and the case was filed in October. The decision came on November 16, 1955. *Elbert D. Felts v. Tyrus R. Cobb*, Case No. 29889, Superior Court of the State of California in and for the County of Butts.

63 The divorce was made final on May 11, 1956. *Frances F. Cobb v. Tyrus R. Cobb*, Case No. 1807, First Judicial District of the State of Nevada in and for the County of Douglas.

64 *Frances F. Cobb v. Tyrus R. Cobb*, Bill of Particulars, dated October 6, 1955.

65 Letter from Cobb to Dr. Daniel C. Elkin dated August 21, 1954, *The Ty Cobb Educational Foundation* by Jerry Atkins, 2007, p. 58.

66 *The Sporting News*, April 3, 1957, p. 3, 4.

67 *The Sporting News*, June 12, 1957, p. 28.
68 The size of Cobb's property was said to be anywhere from 40 to 75 acres. He described the land in a letter to Joe Hauck, dated October 26, 1957, Joseph Hauck Papers (1914–1965), Bancroft Library, University of California, Berkeley, California.
69 *The Sporting News*, September 11, 1957, p. 9.
70 *The Sporting News*, November 26, 1942 and October 5, 1955, p. 28.
71 *Augusta Chronicle*, August 28, 1957, p. 6.
72 *The Sporting News*, August 5, 1959, p. 20.
73 *Tyrus R. Cobb v. Pacific Gas and Electric Company*, Case No. 89689, dated May 28, 1960, Superior Court of the State of California in and for the County of San Mateo. This case was dismissed in January 1970 for failure to bring the action to trial.
74 *Boston Daily Record*, September 22, 1959, p. 38.
75 The best account of Cobb's Olympic journey appeared in *Ty Cobb* by Charles C. Alexander, 1984, p. 232–233.
76 *The Sporting News*, May 10, 1961 and December 13, 1961. The April 27 contest in Los Angeles was the final game Cobb attended.
77 *New York Times*, December 21, 1981, p. C8.
78 *Atlanta Constitution*, July 6, 2001 and *Tribune Business News*, August 9, 2010.
79 *Sports Illustrated*, October 27, 1992.
80 *Augusta Chronicle*, November 24, 1982, p. 2.
81 *Northeast Georgian*, July 20, 1961, p. 1 and *The Sporting News*, July 26, 1961, p. 11.
82 *Northeast Georgian*, July 20, 1961, p. 5.

CHAPTER NINETEEN: "I LOVED THE GUY"

1 *Detroit Free Press*, January 3, 1921, p. 10.
2 Not much was written about it, but the alleged Cobb-Crawford fight reportedly happened during spring training in 1906. *Omaha World Herald*, February 5, 1957, p. 17.
3 *The Sporting News*, March 28, 1946, p. 2.
4 *Salt Lake Telegram*, July 9, 1916, p. 9.
5 *Detroit Free Press*, July 29, 1913, p. 10. Cobb said that he felt his life had been endangered as a result of his baseball success. *St. Louis Post Dispatch*, October 2, 1914, p. 18.
6 *The Sporting News*, May 3, 1950, p. 3.
7 *The Sporting News*, December 26, 1935, p. 2.
8 *Evening Star*, Washington, DC, June 4, 1916, p. 30.
9 *Oxnard Daily Courier*, July 14, 1939, p. 2.
10 *Boston Daily Globe*, June 13, 1915, p. 53.
11 *Aberdeen Daily News*, April 10, 1911, p. 7.
12 *The Sporting News*, May 13, 1953 and February 21, 1962.
13 Following Cobb's death in 1961, Crawford and Jones formed the "Ty Cobb Memorial Association," a non-profit organization "formed to perpetuate Cobb's

ideals of clean, hard baseball through awards" to athletes in the American Legion junior baseball league. *Bakersfield Californian*, March 5, 1962, p. 28.

14 *The Sporting News*, August 15, 1935, p. 4.

15 *New York Evening World*, August 9, 1911, p. 6.

16 *The Sporting News*, February 9, 1955, p. 17.

17 *New Orleans Times-Picayune*, March 4, 1945, p. 21.

18 *Life*, March 24, 1952, p. 73.

19 *The Sporting News*, October 29, 1952, p. 7 and *Sacramento Bee*, October 14, 1952, p. 34.

20 *Detroit Free Press*, January 14, 1910, p. 12.

21 *The Sporting News*, January 4, 1945, p. 11.

22 *The Sporting News*, January 24, 1951, p. 20.

23 *The Sporting News*, April 10, 1957, p. 5.

24 *Detroit Free Press*, June 10, 1908, p. 4.

25 *Norwich Bulletin*, October 9, 1916, p. 3.

26 *Denver Post*, November 2, 1916, p. 12.

27 *Chicago Defender*, July 11, 1936, p. 14.

28 *Chicago Defender*, October 15, 1949, p. 7.

29 *Detroit Free Press*, March 22, 1915, p. 9.

30 *The Sporting News*, May 3, 1945, p. 16.

31 *Pittsburgh Courier*, January 30, 1954, p. 4.

32 *Baseball As I Have Known It*, Fred Lieb, 1977, p. 54.

33 *The Sporting News*, January 17, 1962, p. 40.

34 *The Sporting News*, April 18, 1981, p. 3.

35 Official records on Mlb.com.

36 Article by Michael Bradley, March 25, 2013, sportingnews.com.

37 baseball-reference.com.

38 *New York Times*, December 18, 1995.

39 *The National Pastime*, 1996.

40 *The National Pastime*, 2010.

41 *True—The Man's Magazine*, December 1961, p. 38–41, 106–115.

42 *Baseball Magazine*, April 1916, p. 47–58.

43 Joseph Hauck Papers (1914–1965), Bancroft Library, University of California, Berkeley, California.

44 Letter from Cobb to Joe Hauck dated July 4, 1947, Joseph Hauck Papers (1914–1965), Bancroft Library, University of California, Berkeley, California.

45 *True—The Man's Magazine*, December 1961, p. 38–41, 106–115.

46 *Boston Herald*, July 31, 1941, p. 19. Cobb offered his all-time list in 1941, 1944, and 1955, and didn't name himself any of the times. See *Oakland Tribune*, December 5, 1944 and *Nevada State Journal*, August 21, 1955.

47 *Augusta Chronicle*, May 5, 1995, p. C1.

48 *The Sporting News*, May 26, 1938, p. 7. Also see *New York Times*, February 6, 1963, p. 16.

49 *The Sporting News*, August 17, 1955, p. 14.

50 *Ty Cobb: My Life in Baseball* by Ty Cobb with Al Stump, 1993, Bison Books edition, p. 38.

51 *Atlanta Constitution*, January 14, 1925, p. 9.

52 *The Sporting News*, February 11, 1948, p. 23.

53 Some sources believed that Cobb's net worth at the time of his death was upwards of $11 million.

54 Probate Records, County of Habersham, Georgia.

55 tycobbfoundation.com.

56 tycobbmuseum.org.

57 *Atlanta Constitution*, August 7, 1936, p. 17.

58 *The Sporting News*, December 20, 1961, p. 14.

59 *Atlanta Constitution*, April 14, 1927, p. 18.

ACKNOWLEDGMENTS

In researching this book, I received exceptional assistance from a number of gracious individuals and helpful organizations. First, on a personal level, I want to express my heartfelt appreciation to my wife Jodi for her love and encouragement. Also, Timothy and Barbara Hornbaker, Melissa Hornbaker, Virginia Hall, Sheila Babaganov, Debbie and Paul Kelley, Frances Miller, and John and Christine Hopkins.

My editor, Jason Katzman, was instrumental throughout the creation of this book, and his tireless efforts are immensely appreciated. Also a special thanks to Leigh Eron and everyone at Skyhorse Publishing.

My sincere gratitude goes to Amy Miller and the Interlibrary Loan team, consisting of Margaret Cruz, Alisa Orange, and Deborah Hicks at the Broward County Main Library in Fort Lauderdale, Florida, for their meticulous work in obtaining the resources I needed for this project. Also, the Main Periodicals Department made up of David Hart, James Onessimo, and William Hubly.

A special thanks to Photo Archivist John Horne of the National Baseball Hall of Fame & Museum in Cooperstown, Jane Winton and Tom Blake at the Boston Public Library, Geraldine Eastler, Maria Brandt, Ken Samelson, Don Evans, Derek Blount, Bob Hoie, Gene P. Moy, J Michael Kenyon, Ellen Bowers Davenport, Arthurine N. Turner, Wesley Fricks, and James W. Williams.

Additionally, I would like to convey my appreciation to the following for their assistance: Carrie Tallichet Smith of the National Archives and Records Administration, Dawn Milton of the Butte County Courthouse, Oroville, California, Nicole Webb of the Habersham County Probate Court, Clarkesville, Georgia, Mark McCoy of the Banks County Historical

Society, Homer, Georgia, Allison Galloup of the University of North Georgia, Wanda Stalcup at the Cherokee County Historical Museum in Murphy, North Carolina, Mary Biaggini of the Douglas County Court System, Minden, Nevada, Sheri Berrong, Town Clerk for Mount Airy, Georgia, Tina Rae Floyd of the Augusta-Richmond County Public Library, Augusta, Georgia, Nicole Carmolingo of the DeKalb History Center, Decatur, Georgia, Mark Bowden of the Burton Historical Collection, Detroit Public Library, Detroit, Michigan, Eryn Killian of the Bentley Historical Library, University of Michigan, Ann Arbor, Michigan, Priscilla Colwell of the Putnam Public Library, Putnam, Connecticut, Rebecca Kilby of the Greenville County Library System, Greenville, South Carolina, the Franklin County Historical Society in Carnesville, Georgia, the Athens Historical Society, Athens, Georgia, Clarkesville-Habersham County Library in Clarkesville, Georgia, and the Records Management Division of the San Mateo Superior Court, Redwood City, California.